William Patrick Pitt

*To Susan,
With warmest regards
and great thanks*
Ron and Claire

SPIRITUAL SURVIVAL
IN A RADICALLY CHANGING
WORLD-TIME

WILLIAM PATRICK PATTERSON

Barbara Allen Patterson, Editor
Arete Communications, Publishers
Fairfax, California

Design by Henry Korman, Wordplay Consulting
Korman@wp-consulting.com

Jacket photography by Ron Levitan

Library of Congress Catalog Number is 2007943002
Patterson, William Patrick
Spiritual Survival in a Radically Changing World-Time

1. Technology 2. The Fourth Way 3. G. I. Gurdjieff 4. Lord John
Pentland 5. Title

Casebound ISBN: 978-1-879514-87-4
First casebound edition 2009

Printed on Acid-Free Paper ∞
The paper used in this publication meets the minimum require-
ments of the American National Standard for Information
Services—Permanence of Paper for Printed Library Materials,
ANSI Z39.48-1984.

Arete Communications
773 Center Boulevard, Box 58
Fairfax, CA 94978-0058
www.Gurdjieff-Legacy.Org
Email: *Arete@Gurdjieff-Legacy.Org*

To Mr. Gurdjieff
Mme de Salzmann
Lord Pentland

We are the images of God.

George Ivanovitch Gurdjieff

Other works by the author

Eating The "I"
Struggle of the Magicians
Taking with the Left Hand
Ladies of the Rope
Voices in the Dark
The Life & Teachings of Carlos Castaneda

Video Trilogy

THE LIFE AND SIGNIFICANCE OF G. I. GURDJIEFF
Gurdjieff in Egypt, Part I
Gurdjieff's Mission, Part II
Gurdjieff's Legacy, Part III

Contents

Contents

Introduction

We live in a new and radically changing, high-voltage world-time, one whose technological marvels are as great as its dangers—global warming, dead ocean zones, animal extinction, pandemic diseases, mass famines and migrations, resource wars and nuclear nightmares. But the more immediate threat is Technology itself. Technology is the new ideology of the twenty-first century. It almost totally enframes us. And increasingly we rely on it to make our decisions.

"Well, sir, the computers have demanded it."

That was Treasury Secretary Paulson's answer when he went before Congress and was asked why he needed a $700 billion dollar bailout.

And what was at the core of the worldwide financial meltdown—risk-reward computer models, computer buying and selling of new computer-created financial "products," many so complex that few understood them. The word "product" usually refers to production or other goods, but these financial products were based simply on other computer-generated financial instruments.

Years before the meltdown, one prescient observer warned of the dependence on machines:

> We are suggesting neither that the human race would voluntarily turn power over to the machines nor that the machines would willfully seize power. What we do suggest is that the human race might easily permit itself to *drift into a position of such dependence on machines* [emphasis added] that it would have no practical choice but to accept all of the machines' decisions. . . . Eventually a stage may be reached at which the decisions necessary to keep the system running will

be so complex that human beings will be incapable of making them intelligently. At this stage the machines will be in effective control. People will be so dependent on them that turning them off would amount to suicide.

Human Machines

We are not only in danger of losing our freedom to machines but in becoming machines ourselves. As one observer saw as early as the 1930s:

> People are turning into machines. And no doubt sometimes they become perfect machines. But I do not believe they can think. If they tried to think, they could not have been such fine machines.
>
> Machines, especially big machines, make people work in a certain way.... More and more machines are invented for more and more different purposes, and all these machines have to be fed. I don't mean fed with fuel, I mean they must be kept functioning.
>
> Machines make people serve them, and really machines control the movements and the life of human beings—the place where they live, the food they eat. Certainly they control them, because machines keep them for themselves. But the important thing is invention itself ... the direction of inventions is not controlled and cannot be controlled.

And now, almost eighty years later, neuroscientists foresee the "mating" of human beings with machines. That is, creating a human-machine interface by means of "porting" the human brain and nervous system into robots and computers. A new film, *The Singularity Is Near,* based on computer scientist Ray Kurzweil's book of the same name, posits that human immortality will be achieved by transferring a digital blueprint of the human brain into a computer or robot. And this may happen sooner than later, for already there is a new technology that connects the human brain directly to a computer. Paralyzed people wear a cap that picks up the brain's electrical activity, which allows them to type and use computers and operate their wheelchair by thought. And inside the brain of a monkey, electrodes are implanted which are connected to a robotic arm. Within days the monkey operates the arm as if it were his own. While most brain-computer interfaces are being framed as medical aids, the U.S. military has begun to explore possible applications to augment the research already underway to develop a computer that troops can carry in their backpacks in order to enhance combat performance. Militaries in other countries are already using robots as soldiers, such as Israel and South Korea which use robot border guards.

What Can We Do?

Where are we in all this?

That machines rule our lives is a growing possibility, but it has yet to happen. The same is true of the worst features of global warming and its aftermath. So, yes, it all captures our attention for a time . . . but for how long? No matter how vividly these scenarios are portrayed, they're abstract, not here and now. They cause alarm and might stop us in our tracks for a time, but we keep on walking. The press of our personal lives is just too consuming. Yet in stray moments—what happens? We might find ourselves thinking of limiting our computer use, living a more carbon-free life, donating to eco organizations, even emailing elected officials with our concerns. But afterward another part comes up and we wonder—*will any of this really do any good?*

Isn't it all a way of self-calming? If we take a cold look rather than an emotional one, the forces of Nature just seem too immense. And as for all the national and religious rivalries, and the attendant social problems, they are simply too trapped in history to ever be resolved. But a day or so later we find ourselves thinking of squirreling away food, buying gold, searching for a mountain retreat, even junking it all, buying a shotgun or two, and getting off the grid entirely.

Recently, there was a fellow who did just that, took his family into the wilds of northern Canada, built a cabin hundreds of miles from the nearest reminder of the world, planning to live off the land, hunting and fishing and growing food. It was a great experience until one sunlit morning he was awakened by a low rumble and looked up to see a large bomber dropping heaps of contaminated refuse a few miles from his homestead. Like it or not, the world is simply too small. There's no place to run, nowhere to hide.

We've never before faced the question of physical survival on a global scale. Yes, of course we're going to die someday, either of old age, disease or accident, but this will be personal, not collective, not due to some worldwide horrific event. Yes, we don't think about it, but it's there in the background and every once in a while it bursts forth . . . *I've got to do something, damn it!*

When we think of the world we grew up in—how good and stable it seems in comparison. There's a tendency to idealize the past, of course, but life then seemed to work, not perfectly, but it made sense. It had a certain order, gave a certain security. And if we look back historically, we see earlier forms of human organization were even simpler, smaller, more communal. Yes, geography was a protection then, as it isn't now. Great oceans, mountain chains, jungles and deserts divided peoples, allowed a certain separation and seclusion. Other cultures barely knew each other, if at all. The traditions, religions, values, ways of organizing and living life were relatively stable. Time moved slowly. Nature dominated; the seasons reigned supreme. And people were amazingly few. In 1492, for example, when Columbus first arrived in America, there were only 350 million people on the planet. Now, it's six billion. By mid-century, estimates are nine billion.

In terms of great societal movements and reorganizations, we see how our forebears went from a tribal, hunter-gatherer world to the agrarian, and the forming of villages and eventually towns. Then came the industrial world with its greater centralization, the congestion of cities, fiery furnaces, colonization, the beginning of world trade. Each new world-time challenged the older order of human life, and in doing so each in its way put the question of physical survival. For hunter-gatherers, for example, the change to the agrarian way of life meant to be at the weather's mercy, to put down the spear and pick up the hoe. For the agrarian, the move to cities meant putting down the hoe and picking up the wrench, a loss of freedom, regimentation, new diseases.

What Is Technology?

Technology is not neutral. It seeks, though unknowingly, as it knows nothing in our sense of the word, to remake and redefine everything in its own image. Relentlessly, it is reordering how we live and think and who we take ourselves to be. It poses a direct challenge to our identity and purpose as human beings. Are we facing a kind of Faustian bargain in which for unimaginable material powers we are exchanging our possibility of spiritual transformation?

Is Technology—the term is used in its broadest sense—in itself "bad"? Is there a conscious intent, an "evil god" behind it? Is it conscious of itself? Or, like a great archetypal algorithmic machine, isn't Technology simply mechanically and mindlessly propelling itself forward? That is, for all the talk about its computational powers, it has no sense of itself and its aim. In fact, Technology doesn't know that it exists, much less that we exist. We are simply a certain number among other numbers. Pull its electrical plug and what is it? Dumb and inert, of no use and no value. So to anthropomorphize it as something alien that is intentionally threatening us is simply to indulge a morbid side of the imagination.

Technology is not us. And yet it is us. This is what makes it so difficult to understand. Aristotle spoke of man as "the rational animal." Technology is man's rational part—the logical part of our power of binary reasoning—developed to an extraordinary degree through millennia of experience and experiment. Thus, we are its parents and like all parents had no idea what we were conceiving. But we've been coming to this point all along.

How many times did the First Man (if it was a man), who created fire by rubbing two sticks together, have to observe lightning striking trees and igniting them before he made the intuitive connection that the essence of fire was friction? Experimenting with that idea—rubbing the sticks together—this First Observer of prehistory initiated himself into using his rationality to discover the laws of Nature. The advances came slowly, but over time they began to multiply until in the last century the advances were so enormous as to give birth to powers of communication and calculation once thought unimaginable. We have become so enthralled by our rational part, and the material benefits and powers it has given us, that we, the descendants of the First Man as Observer, are now more and more disembodied, our animal nature misunderstood, judged and rendered inferior. And so our sense of incompletion and isolation has grown proportionately as we have become more and more mentalized, all without our really knowing it.

Technology's Reflection

The part has taken over the whole. Seen in this way, Technology is simply a reflection of this rational part of ourselves. The danger, then, is not from Technology in itself, but rather the part of us that so identifies with Technology that we allow our purpose and meaning as human beings to be defined and limited in this rational part's image so that, unwittingly, we will only want to become better machines. If so, then this part and Technology will have mastered us, and we won't even know it. It will seem natural that we exist merely as bioplasmic machines, a form of worker ants, each stamped with a bar code, totally enframed in a sterile, mentalized-technologized world. Such a machine world running on its "oil"—water to keep it cool and electricity for power—would impoverish all humanity. The human experiment on Earth would be over—a human and a spiritual catastrophe, a binary hell world, from which there would be no return.

Technology, then, simply by being what it is, a gift, forces us both to understand it and in so doing to understand ourselves. Technology cannot know itself; it is dumb to itself. Only we can know it, know its essence, its whatness, for we have the capability of a possible degree of self-knowing that no computation, no matter how powerful, can ever know—*the knowing awareness of presence.*

This is more than knowing as logic, as ordinary rational reasoning. We can only be this knowingness by going beyond the outer and inner trappings of what we take ourselves to be, and seek and work to know our own essence, what it is that makes us human beings, how the basic triad of our organism—the instinctive-sexual, emotional and intellectual—functions and misfunctions.

Our situation is this: We were born bioplasmic machines and have developed through the millennia the logical, binary part of ourselves to such an extraordinary degree that we have "created" ourselves in machine form—the "Son of Man," whose power of computation has dwarfed our own. As Technology and the technological mind-set increase their domination of human activity, we, as bioplasmic machines, lose our possible beingness and become automatons. Having nothing real inside us, false personality and its love of excess and spectacle grows rapidly.

The deeper challenge and opportunity that Technology, the "Son of Man," so to speak, presents then, is that the gift of its reflection returns us anew to the primordial question that has always been at the center of our being—*Who am I?* What does it mean to be a human being? It is for each of us to answer this question for him- or herself, or suffer the consequences of being defined by the part and not the whole of us, the part that has produced the "Son of Man."

The Idea of the Individual

Who am I? However I might describe or identify myself, would we not all agree that we are individuals? The idea has been drummed into us since birth and is constantly reinforced by society. Taking ourselves to be individuals, each of us assumes we are an indivisible I. No matter the time or circumstances, don't we say "I" to everything—"I did this," "I want that," "I should have"? Do I ever really doubt that I am an indivisible I? Sometimes there is a moment of severe shock, when my world-of-the-moment collapses and everything drops away, everything seems meaningless—yes, *then*, the question might arise. Who am I? What have I done with my life? What have I given my life to? What have I invested so much time and energy and attention into becoming, into achieving? It's usually only at or near the end of one's life, when all our ambitions and possibilities have played themselves out, that such self-questioning appears and we stare into the stark emptiness of our answers.

For example, near the end of his life, Alexander Alekhine, the ninth world chess champion, considered to be among the most creative, cultured and erudite players to ever rise to this level, walked into the tournament room, stood in front of the chessboard, and, as his opponent and others looked on, unzipped his trousers and urinated on the chess pieces and the board, and walked out—a chilling demonstration of his self-disgust at having given his life to "the Royal Game." Others, of course, even near death, neither question what they have given their lives to nor their belief in themselves.

The neuroscientist Francis Crick, codiscoverer of DNA, was so obsessed with his ideas about consciousness that even though death was imminent he could never still his mind, but instead poured out idea after idea for experiments that he would not live to pursue.

Disgusted or enchanted with ourselves, we all still live within the world of this "I" that we take ourselves to be. Everything large and small is subsumed under this unchallenged and consensual belief in the reality of an unchangeable, bedrock, unified whole called "I."

But where is this "I"? What is the referent? To what can I point? The primary assumption of my life is that this "I" is real, something substantial, indivisible. And yet all my moods, thoughts, feelings and impulses, even beliefs (though they are more dense) are all changeable and many are contradictory, some extreme, given the circumstances.

So, again, with answers not forthcoming or ambiguous, the question echoes, but now perhaps more immediately, more insistently—*Who am I?*

An Assemblage of "I"s

An ancient, esoteric teaching says we exist only as an assemblage of "I"s—now one "I" thinks, speaks or acts, now another "I," depending on external and internal shocks. And so everything just happens. There is no indivisible, independent, individual I in control. The idea that I am not who I think I am strikes at the heart of my identity. It's so counterintuitive to what I believe and have acted upon all my life that a part of me rejects it immediately. And another part argues that if that is true, then what would I be—nothing! I can't conceive of living life as a "nothing," and in fact look at all I have accomplished, all I have suffered for. And, more deeply, if I was just a group of "I"s, what would know this?

The idea that I am merely an "I" in quotation marks is admittedly hard to swallow. It is not put forward as something to be believed, but, like our First Man, rather as an idea to be rigorously verified by the evidence of one's own observed and direct experience. In observing, we would begin to discriminate ourselves as a cluster of "I"s. This would be the initial step toward the development of real I, an individual I, that which we truly are. For now, let's provisionally accept the idea that there is an "I" in quotation marks and a real I, and explore what each would mean in terms of physical survival.

As an "I" in quotation marks, our physical survival would mean survival would be accidental, the luck of the draw. It would simply happen, as there would be no individual I to which circumstances were happening but rather a zoo of changing "I"s. Afterward, there would be a backfilling, of course, a narrative imposed on what happened (but was not truly experienced) that would make it seem like an indivisible I was there all the time, one who made decisions. Without a real or awakening I who could learn from experience, physical survival, the survival of "I"—an assemblage of "I"s—would have no real meaning. A bioplasmic body would exist in which the "I"s would reside while the body would mechanically receive, transform and transmit energies.

Survival, Conscious & Otherwise

Only the survival of a real or awakening individual I would have value and meaning, for the experiences and decisions would be genuine. Conscious survival—*consciousness of being*—is of a completely different nature and quality. It is a higher level of experiencing in which there is an inherent awareness of the circumstances-of-the-moment and the primordial intelligence and will whose aim is survival at the highest level. The experiences encountered and surmounted (if indeed they are, for while self-awareness, having an individual I, vastly increases the chances of physical survival it is not a guarantee) would develop consciousness and will, a balanced triadic functioning of the instinctive-sexual, emotional and intellectual, to higher and higher degrees. Viewed and related to from this perspective, the radically changing world-time in which we live affords an unparalleled opportunity for the evolution of self-knowledge and being which would crystallize in the degree of understanding and conscience necessary for a genuine self-transformation and transcendence.

But what does it mean to be conscious?

Ask anyone—*Are you conscious?*

Strange question, for if they weren't conscious how could they hear the question?

Aren't we all already conscious?

Doesn't it stand to reason that we must be conscious because we can lose consciousness, be knocked unconscious? But with a little smelling salts, or time, we come to again. There we are, conscious of ourselves, our surroundings, just as we were before. When I go to sleep, yes, I am not conscious (at least not in the sense that I am when I'm awake), but when I awaken, there I am again. It's only when I wake up that I know I've been asleep. (Unless there is a lucid dream state, in which there is consciousness of the dream state within the sleeping state, there is no knowledge of the sleep state as it is happening.)

Thinking I Am Awake

So, when I wake up, in what state do I wake up? Waking consciousness. Only from a state of waking consciousness do I infer I, my consciousness, has been in a sleep state. Consciousness, or my connection to it, has changed. Little sleep, restlessness, hangover, disease and, okay, I'm not as alert and quick as I normally am, but there is a knowingness that I am here again when I awaken.

I *think* I am aware of myself in that moment, but that is almost immediately overwritten by an impulse, feeling or thought. Usually it's not thinking at all in the genuine meaning of the word but associative thought. It's all internal. It's not on display like a street person yammering aloud at invisible creations, yet the mind is filled with random associations, daydreams, fears, desires, futuring, cutting and pasting the past . . . all the while driving the freeway and missing my exit or being surprised that I have arrived at home.

And when with others—what happens? Doesn't the self-talking still go on? Yes, my attention initially might be focused on how you look, what you're feeling, how you're speaking—all, of course, with regard to how it affects me. Waking state consciousness is almost totally self-referential. It's already disposed, conditioned, to see what it sees. Believing and interpreted memory dictate seeing. What I am conditioned to believe is what I see. What I remember is circumscribed in terms of my interests, desires and fears. At a dinner party, for example, I might remember most of the conversation but not what I ate.

Sometimes when I look at you I see you and have a sense of what I am thinking, too. It's all mental and often the attention is switching back and forth between you and what I am thinking, yet there is no awareness of it. If I am captivated by you in some sense then all my attention is on you. There is no awareness of me. When I am focused on myself, my attention is all me; there is no awareness of you. Therefore, if we take myself as the subject and you as the object, then I am *not* in subject-object perception. I am, that is my attention is, *either all subject or all object.*

Further, just as I think I am in subject-object perception, I also think I have a body, but do I have a conscious awareness of it? Do I give the body attention? I am concerned with it in terms of how it looks and feels, but usually I am talking to myself, concerned about the impression I am making, evaluating others, consoling myself, gloating or beating myself... my attention totally lost in the word-world of associations and self-talk—unless called by hunger, lust, fear or bodily shock.

I am so full of self-concern, pregnant with the future, constipated by the past, I often only half-hear what you say. If you are telling me about your vacation, I am only waiting for you to stop talking so I can tell you about mine. I put a good face on it, of course. I pretend I am here, that I am listening; I try to make the appropriate gestures and vocalizations. My attention, though, is constantly wandering off. When moments of misunderstanding happen, I usually blame poor communication. When I do make an effort to communicate, I take for granted the facticity of the moment—if it is raining, it is raining. But you and I both unconsciously superimpose on this facticity a layer of beliefs that are personal, societal and time-bound.

Watch a film from another era. Notice all the unconscious assumptions and values undergirding the story line. It was *the* world according to that time. It was how they thought of themselves, the values they held—all of it taken for granted, assumed. It all happened within the context of that time, a context that was largely invisible to those engulfed in it.

Context & Content

We experience the multitudinous things of life, but do we experience the *context* within which things occur? Like a fish, don't we only see the seaweed, the worm, predators, that which feeds or threatens us? All things, gross and subtle, outer and inner, make up the contents of our experience. Every content is grounded in a referent, a thing that can be pointed to, in some way known, be it visible like a chair or largely invisible like a feeling or thought, or totally invisible like an inner sound. All content occurs within a context. For a full knowledge of the content one must know the context. To make things even more dynamic, the context is always changing; it's only a matter of degree.

Consciousness is often spoken of as if it were a "thing," that is, it has a referent. Yet to what can we point? Surely, waking consciousness exists and is experienced, for otherwise how would we know we are joyous, sad or angry. Neuroscientists are now fast on the trail of what consciousness is, noting the qualia (the qualitative aspect of consciousness, such as feeling pain, seeing colors, hearing a sound), plumbing the cerebrum, cerebellum or reticular activating system, believing that if they can see how it functions they can define its quality of essence. Areas of the brain light up in accordance with different stimuli, but this is the observable functioning of consciousness, not what it is in itself.

Consciousness, however, by definition not being a thing, is the context, the container, in which all things appear and disappear. One can *be* conscious but can't *know* consciousness in itself, for in the act of knowing, I am at a remove from it; the experience is dualized in terms of the knower and what is known. In the sleep and waking states, the context in which our lives occur, consciousness isn't experienced, because our attention is psychologized, discolored, trapped in the person and thing world. Consciousness, then, is only experienced in the third and fourth states, not the sleeping or waking state. (Though these are not separate but degrees of the one consciousness which is.)

Consciousness of Self

The third state of consciousness is self-consciousness. The term "self-consciousness" unfortunately is commonly taken as shyness or embarrassment, but true self-consciousness is a state that is possible only when there is an immediate *consciousness of self*. It's not—in itself—a personal, mental, psychologized, egoistic sense of self. Rather, it's a state in which there is an experiencing of attention divided simultaneously between both the subject, the "I," and the "it," the object.

To have consciousness of self is not only to be aware of oneself mentally (in which case it would be only the mind looking at the mind), but also physically and emotionally; that is, a global awareness inclusive of the facticity of the triadic instinctive-sexual, emotional and intellectual functioning. This demands a certain quality and strength of attention, of a direct recognition of the *Immediate*, of what-is, of having an awareness that is global in reference to oneself. Consciousness of self is a state predicated on self-remembering—a conscious awareness of the body, of being embodied, of being connected with what is happening internally, as well as what is happening externally.

Once embodied, self-observation has a physical support; otherwise, observation is from only a part of us, the head, and therefore entirely mental. As we become relatively more whole, what is observed and experienced also has greater wholeness. Thus, the impressions are stronger, more vivid, and evoke a feeling of what is observed as well as its image. An eagle suddenly flies overhead, for example. Now there is both its image and a sense of myself; both an awareness of the eagle, the "it," and the "I" that is seeing "it," and both *at the same time.*

Only when there is self-consciousness do we experience the world and ourselves in the world. Then, we viscerally sense, feel and know both *simultaneously.* An immediate, sensory experience of the triadic functioning is not only mental, not an idea or feeling alone, but an actuality. However, if I am troubled by or concerned with something not present now, my attention is abstracted from the physicality of the world, while the body, though I am not conscious of it, is walking in the rain. When I abstract myself from the Immediate, the what-is, through daydreams, fantasy and past-futuring, then there is no awared experience of being present *sensorially.* I will only know it is raining when my face gets so wet that the body calls the attention out of the abstraction-of-the-moment into the actuality of what is—the wetness. The awareness of the body grounds us literally in the Immediate, brings us into time; otherwise, living in abstraction, I, my attention, is out of time, in a kind of psychologized time, not grounded in the actuality of the physical.

The Facticity of the Physical

With the experience of wetness felt, I immediately react

accordingly (the reaction is below the level of thought) by making adjustments—pull up my collar, step under an awning or buy an umbrella. But now what? What happens to the attention? Does it stay in the what-is-of-the-moment? Or is it taken again into the abstraction, the what-isn't? Simple observation will show the attention abstracts randomly (or because of fear, desire), switching past-future, future-past, between what has happened or will happen, or some admixture. So, though we appear to be *here*, our attention, and the thoughts and feelings which accompany it, are off *there* in a world of abstraction, not in a *here* whose facticity is a concrete, palpable experiencing. If the rain is of interest, however, then the attention will continue to be directed toward it. But will there be awareness of observing the rain? No, the sense of observing will be lost in thoughts and associations about the rain. In this sense, there is no separation between the observer and what is being observed, for the observer is the rain and nothing more. Much of what we think and do originates below ordinary consciousness. It is nonverbal. When we become aware of the body we begin to experience this nonverbal world. Otherwise, we are unconsciously driven by these nonverbal impulses.

The experiencing, of course, will be of an entirely different quality if there is "something else," that is, self-consciousness. For then there will be a *double attention*. That is, there will be a simultaneous awareness of both the rain, the object, the "it," and the self, the "I," which is observing the rain. Think of it as an arrow pointing in two directions, inward and outward. If we make this experiment, we will see how difficult it is to maintain this double attention. Not only because we have a habit of naming, projecting and fantasizing, building worlds of abstraction out of the material of our experiencings, but also because of the inner self-talk consuming our attention, interpreting and judging everything in relation to ourselves.

How long, then, can our attention stay in the Immediate? This is determined by the quality and quantity of available energy and the degree of will and self-knowledge present. The energy is determined by the cumulative effect of our past efforts to move attention from waking state consciousness to self-consciousness. Will and self-knowledge are predicated on the frequency and degree with which we have experienced self-consciousness—that is, an awareness of a commensurate level of being. The self-knowledge spoken of is not descriptive, intellectual or theoretical but lived material, impressions directly perceived and experienced. The material is vivid and objective in the sense that the impressions are not psychologized, not filtered by the personal, the subjective, but rather awared through self-consciousness itself.

Being in a World of Becoming

As the sense of self-consciousness reveals and informs the triadic functioning (the instinctual-sexual, emotional and intellectual organism), its duration and depth proportionately increase. Each time we say "no" to the ongoing momentum of life's constant Becoming—where everything is in a stage of becoming greater or lesser—there is a *stop*, a shift in which we say "yes" to Being—that which is consciously aware of itself and its contents, gross and subtle, and in which the quality of breath becomes fluid, palpable. Before, we lived in a psychologized time and space. We lived in the foreground. Life was all biography, not biology. But when attention shifts to include both foreground and background then the experiencing of ourselves, others, the environment, and time and space changes, becomes dynamic. Time seems to stop, space expands. Silence, the ever-present background of all that is, is tasted. Verifying ourselves in this way we literally stand in our own shoes. Released from the self-talk of the make-believe world, the ongoing societal hypnotism, we experience the primary—that is, the sensation of ourselves, the breath, the attention, perhaps an interior sound. Otherwise, we live in the secondary, the add-on world of the person—the automatic waking state consciousness.

In embodied presence one experiences—sees, feels, intuits—what-is. No longer is this static and fixed, but, materiality converting into energy and energy into materiality, the world is experienced as it really is: dynamic, fluid, spatial, still, empty, solid, alive. And what is present is both the subject, the perceiver, and the object, what is perceived, that is, subject-object consciousness.

The fourth state of consciousness occurs where the perceiver dissolves in the perceiving. There is no subject, no center, only consciousness. Consciousness-without-an-object. This does not mean the world disappears. But as there is no subject there are no objects in the usual sense; that is, there not being a dualistic subject-object experiencing, the *relationship* with and to objects dynamically changes, as does space and time. Transcending the subject, there is no object in the sense that the foundation of experience has been constrained within the experience of subject-object (how we have unconsciously divided the world and ourselves). As the relationship with oneself is no longer that of a subject in the midst of objects, what remains? The silence of a centerless, panoramic presence of Being. Such an integration is the result of self-knowledge and being developed and raised to a very high degree of understanding through many years of unflagging practice that evolves to an effort that is a noneffort, a negative capability, a conscious and intentional letting-be. The experiencing, essentially timeless and centerless, cannot be willed, and, as it is both beyond and within the time-bound world of centered subject-object experiencing, its recognition is subject to disappearance. Nevertheless, the imprint of no-thingness and nothingness remains. But this is to go far beyond what is at hand.

Breaking the "Water Line"

We are like that fish in water. The water is the world for the fish. Born in water, lives in water, water is all it knows and will ever know unless . . . unless it breaks the water line, as dolphins and whales do, and experiences waterless space (or, less majestically, takes the fisherman's bait). Then, *difference* would be experienced. To break "the water line" of ordinary life, to separate the real from the thin veil of illusion of the real, to distinguish the world of Being from that of Becoming, has been spoken of in religious texts which instruct on its realization by way of faith, prayer, mantra, meditation, yogic practices and so forth. *The Heavenly Ladder*, a treatise on monastic virtues by Saint John Climacus (579–ca. 650), one of the most venerated holy figures in Byzantine monasticism, speaks of this and the temptations one will encounter in breaking the secular world line. In a painting depicting this theme, monks are shown climbing a ladder from Earth to the heavens above and an awaiting Jesus Christ; all the while little black devils shoot arrows of temptation at them. However, like other such texts, the treatise omits, if indeed it was known, the secret of the body as a positive means of spiritual transformation.

It is not surprising, as religion has judged and condemned the body—the part of the triad we take as instinctive-sexual—as negative, something to be dismissed, struggled against, overcome. Society has largely been of split mind about the body, hiding it or flaunting it, and in our time even exalting it to a point of neurotic worship (perhaps an unconscious reaction to how disembodied our mentalized-technologized life has become).

"Do you have a body?"
"Of course I do. Look, this is my body."
"Do you have a right foot?"
"Of course, I do. Look, I can wiggle it."
"Were you consciously aware of your right foot?"
"No, but I am now."
"But before—was there a conscious awareness?"
"Well, no . . ."
"What happened?"
"When you asked I became aware of it."
"You mean, your attention went to the right foot. Only then was there a conscious awareness. Otherwise—from this point of view—you had no right foot, correct?"
"I guess."
"Please, no guessing. You didn't. And if you had no awareness of your right foot, you had none of your left."
"I suppose so."
"And if neither foot, then neither leg. Nor the pelvis, abdomen, lungs—in effect, you had no body really. No body you were consciously aware of."

So, while we have a body physically, we do not have a body in the sense of being aware of it. We take the body for granted. In many respects we'd rather not have a body, if we could still exist. The functions of the body—defecation, urination, menstruation—remind us of a part of ourselves we'd rather not have. Only with these unavoidable functions and times of physical shock, hunger, pain, lust, disease is the supremacy of the body at this level realized. And when these pass: what happens? The body is forgotten again.

Now, to return to what we were speaking about. What happened when the right foot was suddenly experienced? If the question was a shock, then the specific gravity of attention was not in the body but in the head. What did the shock do? It broke the association-of-the-moment, cleared a space, and the attention—now freed from association—went directly to the right foot, giving a seemingly instantaneous sensation of the foot.

The Narcissism of Continual Self-Referral

So, to maintain the experience of the awareness of the right foot requires will, the need to sustain the re-membering, for I am habituated—one might say addicted—to living in thoughts, ideas, fantasies and emotions. Even a casual observation will confirm that I am constantly talking to myself, comparing myself, judging myself—*lost in self-talk*. My attention is captured in narcissism of continual self-referral, self-enchantment and daydreams. Though I appear to be in the facticity of the physical world, I am off into the abstract. Whenever a question arises that is out of the ordinary, say a complex problem to be solved, then the attention is directed. Keeping the attention directed requires will, especially when the problem's solution is not easily resolved, or when the novelty of the experience has played out and boredom reigns.

The truth is—contrary to assumption and belief—*I am not consciously here*. Hearing this, as it was with the right foot, there is an immediate sense of hereness. It's experienced right now. And that is true. *Now*. But what happened before? Didn't the shock of the statement immediately clear the mind space, wipe away whatever the attention was consumed with, and now there is a sense of *hereness*? So, I can say I am here. But, again, what about *before*? Was there this sense of myself then?

At this level of questioning an even more subtle question arises: *Is this hereness only mental?* That is, am I speaking from an integration of body-emotion-mind? Or only the mind with no experiencing of the awareness of the body? This truncated functioning, together with the mechanical unity of the machine itself, is a major reason why we think we are awake when in actuality we are asleep. If we extend this experiencing to the human beings alive now and down through history, then the result is what? So many of the people we honor, the history we speak of, is almost all completely mechanical. This is a lot to swallow, a lot to digest.

As the seminal teaching we will soon introduce holds that *nothing is to be believed before it is verified*, as an experiment, we might begin to explore this idea by experiencing the right foot now and seeing if we can maintain an awareness of it while reading what follows.

The Road to the Supersensuous

We were talking before about the secret of the body. Just when did we in the West begin to separate the body from the mind? With Plato. He divided the sensuous, the body, from the supersensuous, the archetypal realm of Ideas. For him, only the archetypal was real; the body, all physical life, was unreal, a mere shadow of the Ideas. Aristotle spoke of man as the "rational animal." We are two natured. One animal, the other rational. The body needs food and sex, movement and breath. The mind works with symbols and ideas, organizes, adjudicates, speculates. Despite, or perhaps because of, Plato's and Aristotle's intellectual genius, they appear to have had a bias against the body, the "animal." They did not recognize the importance of the physical body as the ground of all higher bodies. Christianity took another step. The body was sinful and had to be purged of its fleshly desires. Then Descartes—"I think therefore I am." Only mind has value. (Though he would later include the body as sensations, impulses, etc., in the word *think*.) This, of course, is all based on Aristotle's definition of man as a "rational animal"; his division of man is not only dualistic but denies the "animal" its crucial place in the self-transformation of consciousness, which entails the development of higher bodies of being.

It is not surprising, then, that the esoteric valuation of the physical body as the foundation of spiritual self-transformation has either been not known or forgotten. Even today the body as the root spiritual praxis of self-transformation and transcendence remains largely unknown. The body is usually taken as a totality of one. The teaching declares that in addition to a physical body, there are other bodies: the *Kesdjan* body, emotional body, intellectual body, and so forth. But for now we need to stay focused on what we can directly experience and thus verify. That, at this level, is the physical body. It has three centers in operation: instinctive-sexual, emotional and intellectual. The thinking center is often a jamming system, filtering out what is not wanted, leveling and reducing it, making it palatable to and in accordance with that which is already accepted as true. And just as our attention moves between subject and object, attention also moves from one center to another—from the intellectual to the emotional to the instinctual-sexual-moving centers (the latter, for simplification, we take as one).

These centers don't always agree. For example, we think one thing, feel another, and speak or act a third. But these contradictions are ignored because of the belief in an indivisible I. One center usually predominates. That is, how we interpret and judge the world is primarily based on one of the centers. Therefore, there is little to no confrontation with the other centers except in extreme circumstances where we find ourselves between a "yes" and a "no." Within the centers, reactive imprints, or "I"s, dart about in waking consciousness like fish of various species, each having its own nature, predilections and agenda. And, not being aware of this, as the various "I"s become active, taking over the centers, we say "I" to each. Thus arises the notion that we are one and not many.

I, the Primary Meta-Belief

What rules the centers is the primary meta-belief that I am an individual—a seamless unchanging indivisible I. This is the basis of false personality. It is the "face" we put forward to the world. At its core is chief feature, or chief weakness, and, being both imaginary and mechanical, it's found in the emotional part of our essence and built upon one or more of the seven deadly sins, an inherency, its deep origin being self-love and vanity.

One way to visualize this system of meta-beliefs is as a computer program (but only as metaphor) with all its defaults, running its routines and subroutines, automatically discounting any assertion or action not in accord with the program—its belief structure. So whatever one does, whatever is thought and felt, the system immediately incorporates and levels to its automatic understanding. It's a seamless whole forever wary of any challenge to its suzerainty. We are caught in it. There is no way out, all exits are guarded, all moves call up a counter move. Within the seamless unity of the notion of this indivisible I and the meta-belief system that runs it, everything is interpreted, filtered, leveled or discounted. All functioning is merely mechanical, based on memory and habit. The stability and integrity of the system is maintained at all costs.

The system prides itself on what it takes to be rationality—remember Aristotle's "rational animal"?—and so if it can't make the irrational into the rational it dismisses it. Thus, order is maintained, the consensual view of the meaning and purpose of life sustained, and the irrational is enframed within its logic pattern. Rationality, as we are speaking about it, certainly has its place, but when the system is so resolutely against anything that challenges its notion of itself as the God of Rationality it becomes what it fears, irrational. But many of life's occurrences simply don't bend to rationality. The existential playwright Samuel Beckett was stabbed on a Paris street by a stranger, and, having recovered from a wound that was almost fatal, he visited his assailant in prison. Beckett asked why he did it. To this query, the fellow shook his head and said— *"Je ne sais pas. Je ne sais pas."*

Personality & the Minds

To deal with the irrational, chaos, the shocks of life, and also in resistance to those around us, as well as the result of wrong conditioning and miseducation, a shield of personality forms. It shields essence, what we are born with, what we truly are—our energy, desires, tastes, proclivities, likes and dislikes—from the vagaries of life. Essence, its development halted in childhood, becomes passive and personality active. Real I can only grow from what is real in us—our essence—not what is unreal. So for growth to occur, personality must become passive, no longer take the lead, be the knower. What keeps personality in place is a series of "buffers," artificial mental compartments that isolate experience so that contradictions in thoughts and actions are not directly experienced. So, before personality can be weakened and dislodged, these buffers must be observed.

The personality informs what we generally call the "mind," the mind of the waking state, its formatory part. This is the mechanical part of the intellectual center (each of the three centers are in turn subdivided into intellectual, emotional and moving parts). This formatory part always goes the way of least resistance, self-calms, avoids immediate difficulties, loves to speak about extremes and has no connection to other centers. It keeps up a running commentary, interpreting, formulating—eating all of our attention—and doing so all on the basis of memory, a memory which it has previously filtered and limited according to its belief structure. So one's moment-to-moment experience is of the formatory mind and its superficial commentary about what is going on inside and outside us in reference to shocks, internal and external. Each shock calls up from the content of the three centers the "I-of-the-moment" that dominates the formatory mind. As outer and inner circumstances change, the "I"s constantly change. Some are subtle and sly, others prominent and outspoken, each taking center stage in a near endless parade.

This is all taking place in the mind of waking consciousness. The waking state mind deals with the everyday occurrences, historizing and futurizing away its energy. What it can't or won't deal with is pushed down into the subconscious mind. This material, as it is not integrated, exerts a subtle influence, largely unrecognized. Though the split between the two minds generally keeps its influence silent, at times it bursts to the surface and words are spoken and actions done that seem irrational. Besides the waking mind, there are two other higher minds. One is the mind of self-remembering and the other is that of the fourth state of consciousness. The mind of self-remembering, the mind of conscious embodiment, lowers the gradient between itself and its subconscious mind. This allows the conscious integration of the contents of the subconscious mind. With duration, conscious and subconscious begin to merge, thus making a connection with the higher mind of the emotional center possible. This, in turn, makes for the connection with the higher mind of the intellectual center spoken about before as the fourth state of consciousness. While all these states of mind are thus differentiated, they are one within another, so, in reality, there is only Mind.

What has heretofore been unknown is that real conscience, the deep feeling of unity with all life—not the learned, societal conscience generally spoken of—is relegated to the subconscious. This is because our actions so often contradict our self-image, and rather than face the truth we feed the lie.

Our unconscious insistence is to live in waking state consciousness—a conditioned state which lives us, we do not live it—and not the third state of self-consciousness. And so we live in only a part of ourselves, the formatory part that has no possibility of evolving. We are then no more than bioplasmic machines and, bereft of a sense of the spiritual, it is only "natural" that we are blind to our mechanicality. However, as both will and consciousness are developed, to the degree where we awaken to our mechanicality and beyond, we cease to be a machine and the true meaning and purpose in life is revealed.

The Thin Film of False Reality

Ouspensky, the Russian writer and mathematician, and seeker after truth, saw early on what was happening to people and searched for what he called "a new or forgotten road" . . . a practical teaching that would give man the knowledge and will to be able to penetrate "beyond the thin film of false reality to an unknown reality," which he called "the miraculous," a teaching that would allow man to learn to separate consciousness from mechanicality.

Following a trip to India in which Ouspensky visited various schools, which, as he said, "promised very much [but] demanded everything at once," he returned to Russia in 1914. The following year he met G. I. Gurdjieff, a Greek-Armenian who had rediscovered and reformulated for modern times an ancient and seminal teaching of self-transformation and transcendence, and whose mission it was to bring the teaching to the West. Of what was happening to people and the world-time we were entering, Mr. Gurdjieff told him:

> We see a preponderance of vulgarity and stupidity of all kinds. . . . There is a clear growth of personality at the cost of essence, that is, a growth of the artificial, the unreal, and what is foreign, at the cost of the natural, the real, and what is one's own. Contemporary culture requires automatons. . . . Man's slavery grows and increases. Man is becoming a willing slave. He no longer needs chains. He begins to grow fond of his slavery, to be proud of it. And this is the most terrible thing that can happen to a man.

Gurdjieff explained explicitly a fundamental illusion:

> One of man's important mistakes, one which must be remembered, is his illusion in regard to his I. . . . Man cannot have a permanent and single I. His I changes as quickly as his thoughts, feelings, and moods, and

he makes a profound mistake in considering himself
always one and the same person; in reality he is *always a
different person*, not the one he was a moment ago. *Man
has no permanent and unchangeable I.* Every thought,
every mood, every desire, every sensation, says "I.". . .
Each minute, each moment, man is saying or thinking
"I." And each time his I is different. Just now it was
a thought, now it is a desire, now a sensation, now
another thought, and so on, endlessly. *Man is a plurality.* Man's name is legion. [Italics in the original.]

Gurdjieff spoke about the world situation and the crucial need
for awakening. As Fritz Peters reported:

He predicted that a day would come when the eastern
world would again rise to a position of world importance
and become a threat to the momentarily all-powerful,
all-influential new culture of the western world, which
was dominated by America—a country that was very
strong but also very young. One should look at the world
in the same way that one looked at a man or woman, or
at oneself. Each individual was a world, of itself, and the
globe—the big world in which we all lived—was, in a
sense, only a reflection or an enlargement of the individual world in each one of us.
    Among the purposes of all leaders, messiahs,
messengers from the gods, there was one fundamental and very important purpose: to find some means
by which the two sides of man, and, therefore, the
two sides of the earth, could live together in peace
and harmony. He said that the time was very short—
it was necessary to achieve this harmony as soon as
possible to avoid a complete disaster. Philosophies,
religions and other such movements had all failed
to accomplish this aim, and the only possible way to
accomplish it was through the individual development of man. . . . The separate, distinct growth of
each individual in the world was the only possible
solution.

The Shock of The Fourth Way

To give us the knowledge and means by which we can become a real individual, to bring the two sides of ourselves together, to consciously survive and use technology and not be used by it—Gurdjieff saw that a major shock was needed to awaken man to a new level of consciousness. And so he broke with spiritual tradition and took an oath to introduce to and establish in the West the seminal and long hidden teaching of self-transformation and transcendence which he called The Fourth Way. Asked why he brought the teaching, he succinctly replied: "To let you know that when it rains, the pavement gets wet."

It is an esoteric teaching, Gurdjieff said, that "has been completely unknown up to the present time."

That is, *completely unknown* in terms of being exoterically known.

"It is completely self-supporting and independent of other [spiritual] lines."

By *lines* he meant the three classical spiritual ways of work with body, feelings or mind.

By being *completely self-supporting and independent* the teaching is not a mixture of fundamental lines, as are Theosophy and Western occultism. These, said Gurdjieff, have "grains of truth, but neither of them possesses full knowledge and therefore attempts to bring them to practical realization give only negative results."

By negative results he meant practitioners would become lost in the psychic world, rather than being grounded in the spiritual world.

Whereas the three classical lines focus on either body, feelings or mind, The Fourth Way works on all three at once. In this way a balance is achieved and the danger of an excessive development of one part or another is avoided.

The Fourth Way is not a rejection of life. It is not a withdrawal to a psychic world, monastery or ashram. Instead, it is centered squarely and practically in ordinary life—using its uncertainties, negativity, suffering, joys and discoveries to come to real life. There are no dogmas, rituals, priests or gurus. Nothing is to be believed, *everything is to be verified*—verified by the evidence of one's own experience. The person is worked with as he or she is. Nothing is to be changed outwardly.

Unlike all other teachings, authentic or invented as the plethora of New Age teachings are, The Fourth Way acknowledges from the start that man is a machine. Gurdjieff said:

> All the people you see, all the people you know, all the people you may get to know, are machines, actual machines working solely under the power of external influences. Machines they are and machines they die. Even now, at this very moment [1915], several millions of machines are trying to annihilate one another. What is the difference between them? Where are the savages and where are the intellectuals? They are all alike. . . . But there is a possibility of ceasing to be a machine.

The Teaching for Our Times

That the teaching Gurdjieff brought begins with the very danger that confronts mankind—*that man is a machine*—and gives the knowledge and practices to cease to be a machine is why The Fourth Way is the teaching for our times.

To repeat, our situation is this:

We are bioplasmic machines in terms of our identification with the mechanicality of our centers. When our consciousness is so attracted by the activity of centers that it loses itself in them, becomes them, then we gradually lose all spiritual possibility and become automatons. It is only by impartially observing our centers that we come to realize their mechanical functioning. In doing so, a process begins in which consciousness gradually separates itself from the activity of the centers. No longer identifying itself with the centers, consciousness becomes the context for all the content and activity of the centers, and we cease to be machines and become conscious human beings. Otherwise, our consciousness transfixed by the mechanical action of centers, there is a growth of personality and love of excess and spectacle and a general dumbing down and coarsening of human life.

The Fourth Way begins by accepting that man is a machine. He can only cease to be a machine by awakening to his mechanicality. The practices of the teaching bring him to this realization and are the preparation for his self-transformation and transcendence. The

Fourth Way, centered in ordinary life and using it to come to real life, is a unique and practical teaching of great scale that perfectly corresponds to the challenges, as well as the great possibilities, of this world-time. Long hidden and now unveiled, the teaching is for those who wish for and will work for self-transformation and transcendence, understanding and conscience.

Technology, giving us a reflection of a part of ourselves that we are in danger of taking as the whole, is thus also a spur to develop ourselves to where it can be truly said, as Mr. Gurdjieff reminds us—*we are made in the image of God.* The meaning of this is to be taken within the context of the teaching. To begin with, being asleep to our real self, we are *negative* images and, like camera film, we must pass through a solution before the positive image latent in the negative appears.

But has this teaching come too late? That was what Ouspensky wondered in June 1917, only months before the Bolshevik revolution that would topple the three-hundred-year-old Czarist control of Russia. Writes Ouspensky:

> "Events are against us," I told Gurdjieff. "It is by now clear that it is not possible to do anything in the midst of this mass madness."
>
> "It is only now that it is possible," Gurdjieff replied, "and events are not against us at all. They are merely moving too quickly. This is the whole trouble. But wait five years and you will see for yourself how what hinders today will prove useful to us."
>
> [Ouspensky continues] Looked at from the point of view of "facts," it was difficult to imagine in what way we could be helped by events in the nature of a "civil war," "murder," epidemics, hunger, the whole of Russia becoming savage, and then the endless lying of European politics and the general crisis which was undoubtedly the result of lying.
>
> But if looked at, not from the point of view of "facts," but from the point of view of esoteric principles, then what Gurdjieff meant becomes more comprehensible.

Why were there not these ideas earlier? Why did we not have them when Russia existed and when Europe was a comfortable and pleasant place "abroad"? It was here probably that lay the solution to Gurdjieff's enigmatic remark. Why were there not these ideas? Probably precisely because these ideas could come only in such a time when the attention of the majority is distracted in some other direction and when these ideas can reach only those who look for them. I was right from the point of view of "facts." Nothing could have hindered us more than "events." At the same time, it is probably that precisely the "events" made it possible for us to receive what we had.

Only a Taste

The foregoing has been only preliminary sketch of some of the tenets of the teaching. The Fourth Way Meetings, a series of illustrative meetings that now follow, can give a taste, but a taste only, of the initial approach. That the focus is on the body's postures and not ideas may seem strange, but, if we reflect on what has been said, it will be realized that a somatic foundation must be established. As Gurdjieff says, "Mechanics is necessary for the study of machines. That is why we begin with mechanics. . . . It is possible to stop being a machine, but for that it is necessary first of all to *know the machine.* A machine, a real machine, does not know itself and cannot know itself. When a machine knows itself it is then no longer a machine, at least, not such a machine as it was before. It already begins to be *responsible* for its actions." While everyone's experience and work on him- or herself is individual, it also takes place in a group, which, to be effective, must be led by an authentic teacher in the teaching's lineage and not an interested therapist or New Age eclectic.

To really become part of the meetings, as far as that is possible without physically being present, it is advised that only a few meetings at a time be read. First, come to yourself in the sense of being embodied as you understand it. This will help to clear the mind. Open yourself as completely as possible to the exchanges.

It's likely that some, or even much, of what is reported will seem obvious, mundane, boring. This is to be expected, but why? Have we truly experienced and starkly observed in ourselves what is spoken of? And could we candidly share our experiences with people we largely don't know? Understand that in asking a question while being embodied the questioner is present to and with the question asked, and so places himself within the question. In this sense, the questioner is the question and not distant from it. An intimacy, a direct channel, is thus created. This allows the dynamism of the interchange to bypass the formatory jamming system and activate the emotional center and, with duration, its higher part.

In Probes and Fourth Way Essays the writer has spoken and written about ideas pertinent to the teaching. Only so much can be conveyed in a print medium, but if one reads with awareness and self-sincerity there may be an opening now and then to another level of experiencing.

So align the body so that it is erect, relax the face, breathe into the body, release the tensions, and enter the real world. . . .

A Warning

And yes, a warning, this has been only a brief introduction. What is given here is a sketch of some aspects of the Work. As Mr. Gurdjieff pointed out—we cannot teach ourselves, for who, what "I," is teaching us? If we try to do so, we will only further entomb ourselves in the "doer-I." What is given here is only a taste of the possibility of self-transformation and transcendence. For those awakened to their wish, it can serve as a bridge for a seeker wishing to become a candidate to enter The Fourth Way, an ancient living teaching, the teaching for our times.

Fourth Way Meetings

I

What I Don't Say

In seeking to know who I am it seems so much harder than expected. I lie not so much in what I say but in what I don't say.

Yes, omission, vagueness, misdirection, half-truth—we lie in so many ways. It's usually mechanical, not conscious, so not really experienced in the moment. It's become habitual. We can't come to the truth through a lie. So the first barrier to self-transformation is lying.

But what if I lie?

Wake up to the lie in the moment-of-the-lie. Get the "taste" of it. Lying has a very specific taste. First we have to verify for ourselves how much of our lives is lived in lying. Look for it in everything. And don't judge, just observe.

Root of Everything

Last week I had a very strong observation of my self-love and how it's from the head. It's completely what I am. In seeing this, there was no experience of shame, although I certainly don't want other people to see it.

To say "it's completely what I am," isn't this in itself a statement of self-love? One has an impression, a deep impression, let us say, and from that we make an absolute judgment. As Mr. Gurdjieff says, we make elephants from fleas. Then the experience of having no shame signals that one has seen this only from the head. I'm so trapped in the head, ruled by it, I psychologize everything. Let us hope you were in a state of self-remembering when this observation happened.

"It" Was Walking

It's been hard to really accept the idea that I'm mechanical. I really resist it. It runs counter to everything I've believed. But I observed myself walking into a room—I wasn't walking, the body was. "It" sat itself down in a chair, I didn't, and so forth. Still, the idea that I'm really so mechanical is hard to accept.

A keen observation. We are being led around by the body and don't realize it.

Not the Body, the Mind

I hear what is said about the body, but I'm really more interested in my mind—that's what gives me all the trouble, not the body. I want to see into the mind, not look at how I'm standing or sitting, which I can easily correct.

We study mechanics first. Do you know why?

Well, that's part of it, but the mind is mechanical, too, isn't it?

Yes, the "mind" you are speaking of is.

What do you mean "mind"?

We'll get to that later. Let me ask you, if you were God and wanted to hide something from inquisitive beings like us—where would you hide it?

[Thinking]

You'd want to hide it in a place no one would think to look, right?

Yes, I guess so.

The more invisible it was, the better, right? What's more "invisible" than our mechanicality—how we walk, sit, eat and so forth? It's all an undiscovered country.

Entering the Subterranean World

I was in the kitchen, making myself a cup of tea, and all the time I was trying to observe the movements involved without much success. When the tea was poured, I caught myself moving my hand in the direction of the book I've been reading. I realized at that moment I acted like a machine that was programmed. I had to make an effort not to grab the book. So, instead, I concentrated my attention on the tea—its flavor, taste, aroma, temperature. I experienced how I was standing, my arm moving, my hand holding the cup.

What you've observed has been going on all your life—and everyone's life—and yet until now it's remained invisible. We're so identified with what we're thinking and feeling that we don't see how we do things, how we get from here to there. It's a "subterranean" world. One way to enter this world is to observe habits—small, simple habits like turning off the alarm clock, putting on your shoes in the morning, brushing your teeth. Are you aware you are doing it? Or is it being done? Observe postures as well.

Postures Are Windows

At the law school yesterday the president suddenly appeared. I was on a personal call. There was a feeling of guilt. I observed that my head lowered about two inches, as if I was standing in front of a judge awaiting sentence. It was amazing. I'd never seen this before.

The mind influences the body, the body the mind. Postures are windows on the mind-of-the moment, the "I"-of-the-moment.

Yes, I see what you are saying.

Stop, don't move. Observe where your head is right now. Take in that impression. No, don't move. You're correcting it. See that you are not moving your head, guilt is.

Washing Dishes, Sort Of

I decided to observe myself doing something I rarely do—washing the dishes. Watching my hands, I suddenly felt my face was reacting to a thought that had nothing to do with washing the dishes.

There's the phrase "the right hand doesn't know what the left hand is doing." That goes for all the parts of the body if there is no conscious awareness. Your hands were in one place, the attention another. So where are we?

Your guess is as good as mine. [Laughs]

Exactly. A life of being neither here nor there.

I Wondered Why

Each time I observed myself I found my posture was slumped, with legs and arms crossed. I wondered why I sat like this, so I deliberately put my feet flat on the floor. An uncomfortable, anxious feeling arose in my abdomen. There is a certain pressure of crossed legs that gives me a protected feeling. What do I need protection from?

We want to observe how we are in the moment, get the "taste" of it by intentionally inhabiting the body. Don't historicize as to why the body is as it is. That avoids the facticity of the moment. In time your question will answer itself. You won't have to think about it.

Reeducating the Body

There has been a change in the body since I began remembering myself and experiencing my postures. The longtime presence of a muscular tension or pain disappeared; now there is only the normal fatigue or tension present. This was unexpected. A few days ago I noticed when starting to pick up something off the floor that the body began to contract, expecting the pain to be present, but it was not there. There is a reeducation going on.

When we give conscious attention to the body-machine it becomes less dense, more open, fluid. With repeated practice, muscular tension begins to dissolve and the body is freed to experience deeper layers of relaxation. Nourishing it in this way increases the body's vibration, reintegrates it on a higher level and, in essence, reeducates it. In your Work Diary have you made a map of all the places your body carries tension?

No, not yet.

What is it that's resisting?

I just forgot.

What forgets?

I guess I don't know.

I have to see that either I'm here or not here. There are many degrees of both, of course, but either there is self-remembering or there isn't. What I'm not here for, I'm not here for. To know is to be. And to be is to be here.

II
Two Completely Different Worlds

I took a sauna and a cold plunge and there was a lot of energy afterward. It surprised me. And in sitting this week the body came to me immediately. I didn't experience all of the body, just the limbs, but it was consistent. Despite this, there's this "I" that doesn't want to be in the body. It resists it. There is something so life giving in being in the body, but this is forgotten completely when I'm in this particular "I." It's like two completely different worlds.

By taking a sauna and then jumping in a cold plunge you gave yourself a strong physical shock. The sauna is a good place to remember yourself. And, yes, it's like two worlds, the one real, the other imaginary. Not one "I" but every "I" resists being present because it wants you, that is, your attention, energy, time, all for itself. Starve the "I"s. The real "jihad" is inner spiritual warfare, not outer. It's desire for the death of the identification with the self-image.

"I" Control

I had to make some phone calls. There was an "I" that did not want to do it. As I sat before the phone after I had oriented myself in my feet, I heard a voice, "I do not like this." I pounded the table with my fist. I noticed afterward that it's true—I am constantly saying "I" to everything.

The "I"s change, of course, but that is usually not seen, for I am always the last "I," trapped in a word cage of "I," its bars formed of "I like this," "I don't like that." Who is this "I"? Don't think about it. Observe it. You may see that it's full not only of self-love but self-will. Will, real will, can only be developed at the expense of self-will. So observe your day and give me a list of habits.

Food

I've been observing myself in terms of food. Each meal has become an opportunity to see myself and try to be awake to what I'm putting in my body.

Of the three foods we sustain ourselves with, the most visible, to begin with, is physical food. What we eat, when and how—and also why we are eating a particular food—can tell us a great deal. Keep observing and we'll talk about it when you have more to report.

Going Through the Motions

I made the effort to focus with intensity on the exercise of observing habits. As the week went on, however, the intensity became weaker and weaker. I saw that I was content with half-hearted efforts, telling myself that at least I was doing it, but really just going through the motions.

When the novelty wears off, the work begins. That is, an effort of will is required, which is how we develop will. Our energy is not limitless. We need to learn to conserve energy. We need to observe how we leak it in needless talk and self-indulgence.

Psychologizing the Posture

I was sitting at a table with a group of people. I noticed that my abdomen was pressed up against the table, with both forearms resting on the table. No one else was sitting this way; everyone else was leaning back in their seats, legs crossed. My posture was so erect it seemed like being back in school. This was observed until someone spoke to me.

I "noticed" my posture, but then compared it with others. Now, could I observe the posture of others and still experience my own posture? That is, could attention be divided between the two? . . . No, not yet. So, I lost myself in how other postures looked, then experienced my posture again, which evoked the association of being back in school. Then a small shock, I was spoken to—someone directed their attention at me. This broke the memory and brought me back to the table, but only mentally. The body had long ago been orphaned.

Jealousy's Body

Many times when jealousy arises there is a strong experiencing of the body. I can't say I observe it, but I seem to intuit that there is a kind of "substate" behind it. There is a quick batting it away, a fear of seeing it, taking it in. So I don't have a question about this, I just see the functioning of this mechanism.

If not the sleep state, we are in the waking state. Other than in rare moments, the third state, the state of self-consciousness, is always intentional. So we first must self-remember, inhabit the body, have a conscious awareness of it. Only then is true self-observation possible. Otherwise, it's only "head-looking," what everyone does, which is commonly mistaken for self-observation or even for consciousness. Self-remembering creates a definite beginning, a new octave, a conscious context.

Tensing Up

Over and over again, when I inhabit a posture I become aware that the left shoulder is tensed upward and forward. Sometimes there is waking up to it as the shoulder is in the midst of creeping forward. I've seen how this tension affects the rest of the body, particularly the torso and neck.

As postures are habitual, not taken consciously, when you find yourself in a posture, use it as a reminder to come to yourself. Then scan the body-machine for other areas of tension. Map the various areas of tension and write it down in your Work Diary.

Observing Personality

What is the right way of looking at personality and the image we have of ourselves?

When we're young we're vulnerable and can easily be hurt, so naturally we protect ourselves by developing buffers—psychological partitions that keep us from experiencing contradictions inherent in the "I" structure, such as saying one thing and doing another. False personality is the whole "I" structure. False personality is the outer presentation, what we are constantly showing to the world; self-image, the prevailing idea, is the inner. Both are centered around our chief feature, or chief weakness, or chief compensation. We have entombed ourselves within it. We live within a "wall of imagination." Everything we see, think, feel, experience is discolored by imagination. Only one thing is not, because it is a silent, inner movement within the wall that changes nothing of the content-of-the-moment, only the quality-of-the-moment changes. Self-remembering, passive, neutral, active, is an inner redistribution of attention, breath, current. So one is freed to observe things as they are and not as we imagine them—though what is seen is imagination.

"I Love My Wife, But…"

I love my wife, but I see I don't really listen to her. What she says usually goes right through me. I make the appropriate gestures, but I'm only half-listening. She calls me on it sometimes and there is a part of me that can repeat what she's said. This drives her nuts.

If she's talking just to talk—inasmuch as she is in the Work—you might have a conversation about this. Otherwise, if she wants your attention and you are off in your own world, what does that tell you? I take it you're listening now.

[Nods]

Why are you listening?

I don't know, I just am.

Well, what did you hear?

Something I didn't understand.

And so you want to understand it?

I suppose so.

You speak of loving your wife. But isn't attention the basis of love? Can we say we love someone and then ignore them?

Well, I think—

Please, don't "think."

People say in the Work there is no love and—

In the Work there is the greatest love. People who say otherwise have never really experienced the Work. Now, if you are listening, isn't what you just said an avoidance. If we re-member ourselves, consciously come to physical presence, then the vibrations in time accumulate and a current is created. "Real love," as Mr. Gurdjieff says, "is a cosmic force which goes through us," but we have to make ourselves available.

III

Bargaining with God

I haven't met the woman I am looking for, and my fear is that I may spend the rest of my life alone. There is a very deep part of me that wishes to have a woman that I will be able to be happy with, who will truly love me, and who will be my partner in the Work. And I want to have children who will have both a father and mother—the mother I never had.

My friend, this is not therapy. You need to bring real material. That said, Mr. Gurdjieff speaks of a space in oneself being created in having lost a loved one—your mother, in this instance—and to let God fill this space. Instead, you want to fill it with a dream image that will love your self-image. Do you really want a partner? Or a mother? In terms of the Work, you hide behind this demand so you don't have to really work on yourself. You want God to give you the woman of your dreams first and then you'll work. So you are bargaining with God.

Peace, Harmony & Violence

I value peace and harmony, but at the same time I see that I am also violent. *This is not in keeping with my self-image, but it's me all the same.*

What do you think about fairness, justice?

Yes, I'm for fairness, too.

Why do you leave out justice?

I didn't know I was.

Isn't your idea of justice what causes the violence?

Justice is the cause of violence?

Look at the world, your life, everyone's life, why is it so violence-filled? We all say we want peace and harmony, but we demand justice.

But if—

Read chapter forty-three in *All and Everything.*

Texture of a Towel

I feel funny saying this. It seems so nothing, but I was standing at the sink and grabbed a towel and turned to the window. There was a thought to observe. I was standing straight, no particular tension. There was a lot of sensation in the hands. I could feel the texture of the towel. It must have been the weave. It was just an old towel I've used a hundred times before. But I never observed the feel of the cloth before.

No direct experiencing is trivial. It only seems so because we're so consumed with ideas, systems, intellectuality—head-tripping. There is a line in Eliot's *Four Quartets* that speaks of being in the rose garden, a garden the poet has been in so many times before, and "knowing it for the first time." Who has been there all the other times? Who has used that towel and not felt its weave? Can we answer? If we think we can, what evidence do we have? Evidence that derives from consciously lived experience, not description.

Do you follow?

Where Does "I" Go?

Listening to the two of you speaking, I observed that my left leg was crossed over my right and my hip became uncomfortable. The thought came to change the position. Then I was taken by something that was said. The next time I observed, the legs had switched, right over left, everything else the same position. I continued listening. Tried to observe moving from one posture to another and couldn't. I kept returning to the body, but when you spoke I'd be gone.

Let's all align the posture. Begin by relaxing the face, letting the flesh fall away from the skull. Now see that the two feet are on floor, pointing straight ahead, knees over the ankles, legs uncrossed, body erect. Experience the sacrum-lumbar. Move it forward a bit. Bring the shoulders into alignment with the hips. Now experience the sacrum-lumbar again and slowly, vertebra by vertebra, climb the tree of the spine. At the top of spine, drop the chin to the sternum. Elongate the neck. Raise the head and neck as one unit on top of the spinal column, keeping the chin down until the very end. With the head and neck thus supported, raise the chin to what is right for you. Rotate the shoulders up to the ears and backward. Now, give all the weight up to the skeletal system, the Earth. Relax the muscles. Take in the impression of the body in alignment. Experience the space, the freedom. Relaxing the muscles, the whole body, is a very strong and necessary work on oneself. Learn to work economically, the muscles relaxed, using as little energy as possible. Experiment when you do physical work. Slow down the tempo, speed it up, relax the eyes, count, and so forth. Work with the machine.

All Head & Hands

I was at the dentist yesterday having my teeth cleaned. It was nothing to be apprehensive about. I knew there would be nothing painful, so I thought this would be a good time to practice. I saw my hands were clenched, which surprised me. I relaxed my hands. Then something took me away. When I observed again, the hands were clenched again.

There are three centers—three machines operating within the

body-machine: intellectual, emotional and the instinctive-moving-sexual. Which center tried to calm you with the notion that it wouldn't be painful?

Probably the intellectual.

Given that, why were your hands clenched?

They just clenched. Some part of me was afraid.

Perhaps the instinctual and emotional centers didn't believe what the intellectual center said?

[Head nods]

We need to verify through our own observed experience that there are three centers. This could be one example. Self-observation begins with first noting which center is active at the moment, how it is functioning. Everything must be verified, not simply believed—that's a fundamental principle.

Things I Would Never Say

I was asked a question and immediately lied. I was surprised as there was no reason to lie. An "I" just shot to the surface with what it felt like saying and stuck me with what it said. You had mentioned making a list of likes and dislikes. I began to see things that I do all day long as "likes," things I would never say like or dislike to, but I must like them because I do them. For example, I dislike people who lie, yet I like to lie.

The "I" that lies never pays for it. You know better and yet you indulge. You have a certain influence over people. You can get them to follow you. You can easily lead some people astray. There needs to be a connection with conscience. You do not trust what is real in you. You know this yet you persist. Underneath the smiles is a hard self-will. You must understand—time is counted. There is no one counting, but we need to seriously work on ourselves. Otherwise, we'll know the words, the Work language, and be able to "talk the talk" but it's just empty concepts—there's no body to it. The Internet is full of talk like that.

How do I work with self-will?

Self-will can only be broken by doing what it will hate—doing what you are told to do in terms of the Work. Self-will always knows better, always insists on doing things its way. It stands in the way of coming to real will.

Where Are My Feet?

Sitting at the computer the thought came to observe my posture. I noticed I was up on the balls of my feet. I put them flat on the floor and decided to keep observing them. I glanced at the time displayed on the screen. Several times my attention went to the head then back to the feet. I felt maybe fifteen minutes had passed. I was surprised to see only a few minutes had gone by.

You acted on the mental reminder to inhabit the posture and so saw your feet. Instead of deeply experiencing the posture, you changed it, made it more comfortable. As you say, attention kept going back and forth between the head and the feet. It shows you were primarily still in the grip of the head. You don't speak about what happened with the feet after you stopped observing. Do you know?

No, I became too involved in what I was doing.

What Takes Me?

I was sitting in a swing on the deck. In a previous attempt a few days before I had been taken by the sound of a siren. I wanted to try again, not be taken. I was rocking back and forth heel to toe. The soles of my feet could feel a texture that felt like corduroy. It was the inside of my tennis shoe. I stayed with this. There were various sounds, birds, more sounds than usual. A loud motorcycle roared up a ramp. It didn't take me. Then I was taken when a breeze came up; I felt cold then and went inside.

You say there were "more sounds than usual." But what is the reference? Only the last time, or times that I tried to be present.

And these were fragmentary at best and without duration, yes? So my basis of objective comparison is minimal. I can only use the word "seems" as in "it seems there were more sounds than usual." Because "usually" I am not there or only partially so; that is, the specific gravity of my attention is all in my head, taken up with the thoughts of the moment and their projection and reaction. Now you were taken, but for how long? You have no idea really. You don't even know when you left. The cold breeze brought the attention back to the body. The body ordered you to go inside and you obeyed. This said, there is a lot of valuable material in what is reported.

A World Gone Mad

Since 9/11 the world seems to have gone mad. The violence and greed keep escalating along with the self-righteousness on all sides, no one taking responsibility, no accountability. It's depressing. I try not to be influenced but I am.

We're in a transition zone between the new world-time and the old. It began before 9/11, but that was the big shock point. History, in my opinion, will be divided between what is pre-9/11 and post. Understand that there is nothing you or I can do to change the world on the level of the world. We can work to change our relationship to the world, to become conscious receivers and transmitters of energy. In so doing, we help ourselves and the world.

IV

Observe what happens when someone begins to speak—where does the attention go? Isn't our habit to "understand" from the head? Observe that. When we leave the physical world, we become what? Uninhabited space stations, spinning around in space, reacting mechanically to external and internal shocks, and at the same time believing we're here.

The Body Rules

I see that I am controlled by my body. I give into it without protest. It rules me almost completely.

The machine always seeks its "comfort zone." Unless educated, it lives in inertia, passivity—it's only activated by the need or desire for food, sex, shelter, security, status. So our first work is with the body, with inhabiting and awakening the body. Work with postures is primary. Postures are physical, heavy; not like thoughts, feelings, impulses which are light, mercurial, difficult to really experience first-hand. Unless we have intentionally taken a posture, when we wake up—what do we wake up in?

Well, another posture.

Yes, so I can't know the posture I was in, but I can know this one if I inhabit the body, experience it from both the inside and outside. It's really an amazing revelation—I'm not here, it only looks like I'm here. Same with most everyone.

Likes & Dislikes

In looking at my likes and dislikes, the self-will of "I"s has been seen. What I had thought was a lack of will is actually self-will of "I"s.

A keen observation. Yes, there is the self-will of the "I"s. Only in self-remembering do I enter the realm of real will. You might ask yourself why this is.

Yes.

Do you know what self-remembering is?

To begin with, it is dividing the attention.

But before the attention is divided what must occur?

I don't follow you.

Had you inhabited the body?

You mean was I aware of the body?

Yes.

Sort of.

There are many degrees of self-remembering—you can do so on the level of the Moon, the Earth, the planets, and so on, but "sort of" is not one of them. Please understand, there can be no rightly conducted self-observation without self-remembering.

Too Big to Work With

An experience has generated a good deal of frustration and anger. The emotional reaction completely takes over. The experience seems too big to work with.

To work in emotional moments requires a great deal of self-study and practice. So prepare by working in small, neutral moments, ones that have a definite beginning, middle and end. For example, washing your hands, taking off your shoes. Work often. Extend the duration; the depth and separation will follow.

It Makes Me Feel Awkward

I find that in self-observing there is almost always a sense of awkwardness, of being peculiar.

Yes, in the beginning it's a taboo to actually be present. There's even a sense of disloyalty. You're a black sheep, not one of the group. It shows you how much we see the world topsy-turvy. See where the attention is, where it goes, and why.

The Exact Same Posture

I was driving home from work and observed a familiar posture. My right foot was resting on the heel, the toes lifted. The left foot was on the brake. My left elbow was on the armrest, the arm up and the nail of the thumb between my front teeth, the right arm on the steering wheel. Then the light changed and my attention was taken. Later, at another light, I found the body in the same posture. Observed this several more times, the exact same posture every time!

Our postures are our "clothes." Like our movements, we only have so many postures in our wardrobe. As circumstances and shocks repeat, so do our "outfits." We rarely see the "clothes" we are wearing. Our wardrobe gives us a subliminal sense and feeling of identity. Just think of it—all this is going on with you and everyone else all the time and no one is conscious of anything below the chin. Now, participate in the postures you observe by really inhabiting them, breathing into them, amplifying the awareness.

I, Myself & Me

What another student said at a previous meeting I am beginning to realize is true with me as well. In talking to people I'm not really interested in what they are saying. Of course, I pretend to carefully listen so they think I am a good listener, engage in gossip so they like me, and express compassion so they think I care. But deep down all I want to do is get to the point where the focus is on me. It's really chilling to see this.

Before you entered the Work was there any awareness of this?

I don't think so. If there was it made no impression.

This is an individual and a group work. We meet together weekly to share the material we've unearthed in working to be present. What one person discovers alerts others to that as a line of observation; that is, to look for that once the body-machine is inhabited. As much as we talk about ourselves, are concerned with ourselves, we truly do not know ourselves. Once the attention is rightly redirected out of the head brain, its usual locale, we feel what is observed. The impressions are much stronger, deeper, more lasting. Otherwise, we are only seeing from the ordinary mind, the formatory mind. Behind this is the real mind.

Psychic Murderer

I had a meeting with my boss's boss. I observed the reaction of swelling with pride—I actually "puffed up"—when he said how impressed he was with how I handled a meeting. It seemed a good time to bring up the rather sizeable raise I had been promised. He gave me the corporate "not yet." I played the yes-man, and so forth. Inside though, I was raging. An "I" emerged that wanted to strangle him. This was kind of scary.

Push the right button and beneath the civilized veneer a psychic murderer may emerge. Perhaps that's why murder mysteries sell so well, no? As long as the animal is not consciously integrated, it remains wild. For all the trappings of civilization, we live in the Wild Kingdom where money rules. Remember, St. Paul says the root of evil is not money but the love of money. This is a work in life, not a monastery or ashram, so we don't divide life up into times to be present and not. But, as I mentioned to you earlier, it's too soon to mix the Work with your job. Lastly, you speak as if you were present during this whole meeting. Is that the truth?

I tried to be.

Changing of the Guard

There was a moment when the "I" changed from one "I" to another. It was noticed but immediately identified with.

If there's duration, this millisecond switch—"the changing of the guard"—can be apperceived. You'll discover that not only do the "I"s change but the postures and other manifestations, as well. It's all happening without our knowledge on a "subterranean" level if we are not present. Did you notice the identification in the moment? Or was it long afterward?

Long afterward.

If you see it in the moment, then observe the identification. Or, if you realize what happened long afterward, then take that as a reminder to remember yourself. Use everything!

Ode to the Cantilever

I was standing at the sink washing some dishes, standing away so as not to get my clothes wet, leaning forward on the balls of the feet. Thought to observe. The body was leaning forward in an arc. I observed tension in the front of the body, the contracted part, relaxation in the back. Toes curled. Reaching out. Cantilevered. The thought came, "cantilever." I began to remember all I knew about cantilevers. I was so taken with "cantilevered," proud of knowing what it is, that I forgot all about the observation.

Again, did you forget? Did you actually choose to forget? Or were you, your attention, taken? Our language always assumes a conscious "doer." The consensual assumption is that our lives are a seamless stream of consciousness and doing by an indivisible I. We need to verify the truth or falseness of this by the evidence of our own observed experience.

V

The Great Illusion

While driving I remembered myself and noticed voices chattering. As the voices became clearer, it was as if there were two or three people sitting in the car with me, each with its own agenda and priorities. We've talked about "I"s, but I'd never really seen them in the moment.

The fundamental illusion, the meta-belief, is that I am an indivisible I. It's a hard nut to crack, so forgive me if I keep saying it. In reality I am a "zoo" of different "I"s, each having its own agenda, some quite contradictory. We need to verify this time and again, as the "I-illusion" is strong and constantly reinforced by society.

Self-Calming Is Good

Identifications have one content and self-calming another. Without thinking about it, I've felt self-calming was good because it stopped the mind from stressing. But now I see that self-calming is just a deep form of lying.

Observe how often we say "I," as in "I like," "I don't like," "I don't care." This "I" is invested in everything. Our identifications completely coat us. To self-calm, this "I" runs the gamut from manic activity to walling ourselves off psychologically, even physically sometimes. So self-calming has many permutations. At base, yes, it's lying because it is soaked in avoidance. Deeper, ask yourself what self is being calmed?

What's So Wrong About Being Wrong?

I was told I'd done something wrong. I wanted to make myself right. When I calmed down I saw I was wrong, and then I wanted to hide.

I realized I couldn't hide forever, so I emailed the person. My message was more contrite than I really felt. Now, as I speak, I wonder if I hid behind that so as not to express negativity?

You were expressing it but not verbally. You read about not expressing negativity in *In Search of the Miraculous*, yes?

[Nods]

We should first observe ourselves expressing it. This goes against what is ordinarily believed. I'll speak to this later. As to what you say, I hide myself away in the little video game that the formatory mind likes to play out. Why can't I accept being wrong? Why the drama? Please don't "think" about this—observe it in the moment so it can speak to you.

Analyzing & Judging

When something happens I see my mind wants to immediately analyze and judge it. The only time this doesn't happen is when the mind is quiet and when the experience is all encompassing, overwhelming and intense.

The "mind" you speak of is the formatory mind, the mind that is always forming associations, opinions, comparing, judging, backfilling, worrying, gloating and constantly commenting. Real mind has no clutter. By the way, how's it going with observing habits?

Well, right. I remember now. Sorry.

If we're to speak rigorously, you can't be sorry. You didn't deliberately forget. It just happened, yes? Like everything else happens.

Intoxicating Power

I was put in a position of power. Externally, a mild mannered "I" appeared that was cordial and nice to everyone, but internally there was this celebration of the power. Throughout the day reminders came to remember myself, but the mind was so intoxicated that it took all the attention and the body never had a chance to exist.

On every level with every animate thing there is a will to power. Schopenhauer was the first to formulate this and Nietzsche later expanded on it. Instead of using this in the service of the person—with all the attendant and never ending problems that brings—what if we used the will not for power but for the will to be?

You say "the mind was so intoxicated that it took all the attention." Ponder what this means.

Ponder?

There are three smaller machines within the body-machine—three centers: intellectual, emotional and instinctive-moving. Connect them through self-remembering and then think, feel and sense whatever is to be pondered.

Who or What Takes the Posture?

While observing the body there was a small shock and the body automatically assumed a pose. Who assumed this automatic posture?

Was it a "who" or a "what"? And was there observation of this? That is, did the shock break your attention and only later did you find the body in a new posture and make the inference that someone or something had to have moved it? Keep observing. The answer is in the Immediate.

Not Revealing Myself

At last week's meeting I didn't say anything because I didn't want to reveal myself to the group. I didn't want to show my embarrassment and shame. There also was a fear that I might cry in front of the group.

There's a Work term for what you just described. Do you know what that is?

Internal considering.

Yes.

"Are You Enjoying It?"

I had a strong experience of internal considering, sorry, I mean "internal," at a theatrical performance. I wanted to see the performance, but I found myself caught up in considering if my husband was enjoying it. Did he think it was a waste of time, boring? The considering colored my own experience and at intermission I nearly suggested we leave. Only after asking and being assured that he was okay was I able to relax and experience the performance for myself.

Internal considering is a killer. It entwines us in its machinations. Your husband was there with you, so there was an agreement on that level. But you psychologized. You were not there yourself. It was good you spoke to him, as it surfaced your fear. Understand the difference between internal considering and external considering. Relationships are built on the latter, destroyed with the former.

How Did I Get Here?

Last week I went to an art show. I wanted to conserve my attention for two or three objects and not be bled dry by scattering it. In various locations I would stand before a painting and pretend to look at it while observing myself. At one point, I was sitting on a bench and an old man, feeble and unsure, sat down near me. Shortly, a woman, probably his wife, came up and asked him in an anxious voice, "Are you okay?" "Yes, I am fine," he said in a tired voice. All of a sudden I experienced a fear in the middle of my chest. I knew these two selves that had appeared before me and felt the fear of my own mortality. And then I apparently got up and walked into the next gallery. I say "apparently" because I suddenly realized I was in the gallery and really didn't know how I'd gotten there.

This is an illustrative cameo of how we live our lives, thinking we are here, worrying about one day not being here. But the question is not "Who am I?"—which presumes a certain hereness—but "Am I here?" And if so, "How am I here?"

Yes, we all have only so much time in the body-machine. None of us knows how much time. We head-worry about dying, but it's just another way of avoiding what is. Up until now most of our observations have been from the head. The body-machine, its habits and postures, haven't really been observed. We are not in physical reality; we only appear to be.

VI

The stronger the vanity and self-love, the stronger the identification with being right. Why the insistence on being right? The refusal to be wrong? Why are we so afraid of being wrong?

The Hollow Man Awakens

Talking with a friend there was the stark realization that I had not been listening and had been completely asleep. Externally the body was making all the gestures of listening, but internally nothing was being absorbed. In that moment it was seen how I was positioning myself to talk at the first opportunity. As soon as I saw this, there was an effort made to remember and to really be there, to listen. There was a change in the environment, the space grew larger and there was a feeling that the person on some level noticed the change.

This is genuine material and rarely seen and even more rarely acknowledged. The hollow gestures, the self-positioning, the hypocrisy of looking like you were listening. Of course, none of it is intentional, conscious. And, yes, at some level the fact that you became embodied and so were truly listening had an effect on your friend. Isn't it interesting that we want and need relationship—isn't that what most of us are constantly seeking? Why then do so few have it? We must first relate to ourselves before we can relate to others.

Body Takes a Posture

I had an experience walking and experiencing the pelvis as I did. There was a point in the walk where I saw the body take a posture. There was this inner feeling of the posture and then the leaving of it. The impressions were very subtle but strong, and this experience has given me an interest in working with postures again. It was very surprising to see how much information was received from the impressions of just one posture.

After a few observations most students resist working with postures. The attitude is, "Okay, I've seen it, now let's move on."

But there is a wealth of data in postures. They are concrete, physical and observable in the way thoughts, feelings and impulses are not. We don't take postures, they take us. We are moved through the whole day from one posture to another, and it's all mechanical. I am too busy with my thoughts and feelings to observe them. Postures are directly connected to our states and cannot be denied the way more subtle reactions can be. Please continue. This is the way to build a strong foundation.

Alignment

There was an experience with postures this past week while trying to read. There was trouble staying awake. I knew I couldn't read while lying down. I tried sitting on the couch, in a straight chair, at a table. Sitting at the table, one leg wanted to rest on the other, my upper body wanted to lean to one side or sprawl. Each time I found myself falling asleep and not having the attention to read more than a few sentences. Up until the very end the body resisted the correct posture: sitting at the table with my feet flat on the floor, knees over the ankles, my back aligned properly, the shoulders over the hips. Once I got into this posture, attention was easier to control and there was more energy for the task.

Physical alignment brings inner alignment. The first struggle is with the machine. It is the denying force. Later, it may become the affirming. In a quiet time do this exercise: tense the arms but keep the rest of the body relaxed. Do this when sitting, standing, lying down. Practice this every day. After several weeks do the same when you are out in the world.

Experiencing the Shock

I was in a meeting with someone who I have a lot of judgments about. So I made it my goal not to let anything she said get to me. I felt that I was fairly successful at it. But after the meeting I realized I was not embodied. The whole scenario had taken place in the head.

So the "material" you report is in itself worthless, but that you have the sincerity to report is worth a great deal. Your face is flushed. Are you shocked?

Yes.

The shock has connected you with the body. Experience the shock directly. Don't mix it with thought. Do not say "I" to it. Stay separate. Give the shock its energy, the freedom to act itself out— but keep it below the neck.

"She"

There was an incident with another person and later I intentionally sought him out. Speaking to him, I became aware not only of postures but other manifestations. The falseness of the "she" that was there, all the personality manifesting, was amazing and sickening, even though to the ordinary listener "she" probably sounded like "she" always does.

"She" is a good name for false personality, "she" as in "she who must be obeyed." "She" is very concerned with being the "fairest," the "purest," no?

I don't understand.

You will if you keep working with this intensity.

The Wages of Fear

I see that I live in fear to an extent I never realized before. It leads to my guarding myself emotionally and physically and not being vulnerable. I do not want others to see who I really am. But there is a sense that there is something else that is more primary that is lying underneath the fear.

As we work to see ourselves, we become less opaque. Take this as a line of observation. Work small, the smaller the better. Observe all the little ways fear arranges your life, how you insist on making yourself right. Keep the question of something deeper than the fear, but don't pursue it. Let it come to you in its own time, in its own way.

The Therapist-Patient Game

A woman at work who is very curt was walking toward me in the hall. There was an impulse to treat her curtly, and also the thought to smile. The feeling came up that it would "kill" me to smile. As she came near, I smiled and we passed one another. So I saw this very pretty "I" I put on.

This is just description. But there is really no material in what you say. You weren't embodied. This is what people say to their therapists, but no one is there, embodied and observing impartially, so it's just two persons playing the therapist-patient game.

Where Is the Mind?

As I sit here, I am experiencing a high degree of being embodied. Where is the mind?

Experience, don't question. You're avoiding by intellectualizing. Overcome your fear. Open to the Immediate, breathe, relax, allow yourself to go deeper.

Your face is changing.

Of course. We are energy. Energy converting into matter, matter into energy. Life is dynamic, not fixed, not static.

I Felt Stripped

I was remembering myself while walking toward a door where some people were standing. They looked at me and I felt stripped, like they could see right through me.

You became self-conscious at that moment.

What do you mean "self-conscious"?

I am not using the term in the way Gurdjieff did—as a stage of self-remembering. In this case, you took the shock personally, and so the person reacted and felt vulnerable, embarrassed. Do you follow?

I think so.

If thinking, you are not following. Now the same can happen

when the attention becomes embodied. But then the impressions are much stronger and involve two centers, perhaps three. In any case, there was a shock and a stop. Instead of being able to keep the forces separate, they were personalized. Hence the reaction of feeling naked, a bit like Adam in the Garden, no?

VII

Patterns upon Patterns

I noticed people I was with expressed themselves in predictable patterns. I mentioned this and someone pointed out that my response was just as predictable. It was a shock. I thought I was being "fair." Even though this tendency has been pointed out to me before, I have never really seen it as my pattern. I have always seen being fair as a "good" behavior and not a habitual pattern.

Mechanicality is predictable because it is simply patterned reaction. We are bioplasmic machines. The only difference between us and animals, as Mr. Gurdjieff says, is that we have a greater complexity of reactions to external impressions and a more complex construction for perceiving and reacting to them. Complicated, yes, but a machine nevertheless, defaulting in predictable patterns, reacting to circumstances, real and imagined, from interpreted and conditioned memory of what the machine takes itself and the world to be. The "fair-I," like all "I"s, is circumscribed by a "magic circle" of "I"s fulfilling ideas and the patterns of reaction they impel. In bringing awareness to the machine another body begins to develop which exerts an intelligent stewardship over the machine. So it is two bodies in one. At that point I have ceased to be a machine. Do you follow?

No.

Good.

How "I" Gets Its Way

Speaking with someone, I saw this "nice-I" manipulating to get its way. It was like, do this for "me" because I am nice and should have things done for me.

How we get our way gives a real insight into what's beneath the floorboards. Your "I-of-the-moment" meets another's "I-of-the-moment" and the manipulation begins, usually unknowingly. There is so much to see. For example, besides the smiles how do you position yourself in regard to space?

If the situation begins to turn against what you want, do you overpower the moment? Turn up the flattery? Turn cold, resentful? Remember, it's all mechanical, no judgments. Or if judging yourself, see that as well.

Bad Mood Rising

I was in a negative mood. I tried to change my mood but couldn't. The thought came that this would be a good time to observe. I was sitting in an armchair. My abdomen was tight, the usual tensions in my upper body. The breathing was not constricted. Then I realized that the observations were from the head, that I was doing a mental inventory of the body.

We are always in a mood, but we only use the word for its extremes. We have such a habit of observing everything from the head that we don't realize it. It is only in waking up to it time and again that one can come to true self-observation. We must strive to observe like scientists. A biologist looking at a virus under a microscope, for example, isn't hoping the virus gets better. He or she wants to know what it is, how it reacts. There's no identification. The observation is impartial.

"I Don't Have the Time"

When I remembered about writing my question down, my initial reaction was "I don't have time," and so forth. The next day there was the memory of why I came to the Work, then I felt remorse. It's like the head struggles with the head.

Ask yourself, who is it that doesn't have the time? What "I" is this? Almost as much as money, what's important to us, what we're loathe to give away, is "our time." And what do we do with this time? Do we really use it to our advantage? Or is it just living the selfish animal life? When the Buddha addressed his monks, he said, "Oh sentient beings..." Today, he might say, "Oh mental beings..." As to the word *remorse*, that's a very big word.

Scrambled Eggs

During the morning exercise suddenly something came up that happened between my mother and me when I was a five or six years old. I was sitting at the kitchen table with a plate of scrambled eggs in front of me that I wouldn't eat. My mother became exasperated and said, "If you don't eat those eggs, you're gonna wear them!" I shook my head that I wouldn't and she dumped them on my head. What I see now is that this is probably one of the few times in my life where I have really asserted myself.

Did you feel that was unfair?

Of course.

Do you see a connection between that and your work as an interior designer?

No, not really.

You're very concerned about doing the right thing, aren't you?

[Silence]

Everything is connected on every level. What we are today is what we were yesterday. We can only change tomorrow by changing today. And the only real change we can make is in how we consciously relate to ourselves. This is very fertile material you've reported. Keep pondering it.

The Emotional Body

My wish was to observe the machine during times of emotion. For days afterward I kept that wish with me, repeating it over and over to myself. Then, when winding a watch my father had owned, I noticed this sadness in my chest. It was as if it was being stepped on, a heavy weight. Well, after that I didn't see much and completely forgot my wish.

Your wish was answered. And your father was the means. The father was your first contact with the masculine. Your deep feeling toward your father, your loss, makes a place for something higher. We have only so much energy for work and when that is used up no work is possible. So it is not surprising that you completely forgot your wish. But, speaking as you have, your wish can be renewed. Now, to explore more deeply—and not only to observe the body but to become the body—you need not only to observe but to first re-member yourself.

All Object, No Subject

There has been a lot of distaste for people, all the lying, venality, aggression, hubris, the lack of shame. At one point I saw that I was so projected outward that there was nothing of me. This allowed a centering or balancing to take place and the distaste disappeared. In saying this there was a sensation in my chest and abdomen like a fire was started, but no pain.

Before, I was completely lost, eaten up, in a world that was all object, no subject. We think we live in subject-object orientation, but do we? If we watch our attention we are all object; that is, our attention is completely identified with the object. Or we are all subject, completely identified, indwelling, full of self-concern. But because you are now being introduced to the idea and practice of having a double attention—having a recognition of both the subject and object simultaneously—it was suddenly realized how swallowed up you were. Before, no such discrimination would have been possible. Having a true subject-object perception is the third tier. And then perhaps, after a long work on yourself, the fourth appears, which is centerless.

"Joker-I"

The past week there have been several occasions when it was observed that I say things on a superficial level. What I say is not what would be said if the thought, idea, or subject had been reflected on even briefly. It feels as if something is sitting in the top of my head and speaking for me. It speaks very quickly before the rest of me is engaged or even knows what is being said. It will say just about anything—true or not—to be funny. This trait has been there a long time and seems to be very deep and pervasive.

One of the interesting things about the "joker-I" is that he both deflects attention from the situation or subject being discussed and from yourself. And at the same time he attracts attention to you, the joker. The "joker-I" has been robbing you blind for years. Take his role away from him. Intentionally joke.

Other Bodies

I entered our office elevator after swimming. I was trying to move my "I" awareness from between my eyes down to the abdomen. Two attractive women got on the elevator. I immediately became conscious that my body was making a number of extremely rapid "adjustments," of which I am normally unconscious. Like straightening my posture, moving to "correct" social distance, keeping the visual field, but not directly looking at them. But there was something else. I had the sense that our bodies were rapidly "exchanging data" and reacting. The awareness was physical and centered in the abdomen. We didn't directly look at each other nor did we speak. I was aware of an olfactory perception, but not any specific odor, perfume or scent. Just the presence of it. I left the elevator with an intense physical, though not sexual, sense that our bodies had somehow had a significant encounter. To remember this, I have to return to the solar plexus–and immediately the scene in the elevator returns—along with a sense of energy in my hands (maybe associated with swimming earlier?). I can't immediately decipher what the specific content of the body exchange involved, except that it was generally positive and very rapid.

There is the idea of "thinking in different categories," though that's from a different model. But to actually think one must first experience in different categories. Once we get out of the word cage, we leave the level of the Moon world, heavy with dualism, irrationality and agitation, and enter an entirely new domain which has been there all along, but which our identifications, our self-love, have blinded us to. We live in a sexual world, not only physically but emotionally and mentally. It's ongoing, though we usually play dumb to it by circumscribing it. Mr. Gurdjieff called it "reciprocal maintenance," but we generally refer to it on a much larger scale.

VIII

New World, Old World

I ran into a former colleague I used to work with years ago. The experience was very deep on many levels. As we spoke there was a strong sense of the old world I had been in. There was also the strong organic taste of the current world that I was speaking from. So there was the old world and this other new world awared simultaneously. I say "world" because the organic taste was that it was more than "I." What was being experienced was a whole way of being in terms of postures, facial expressions, perceptions, beliefs. I hadn't known that I was still carrying the old world and meeting this person called it up. I wonder now as I speak how many other worlds I am carrying that I don't know about. Deeper was the beginning of real understanding of how I hadn't let go not only of this old world but what I was carrying against someone.

We pass through many worlds in our lives. To the extent we have integrated and understood them, we no longer carry them. We take the weight off our shoulders, literally as well as figuratively—a reason, perhaps, why so many people are bent with age. We don't "do" this but rather we make ourselves available by being present and allowing the integration to occur. What impedes this, of course, is what we hold against others, what we think has to be atoned for. But we're just strapping ourselves to this person. If we wait for this, we may well wait all our lives. And remember, it is your narrative, your subjectivity, by which you are fixing and insisting. In this way, you are judging yourself. Remember what the New Testament says about judging.

Every Posture Has Its "I"

I see that just as I am always in a posture, every posture has its "I."

Yes, the machine is never without a posture and each posture is a representative of an "I." Now, can we observe the posture impartially without judging it, wanting to improve it, move it to a "better" posture? Can we inhabit it; that is, look first from a double attention, a subject-object orientation, but then be the posture, merge with it without identifying with it?

Body Work, Computer Work

There was a question tonight about how to work with the influence of the computer. I have set up alarms to remind me to stop and come down into the body, but very little sensation has been experienced and the computer would just suck me back in. What came up after having the question in my mind was to step away from the computer and go in the other room and then try to come down into the body.

Mr. Gurdjieff says that if people learn to think with the proper mind they will be able to think even better in their work with machines. One of the fundamental questions of our time is how to work with machines. So we must experiment.

Doing It Right

After leaving the Day of Exploration I noticed that I was confused as to the seven steps you gave to become self-conscious. I felt a kind of panic. I couldn't remember and I didn't want to be seen as having confused the instructions. I didn't want to call anyone and ask for help. So I tried to remember on my own, but I wasn't sure that I was doing it right. The feeling of panic that was experienced seemed tied into doing it right, doing the work perfectly.

Ahh, but remember—we are perfectly imperfect.

You're not going to tell me?

No.

Supermarket Checkout

There was a lot of attention and energy in the body and there was this experience of the pelvis while walking that I've never had before. There was a point in the walking where it was observed that the body just took a posture. I was able to observe the body going into the posture, what it felt like to be in the posture and leaving the posture. In the moment the impressions were very subtle but strong, and this experience has given me a drive to work with postures again.

There's a wealth of data in postures. Postures are concrete, physical, and observable in the way thoughts, feelings and impulses are not. But they are all connected. So in observing the posture, also observe what you are thinking, what you are feeling. Now, it's time to experiment. Inhabit a posture and then intentionally move to another, inhabiting that as well. Practice at home. Then take it to the supermarket checkout line.

I Cried in Public

The past several days have been very emotional. Usually, I keep a tight lid on emotions, especially in public. But this week the emotions were so strong that I cried in public—in restaurants in front of waiters and other people dining, and in front of a bus driver—and I felt ashamed and thought that they would feel uncomfortable being around me and keep their distance. I was actually surprised to find that people were very sympathetic ... and I felt this emotional bond with people that I don't normally have. And I recognized that there is an "I" that gets in the way of this and keeps an emotional distance from people.

Self-remembering allows us to take in impressions directly, unfiltered. That makes us more emotional. The hypnotic momentum of ordinary life is broken. Out of nonbeing, one enters being—a being present in the midst of all the mechanical becoming of life. Becoming without being is sheer mechanicality. Being, we consciously receive and digest impressions, rather than simply react to them. And, yes, all people, except sociopaths, have an innate understanding of tears.

"I" Voices

A few days after last week's meeting I heard a voice say, "You have nothing to report for next week." Then suddenly it was the day before the meeting and still nothing to report. There had been some moments that were intentional, but this voice seemed to be a general attitude. As though something will come, just wait for it.

Voices are the talking part of "I"s. They need to be listened to, impartially. Instead of acquiescing to the attitudes they represent, we need to resist them, act the opposite. That you will be rewarded for making no effort is as irrational as a voice that purports to know the future. Be active, not passive.

Staying Above the Fray

My mother always told me to "Stay above the fray." My father was prone to emotional outbursts that quickly escalated to rage. His temper could be triggered by something as simple as a light bulb that needed changing. "Ignore it," mother would say. I went one better. I developed "self-control." The only thing I could control was what I took to be "me." At one point I was down to eating only eight hundred calories a day. While an overachiever at school, I had eating disorders at home.

As a result, one has developed a powerful "controller-I." It's like the Mafia, it offers protection, security of a sort, but in return it takes your life by keeping you "above the fray." It appears not to react, puts on a good front. Take the need to control as a line of observation; see its influence in even the smallest areas of your life. In your work on yourself you've come to something important. Observe now who makes your decisions. It's going to take courage to continue to observe. If you come to feeling hopelessness and futility don't fall into it. It's a sign this "I" is weakening. You must apply your reason to your feelings, master them. But this can only be achieved if you first become embodied. That will mean the hopelessness will seem to become even stronger. Keep it below the neck, ride it out.

Head Case

I was given a task to do. Immediately, there was the thought of an excuse. A number of excuses were run through, all with possible objections; it was like a court trial being played out in my head. Finally, there was an "I" that denied the task had been given to me.

People often think they are not creative. But just watch when I'm told to do something I don't want to do. Our "creator-I" is world-class and without shame, even to the point of pleading amnesia.

IX

"I Completely Forgot"

I didn't do the exercise. I completely forgot about it. When you gave it last week I made a point to come into my body and really hear it so that I would remember it. But it wasn't until today that I remembered.

You did not remember as an intentional act. It just happened, no?

Well, my memory produced it.

But memory is only one part of us. And to what extent is it yours? Is it yours like your car?

What do you mean?

You claim ownership of both your memory and your car. But they exist on different levels. One is concrete and outside you. The other is subtle and inside. Can you manipulate your memory like you can your car?

I don't know. I've never tried. I've studied for tests.

We all have a small amount of energy and freedom to wish to be, to remember. The energy has to be husbanded and spent judiciously. We have to keep our wish alive by reminding ourselves how easily we forget. Let me ask you—Are you mostly awake in life?

I don't know. I think so. I mean I have a job, obligations, all that.

When you first heard the idea that we are asleep, mechanical, cannot do, have no indivisible I—did you apply it to yourself?

I could see what was said, yes.

But wasn't there a sense that because you could mentally comprehend it that it somehow didn't really apply to you...or at least not as much as to other people who don't know about these ideas?

Yes, I see what you mean. I did do that but not consciously.

Of course not. So, despite what you've read and your practice of the teaching, you still take yourself to be mostly awake and only sometimes asleep. Isn't that right?

Well, I got to this meeting.

The truth is—and this must be verified by repeated self-observation—that what we call being awake is usually only mental.

If that was true, I feel like I would be left with nothing.

Let's say that's true. Now how do you know it's nothing?

I don't follow you.

If I say "I am nothing," that which knows and says that it is nothing cannot by definition be "nothing."

What is it then?

Directly experience what you call your nothingness. The answer is in the experiencing. Look up in *Search* what Mr. Gurdjieff says to Ouspensky about this.

Totally in Love

So many times I've heard the idea of only living out of the head, and I always thought I understood—that was the trouble, I only "thought." Now, inhabiting the body, there is the realization that I've been looking at everything from my head. I've been totally in love with my thoughts. Now I want to stop thought.

To stop thought one must first experience oneself in thought and not in thought, to discriminate the difference. That means inhabiting the body and observing. When we do so initially the mind becomes spacious because of the redirection of the attention out of thoughts that have been thinking us. This is a shock, albeit a very subtle shock. The shock clears the space of the mind momentarily. And then what happens?

The mind fills up with thought again.

Yes, but now one is experiencing this arising of thought from a mind without thought. So a discrimination is born.

The Envy of Others

Today the exercise of self-image came up. What was seen was an "I" that wants to be envied by others. At first, I couldn't acknowledge this; it was too strong, too much to be eaten. I wanted to be admired, respected, but "envied"? This "I" remained and it was seen that I did desire the envy of others, to be esteemed by them so that they would want to be me.

That's a big snake around your neck. It took a great deal to admit it. It shows the seriousness of your work on yourself that you could bring this to the meeting.

There was an "I" that said since I'd seen it and admitted it to myself that I didn't have to speak about it here.

That snake has been strangling you, taking your energy, distorting your relationship with yourself and others. To get it off your neck you have to weaken it. That means having the sincerity to speak about it here, share it with the group, each of whom is working with their own serpents. Now, take this as a continuing line of observation—that is, look at the "envied-I" in the smallest things.

The Sensual Body

These past days there's been a deeper connection with the body . . . I have to say "body," as "machine" just doesn't feel right. It has been a very sensual experience. Then something happened a little later; there was the recognition of being completely in the head, filled with thoughts. The sensation was as if my head was going to explode. So there was the recognition that the energy needed to be embodied. Then the feet appeared and there was the energy moving down, becoming relatively balanced. So there was a deep gratitude for the practice.

We live in a very mental, technologized world-time. The head is taken for all. It keeps all the attention for itself. So, again and again, machine or body, I need to redirect the attention into the body, breathe into the body, connect to the ground, amplify and breathe the current up, and so forth. Make a conscious contact with the world. The world is alive, sensual; open the pores of the body and breathe it in.

"Work-I"

There has been an "I" that has developed out of the Work and functions differently than I am used to. There will be a Work situation where there will be a "yes" and a "no" where I would usually side with the "no"; this new "Work-I" argues for the "yes." It seems not to go through the regular channels.

The continual grounding in the reality of the body and the material that self-observation unearths develops a new "I," a "Work-I," that begins to allow a new valuation and perspective that lets me begin to see things as they are and not as I have imagined. Welcome.

The World, Me, Everyone

I am so negative about everything. There is a constant litany that the world, me, everyone is not good enough. I want to work with this.

Negativity is almost a default condition as long as we are asleep, for we personalize, psychologize everything. It colors our whole life—nothing and no one is good enough, including me. Simply experience and observe it, don't judge it, or want to improve it. Let it express itself. At this stage express negative emotions so you know what they are and how they function.

Forgiveness

I've been thinking about forgiveness, what it is. There was a deep wish to know what this word truly meant, so I looked up the word in the dictionary. One of the meanings was "to thoroughly give" and when I read that it was like an ocean opened up, it was as if I had stepped into a clearing. There was an understanding that this called for a giving up of my judgments, ideas of others, my beliefs about them. It was very clear that what was important was what was happening inside of me, and not outside.

The work to forgive others begins with the work to forgive myself. First we need to recognize that forgiveness that comes from wanting to forgive is bogus. It's only one "I," a thought or feeling of the moment evoked by a situation. It's when the need for forgiveness won't let you alone that the boiling point has been reached. What is it that prevents forgiveness?

I want to, but something won't let me.

It could be the wish for revenge, for a settling of accounts. Go deeper into this—not by thinking about it but directly stepping into it.

Putting a Plant in Your Life

You had recommended that I buy myself a plant. I picked out one that I seemed to have an affinity with. The saleslady showed me how to water it, that you dip and keep it submerged until no more bubbles come up. It was so simple I was kind of wonderstruck. When she was ringing me up, a shock came and the realization that from this moment I was responsible for this plant's life. I felt like there was an energy channel between me and the plant. I live with a person who loves plants, the bathroom has about a half-dozen. That night when I went into the bathroom I felt for a brief moment that I was resonating with all of them. I'd lived there for almost three months and this was the first time this ever happened.

So much of life we pass by, never see or relate to. Everything is energy converting into matter and back into energy. The world is alive. Let it speak to you.

The Drifter

When I do the morning exercise I find my attention drifting.

Only will and consciousness can develop. First make sure you are in alignment. Take it step-by-step, beginning with relaxing the face, letting the flesh fall away from the skull. Give up all the weight to the earth, to the skeletal system, free the muscles from the bones. Settle in. Experience the body, work with the attention and the exercise as given. Welcome whatever occurs.

But the attention keeps drifting.

Our attention is usually invisible to us. Whatever takes our attention…that we are. It's directed by either our will or desire. Identified with the person as we are, it is drawn, captured, drained by outer and inner worlds. Then, exhausted, we numb our way through life until the next "attraction." Once again, the attention bites and again we are leeched. Observe the frustration and how it may turn into self-disgust. Be with it. Just intellectually "knowing" is not enough, the emotional center must be activated. Then a genuine wrath arises. That is the basis of a new move.

But what if I can't do it? I wonder if it's beyond me at this stage?

Why hypnotize yourself. You have yet to really make an effort. You are "end-gaining," looking for results. Do not be concerned with results, for who is it, what "I," that demands results? When the need for results is seen through and given up one moves to a new level of work.

I find that I don't practice unless there is a reward.

We feed on the world's "carrots." Like an animal, no carrot, no work. You are only a year or so old in the Work. Still a baby. But the "baby" is observing herself enough that she is beginning to see something of why she acts and does not act. Hard on the self-image, good food for essence. By the way, how's the work on habits going?

I'm ashamed.

Forget the shame. Resolve.

X

People Fear

There was one person waiting when I walked into a doctor's waiting room. I thought of doing otherwise and sitting next to him but instead sat so there would be an empty chair between us. Then someone came in and sat in the empty chair on the other side of me. This immediately created a new tension. There was a relaxing with it. Then the smell of this person was noticed and their energy felt. Another person came in then and sat down in the empty chair on the other side, so now I had people on both sides of me. I made an intentional effort to smile at the person and make a connection. These few moments of observation were experienced as a great exploration.

Were you embodied when this was happening?

Not for all of it. It came and went.

There was the thought of doing otherwise, but it was overcome by the instinctive fear of sitting close to a stranger. If you had been embodied at that point, you would have been grounded in the body, not the head, and might have negated the fear. Now, why this fear of others? Being near a lion or cobra, yes . . . but with our own species? Is it because most people are really so mechanical, so subhuman, that they are living on the animal level?

I've never thought of humans as animals.

Study the Diagram of Everything Living in *Search* to see where it places human beings. It shows, too, the possibilities of what we can ascend or descend to.

I Love to Suffer

There is a lump in my throat because there is something that doesn't want this to be said. But it needs to be said and it is necessary to say it. There have been many observations that I love to suffer. It's a thread in my life. When the body has an ache or pain, I see an immediate identification, and a whole world of suffering is created.

Our "Lady of Sorrows" is very strong. Not only is she a thread, but a major thread. Now take "her" as a line of observation. See the influence in the smallest outward things, also in what you think and feel, in how life is interpreted. Don't try to change "her" or ignore "her." It's too early for that. Simply observe as impartially as possible.

My Dog

When you spoke about the "animal," it really resonated with me. I've been seeing this in myself. I've got a "dog" that really likes to be petted, admired, told how important it is. It doesn't matter where it comes from. As an example, I was at an alumni meeting today with a fairly large group of people. I was in the position of a kind of moderator. At some points I could actually see in the moment that I was drawn to the people that agreed with what I was saying. And at the same time I could see that I wanted to "get" the people who disagreed with me. It was as if I was marking my emotional territory—kind of like an animal does.

The animal divides the world up into that which it can eat and that which can eat it. It's a highly dualistic world. Mr. Gurdjieff says we must "make friends with our animal." Not only did he speak about what type of idiot a person was but he often named their animal—like Krokodeel and Kanari.

There's an animal in the machine?

Of course. Now I can't make friends with an animal I don't know. So the first step is to become aware of the animal, to observe how it thinks and acts.

"Don't Tell Me What to Do"

Something was said to me and I saw this anger come up—"Don't tell me what to do." There was the experiencing of a chaotic sensation in the torso. Impulses arose to end it by explaining it or manipulating it in some way.

Yes, work not to manipulate it in any way. Simply struggle to keep it below the neck. That is, don't say "I" to it; keep the emotions separate from the head brain. Simply observe. It can be like trying to tame a wild stallion. But in this way we come to appreciate why the emblem of the society Akhaldan had an amber neck. It is completely in its essence, balanced. Also, ask yourself: what does amber not conduct?

Like Mother, Like Daughter

I had an episode of great anger with someone where I went into a rage. As I was ranting I was watching myself in disgust. A part of me was repulsed by the way I was behaving, but I had no control or ability to change my venting. The next morning my mother called. She was in a bad mood, complaining and blaming, full of self-importance. I was repulsed, but saw how her attitude was so similar to mine. I see that I am both attracted to being angry in that same way and repulsed by being that way.

Our parents are the primordial images and influences in our lives. They represent our first images of the feminine and masculine. And it's not what they say so much as what they do that influences us. How our parents cope with life, interact with others and with each other is what makes an imprint. Then we imitate them or rebel. Either way, it's all identification. Your mother's call was a great blessing. What did it show you?

That I can't control myself. That I'm a lot like her.

It showed your behavior is learned. It's not in essence, what you truly are, but in false personality—an imitation, compensation. Take anger as a line of observation.

Observing Face

You once suggested observing the face as well as the posture. Observing the face without changing its expression is very unpleasant. The expression on my face is one of anger. I don't want anyone to see this.

Who is this "I" to whom it is "unpleasant"? You talk as if you still take yourself to be an indivisible I. What you protect, hide or argue for you get to keep. This is one reason why people seem so weighted down. Keep working to be embodied, guarding the mind from associative thought, dividing the attention between subject and object, observing. You'll see the face is the seat of false personality.

Thinking I Was Present

I thought I was present, but then saw I was only thinking I was present.

Thinking is not presence.

What?

The thought of the object is not the experience of the object.

Right! I think—I mean this could be a breakthrough, right?

It's just the beginning, but it shows how we must question everything. The head is constantly producing shadows and calling them real. Once you see through the shadow, there is space for the real to arise. The head thinking it was present has to be observed again and again, as it is quite canny. Your question was clear tonight. Usually it is like a car windshield that has to be defogged.

Eating the Packaging

The more I strive to remember myself, to be embodied, the more I find parts that are not. For example, I became aware that I had never actually sensed the neck and throat area nor the lower abdomen. Focusing on these parts, there was finally an experience of the muscles surrounding the neck, the veins and arteries, as well as the awareness of the saliva being swallowed and the air moving toward the lungs. This sensation became very intense.

This was a keen observation to recognize that some parts of the body are not readily accessible. Too often I hear an idea, which can only be a concept no matter how well formulated or how true, and think I understand it. But the idea has no legs, no body. It's just part of the word-world. In this way we constantly hypnotize ourselves linguistically. We eat the packaging and not the food.

My Name Is Guilt

I have a habit of feeling guilty. There was a reaction of resistance to seeing that and admitting to myself that this guilt is me. It's what I am.

To be truly guilty one would have to be responsible, to be present, not mechanical. Otherwise, it's a form of self-love and vanity. So be this guilt, experience it. See that any desire to be different than what one is at the moment is an avoidance. Observe like a scientist.

But I see that I immediately begin to react.

Observe the reaction. The reaction is based on identification.

Then what?

See that it is tied to the content. The content is what you are still identified with. All content has a context, but it can't be seen as long as I am absorbed in the content.

XI

I live in parts thinking I am whole, superimposing that idea and creating a false unity. I compartmentalize everything so one part does not know about another part. This is simply another way of speaking about the "I-structure" and buffers.

Life as a Pinball

I have been especially aware of how I don't make decisions but decisions make me. For example, the body wants sex, so a "decision" is made to get that. Then the emotional part is turned off and repelled by perceived incompatibilities and moves away, creating distance. Then the mind experiences loneliness, "deciding" to move again toward relationship—and the cycle continues. It feels so hopeless, yet I continue in this repetitive cycle.

One of the age-old debates is about free will and determinism—which is true? They both are. Asleep, I am determined. There is no choice. Like a pinball, I carom from one cushion to another, bells and whistles going off, racking up an imaginary score, until finally, velocity diminishing, I disappear down the black hole. Game over. Awake, a different story entirely.

Feeling Proud

Whenever observation takes place there is this "I" that feels proud of the observation. It occurs to me that what I'm experiencing is not self-observation but another "I" observing itself at a more subtle level. I guess I'm seeing that most of the so-called observations are from the head.

The aim is to observe impartially, like an astronomer. He looks at the world through a telescope. He observes dispassionately, recording as factually as possible what he sees—the movement of planets and stars, the action of "black holes," and so forth. Then this is verified through continued observations. What is observed is neither liked nor disliked. Emotivity only obscures and exaggerates.

Locked In

I am always so identified. I'm completely into everything I do, everything that happens . . . or doesn't happen.

Identification can happen in any one of the centers. But one center soon infects the others so that I'm quickly in a full, three-center state of identification. Completely lost. As long as the intellectual center remains neutral—for its agreement or denial at once unifies all the centers in identification—there can be a possible distance, separation, a confrontation of centers. Once I say "I," as in "I am angry"—instead of "there is anger"—the cell door shuts. I'm locked in.

Owning the Experience

While sitting in a chair I became conscious of sitting. What took me away was when I ascribed the experiencing to myself. After this shock many memories came to me of the same moments. Every real experience is aborted. It's the same in observing habits. And I have so many of them. I live in habit.

When I remember or am remembered that's the beginning of a new octave, a new doh. Now, can it be sustained long enough to pass the interval? Otherwise, I, a part, owns the experience and so lives in broken octaves. Now, having seen the habits, take one and do the opposite. If you put your right shoe on first, put on the left.

Jealousy & Guilt

This past week jealousy came up, but it was more subtle, not what I have experienced before as the full-blown jealousy I'm familiar with. These reactions were quieter and seemed smaller, but they were recognized to be how jealousy begins. What was common was an "I," a part of me, that is never good enough. There is a lot of guilt in my life.

We need to distinguish between "jealousy" and "envy." The first concerns that which I have, own, in some way consider mine. The second is that which I don't have but intensely want. So, whether it's one or the other, it's to recognize this particular "taste," acknowledge it, and strive to observe it impartially. If still identified, then observe the identification impartially.

Consciousness Isn't Personal

I have noticed that when speaking to someone my voice sounds like it's originating from a specific place in me. There is a vibration in the solar plexus. When my voice speaks it's as if I am a separate person from that voice. I am speaking and at the same time hearing myself speaking. Time appears to be of a different quality, and the words coming from my mouth are simpler and have more weight. But then I identify and become trapped. Does all identification have an emotional component to it?

What is said is right. Except that the interpretation is still framed by the notion of the "person." Certainly there is an "I" speaking, a person, if you like, but why a person listening? Isn't there just listening? Why make a person out of it? Remember, the person is a construct of parts. Listening, consciousness, isn't personal.

The Force of Sleep

In working with the postures and making efforts to do otherwise I would take a posture that was different than I would ordinarily take. This was a "doing otherwise," as you suggested, and it was a great help in attempting to stay awake. But now I see it's become "old" in the sense it has become comfortable and no longer is of any help. I found I had to change the posture in a small way, such as moving my finger to an uncomfortable position, in order to maintain relative presence. It was a shock to see how fast this force of sleep adapted to new postures.

It's the way of all impressions. What was once new with repetition becomes old. It moves to the instinctive center. So "reminders" only have a certain life span. That you saw you needed to add something was intelligent application of the teaching. Since the posture was static, now try walking and doing otherwise. Change the gait, the tempo, and so forth. Deny the "doer-I."

"I'd Like a Mint Julep, Please"

I was eating in a crowded restaurant and the thought came to observe myself during the meal. There was no one in my direct line of sight, so I was not distracted and kept my gaze soft as I waited to be served. My feet were flat on the floor, elbows on the table, fingers interlaced, with my chin resting on the back of my fingers. When the waiter approached to take my order, I fully intended to stay present but was taken by my "need" to be polite and respond to him. After telling him "I'd like a mint julep, please," I returned to the observation and I saw myself glancing at the local paper sitting next to me, which I had picked up upon entering the restaurant. Part of my personal work is not to read during meals, so there was no immediate urge to read the paper, but I remembered why I do this. When I was newly divorced, I was painfully aware of being alone wherever I went, and one of the things I dreaded was going to a restaurant. A friend had suggested I always take a book, so it looked like I was "doing" something, and it would keep me from having to make eye contact with people.

To be polite, I had to interact. Why did this short-circuit the observation? Now, in what I describe as "returning to the observation," did I return to the body or was the return only mental? Is that why the attention went from the newspaper, to my personal work not to read while eating, to my divorce, and how I protected myself when out in public? As to the waiter, try to differentiate between a response and a mechanical reaction.

Victims & Kings

When we spoke you suggested that I listen to myself when I am speaking. I almost immediately forgot about it. Then when it came up I resisted it, but finally began to listen. What I heard was an underlying self-pity in my voice. I often play the role of the victim. But I also heard how I am I continually blaming others. I see a recurring pattern of blame in my relationship with my wife. I am full of judgment toward her and haven't recognized that I am reacting from a place where only my own desires are important.

We're almost constantly talking, if not to others, then silently to ourselves. And what are we saying? Yes, it changes with circumstances but how we relate to them is pretty much the same. We swing between the "victim-I" and the "judge-I" and if blamed ourselves what do we do?

We plead for mercy?

No, that's just a side of the "victim-I." We bring out the "lawyer-I," of course. We live in "I"s. So observe them, taste them, get to know their voices, name them. That will begin the process of separation.

XII
Many Kinds of Love

I have lived a lie regarding my marriage. Outwardly appearing and pretending that it's all okay, but inwardly not. I've discovered that there are many different kinds of love, and I do love my wife but in a very different way than I wanted to accept, because this contradicted beliefs regarding what was right, what marriage was. Reading Ouspensky's New Model of the Universe *I shut the book after reading a certain section. I didn't want to read any more. It was a shock to my body—I didn't want to hear it and yet what I read was my experience. I read:*

No moral principles, no feeling of duty, affection, gratitude, friendship, sympathy, pity, no community of ideas and no community of interests, can create a sensation when it is not there, or stand in its way when it is there; that is, nothing can change anything in this truly iron law of types.

This helped me to actually see and understand the reality of my situation. That in the world of the physical, where I am, it's not possible to do what my mind asks. There was, of course, working with my own judgment and the fear of other's judgments. I had to let go of all that, not once, but again and again. What I do now I do for myself in a selfish way. That is, selfish not in an ordinary way, but in a way that gives permission, allows freedom to experience. And with it a sense of responsibility.

Your children are grown, otherwise I would counsel that you take the marriage as your work and consciously live the marriage for their sakes. Given that, I would first ask myself how it was that I came to marry someone whom I thought I loved and how that waned. Was what we call love primarily emotional, intellectual, instinctual? What dampened it? What was it that you were taken with? We need to reflect on this deeply and to work to awaken, for otherwise, as in Ouspensky's book, *The Strange Life of Ivan Osokin*, we'll just repeat ourselves. Also read Orage's *On Love*, where he speaks about conscious love. As a side note, you say "in the world of the physical, where I am." From the point of view of the Work, I am only in the physical when I am aware of it; that is, when I am is embodied. This helps to realign the centers so that when there is a "yes" or "no" it comes from unity, not a fraction.

Father's Temper

I talked to my mother about my father, as you recommended, easing into it with questions about where they had met and so forth. Then I asked if she had ever been afraid of him. She was surprised by the question and asked what she would have been afraid of. I said his temper. She completely rejected that. She said he'd been very gentle and she still thanks God every day that she met him. She also said he was a devout Catholic and got down on his knees every night before he went to bed and said his prayers.

I know that last part is true because I sometimes saw him doing that, but her memory of him being a gentle man without a temper doesn't match my memory.

I don't really feel this is important. Actually, I'm wondering why you wanted me to pursue this since the Work is about observing in the present and not psychoanalyzing the past. Also, my father's temper wasn't of a violent nature—I wasn't abused in any way. It was just that it frightened me enough that it kept me from being close to him and it's sad that I missed that relationship.

The Work explores all avenues, but from the standpoint of presence. Esoteric psychology is far older than today's Freudian psychology and its many offshoots, including the au courant "transpersonal" version, simply a grafting of Eastern thought onto Western egotism, with the result that we have a lot of people running around calling themselves "the Self" who've never experienced their selves. That said, that your mother protects your father's image is not uncommon. What matters is your experience. You were obviously afraid of him and his temper. Note that you say that you "weren't abused in any way," but abuse doesn't have to be physical. Also, after denying any abuse, you then abstract your father and his temper into an "it" in saying "It was just that it frightened me."

So now take fear and temper as a line of observation to see how you are living your life, what choices you make, and why. You'll perhaps see that if there are four possible choices, you only consider two. The others you unconsciously eliminate. And of the two it's quite predictable which you'll choose given the situation. Ponder why this is.

Blood Father, Spiritual Father

There are observations tonight when you give attention to other students. I feel jealous and angry. This "I" is ruthlessly selfish and doesn't care about any community, spiritual or otherwise. It's interesting that at the Day of Exploration, when it was mentioned that "the Work doesn't come cheaply," I experienced that both as acknowledgement that the person had to pay and also that the Work in itself is not personal. I see that this is really about my father.

The Work will enable us to relive our lives by working to be in the present. If we do that strongly enough, if we can sustain it, the past will surely arise, for in many ways it has never left. See the connection between your father and he, as Mr. Gurdjieff says, "who takes the role of the teacher." That is, between your blood father and your spiritual father. For a long time the two will be confused and we'll project and play out on the second what we had with the first.

Mr. Rebel

There was a lot of reaction to what you said to me last week. Intellectually I knew what you were saying was true, but emotionally there was a lot of anger and a desire to rebel. This week I stopped sitting and stopped my other practices. I rebelled and a part of me really enjoyed it.

Yes, the person personalizes everything. It cannot do otherwise. So, what was said was taken to be an attack. This set up a struggle between the self-importance that has dogged you and the development of sincerity. The fact that you are sitting here tonight shows what won out—this time—for the struggle is far from over. As to the rebelling, my friend, who are you hurting when you don't sit, when you live to your lowest aspiration, not your highest?

In a way "the rebel" brought you to the Work. Everyone who comes is a rebel, that is, they haven't been entirely hypnotized by society's carrots. Now that we have found a teaching that can lead us to the truth, the rebel has served his or her purpose. It's time to commit. Otherwise, you'll keep one foot in, one out, and go nowhere.

"I Love You, Dad"

I visited my father who is old and isn't well. I hadn't spent much time with him since I was a kid. He was in bed so I pulled up a chair and we talked. From time to time, waves of emotion would come over me. It was hard not to be taken by them. Something in me arose that told me, "You should tell your father that you love him. That would be good." I couldn't do it. As I was leaving my father got out of bed. It confused me. I asked if he was going for a walk. He said he wasn't and just stood there. I realized he had gotten out of bed to say goodbye and give me a hug. I gave him a hug and told him, "I love you, Dad."

Conscience speaks, conscience heals. That's wonderful to hear.

The Predator

While out walking the dogs I had a shock—

I thought you were going to talk about another shock. Do you know which one?

Yes, you had asked if I wanted to see you and I said, "I'll sit on it." The other day you asked, "Are you still sitting on it?" I said I'd talk to you then, but you told me, "Continue sitting on it, maybe something will hatch."

You seem to live in compartments, always ignoring or fleeing from what you deem disagreeable, thinking if you pay no attention to it, it will go away. But your closets are full. Do you remember that after you observed what you called "The Predator"—which was a keen observation and a courageous report—I told you to paint it. Did you?

No. . . I cannot paint in my present environment . . . [loud coughing] but maybe that's an excuse.

There is no "maybe" about it. You've seen my paintings, yes? Painting is, or can be, a sacred channel of self-transformation. If we hold ourselves to paint the stark truth, then we objectify it, integrate it. We eat it rather than letting it eat us. But you made excuses as usual. So what happened? For three weeks you've had this deep cough. It's time to commit to the Work. Or, I'm sorry to say, to leave. But you live a life of one foot in, one foot out—with everything. You're wasting your possibility and your talent and time is counted.

The "God Problem"

A person said something that I understood on a deeper level than what the person understood. It was something that implied that I didn't understand. I reacted defensively, saying I did understand. There was a moment of silence that felt very uncomfortable. I felt a nervous energy in my stomach and chest.

The report of any value—as stated endlessly—is when I am embodied. Otherwise, it has no value. The exchange was purely psychological; one center was shocked into wakefulness, that's all. Is this understood?

[Nods]

Now, leaving that distinction—and it's crucial—what do you make of this?

That I frequently consider internally about how I am being perceived. I don't want to be seen as not understanding something. I always want to be on top of things, to be seen as being unlimited.

It's the "God problem." Everyone carries the *Kundabuffer* virus, but some are more infected than others.

How to disinfect then?

Observe the perpetual rating game being played out, being so concerned with being one up or one down. One up, a secret sneer. One down, being found out, paranoia, revenge. Don't judge it. Consciously live it. It's the true homeopathic cure.

Attention Shifting

Driving my car I observed how attention can shift seamlessly from one level to another. I was involved in a conversation with my wife and my attention was focused on the topic. Meanwhile, a more mechanical part of the attention was scanning traffic. Suddenly the traffic demanded more attention and my attention went from the conversation to the road. Then, the traffic situation dealt with, back to the conversation. There was an awareness of the smoothness and effortlessness of the transition, and a similarity was seen with the sitting where the attention is with the body while the formatory mind is occupied with its exercise.

The observation is keen. The shifting of attention was seamless, but it wasn't "different types of attention," rather different contents were given attention. Attention shifted on the same horizontal level. There is a vertical level.

Sleeping Next to a Woman

I took sensation to always be pretty much the same until I began observing it. The change in intensity and quality varies according to circumstances and even abstract thoughts and feelings. The circumstances needn't be acute. For example, simply sleeping next to a woman seems to affect sensation, though on a temporary basis. Sensation also seems to be cyclical according to the time of day. I don't really have a question. It's just that I've never paid attention to any of this.

There is a great deal of material in what is said. Connect the observation of sensation now with the observation of the "I-of-the-moment." See where that leads. You have a scientific bent; that is good in itself, but it can easily be used to avoid observing the messy things of life, like self-image, false personality and internal considering.

XIII

Have you seen the cartoon strip showing a fellow underground, digging a deep and winding tunnel? He digs and digs until finally in the last frame he lies down on his back and, holding the shovel to his breast like a crucifix, thinks to himself, "Now, if they really love me, they will find me."

The "Chosen One"

My boss convened a meeting to talk over the assignments for our group while she would be away. She went over the workload and then turned to me and said, "You will be in charge." I felt awkward, as though a spotlight had been turned on me. A colleague smiled. I considered internally: What would my colleagues think of me? That I was trying to be better than them? I uncrossed my legs and tried to come down into my body. Logically it made sense she would choose me since I had been there the longest, but that part that wants to remain in the background was protesting. I simply tried to absorb the conflicting feelings—unease, vanity, "Yes, I'm the chosen one!," and not wanting the responsibility.

I psychologize everything. Nothing is observed impartially. Everything and everyone is an appendage of my egotism. I live in parts. A part wants and a part doesn't want. I live in the "background" yearning to be in the "foreground," and when that happens—what then? I pine for the "background." Conflicted, the tension grows. I outfox it by off-loading the energy into imagination. I don't do this consciously, of course; it's how I function. My relationship with myself is incestuous, a secret love, a sort of intellectual onanism, of which I live in fear of being found out. Only by sincerely submitting fully to *being-Partkdolg-duty*—recognizing that self-remembering and self-observation is a duty, and working to be there for this dysfunctioning—can I bring the intelligence and will necessary to correct the situation.

Battle of the "Knower-I's"

Someone called me to see if I remembered something you said at the last meeting. Immediately, there was a recognition that I didn't remember. I gave a summary of what you said, though it was an interpretation of words that I couldn't remember. And while I was speaking there was a kind of insistence that I did really know. Throughout the conversation there was this undercurrent of knowing that I couldn't remember and yet some "I" kept insisting that it did. And then there was a sense of shame that this had happened. And this shame also had to do with the idea that I somehow messed up this person's question. I couldn't just simply say, "No, I don't remember."

One of the strongest "I"s is the "knower-I." There is such a fear of not knowing. We are always positioning ourselves, leading the conversation into areas where we know. Sometimes we encounter another person who challenges our knowing. Have you ever watched two "knower-I"s doing battle? It's like big horn sheep knocking heads. Tell me, have you called this person to admit you were lying?

Not yet.

One-Centered Life

I've finally realized the obvious—that if an observation is only from the head, then the experience of the moment is only the head. This was also seen when there is an experience where only the emotional center is there taking in the experience; it is just as partial as the intellectual center having the experience alone.

The one-centered life is no life at all. It's only a partial life. It's only when I have remembered myself that I am in two centers, intellectual and instinctual, with the possibility, if sustained, to contact the emotional center.

Craving Attention

I was in a state of internal considering. There was also a craving for attention from others. Though I was very much in my head, there was something physical going on. There was an oppressive feeling, a hole in my chest. Later I stood and came into the body. I breathed into that part of the chest and the feeling dissipated in time. There were many moments when I became angry with someone. I saw I use anger as a tool, a tactic. I can then keep a distance, things are safer. It puts me in a superior position.

Anger is used to maintain my world. It controls relationships. Others are just pawns in the game I'm playing. It is like chess. I play white or black, depending; all the time trying to occupy or control the center of the situation. Anger is a high state of energy. This level of energy, rightly directed, could open many possibilities for me, but I am dug into my self-love, waiting for someone to find me.

Energy in the Palm of My Hand

At the seminar, I had a high temperature and a cold and cough. During the CBI, they disappeared and my bad knee never hurt. It was like being in a higher state, difficult to explain with words. When you adjusted my position there was an explosion of energy in the palm of the hand. It was so strong I could hardly contain it. And then there was the experience of no body there—just energy.

We begin the CBI [Conscious Body-Breath Impressions] in the stillness of silence. Relaxing and redirecting our focus, all the movements, both of body and breath, take place within a context of silence. There are three types of breath: normal, inflation, and breathing assisted by body movements.

Yes, breathing with movements. And I remember you saying to observe that the movements were in the foreground, and the stillness of silence, consciousness in the background. To observe both at the same time.

Experiencing the direct impression of being in Being, psychological time stops, space appears, and we are self-healed.

Separation of Sounds

For the last couple of days I have been observing separations in the sounds that I hear. For example a separation of birds and wind and cars driving. This was a small shock to know that most of the time I am not hearing any separation, only combined ambient sounds. Then I realized that most or all of my observations are external observations. Observing a reaction, emotion or feeling seldom happens, and when it does the observation is so quick that nothing is remembered. Something has a lot of resistance to seeing internal reactions, feelings and emotions.

Sights, sounds, smells, sensations are all living me, turning me here, turning me there, because I am not. I live as a ghost. I am disembodied. Once I learn to inhabit the body then the gaps, the spaces between phenomena, are observed and much else as well. Why is there such resistance to seeing oneself? In time, with repeated effort to remember and observe, you'll see why. We wake up to higher and higher levels of sleep. Knowledge is state specific. When our state changes so does the level of knowledge. Have you ever looked at the space between yourself and an outer object?

No.

Try it when embodied and the mind is very quiet.

Rewriting History

There were two shocks. The first was when you asked that I write down my question and your answer from the meeting. It became clear that I do not know how to listen. It may have been the quote from Ouspensky in your answer, which I had never understood. It captured my attention and caused me to go into associative thinking and stop listening. The second shock came after writing my question and answer and seeing I had altered it in a way that made me look better. A feeling of shame at having done this arose and it felt like what had been a powerful experience was diminished.

History is being rewritten all the time in terms of our self-image. As it's said, "The victors get to write history." And there's nothing the self-image won't do in order to win. How is it that we don't wake up? The answer is we really want to stay asleep. One becomes responsible when one awakens. By the way, what is the self-image?

What I think of myself.

Yes, both positive and negative. Ask yourself the question—how do other people see me? What don't they see? How do I cover myself? Is that the test? That in some way, someone will find me?

Working with Anger

A shock was received and anger felt. I didn't do anything about the anger, just breathed into the body, and allowed the anger to be. I experienced a change as the breathing into it continued. It didn't go away, was just there. Impulses to react arose, were seen, not acted on. I came to a kind of balance, the anger simply a part of things.

Breathing is healing, if conscious. It is also a second being food. This is a good example of keeping the experiencing below the neck, not saying "I" to it.

The Tuning Fork

At the end of the seminar when the Gurdjieff/de Hartmann music was performed, I found the vibrations of the music interacted and affected the vibrations of the body, the body becoming something like a tuning fork. At one point, tears came to my eyes, yet there was no perceived emotion. I have never experienced music in this way and

I've listened to a lot of music.

Yes, listened to a lot but not heard. Now that you've experienced the difference between "it" listening and listening-without-listening, take that out into life.

What's that?

Listening without an "it."

XIV

The Dummy & the Ventriloquist

An "I" was observed making a mean and rude comment. The really striking sensation was that it was as if the voice wasn't mine. There was hearing of the comment as if another person in the room had spoken. There was a separation between it and the experience of being present. The image comes to me now of a ventriloquist. Did my lips move? But I heard the voice and then the shock of the "shame-I"s in embarrassment. I have heard myself speak from mean, insensitive "I"s before, but they had not been experienced like this in several years.

Usually, we're not present at the "moment of creation." That is, when "I"s erupt and dominate. It's only afterward, faced with the results of their actions, that we self-calm or beat ourselves. But the "I" that is reacting is not the "I" that acted. Because of your work on yourself, you weren't completely taken over. You witnessed how the "ventriloquist" uses his "dummy." That this hasn't been observed for several years doesn't mean it was not taking place, only that you've been asleep to it.

Mother-in-Law as Teacher

Last week I was organizing the closets and drawers at my mother-in-law's house. There was a feeling of frustration, sensed in the chest area, with the disorganization and illogical way that things were arranged. This week I have been attending a training on software design. When I saw the template for the software specifications, there was a feeling of pleasure over its organization. There was a pondering of this valuing of organization and logic and where it was seated in me. Did it come from essence or was it a mechanical response of false personality? Where did the emotion come from? Was it from the emotional part of the intellectual center or from the intellectual part of the emotional center?

You have observed the effect of order, harmony, proportion—and their opposite—on one level. Now continue this line of observation. As to centers, you must first be sufficiently embodied, both in duration and depth. Then observe the functioning of each center and later its parts. But this is all for the future. Do you follow?

Glimpses

At the last meeting it seemed that everyone was being who they are, and that I could describe how each person in the group manifests except for myself. But at the times I've had glimpses of myself it has been sickening.

We need not only to study ourselves but others as well. In listening to them, watching them—but only when I myself am in a state of self-remembering—we get beyond the mask everyone wears and not only see them as they are at the moment but also aspects of ourselves. Ask yourself: From which center does this or that person interpret and react to life? Which center is usually dominant? Which interprets? Which decides? Is it the intellectual center? Emotional? Instinctive-moving? Is this how you were seeing them?

Well, not exactly . . .

Study the books, get a grounding in the basic ideas, and seek to observe them in life. Put flesh on the ideas.

"Programmer-I"

I briefly saw the "programmer-I" in action in the moment while he was working on the kind of clerical job that a programmer "does much better than other people." I was into total identification. Later, when I was raking leaves, the identifications kept coming up persistently. When I was able to stay in the body—which came and went—I realized that I do this whenever I am challenged in an intellectual

*area where I consider myself "an expert." This includes, but is not
limited to, computers, film, Scrabble, and so on.*

Interestingly, you are such an emotional fellow, not intellectual at all. That doesn't mean you don't have a strong intellectual
center, just that you live in feelings, emotions, moods, while taking
yourself to be intellectual. You believe your decisions are intellectually based when the context in which the decisions are made
is emotional. When you are between a "yes" and a "no" see what
makes the decision. It will give a look at false personality and also
your dominant center.

I Don't Want to Be Present

*I was driving home from work and lost in thought. I noticed a feeling
of being very contracted. When I did, there was a sense of expansion,
but with that there was a strong voice saying, "I don't want to do
this right now . . . I'm too tired . . . I don't want to be present." The
resistance was very strong and I struggled with it for a while, coming in
and out of awareness. What I found interesting was the distinct feeling
of being in two different worlds. There was such a different quality
between the two. I was also surprised at my level of resistance.*

Resistance, the Holy-Denying, is part of life, as it should be. If
there was no resistance there would be no world.

I don't understand.

Three forces are needed for any genuine phenomena to exist—
affirming, denying, neutralizing. If there was no denying force you
wouldn't be alive. Or take the neutralizing force away, for example,
and you get artificial light. In terms of the Ray of Creation, if one
level of reality didn't resist being absorbed into a higher or lower
level, it would disappear. There would be no universe. It's interesting that the three forces are spoken of in Eastern teachings, but they
are taken as static. We take them as fluid, changing. So which came
first, The Fourth Way or the Eastern? Interestingly, the denying can
be affirming, but we will talk about this later.

Now to respond to your question. We are two-natured beings.
Therefore, we live in question as to which of these natures we will

feed. So I need to question to what am I giving my attention, energy and time—is it an ascending or descending octave? If I choose the ascending there is certain to be a resistance from the lower. This is useful. It develops real will if I struggle with it. All efforts have merit, as they serve to short-circuit the automatism.

Pelvic Space

I was speaking with an older student about postures and she asked if I experienced the space in my pelvis when I was walking. There was a memory of hearing this idea before, of experiencing space in different parts of the body, and the realization that it's hard for the mind to grasp this. I usually think of space in terms of what I experience outside my body. I can understand the difference between having my awareness focused inwardly and outwardly, but it's difficult to imagine a space in my pelvis.

We really don't know the body. To begin to experience it, we must go beyond words into the wordless. As long as attention is submerged in words, there can be no merger, for words, by their nature, are only symbols, not actualities.

Dynamic, Not Static

At the last meeting you answered a question that I had not asked. Earlier, I had spoken about my experiences with self-remembering while on a hike. I felt I was coming to a "wall" or place from which I could go no further. Later in the meeting, in response to another's question, you spoke of how the experience of the remembered body changed, that at first the resistance is usually coming from the body, but if the body awakens and begins to experience beyond what the head believes is normal, then the head resists. Hearing this it became immediately clear to me that this was exactly what I had experienced. In sitting in the morning after completing the morning exercise, I saw that the same resistance occurred. There came a place where the mind would not release and I could go no deeper.

A mental reminder occurs. The head denies or assents. If it denies, the mechanicality continues. If not, the octave of self-remembering begins. If sustained long enough, the body may become active, the head now becoming either neutral or denying.

As it is used to being in control, the head may become fearful if the body begins to experience too much life. We can spend our life trying to make ourselves better, pruning the "I-tree," so to speak, but it's only when the roots are cut that we free ourselves.

How do you cut the roots?

Don't water the tree.

The Body "Speaks"

Observing my movements I find that the lower part of my body is desensitized. It sometimes feels like the lumbar spine has fused together. Bending, for example, happens mechanically from the head, and only parts of the body closest to the head seem to participate. It's a revelation to move the body from the lumbar spine.

By remembering and working with postures, we begin to first observe the posture as it presents itself. Experience and observe it from the inside. Then intentionally move to a new posture. That is, having participated in the experiencing of the body, now experiment with it. Observe how the body moves. Being attentive, we bring a finer level of intelligence to the body and it "speaks" to us, as it has done with you. Working with the impressions of the body is a very fine work.

Self-Isolation

You spoke about the way we live in isolation at the talk on the Day of Exploration. I recognize that in myself. I noticed during the day that I usually don't meet another's eyes when I am spoken to. I've also noticed that I hold my breath when someone unfamiliar enters my space. It's like I live in an isolation tank with little real interaction.

If I am raised in a family where the irrational can erupt at any time, even over the slightest thing, I protect myself by living carefully, not drawing attention. From experience I know sanity is just on the surface. So what was intelligent as a child—being invisible—as an adult is irrational. Ironically, this irrationality is just what I was trying to protect myself against. I need to admit this to myself deeply so that the "isolation tank" I unknowingly put myself in has

no credibility. I observe it for what it is—irrational. From the way
you speak, I sense you have done this. In Alcoholics Anonymous,
I am told, when someone speaks they first introduce themselves
by saying "I am an alcoholic." Do the same every morning and
evening. Look in the mirror and say aloud: "I am an isolationist."

XV

Postures, States & "I"s

*In observing body postures, a correlation was noticed between my
postures, my inner state and "I"s. Often I would be in a negative
state and the thought would come to observe the posture. I saw that
my postures, even my facial expressions, were an expression of my
inner state and the "I-of-the-moment." I found that changing the
posture could dramatically alter my state and so change the "I." This
was especially true in an unpleasant situation this morning in which
my husband was speaking to me. I noticed that I was slouching and
looking away as he was speaking to me. I changed my posture. I sat
up and looked him in the eye and my inner state changed, and what
was a potentially negative situation ended with a good outcome. But
usually I have no awareness of my posture whatsoever.*

Everything is connected. It is true on all levels, macro and
micro. So it is with postures, states and "I"s, as well as breath, tempo,
body temperature, and so forth. Keep working in this way.

The Maskless Man

*When you told us that we all have masks there was a resistance and a
voice that said, "No, I don't wear masks." So I tried to observe whether
this was true and found that I don't wear masks of expression but of
nonexpression. I see that I wear this mask when I want to be perceived
as being in control. I realize that this mask ends up stopping any
real connection from happening with the person who I am talking to
because it keeps it closed on my end.*

I didn't say "have" masks, I said "wear." Note the difference.

I don't see what you mean.

If we "have" masks, we may or may not "wear" them. That said, your experience is a good illustration of why we need to challenge our reactions, not accept them. You did so and were rewarded with a very keen observation. You now need to go further and observe what's under that mask.

Talking with Hands

I was given a task last week and was talking with someone who was still within himself. After a bit I noticed that I was waving my hands around while talking, using my energy that way. Afterward it was noticed that energy was being expended in many small ways: humming, whistling, music in my head, fidgeting. A constant waste of energy.

Apparently, the identification with momentum was so strong that even the recognition of another's quality of being only momentarily stopped me. I am constantly off-loading the energy through a thousand little nervous habits. Pick one, like talking with your hands. Each time you find yourself doing it use it as a cue to remember yourself.

Moral Suffering

The more I see of myself I get a sense of, not really despair, but very intense dissatisfaction and sadness.

Physical and psychological suffering is useless for self-transformation unless accompanied by presence. Moral suffering—the deep recognition, without excuse or blame, that I am as I am and will always be so unless I become conscious—prepares the ground for an inner separation.

Working with What-Is

Someone broke into my car and stole my case of CDs. I felt fear and self-judgment. I drove home and covered my windows . . . but I was still afraid. I turned on the TV, but realized there was this nervous energy and that it was just escaping. I turned off the TV and came down into the body and sat for several minutes until the nervousness subsided. When I got up, the nervous energy came back, so I sat down again and redirected the attention. The feeling didn't go away completely, but it did diminish quite a bit.

Instead of allowing the reaction to overwhelm you completely, you worked with it. Many people, not knowing how to work with it, off-load energy of this kind with drink, drugs, sex, overdosing on TV, excessive talking. All a leaking, a descending octave, a waste upon waste. Begin to see life in terms of ascending and descending octaves. Life is never static. It's either moving upward or downward. Remembering yourself is upward, moving against the hypnotic momentum of life. Note where the initial thrust of energy begins to wane. Just there make a greater effort.

To Be or Not

A speaker at a conference had written a book on a subject I am familiar with, and he had interviewed me. I expected he might mention me and thought if he did I would look important in front of my coworkers. I saw this as a fantasy, but instead of it getting weaker it got stronger. During the talk there were moments when he might mention my work and there was a voice saying, "Okay, here it comes . . .." But he never did. Afterward there was a feeling of emptiness and a strong experience of my self-love and need to be important. I felt empty and sad.

Can I work with this "emptiness and sadness"? Can I let be what-is and, at the same time, not be what-is? Can I separate from it and see how it lives me? Or do I indulge myself, leaking into fantasy, another form of onanism? Can I consciously stand in my own shoes experiencing and countering this thirst for recognition? I told you how to work with this escaping—not to deny it but to remember yourself. Have you done that?

No.

Why not?

It takes all the fun out of it.

The Belief of "I"s

I've become aware of "I"s that do understand that I am not really able to listen to myself speaking or to others speaking. But I was shocked to observe "I"s that believe they already do listen to others, and even more shocked to observe "I"s that have absolute certainty that they are awake. I saw that these "I"s believe that they certainly can do this, and that they already knew how to do this before coming into the Work. So this week I made efforts in smaller moments to listen to myself speak. I was aware of an urge to speak very quickly, to over-talk and also to repeat myself.

Our beliefs live us. "I"s are born not only of imitation, compensation, but beliefs. Observing how we interact with others—that is, what's happening on the outside and how we're thinking and feeling on the inside—is a necessary division. There is a Gnostic saying that if one would become One, they must first become two. That's what happens when we self-remember and observe. This division takes will, real will. Will, like consciousness, can be developed, if we exercise it.

"No, I Have No Excuse"

I opted out of doing something and was told by email "to reorganize my life" so I could do it. I felt anger, not at any person, but because I thought I had already done so. I felt a need for justification. I wrote an email in return but saw I was making excuses. I let a day or so go by and wrote another email that I thought was free of excuses. But on rereading it I saw I had made another excuse. Later, I had an appointment with a fitness trainer. She asked if I'd been to the gym since our last meeting. I immediately started to make an excuse, but stopped midsentence and told her, "No, I have no excuse. I could have been here if I'd wanted to; I could have made the time." I feel like I'm just one big excuse.

This is quite a lot to have come to and in such a short time. How old are you?

Three years old. [Laughs]

Okay, you're giving everyone hope. It took real will to inhibit the impulse to justify yourself. You were burning inside and instead of projecting it you ate it. That allowed you to see by extension that you were doing the same thing with the fitness trainer. When we organize our life in terms of the truth, and not excuses and waivers, it's genuine and we enter a realm of power, power over ourselves. The only power that counts. Read in *Our Life with Mr. Gurdjieff* what Thomas de Hartmann does when Mr. Gurdjieff calls him "Balda," that is, "Stupid." As a Russian aristocrat and a famous composer, I'm sure he had never been called that. It was a lot to eat.

Prince of Lies

Last week I saw that there are different kinds of lying. Lying by confusing oneself. Misinterpreting. Forgetting. Not committing. Refusing to see. By quibbling. Being vague. Projecting. Changing levels. Enlarging to the extreme. By not acknowledging what is seen. When the reaction to seeing this came up there was more lying by not accepting.

Your "Prince of Lies" is quite creative, so don't rest content. You've made a sincere effort. It's produced valuable material. Now, it's time to take an essence oath that you will no longer lie in terms of the Work. Remember, the first barrier to overcome in the Work is lying. Take this oath at the beginning and end of the morning exercise for the next forty days.

XVI
How Do I Live My Life?
If I'm asleep, then how do I live my life?

You don't live it, it lives you. Picture yourself in a sail boat asleep at the helm. Instead of being steered, the boat is taken by the currents and winds.

Looking-Without-Looking

I was walking to a grocery store about a block from my apartment when I suddenly noticed my vision was in sharp focus. It's a habit I'm trying to break, so I softened the focus and became embodied. I noticed the soft focus helped to bring me down into the body, relax

it. It gave me more of a sense of myself in space. I decided to walk the
rest of the way like this. The next thing I knew I was reaching for a
box of cereal in the store.

Everyone's vision is almost always in focus, always fixed on objects. We're not with ourselves but out ahead of ourselves. So you were already "there" before you got there. We only have so much energy and though you worked in walking to the store—relaxing, remembering, keeping a soft focus—the energy ran out. This is why we need to watch how we spend it. Be as economical as possible. As an experiment, you might try crossing the eyes and see what happens with the mind.

Behind the Eight Ball

I went back home for a long weekend and played pool with an old
friend whom I'd once brought to a seminar. I missed a lot of shots and
found myself in postures that were familiar but tense and closed. My
friend began to play well. He told me that my ex-wife was disappointed
that I hadn't seen her to speak about our daughter while I was in town.
There was an immediate reaction to this and an "I" came up that felt
badly I hadn't done this, though I had intentionally decided not to.
I came to myself, centered in the middle story, and explained why I
hadn't spoken to her. This somehow changed everything. My energy
grew and his diminished, I began to win while his game fell apart.
There was a solidity that was experienced. When we parted I felt full
and connected while he seemed depleted and in parts.

How different the two experiences were, yet you were in the same space, at the same table. Yes, I remember him. He never spoke during the seminar. When I asked afterward why he hadn't spoken he said he had no questions. He was an amiable, intelligent fellow, but his suitcase was closed. It's interesting how people can come to the door but never open it. Everyone has a very small measure of opportunity and then they are sucked back into ordinary life. You say you "felt full and connected." Did you feel vindicated, too?

What do you mean?

You're in the Work, he's not.

Yes, a part of me did feel that.

Watch that "I." It's the seed of arrogance.

Being Perfectly Imperfect

I have a desire to be perfect. I think it comes from not wanting to suffer in the present the results of the actions that I have committed in the past. There is also fear of making mistakes in the future, as if I have a choice to act differently if I am not present.

Perfection is what? As long as it is a concept it is not perfection. In fact, you are perfect. You are perfectly yourself, that is, perfectly imperfect.

I don't follow.

Whatever you take yourself to be, isn't that what you are. Isn't that what is being lived out?

Yes, but it's not very perfect.

True, you are perfectly imperfect. You've played what you take to be yourself perfectly, warts and all. You simply haven't been conscious of what a great actor you've been.

So then what?

So then I have a choice, either to wake up to it, accept myself as I presently am, or stay asleep to it. If my wish is to wake up, I will suffer the perfection of my imperfection. This will create resistance, heat and possibility. If not, there is no possibility other than unconsciously having my perfect imperfection live out my attention, energy and time.

Being on Automatic

I've tried the exercise of noticing when I am in an automatic state of worry or anxiety about the future, and then allowing the process to continue, but consciously observing it. This has brought about the definite recognition that I normally judge worry as being negative and attempt to censor these thoughts. The effort to consciously include the worrying, without interference, had an unexpected feeling of liberation or freedom.

There are two ways of working: either stop the thought and redirect your attention or consciously observe it. Watch how the worry fights for your attention, how it moves, how your breath and postures change. Get as much material as you can.

Strengthening the Wish

I want to ask what I can do to strengthen my wish to be present. If it is true that I have no will and that I cannot "do" anything myself, it seems that this question isn't valid. I go through these periods when the resistance is strong and my efforts are very weak and my level of sleep increases. I have had this belief that if I just try harder I can overcome it, but I am beginning to realize that maybe this is all I'm capable of doing.

Every day, at the end of the morning sitting before opening your eyes, say to yourself three times: "In the name of the Father and of the Son and in the Name of the Holy Ghost, please strengthen my wish for Being." The origin of real will is Being—Being in itself, not being something or other. We have a small amount of freedom. Use it and capability will grow.

Trust Issues

May I be blunt?

Of course.

I have trust issues. Why should I trust you, or the teaching. I don't trust myself or anyone really.

You think in order to do the work you have to trust?

Yes, how else?

You don't have to change one thing about yourself. If you don't trust, fine. It's not bad, it's not good. It's fact. But what kind of fact is it?

If nothing's going to change, why do this at all?

The assumption is you're going to change it, no?

Yes.

And this means you are still taking yourself as an indivisible I. That's okay, too. But back to the question—what kind of fact is it that you don't trust?

It's simply what is. I've lived my life not trusting myself or anyone.

It's a mental-emotional fact, isn't it? It isn't a body fact. That is, can you come into the body, remember yourself, and simply observe the lack of trust without judging it or reacting to it in any way.

That would be tough.

You're futurizing an experience that you haven't done yet. You have a body. It's not foreign to you. You certainly can trust that. So inhabit the body and strive to observe impartially.

But what if I can't.

My friend, you're not listening. Next question . . .

A Thief in the Night

On the way to the meeting tonight, I was traveling a different route and there was a sharp pain in my stomach and a moment of nausea. For a second I didn't know where I was. I remembered turning on to this new road and that was it. It was all sleep for miles and miles, the car being driven but no one there.

We never know when we are taken. We're here one nanosecond, gone the next. And we never know it. A thief in the night. We only wake up to an instant of the dream, the identification in progress.

That's the defining moment. For either I return to self-remembering or not. Often I think I'm awake when I judge and blame myself for being taken, and make vows it won't happen again—but what "I" is doing this? That needs to be seen as well. The Work becomes more and more subtle. The demands also increase. For example, the pressure to lie at one level is more intense at another. Working with the intensity creates a right crystallization.

Starving Woman

I asked someone to see my painting and was looking for him to recognize how good it was. I feel like I'm starving, running around with my tongue hanging out.

Could you remember yourself and empty out and listen? We can lose an arm, our loved ones, our job, our savings, our reputation, and so on, but we will still exist. What is it that we still have?

We have time, yes? Time in the body. We can never know how much. And we have energy of the centers—vital, emotional and intellectual energy. Our essence is the original energy of these centers. And along with time and energy we have attention. Again, the attention of the three centers.

Now, having stated the context, let me ask you: How is it that you have attention but you want attention, feel you need attention?

I don't know. But it always seems to be the case.

Why do you need what you already have?

You mean that if I have attention, why am I needing other people's attention?

Exactly.

Well, maybe I don't have enough of it.

Yes, but why would you not have enough?

I must use it up. Or I don't have enough to begin with.

We all have enough attention, though of course it varies with one's health, and so forth. But, given that, each day I begin with the requisite amount of attention—why would I need more?

Because I am using my attention throughout the day.

Yes, I am constantly spending my attention, rarely intentionally using it, especially to be present. But I'm spending it on myself, the person with his fears, desires, self-concerns. And so the person is always hungry for attention. He lives in a state of compensation. He wants attention, even negative attention, he's so desperate to be fed.

I need your attention because I do not give myself enough attention. If I did, then I would have no need of your attention. I live in a world of attention deficit disorder. If I'm present, then we could share our attention, enjoy it, live it, enter realms of attention beyond the word cage.

XVII

Inner Influences

Reading about influences there was a recognition that influences are not just from the outside but also inward. This was a new way of seeing them. Gurdjieff said that in taking in impressions we need to take them in with two centers. You've talked about this many times. But this time the listening was different. Later there was something that needed to be read. Suddenly there was an all-at-once recognition that I was reading the material through the emotional center. It was very clear. There was the sensation of having been out of balance. The emotional reactions were extreme. This was a shock, a stop. Then a breathing and a coming into the body and a conscious effort to engage the mind. The experience then was much richer. There was a sense of balance. A sense that much more was being taken in, not only of what was written but also the listening to the inner impulses, and at the same time there was something conscious, aware of all that was transpiring in the organism.

There is a great deal of material here but no question. Do you have a question?

No.

You need to ponder the material—what does it mean? Where does it lead? Bring this and we can have a real exploration.

Why Can't Attention Be Divided?

I looked at the front page of a newspaper and thought to observe myself. I was holding it in front of me, between both hands. Going to the feet, I noticed that my weight was on the outsides of both feet, though my shoes were flat on the floor. It was a pleasant and stable sensation, one I was not familiar with. I felt relatively balanced and erect, though with my usual tension at the shoulders and neck, including a forward head position. I felt the newspaper against my abdomen, and became aware that rather than the paper resting against my abdomen, my abdomen was against the paper. Though I had been looking at the front page I realized nothing had registered. My eyes were one place, my attention another. Why couldn't there be a registration of what was being seen—the newspaper—and the observation of the body at the same time. Why couldn't both be taken in?

Experience yourself now. No, don't look away. Become embodied. Okay, now look at me. Right. Now, experience your feet on the floor, as well as what you are looking at, in this case me. Are you doing so?

I think so.

There is no thinking. One does or doesn't. Right?

[Silence]

You're looking down. So keep your eyes focused on the rug. Now experience both yourself and the rug at the same time. Are you?

Yes.

That's a taste of divided attention.

"I'm Special"

I have come to see that an "I" believes it is being helpful, considering externally. But it's not. Instead, it takes on the "good student role," which is actually a disguised usurping of the teacher role. This "I" demonstrates to itself that it has made progress.

Once the "I" structure realizes it can never become self-realized, never come to true individuality, it will fight, no holds barred. Deeper is false personality and chief feature, or chief weakness. We entered the Work because we thought we would gain what?—power, knowledge, end of suffering. Once the false personality realizes it's not going to get it, and that itself is under scrutiny, the battle begins.

"You Should Have Done This"

I find I continually talk to myself, and a lot of it is some sort of self-judgment or blame. I'm telling myself, "You should have done this" or "You did this wrong" or "You are going to do this wrong."

One of the main reasons we do not remember ourselves is negativity either toward ourselves or others. It sounds like you are carrying around one of your parents.

Yes, my mother. Always concerned with how I was doing.

We need to honor our parents but also to "kill them." That is, know that what's talking inside me is not me but, in your case, the mother. Starve "her." Don't give "her" any attention. Instead, do something, take a walk, direct your attention on something else. When you really come to being embodied, when there is enough duration that an inner separation occurs, then intentionally do something wrong.

Getting My Way

There were two situations in the past week when getting my way was significant. In one, I didn't respond externally, but acted as if I hadn't heard the other person. I withdrew psychologically, and then I physically distanced myself, left the room. In the second situation, I tried to get my way by force, by using energy. I made a forceful argument for my point of view, what I wanted to happen. There were concentrations of energy in the back at the shoulder blades, in the whole upper torso, in the chest just below the clavicle. There was an increase of tension in the room, in the other person, in the other people as well.

This was seen and a different "I" tried to get my way by being charming, smiling, putting on a warm face and tone of voice. The head rehearsed the reasons why, "objectively," what I wanted to do should be done, why it was good that I get my way. This was connected with wanting to be liked.

This was also seen and there was a letting go of what "I" wanted and a listening to the other person began. The body relaxed and the tension in the room eased. The other person also relaxed and began making useful contributions to the meeting.

What was your experience of the other person?

He was the enemy, the other, the person who wasn't considering my thoughts and feelings. There was an inner movement away from him, a feeling of more distance between him and me. As long as there was identification, there was wanting to get my way.

So I belittled him. Made him smaller to make myself larger. This psychologized jousting and manipulation is all of the "person," the supposed indivisible I. At root, it's all compensation, a tribute paid to the lie that lives me. Now, having seen this much, begin to act otherwise; act against these patterns. Create friction, release energy. That will open up new territory.

Some people never get their way. I once asked a woman how she got her way. She couldn't answer me. Her aging, fearful husband, who had been her university professor, didn't want her to be in the Work and made it difficult. She had really come to a lot but couldn't stand up to him.

Shadow Conversation

I was a standee at a public performance, standing shoulder to shoulder with people. I felt an impulse to connect with the woman to my right, to say something pleasant. But what I said had a negative tinge. I often express myself this way even though I want to be pleasant.

Look at the functioning. Between the impulse and its expression an "I"—unbeknownst to the speaker—cut in. What kind of "I"? Likely a "fear-I" as you were speaking to a stranger. As you say, you often find yourself expressing yourself with a "forked tongue." I take it that it happens with people you know, too.

Yes, though I don't like this "forked tongue" image.

That was a direct communication, untinged. So you can speak this way, if you are present to what you say and not speaking mechanically. Gurdjieff says that when two or more people are talking, underneath what is being said there is a "shadow conversation," one that is not being said. Listen for it.

The Darwinian Choice

When I speak with others—particularly men—I do so in a very critical and condescending manner. I observed this urge to rip into them, but I'd change what came out of my mouth midsentence to make it more neutral. But it was a real shock to see this sort of unconscious, negative "vigilance" that looked out for any ignorance or perceived weakness that I could jump on and pound them with. Then I went to a music festival on a date, and as we were walking around and talking, I observed this impulse several times to really put him down. I denied it, didn't act on it. I saw then a space between thoughts, the impulse, and the action—there was a choice not to react.

If the reaction is observed, we can absorb it, rather than have it absorb us. In this sense, life is very Darwinian, eat or be eaten. Don't psychologize about this. Simply recognize this as a pattern and don't feed it. When you speak with your father observe where you are, how you are speaking and not. Simply observe, relieve him and you of any blame.

"You're Not the Person I Married"

I was the youngest of three children and enjoyed being "buoyed up" emotionally by the love that naturally comes to the baby of the family. Later, these manifestations became a compensation, especially after each divorce when my person was hurt. I sought connections with people, hoping to find emotional support and to have reflected back to me my picture of myself as a lovable person. I see that there are "I"s that need to be loved and want to please others. This was a shock and it went in deeply. These were seen as a lifelong pattern beginning in childhood.

We live in images, not in actuality. Relationship is based on images, expectations, type and polarity. We call this "love." We "fall in love," but where do we "fall from"? And where do we "fall to"? Time erodes all images. Then we are left with the substrate beneath the images and we are surprised, disappointed—"You're not the person I married." We blame it all on the other person. We feel cheated, conned, angry. We withdraw and fall out of love. How many times does this have to happen before I realize I live in images? Healthy self-images, negative ones, have been formed and fed since childhood.

Working with Illness

At the end of the morning sittings, as advised, I have been visualizing being present during radiation treatments. At the clinic, I can walk off the elevator, check in, and go to the dressing room being relatively present, off and on. After changing, I sit and meditate and am relatively present again. But if another patient talks to me, or when my name is called, I immediately fall asleep. I am never present on the table during the treatment, and I don't remember trying to be present until much later the same day, or the next morning.

The Work needs to enter all aspects of my life. That you have been able to work on yourself in regard to a situation which most people try to deny and avoid any way they can, shows how far you have come. I remember someone who was so afraid she could not even close her eyes during body impressions. We rarely see how far we have come, because we take how we are now to be how we have always been. It's a deep form of lying.

Yes, I remember. I kept my eyes open the whole time.

And now you don't. Value that. Be grateful, don't level it. Remember this when you are having, as Mr. Gurdjieff says, "five Fridays a week."

XVIII

I say "I" to every thought, every feeling, no matter how contradictory. Now who is this "I" that says "I" to all that?

War of the Worlds

I experienced what felt like a war between the worlds, the different centers. I wanted to go somewhere interesting. My emotional center was engaged and my body felt light. I had to make some decisions before going. The intellectual center took over and I felt the body grow heavy with thought and indecision, so that it was difficult to even get out the door. Once I took care of the mental task, the emotional center came forward and the lightness returned to the body. The lack of balance between the centers was apparent.

This observation could only come after long work on oneself. We need to separate the observing from the manifestations of the "I-of-the-moment," but self-observation only truly begins when we observe which is the "center-of-the-moment," that is, which is active. Observing the lack of balance between centers is the first step in bringing them into balance, in becoming number four. Otherwise, we tend to live out of the most dominant center, the instinctive, emotional or intellectual, one, two or three.

"I'll Never Get Anywhere"

There is this continuing belief that I'll never get anywhere in the Work. This is a belief in all of the "I"s that come up in the moment, even though there are conflicting desires and viewpoints among them. They are all still taken as "I."

Yes, you're right. So relax. You will never get anywhere. Accept that. That would be a breakthrough, as you, the person, the self-image, the false personality, insist on indulging in this world of self-absorption, trapped forever in projecting a "something" to be gotten or protected from. As has been said countless times, this shows how strong the identification is. As long as you believe yourself to be an indivisible I, you are asleep in this dream of the "Great I." It is simply an animal dream. To become a human being, one must see and sacrifice their illusions and infantile self-love. Just as everyone appears to have a body but has no conscious awareness of it, is not embodied, so everyone believes they are an indivisible I. It's a mass hypnotism. But to actually recognize the truth of this for oneself requires a great payment.

Deepest, Darkest Secret

What's been experienced is judgment. And the experience is like having a large ugly animal inside. It's been seen with the experience of having judged and the need to be impartial, that this is what is needed to learn, but this means remembering myself. And this has acted as a reminder, yet this animal is very large. It feels like, I want to say, like it's infiltrating inside—but that's not right. It's not that it's infiltrating as if it wasn't there before, because it actually has been there all the time; it's that it's just now beginning to be seen.

What's behind the judgment?

Self-righteousness.

And behind that?

Self-love.

And behind that?

Vanity?

Let's try our deepest, darkest secret—*superiority.*

False Woundedness

There have been a number of observations of my being covered in self-love. Not that there are long periods of duration, but this self-love feels like a coat . . . but it's more than that, it's big and thick, like something is stuck to me. And for many years, whenever I would listen to myself speak the words "self-love," there was a disconnect; I didn't really believe it. It was the self-image talking . . . the self-image cringes inwardly at this being said. Nevertheless, it is recognized that the words need to be said. There was a walking into a situation, and having come to myself, breathing down into the body—but when I opened my mouth I could hear the voice and all the intonations and the awareness of the inner postures. It was felt deeply that this was self-love. And there is a feeling of woundedness. It's not like the woundedness stems from essence. This is a false woundedness. And there is a burning, a continual burning in the chest. And it is experienced that it is directly related to this self-love that feels so thick.

Everyone is wounded in some way. The mind is split between waking state consciousness and the subconscious. What "comet" hit us that caused this rupture? With time and right effort we will come to it. But we compensate for it with an excessive self-love and, what was not mentioned, vanity. Perhaps the woundedness stems from a belief that one was not loved in the past or will not be loved now—a rejection of love because of a feeling of unworthiness.

Seeing the Movie

I was standing in line at the bank, in a usual posture, weight on one leg and hip, the other out. I decided to maintain the observation when the line moved forward. The line moved and as I moved with it—it was like slow motion. It was like I saw every movement.

Your attention and will must have been very strong, because as soon as you and the line moved, the instinctual-moving center—the most powerful of all centers—was engaged. Because it didn't take your attention, you saw the context as well as the content, the motion within it. Instead of seeing still frames, as it were, you saw the "I-movie."

The Question of Sincerity

In this relationship I have with you the question of sincerity comes up. There is a level of communication that "calls out" what is considered not sincere between us. At the beginning, there was immediate identification so I couldn't see it, I could see only the reaction—that of anger. Now I am seeing an "I" that has not been seen before, one that doesn't like to be questioned in its sincerity or its rightness. It feels like it is a new "I" that is being seen.

Relationship? "I"s don't have relationship. They use and abuse and discard. And, yes, with repeated efforts, one sees deeper and deeper into the pool of Narcissus. Sincerity is a function of conscience. Conscience unites essence and personality. Ask yourself why it is said that "sincerity must be learned"?

"I Work Like a Dog"

I work like a dog for appreciation. I observed I was appreciated like a dog, while my immediate superior works like an aristocrat and is appreciated like one.

The need to be appreciated—to always be looking for appreciation from others—makes me a slave. The need for appreciation is really the need for attention. As long as I do not give myself the proper attention through remembering myself, I will look to others to satisfy this need and so be in their control.

My need for appreciation started way back in my life.

Yes, but now is not the time to focus on that. Instead, I need to observe all the ways I seek appreciation. Who is this "I"? Take that as a line of observation.

Exposing Too Much

Something happened and it was a question of whether to report on it or not. There was a feeling that it was too risky, that I would be exposing too much. And so I consider internally, say nothing, or shape and paint over what I report.

Of course, truth exposes the lie, which is why I live in half-truth and lies. We come together here to wake up to this general state, to see how it holds me. We can say whatever we like here. Personal matters, of course, should be discussed privately. But everything else should be reported.

As I was speaking I could hear in my voice that I wasn't telling the truth . . . not completely. There was a lot more that I wasn't saying.

To hear myself as I am speaking takes a special inner effort and division of attention. Adam naked, that is, without false personality, ate the apple and so had to leave, put on clothes, assume different faces, take on an identity, a self-image. All this has happened mechanically. Here we are learning to see and admit what we are wearing, what we have assumed—what keeps us out of the Garden.

Dancing Mechanical Dolls

I always took myself to be myself, a unity. Sure, sometimes I'd be arguing with myself about something, but it was always "Me." Now I see all these "I"s, triggered again and again by the same events, subjects, what have you, and all performing like dancing mechanical dolls. Am I anything else?

We live in "The World of Name," constantly reacting in terms of names, our own and others. Others continually reinforce this by calling us by our name and speaking about themselves, reminding us of their name. The three centers, intellectual, emotional and moving, are connected and always working in unison, so a given thought has an equivalent feeling which has an equivalent posture, and so it is with feeling and postures. Whatever one center identifies with, so do the others. Sometimes they argue, but usually they are in complete agreement. Given this unison, it's no wonder that the mass hypnotic spell of being an indivisible I is one very few wake up to. Through inhabiting the body and observing, we see the carousel of mechanical dolls that live our life in our name. The question "Am I anything else?" is genuine, as it arises from observation. Let us ask in response—What is it that observes?

XIX

Examining the Unexamined

I've experienced a very big shift in the past week or so. Instead of all the internal considering, looking away and fear that usually occurs, all of a sudden I've wanted to relate to people, to reach out to them and look them in the eye when I speak.

Socrates spoke of the unexamined life. We speak of the unobserved life. To truly examine, one must first become self-conscious. What existed in darkness, unconsciousness, is now lit by the light of consciousness. To directly experience what is observed—without softening the image, changing it or self-calming it away with hopes or vows of improvement—evokes genuine moral suffering, not mental, emotional or physical suffering.

One's life is examined in the light and facticity of what life is. This is compared to what we think life is. This suffering causes an essential healing. We don't do it. We only need to have the faith and courage to make ourselves available, to have the will to bear with it.

Mirror, Mirror

Today, I stood in front of the mirror putting on my blouse and skirt and styling my hair, and all at once I saw what I have been denying—my self-love and vanity. When I began to observe, the gestures started, something knew it was being observed, and then the gestures were no longer genuine but made up. The biggest shock was how incredibly identified I was with the image in the mirror.

The mirror image is a doorway if you "eat," absorb, the energy of the impression. Otherwise, the impression eats you. But you can't be in the head, you have to be embodied. "I"s do not like to be observed. They like the shadow life. When seen, they run for cover.

Suffering the Group

I notice that when I am with other members of my group, I see their worst characteristics or features. I don't know how to say this, but I hold them in a kind of disdain. And in that way I see I isolate myself from others.

There is a difference between "noticing" and "observing." One is of the mind, the other of self-remembering. That said, you will remember the people in your group as long as you live. You are all going through a self-initiation together. In this sense, they are your brothers and sisters, your spiritual brothers and sisters. Their weak and inferior sides are on view here, as much as yours, because that is the initial aim—to unmask our self-love and vanity. The work is to report as sincerely as possible what one has seen. This calls for and develops sincerity, courage, real will. Go beyond the usual way of relating in terms of likes and dislikes and affinity and disaffinity, and value what others offer you in revealing their suffering of themselves in trying to speak the truth of what has been seen. So it is just the opposite of what you say. Please ponder this.

Mary Jane, Acid & the Messianic

I did a lot of Mary Jane and acid before I entered the Work. I was able to experience such calm and beauty. Now it is all suffering. There is a part of me that says, "Why suffer?"

Drugs create imagination in higher emotional center. Besides the intellectual, emotional and instinctive centers, there are two higher centers, the higher emotional and higher intellectual. Drugs change the chemistry, one's vibration, allowing a possible contact with the higher emotional center. But if you have not sufficiently worked on yourself, haven't integrated all those strange fish swimming in the subconscious, they are going to be projected onto the higher emotional center.

Whatever happens will be taken as "real" because of the power the drug has opened you to. If you talk to the "devil" then that will be real for you. And when you come down, it will still be taken as real, because it's been chemically imprinted on the higher emotional center. The same goes for having "a conversation with God." A lot of messianic types got their start talking to God. And, of course, some people go "up" but never come "down." They get stuck between states of consciousness, trapped in the dramatic universe.

But let's say you could take that little Matrix pill and become conscious, even to the degree of consciousness-without-an-object. You'd miss out on the entire adventure of learning about yourself, the "I"s, false personality, internal considering, daydreaming, imagination, essence, being, centers and how they work, their dysfunctions, and so on. What would you be? At best, a stupid saint or another of our "acid-head messiahs." Why are we here? What is the sense and significance of life on Earth, human and otherwise?

World-Creation & World-Maintenance

I took as a line of observation looking at where I get my strokes. I'd thought it was mostly from other people, but I've begun to see how I've created a whole world based on this. As an example, I was at the grocery store and the clerk asked me about "the game." At first I didn't understand, but then I realized he was talking about the Super Bowl. I told him I didn't keep up with such things. Inside I could see there was this feeling of superiority. Walking home all kinds of memories from my late teen years and early twenties came up and I could see that I had started building this world then. It was in reaction to my feelings of alienation. No one understood me.

Imaginary world-building begins when we are children. It soon crystallizes into a self-image—how we want others to see us. It's all self-stroking, self-calming, *Kundabuffer*. The teaching speaks about knowing more and more about world-creation and world-maintenance. This is usually taken in a positive sense, but what of our imaginary world creations and world maintenance? As to "alienation," that can only be psychological. Like it or not, you've been here all the time. There's no cure for it other than to put your feet on the ground, become embodied. But, of course, this would challenge your "superiority," your last defense against your fear of trusting.

The Original Mistake

I've been reading All and Everything *about our situation and how it came about. During the evening sitting I suddenly felt rage about having to live in the far reaches of the universe, the implantation of the organ Kundabuffer, its removal but its specific properties persisting, that there is no Original Sin but an Original Mistake and it is not ours. We're having to pay for an "unforeseeingness."*

The picture Mr. Gurdjieff gives of the creation of our solar system, the comet collision with the Earth, the "Original Mistake," as you call it, is entirely different from what has been passed down to us. The idea that there is cosmic hazard, cosmic mistakes, that all is not perfect, not *Autoegocrat*, that we see things topsy-turvy is part of, as he says, his "merciless destruction" of the subjectivity we have taken to be objective. That said, it is also important to realize the essential truth that a freedom and knowledge to evolve or involve has been granted us; the choice is ours. It is not a time for rage but rejoicing. In the meantime, there's nothing wrong with rage. Live it, eat it, don't express it.

Dissipating Anger

The other day there was a realization that created anger. A voice said, "Observe the anger." Then the body appeared and the anger dissipated. Afterward, there was thinking about what the anger was and where it came from. How can the anger be observed in the moment when the body appears and dissipates the anger?

When it does, what is present? With the shock of self-remembering, the body appears in what? Consciousness. So now, with the evoking of self-consciousness, self-observation can take place. It has a foundation. Note that consciousness does not appear in the body. Just the reverse. The body appears in consciousness. Ponder this. It's an important and keen discrimination that few recognize.

Seven Degrees of Relaxation

Last week at the meeting I noticed a strong reaction to your response to what I said, particularly hearing you say "one-centered observation" and "the mind observing the mind." I saw a strong negative reaction in myself and a defensiveness. At first I thought that because there was some experiencing of the body that this meant the observation was more than one-centered. This was seen as a reaction and that there was truth to what you said. I wanted to explore this and took walks after my morning meditation a few times in order to connect with the body and to look at my observations. I saw more of how the mind wants to take over. It made rhythms out of my footsteps, even counted them. There was also a lot of worry about things that had not been completed, and it was seen how this keeps me from relaxing into the body.

The formatory mind will never relinquish control on its own. It's too literal and neurotic. It's completely centered on itself. Everything and everyone is an appendage of its concerns.
Everyone make a fist now.
[Holds up hand, slowly makes a fist]
That's how we are when we are uptight, angry and so forth. Now relax the fingers a little bit. That's what we usually call being relaxed. Compared to this . . .
[Hand closes into a fist]
. . . it is.

[Fingers open slightly]

But it's still in tension. There's simply less tension and we take that as our benchmark for being relaxed. But compared to this . . .

[Fingers open completely]

. . . it's not relaxed at all. And look at how much more is possible with a relaxed hand.

[Moves hand about, opens, closes fingers]

So when we use words, let's be careful not to hypnotize ourselves with them. Realize that words are not that to which they point, they are symbols. "Sugar," as my teacher would say, "is not sweet." That is, the word is not sweet. However, words are "magic" in the sense that this word can start you salivating.

Wrong Path Walking

There was an experience of going down a path I felt was wrong, and at the same time I felt I had to go down it. This experience from the start to the finish lasted about three weeks. Many very strong emotions were experienced directly, such as desire and lust, and it was seen that these emotions were coming directly from the self-love and vanity. Still I persisted until a very strong physical shock woke me up to the situation. In the moment of the shock there was a complete separation of the self-love world and the relationship I had with it, and the world as it was in the moment of the shock. This allowed me to see the situation for what it really was and the hold it had on me. It stopped me from possibly doing something I would have regretted. The shock was so deep that the relationship was completely severed and no longer had any pull or control after that moment. There was a moment when there was nothing, everything just was. Then an "I" came up that wanted to keep the moment and it was gone.

Sometimes we find ourselves being drawn down the steps to the cellar doorway. But we're not completely compelled, something is there observing. The feeling isn't right. We put our hand on the doorknob and we wake up and turn away. Other times we open the door. The work you've done on yourself has been serious and sustained and so there was "something else" that could wake up. There was a certain seeing of the situation, but it wasn't so deep that you stopped yourself from going down those steps. It was only when you put your hand out that the shock split the forces and you were awakened.

And, yes, in that space there is no personal consciousness. Everything is. There is no psychologizing, no personal relationship. It is empty of that. Even empty of time, though you make reference many times to "the moment." You didn't speak of silence, but it was also that on an even deeper level. That this wasn't awared allowed the "I" to appear that wanted to own it. So begin to work more now with silence in your everyday life. It's always there in the background behind all the noise and sound.

XX

With self-remembering, I actualize myself in physical space. Before, what was I? Simply a thought, a feeling, an impulse, all subject to external and internal shocks. There was no body awareness, so no visceral context, no conscious connection between centers, no space of mind, no sense of myself. My sense of unity is only in my mechanicality, not in consciousness. It's a difficult hypnotic state to break.

The Listening Body

As I sit in the meeting tonight and listen to the questions and answers I feel my body responding by tightening and loosening. I am not thinking about what is said, but there is an emotional response to what I am hearing and my body is participating in this response.

It is a sign that the body is inhabited and there is a listening. Now, can we listen-without-listening?

What do you mean?

Just what you reported.

Denying "I"s

I noticed in working with the exercise to deny myself something, a lot of "I"s came up that gave excuses not to do it. Several times I did deny myself something, but there were more times when I didn't. There wasn't any consistency. I denied myself coffee on several occasions and listening to the radio in my car, but overall I didn't really struggle with the exercise.

Are we "noticing" or "observing"?

The latter.

So what do you need to do?

I don't know.

You don't know? You just said that there wasn't any consistency. How could you not know?

I guess I need to be more consistent.

You "guess." . . . Why do we say we "guess" when we know?

Expecting Something Great

After I take a cold shower between the two sauna sessions, I return to the sauna to sit and observe the pulse. All that's been noticed is that it is more rapid, otherwise it seems no different than before.

You're expecting something?

Yes! I thought there would be some great discovery.

It's to remember oneself and observe the pulse.

Yes.

So, I observe it, but I begin to go more deeply into it, and perhaps I might . . . well, why spoil it by naming it? At the very least, you'll be strengthening the will, the attention, and you'll begin to be able to access deeper states of mind. The ordinary mind, after all, is like a monkey. It has to be tamed, put in its place, in order to open to deeper spaces of mind.

The Eraser

It has been seen that the personality erases certain observations that happen which the personality does not like admitting to. This week there has been much judgment seen, and when it is observed there is a familiar feeling that this happens all the time, and sometimes a voice says, "You have seen this before." The judgments have been happening all the time, but just recently there has been a strong awareness of it. There is a sense that what I am is made up.

It is important that you write down observations, because one of the ways the false personality manifests is to erase. There is a genuine personality, but its origin is essence and being, not conditioning. Play a role externally always, internally never.

Secret Life of Small Men

Standing in line at the deli there were two very tall men in front of me, taller than normal. These feelings started coming up about being inferior and insignificant. Seeing this shocked me into my body somewhat and that created some distance. These guys weren't doing anything that would cause these feelings in me of insignificance about my size. It was a very interesting experience.

Well, now you know the secret of small men. They live off their envy and resentment and often use the energy to conquer others, bring others down to size—their size. It's really too bad you are of medium height. Think of all the worlds you might conquer. And all in reaction. And then who knows—you might end up sucking your thumb on the island of Elba.

Holding the Breath

I've noticed repeatedly that while in a conversation I hold my breath and do not breathe regularly.

When you breathe regularly, what happens to the diaphragm?

I don't know. I never looked.

Well, observe now. What happens to the diaphragm when you inhale?

It comes up.

No, it should descend on the in breath. This creates an inner space and massages the lower organs. On the out breath, it moves up helping the outward flow. Tell me, have you ever been knocked out or lost your breath?

Yeah, playing football. They had to use smelling salts to revive me.

It might have been then that you were knocked off the normal pattern of breathing. So, as it's become a habit to breathe as you have, practice breathing from the diaphragm—you obviously breathe from the upper chest—and breathe as we've spoken about.

Get the Gold & Run

There's an "I" that wants to be seen as my working on myself, but it doesn't want to do it. Just wants to get the gold and run. So I find myself pretending to others and even myself.

Ahh, the "Great Pretender." Join the crowd. And there is also another one, the "I" that plays dumb. And the ones that use "I don't know," "I don't remember" to evade the truth. Remember that each center has its "I"s. They run in packs like dogs of the night. When one becomes the alpha-male-of-the-moment, it thinks it is the only "I." The "I"s have their needs, their agendas. They play with or against the "I"s of other people. It's all a pretense, a fight for the space-of-the-moment.

"I Thought . . ."

Doing the morning exercise there were associations whirling around my head, so I thought I would refocus on the body. Then there was a shock of realization—it had all happened in my head. I had never made the move down to the body. I just thought I had.

We live in thought. We conceptualize everything, systematizing, organizing, building great edifices of thought dedicated to what? Ourselves, of course. To break out of the thought-world takes aim, knowledge and effort. The aim is to awaken, but as long as I think I am awake how strong can my aim be? So I must verify through the evidence of my own observed experience that I am almost always asleep in the dream of myself, rarely awake. This observation must be a self-observation. That is only possible if there is self-sensing, a conscious attention. So this is not an "effort" in the usual sense of the word. It's not an outward effort but inward. We need to get the taste of refocusing, grounding, breathing, guarding, dividing attention. Do this not only when sitting but in neutral moments during your day, so that you come to a direct and unmistakable impression that you can't confuse yourself about.

"Don't Ignore Me!"

I saw some contradictory parts of myself. I usually want to be invisible. I was working in a large room with several other people. They decided to order lunch and no one asked me to join them. I saw the "I" that didn't want to be noticed, but another came up and said, "Hey, I'm here too. Don't ignore me!" I started to feel left out and sorry for myself, then I resolved to act and speak up. I ordered a roll just to participate.

Self-remembering is not enough in itself. The next stage is where there is active participation, where one acts and relates consciously. Then we can begin experimenting. Invisibility was a useful way to cope given the irrationality with which I grew up. But I must go against the grain of that habit.

XXI
Playing to Lose

You said something which resonated with me. You said we often play to lose, not to win. After thinking about this, I have to admit I have often played to lose. But the question remains: why would I play to lose?

Don't ask why. Too mental. Remember and listen. We speak of self-observation but much deeper is self-listening.

Reaction, Reaction

I have been noticing lately that everything I do is reaction, my relationships are reaction, my career is a reaction. I have been trying to not act out of reaction, but when the time comes to act differently, I find myself functioning out of reaction. There was an experience this past week where there seemed to be an opening and I saw an overview of all my reactions . . . words cannot express the seeing. The observing took place in a millisecond, and I immediately identified with it and was terrified that someone else would see what I saw, see that I am a nothing, a mess, and have no control—that there really is no indivisible I. It's been shattering.

It's said that "The truth shall set you free." But free from what? From the lie, the illusion. To be set free I must first die to what I have presumed. Now, not being that someone, who am I? I am no one, nothing. But what is it that knows this? Work on that.

Eating Feelings

I have been living in dread, and hope, of seeing someone from the past I've had a strong attraction to. We had a brief relationship that ended about a year ago, not without some regret on my part. I heard she was going to be at a party I was going to. As it turned out, she didn't come, and I found myself greatly relieved. It was a shock to see how much this had been weighing on me—the anticipation taking my energy and attention and eating away at my feelings.

Intellectually, in this instance, I may be free of a person but the other centers are not. So, two centers want her, one center does not. Can I experience the "yes" and "no" of centers. By the way, what posture was the body in when this was experienced?

I don't know.

"Old-Dog-I"

I have been observing a particular "I" that came out of the instinctive center. This "I"—which was first noticed at a seminar a few years ago—looks to be the leader of a group of instinctive center "I"s. It's very solid, unified, certain, powerful. Previously, it had been a goal to be in this "I" rather than in the fragmentation of "I"s. However, this "I" is now seen as having no compassion and is derived from egotism.

This is an "Old-Dog-I" that's been barking a long time and only now has it been heard. You would have crystallized in it had you not entered this Work. As in Ibsen's *Peer Gynt*, it will have to be melted down. One could say, "Now, don't take it personally, old boy," but, of course, the personal is what is going to be melted. As Mr. Gurdjieff said, "Thank everyone who helps you to wake up." Can you do that?

Thank you.

But don't you really get angry at people who try to wake you up?

Thank you, again.

Living in Shame

I recently observed how much of my personality was based on shame or fear of shame. My reaction of course was to say "Stop it! Stop it!"

I have seen something significant. I've seen what's beneath the floorboards. I have lived in shame. It has ordered my life, what I do and don't do, how I interpret, what I focus on, what I value. Take this as a line of observation. See it in the small, everyday things, those things which you most take for granted. And recognize that that which is seeing is not what is seen, if I am present. Recognize that which says "Stop it! Stop it!" is just the other side of shame.

Need for Sympathy

I had an impulse to go to my neighbor's house and tell him about something that had happened, to keep it alive. There was this need for sympathy. When the thought was heard, a voice said, "No, you're not going to do that." Then, there was the recognition that going to his house was a way to work by not talking about it. Sitting with him in his kitchen, I noticed "she" was positioned not to talk about it. And so there was a subtle "to talk-not talk" internal game going on. Time passed and with it a self-praising. When I was about to leave a voice said, "Look how long I've been sitting here and I haven't talked about it!" And with it the shock came that I had been asleep all that time.

There is the phrase "Get wise to yourself." It's usually said pejoratively, but we want to take it seriously. What do I deny constantly, despite all evidence to the contrary? That I am asleep. Asleep to what? Asleep to the deep compensations born in the past that still play themselves out in the present. I think I am here, it looks like I am here, but what is here in mind-feelings-body is my past. For example, if something dirty happened to me in the past, there will be an overreaction to anything not clean. Always look for overreactions. They are telltale. Now, it took you to your neighbor's by a clever use of the Work. It kept you in your head struggling with whether to talk or not. You didn't. But it was all from the head. Then you fell in love with yourself . . . all the time thinking you were awake. Ponder this.

Taking the Bull by the Horns

There's been a lot of frustration and anger at not being able to have much experience of the body. It was a quiet day at work, so I decided to take the bull by the horns and observe my postures every hour. One posture was sitting with the spine curved, head to the left side, the right shoulder dropped. Observed this many times. I was surprised to see a posture of folding the arms over the chest. This was pointed out to me at the first seminar I attended, and has been subsequently pointed out. The meaning of it has been resisted. I didn't always remember to observe every hour on the hour. A lot of judgment. I decided to deliberately take a posture that I know is habitual. That is, sitting with legs extended, leaning back, arms behind the head. Then today at work, I had to go to the office of a superior. We sat talking amicably. Then I realized that I was sitting arms folded and so was she. We were in fact in conflict, but I hadn't been aware of that.

This is rich material. You were active toward yourself, not passive. And look at all that was observed with postures and the attitudes, the way the attitude guards itself. The first step in coming to an experience of the body is to be sincere with ourselves and admit that we have little to no experience of it. The next is discrimination between being embodied and not. Keep working just as you are working, and in time, it's lawful, your wish will become reality.

Love of War

Yesterday I made a tech support call. I know what you say about not mixing the Work with one's job, but this, I think, is an important insight. I like making these calls not only because they help me get my job done but also because they give me a sense of power. On this particular call the agent was being idiotic . . . at least from my point of view . . . and I warmed to my agenda—light sarcasm, which goaded the agent into being less polite so that I could then escalate our disagreement. Then I rattled off information which is of course "gospel," which caused the agent to dig in her heels. Finally I could openly attack her lack of understanding and rudeness to me, the customer. This is what I love. This is where I was headed in the first place. Afterward, I felt drained of energy.

I love war. Physical or psychic, it makes me feel what? More alive. It is a way of unifying the parts of myself, changes the breath, sharpens the mind. Makes me feel like somebody. Gives me a story to tell. But I've paid for my little game. The time, energy and attention are gone now. My identification with my game player is increased. I can see all this now, but wait until I'm bored again or feeling a lot of energy, then what excuse is given? Take the need for combat as a line of observation. Also, I tend to live in "exceptionalism." Yes, I understand the rules but still . . . One last thought to ponder. Why does Gurdjieff say to never take the life of another even when your life is threatened? Could that have anything to do with self-transformation and what we kill we carry with us?

Hiding the Bad, Showing the Good

You've pointed out how I hide from seeing myself by splitting myself up into what I judge as "bad," which I call by my name, and what is "good," which is attributed to what I call "I" and take to be essence.

You will never come to reality as long as you divide the world and yourself up into "good" and "bad." Strive to observe impartially. Observe as you would observe the motor when you lift the hood of your car.

I notice that tonight when you speak to others I am open and receptive to what is said. But when you speak to me, a defensive feeling comes up and there is a filtering of what is said.

Yes, exactly.

Sometimes when you speak to people, instead of addressing them as "you"—you use the word "I." It's like you're talking about yourself but you're really talking about them.

You listen well.

XXII

We have too many answers and not enough questions. Questions are usually not about what one does not know, but rather asking for affirmation of answers we already have. True questions are the result of the material of observed experience. They have been lived. Otherwise, questions are merely of one center or another.

My Life in Earrings

I was going to buy some earrings that I had almost bought several times, but thought them too frivolous. I became distressed when I couldn't go to the store when I planned. When I did go, I thought that I shouldn't buy them, since I was so identified. Walking into the store, I thought "What do I do now?" As it turned out, the earrings had been sold, but there were some others I liked and so I bought them. On the way home strong "I"s came up, denigrating the body.

This was a head experience, not an embodied experience. I apparently still do not know how to work. Now what happens when you become embodied? The state is changed, the breath, the chemistry, one's potency. There is a change in the quality of one's materiality. Remember, everything is material, only the level, the density and frequency of vibration changes. So self-remembering is the beginning of the alchemical process of changing a sow's ears into human ears. Do you follow?

Yes.

Unfortunate.

Absolute Chaos

I got lost driving, not knowing whether to turn right or left. So I turned left, but it didn't look right, so I turned around and went the other direction. Traffic was heavy and I spent twenty-five minutes going only a few blocks. It was dark now and nothing looked familiar; all I could see were the street lights. The emotionality was so strong there was intermittent crying. All the time there was this fear and futurizing. Then your words came to remember myself in the midst of conditions. With that there was a coming back to the body, relatively speaking, enough so there was a sensation of the core and a sense of grounding. It wasn't that all the stuff went away, but it was possible to simply accept where I was and work with it . . . but initially it was absolute chaos.

Outwardly, I live in a relative degree of societal and personal order. But then there is a shock and what happens? I'm thrown into chaos, uncertainty. It usually eats me alive. But I imposed order, an inner order on myself, and that gave me a ground. Otherwise, I was like a kite in the wind. I must remember myself in neutral moments again and again, so that when chaos, real or imagined, occurs I can establish order by remembering myself.

I Didn't Say Anything

Somebody said something that shocked me, mainly because there was some truth to it, and it was something I'd never spoken about to anyone before. Though I didn't react outwardly, there was an inner reaction of defensiveness and anger. I didn't say anything, which is typical, as I'm afraid that if I speak my reactions will show.

What am I afraid others will see? I live like a fugitive fenced in by self-judgment. When someone shows me they see something about me, this evokes fear—the fear that what I am hiding will be discovered and my whole world will crumble. What I hide I get to keep and it keeps control of me.

Vicious Circle

I sit here and work to be present. The body is inhabited, but then others speak, thoughts come and there is identification. Then that leaves, things settle and the body appears again, but again I'm taken by the thoughts. What can I do? I feel powerless. It's a vicious circle.

Who is the "I" that feels powerless? When I am not talking to myself, I am out of the word-world. Recognize and value that. Break out of the magic thought circle. See that I am so identified with words, so addicted, that to be without words is interpreted as being nothing, being of no value. Work on oneself brings a new set of experience-based values, the experiencing of what is needed for self-transformation. What is happening here with the support of the group, how much less is it happening in ordinary life where there is no support? So we begin here. No matter how many times I am taken by thought, judgment, I return to being embodied.

Pushing It Down

Earlier today I had a thought, "What am I going to say at the meeting?" I have nothing to say . . . then as I reviewed my week one event stood out. But almost immediately there was pushing it down; there wasn't even a consideration to talk about it. And it was as if there was a resistance to look at that event.

It wasn't "as if there was," there was resistance. Why be vague? Why not say it? "I have resistance to talking about this." You are under no compulsion to speak about anything you don't want to bring up. The Work on all levels is and must be voluntary. The difficulty with answering is that it is usually received on the level of the formatory mind, put into memory, spoken about—and, thinking we know it, it's never explored. Answers are dangerous.

The Obese Woman in My Life

I entered the communal shower at my gym and saw a morbidly obese woman. I felt a revulsion and averted my eyes. After showering I went to the sauna. Soon she came in as well and sat down; the bench creaked under her weight. I withdrew into my own space and closed my eyes. The thought came to go against my negative feelings and engage her in conversation. There was the thought, too, to stay in my space and not include her. I decided to work with the revulsion and initiated a conversation. There was a freedom experienced in going against the impulse to hide.

We need to take the work on ourselves into ordinary life— remember ourselves, participate, experiment, do otherwise. It may seem awkward at first, but it is only psychological. Working in this way, our whole life can be an opportunity for self-transformation. And look what you gave this woman by going against your reaction. Think of what she has to endure every time she leaves her home. Many obese people cannot help it; it's genetic. And even if it isn't, it's no reason to not treat them with respect.

Goes Right Through Me

I know others have said this—it was a great help that they did—but, I, too, find I don't listen to others. I thought I listened, but what others say goes right through me. I am always making gestures and movements that convey I am listening, but internally I am thinking about what I am going to say next.

We entomb our life in the formatory mind.

This even happens with people I love.

Of course it does.

Of course. What do you mean—of course?

I take it you're listening.

[Nods]

Why are you listening to me when you don't listen to others?

I don't know, I just am.

Well, what did you hear?

Something I didn't understand.

You speak of "people you love." Who loves?

Well, I think—

Please, don't "think."

Loving My Cat

Gurdjieff says we should practice unconditional love on houseplants and pets. My cat was going to die. I made a conscious decision to love my cat unconditionally. Many times when I became irritated by my cat, I realized he was just being a cat and was incapable of doing anything "right" or "wrong," and negative feelings would just evaporate. Closely related to this are my experiences of following another of Gurdjieff's exercises: that of being conscious of the death of others and of oneself. When this is felt deeply, I experience a feeling of compassion along with a sense of expansion. Identifications seem unimportant and a feeling of connectedness to others seems to predominate. My problem is that I am having difficulty integrating these experiences with my approach to my personal relationships.

To have a genuine feeling for plants and animals is a sign of having a healthy relationship with life. But if it stops there, then aren't we using plants and animals as a compensation for our lack of regard, our fear, of other people? I would consider getting involved with children in some way, like coaching an elementary school sport, or being a Cub Scout leader, something that would connect you with children, but in a position of authority.

"I'm Not Understood"

The other day when you said something to me there was an anger toward you. It was an "I" that said I'm not understood. I put it all on you. This lasted well into the next day.

Projection is suggestibility's brother. The anger we don't eat, we project. Why the emphasis on being understood? How is it that I always think I am not understood—"If they would just understand me. . . ." Then what? I wouldn't be responsible for what I do and don't do. Is that it? Remember what St. Francis said: "Seek to understand, not to be understood." Deny what is active, but also be neutral, impartial, toward it, and so give rise to the active which is higher than the previous active; otherwise, one falls.

He also said, "Preach always and if you must, speak."

The saying is excellent. Thank you.

XXIII

The Veil of Vanity

Throughout the Day of Exploration there was an experiencing of self-love, the taste of it. Behind each thought or attitude, there it was. There was nothing "I" could do, no place "I" could go to get away from it. It was like a veil covering everything.

Why didn't you talk about it then? What was it that said you shouldn't talk about it?

Well, I wasn't going to bring it up today, either.

So now we should be thankful to you for reporting it?

No ... it's just that there was something that didn't want to talk about this and was going to talk about something else instead. So I knew this was what I should speak about.

Next time you might put a little more flesh on the bone.

Trapping Attention

As I sat down here tonight at the meeting, there was the lifting of a fog that's been with me for the last few days. I feel like I'm suddenly here, relatively speaking. There's something here that's not out there.

What does the world want from us? What's always in play? What's everyone competing for? Our attention. Trap the attention, you have the person. You can suggest anything you want and it will make an impact. Until we entered the Work, there was no conscious influence, no call and support to awaken. Here there is that support. It needs to be valued and protected.

Giving Testimony

At seminars I write in my journal and then look back over what I have written previously. There is always an observation or insight that is valuable. I see that writing down what I have experienced objectifies it and keeps the observation from simply fading away. When I am home I rarely write. There seems to be a resistance, a kind of sense that someone, maybe even me, will read what I write. A reluctance to put my own thoughts in front of myself.

Any serious self-expression objectifies—brings into physical reality—our relation to the moment. Where we are writing from in ourselves, the words used, what is emphasized, what is left out— these all stamp the experience. This is where I am at the moment, this is what I think, this is what I feel. We honor that when we express ourselves, rather than keeping it in the unexpressed. It's interesting isn't it, that even though I am always in thoughts of myself I am reluctant to, as you say, "put my own thoughts in front of myself." I hesitate to give testimony. Could it be that I am afraid of being judged? And if that is true, could it be that I am always judging?

Highest Aspiration

I find the illusion of using the head brain for self-observation very strong. It easily leads to analysis and philosophizing and never penetrates beyond the surface. When it does genuinely occur I see the limited nature of all my manifestations, be they thoughts, emotions or postures, particularly postures. Despite all the emphasis on them, I really didn't take them seriously, but I see now that they move always from one point of "comfort" to another. To take a posture intentionally meets immediate resistance once the novelty stage is over. There is something very shocking about the recognition that we are machines, that this isn't just some concept but a living truth. That it has taken me so long to genuinely see and admit all this gave an initial reaction of disgust with myself and futility. You've sometimes spoken of making a commitment to our highest aspiration. I see now how important it is.

As it says in Proverbs, "For as he thinketh in his heart, so is he." True, and also what I give my attention to, that I am. I observe something about myself and the first reaction is to want to change it, make it better. But this is the "self-improvement-I." Now, simply be with what is observed, get to know it, take it as a line of observation. Increase of self-knowledge and change of the level of being happens of itself simply by again and again bringing the light of our attention and intelligence to what we have been blind to. Your work has been serious in that you didn't trap yourself in the self-pity that underlies futility but saw it for what it was. And now you see the need to commit to working to fulfill your highest aspiration. To do that, you must put the Work first. If you do, there will be no confusion, for you have an aim, and everything then takes its place in the fulfillment of that aim.

Mechanical Rewards

I've observed myself again and again over the years, and in many situations, and I've come to realize that it's true that we are bioplasmic machines. We're certainly imperfect but perfect as machines, and so we are, as you say, "perfectly imperfect." My life is expressed perfectly mechanically. And there are continuous rewards with our personal mechanical successes—money, power, respect, sex. It's very self-calming and increases the level of sleep. The refusal of our mechanicality will exist as long as there exists this satisfaction with mechanical rewards.

Now that this has all been verified a new level of work has begun. I'll speak about this with you later.

Denying Myself

For several weeks now, each morning after a meeting, at the end of sitting, I think about not drinking coffee, to see if I should continue, if there's still a "no." At the end of the first week there was a small "no," nothing like the big "no" when I was thinking about what to deny the body in order to better observe it. But although the intention was to stop for a week, I kept on for another week. At the end of the second week, there wasn't any "no" at all, but I felt I ought to continue anyway to see what would happen. During the week, there were no strong impulses to have coffee. Like the week before, there were other impulses, some given in to, others not.

It can't be day by day, or week by week. You give something up for a definite period. Read *Undiscovered Country* where Kathryn Hulme tells how Mr. Gurdjieff worked with her on giving up cigarettes. If you want to take another step, imagine that you are drinking coffee, "taste" it. But keep it as an image, not an actuality. That will bring your inner and outer worlds together.

What Is the Meaning of Life?

Shopping at yet the third grocery store in my area and finding no fresh shrimp, I became aware of my saying over and over again out loud, "I can't believe it! I just can't believe it!" The clerk, who was clearly making an effort, explained that there had never been any fresh shrimp for sale since he'd been hired eleven months before. Still, I couldn't let go of the picture in my head of fresh shrimp on ice in the seafood display. One "I" insisted it was right, and another was embarrassed that "I" was so out of touch with the new prepackaged frozen shrimp "units," as they now call these things.

A couple of days later as a clerk scanned the third set of Christmas tree lights, I said, "Can't you just scan one package and multiply?" I saw my attitude was of some haughty superior "I" who figured the clerk had a below-average I.Q., and believed that if it had designed the cash register, it would have made it much more efficient—though of course nothing is known about cash register design or inventory control.

Then last evening while dining out with two girlfriends I heard myself pontificating about "What is the meaning of life?" and ending with "It surely isn't shopping!" I realized then the truth was both that I didn't want to see "the bitch," and neither did "she" want to have to endure shelves of new packaging and wrangling with clerks.

Ahh, yes, ordinary life seen at its best. Thank you.

Self-Will & Breath

Self-will has been seen with breathing, a forcing, an interfering with the body's breathing.

Self-will is pervasive and neurotic. It interferes on every level. Its one aim is to keep control, keep separate. See that the body is properly aligned, that the knees are not higher than the hips. Sense the face. Let the flesh fall away from the skull. Then experience the sacrum-lumbar, the lower spine, and move it forward slightly. Experience the end of the spinal column and slowly with the attention climb the tree of the spine. At the top of the spinal column, drop the chin to the sternum, elongate the neck. Then, keeping the chin down, move the head and neck as one unit on top of the spinal column. Thus supported, now raise the chin to what feels right for you. Give all the weight up to the skeletal system, the Earth. Sense the face again. Experience your verticality, the freedom, the nobility. Then relax the face, the seat of false personality. Take some deep breaths, filling the whole rib cage and back of the body with breath. Then totally relax, opening up the pores of the skin, so that the whole body is breathing. After a while, take note of the breath, where it is originating from. Most people breathe high up in the upper chest. If so, redirect the attention to the diaphragm and the breath will follow, as the breath follows the attention and vice versa. Experience the rhythm of the breath, relaxing the body, letting the muscles fall away from the bones. Understand that you are absorbing second being food. Now, aligned and present, begin the morning exercise.

Being My Own Teacher

I've been experiencing more resistance than I have thus far in the Work, and I am hoping that telling you about it will create a shock and enough desire for me to work through it. When I was fasting for a week I was very focused on the Work, and the fast provided a great shock. I was getting up and doing the morning exercise every morning and observing myself with much greater depth and frequency during the day. I did this fast to clean out my body, but I noticed that my level of vibration seemed to become higher, and I figured that in this state it would be beneficial to "purify" myself in other ways and to conserve as much energy as I could. People noticed a positive difference, despite the fact that I didn't talk about what I was doing. I thought I was building a good foundation to continue working on myself, but I lost it all soon after I ended the fast.

I went on a short vacation with my family and only sat one of the four mornings I was there and I haven't sat once in the week I have been back. I have felt overwhelmed and unable to "do" small tasks—life tasks or Work-related. I am trying to see the resistance and continue through it, but I am having a lot of difficulty. I know there are many forces keeping me here, many "I"s, my identification with what I had thought I had obtained, my belief that I could continue conserving energy without growing resistance, and probably greatest of all—not having to attend group meetings.

On the face of it, your report sounds like that of a "good

student." Is it?

[Confused silence]
I don't know. I guess so. It's what happened.

Who told you to fast?

No one. I thought it would be a good idea because—

I? What "I"?

The one that's interested in the Work.

That's an "I" in magnetic center which is in personality. It can change in a flash, nothing is fixed. I see that you take yourself to be a student.

[Nods]

But you are acting like your own teacher, no?

I guess so.

To guess is an appropriate function, if the situation calls for it. Does this situation call for it?

I guess not, I mean . . . well, I don't know what I mean.

The word was used to avoid what I knew to be the truth—that I am trying to be my own teacher, creating my own exercises, stopping them when I wish and so forth.

What's wrong with giving myself an exercise?

If you are asked to do that, fine. But you weren't, so, again, what "I" is giving the exercise? At this stage we are still learning to discriminate between "I"s. By trying to be my own teacher—a common strategy of the person—I maintain control. So I play the "student card" in meetings and the "teacher card" outside. It's all self-will. Do you follow?

I never saw it like that, but, yes, that's what was happening.

To become an individual—and the word is used in Gurdjieff's meaning—is to become independent. But this is an example of premature independence.

Okay. I see that now.

That recognized, there was an interest, an initiative taken, a certain effort toward creativity. This is to be cultivated, but from the right starting point. Remember in J. G. Bennett's book *Witness* where Ouspensky is leaving for America—Bennett has been a member of one of Ouspensky's groups for eight years or so—and Bennett asks about his work. Ouspensky tells him, "You always begin from the wrong place." Bennett never explains what he understands by this, but earlier he writes about Ouspensky having given students an exercise of repetitive prayer. After a few months he then told everyone to stop. Bennett says he continued the prayer on his own for seven years.

XXIV
"Pumpkin"

I called my parents and my father answered. He seemed very "happy"— they were having a party and he had apparently been drinking. He called me "Pumpkin." Never in my life had I heard this from his lips, and I never would have associated him with that comment.

We are all connected, and a deeper connection is the bond of blood. The work that we do on ourselves reaches those we are connected to and bonded with. Perhaps you have forgotten, but you have said that your father adored you as a little girl, so it's quite likely that he did call you "Pumpkin" at one time. That is, until you began to criticize his behavior and, in your eyes, he "fell from grace." If we only knew the extent to which women are living out their dysfunctional daughter-father relationship, and how men are living out their dysfunctional son-mother relationship. As long as there is not wholeness, we live in parts. We live—rather are lived—by historicizing, by justification, by having to make ourselves right, so all relationship is skewed.

Roller Coaster Ride

I feel like I'm on a roller coaster ride. I go through these periods when I'm all gung ho for the Work and I'm practicing regularly. Then there's a real plunge where my resistance is strong and my efforts are very weak. I've had this belief that if I just try harder I can overcome it, but I am beginning to realize that maybe this is all I'm capable of doing.

You started out trying to do the hundred yard dash in 9.5 and now you find you're barely in the race. It seems as though everyone is passing you up. So you come to a place of futility that this is "all I'm capable of doing." What do you think about that?

At this point I don't really care.

Do you feel like something is being taken away from you?

I'm not sure what you mean.

You're resisting the question. What's not to understand about "Do you feel like something is being taken away?"

I don't know if you mean in general or in a particular situation. There is a resistance to letting go of imagination, so I suppose I do feel like something is being taken away.

You use the word *imagination*. Is this a mask for the word *fantasy*?

Probably. It depends . . .

No one's asking you to give up anything. No one's taking anything away from you. We're meeting here to practice being present, to learn how to listen, to speak, while being embodied. We are working to come out of fantasy, not indulge it.

The Ability to Do

I'm wondering what in myself makes decisions. I've observed that there is a difference between "will" and "desire" and their effect in motivating actions. I am reminded of Gurdjieff's aphorism that the highest attainment of man is the ability to do. Also, he has said that when man knows his place, he will know what to do. I see in myself that my actions are motivated primarily by desire from various "I"s.

To decide and do, one must first be. Otherwise, it's deciding and doing. To be is to be free from the person. That doesn't mean disowning it. It means knowing what it is and what it represents and using it when the occasion demands rather than being used by it. The person is coated in self-will. Self-will is propelled by desires, and the desires—except the wish to be—are all of the person. So it's a constantly spinning wheel kept in motion by reaction upon reaction. Instead of living on the circumference we need to find the center.

Remember the film *The Truman Show*? The character is deep in the societal dream in which all the decisions about how to live are already made and everyone conforms. He wakes up but realizes there are cameras watching him wherever he goes. So he's got to be sly. He makes his bed so that it looks like he is in it. He slips out and rows across the water. Terrible weather. He almost drowns but he does not turn back. Only at the end, when he is just about to leave the bubble of his former life, does he hear the director's voice, the part of him that has been controlling his life, commanding him to turn around. His desire for a real life, his clarity and will, are such that he doesn't obey and so bursts the bubble. He's free and awake to what was. Now can he be awake to what is?

Yes, in the world he enters the people are still asleep, drugged out on TV and fast food.

Have you been listening? That's *The Truman Show Part II*.

Day of Poetry

The day of poetry brought several interesting observations. I saw that during the part of the day when we were directed to read from each center, that even though there was intent and effort to do so, that

I read largely from the formatory mind. It seems that intent isn't enough, that it isn't enough to think or intend that I am in any given center.

It shows how strong the grip of the formatory mind is. You need to first come to remember yourself, become embodied, breathe fully, stop all thought, divide the attention, highlight the center you intend to read from in the global awareness of the body, begin to read. Read the same line over and over again.

Self-Calming the Negativity

I don't know how to say what I want to speak about so I'm just going to start talking. It's been seen that with negative emotions that while there is an initial flash of awareness a shift occurs very quickly. There is an "I" that takes over. So rather than a transformation of the energy of the negativity, there is a pushing down, a self-calming.

Yes, to see this you've had to develop your attention to a fine degree. Usually the discriminations we make take place long after so much else has happened. We have been trained not to express negative emotions. It's mechanical, not a conscious decision. We push them down and they fester and eventually explode socially or make us sick physically. So instead become embodied and do otherwise—express them.

I Have a Body

Observing my postures begins with remembering that I have a body. The body appears to me in a posture that was taken without my awareness. It might be more correct to say that I appear with a body, or even that sometimes my body calls me to it. When I can sustain my attention, having a body instead of being it, I impartially follow the movements of my body as it responds primarily to my instinctive center. It is as if my body is living its own life without me. Preparing for sitting meditation is almost the only intentional posture that I ever take. It was a shock to have you point out that a specific "I" was speaking and to listen for its voice. This bard has a facility with words and it has appropriated the language of the Work. This "I" thinks that it is real, thinks that it knows. I have recognized it only after it has painted itself into a corner at the end of its train of thought.

It's self-comforting, offering the illusion of the solidity of words and logical explanation. It's seemingly able to explain up to a point. Being one-centered, it can't see itself and falls apart leaving the emotional energy of the personality wanting to be something.

These are keen observations. You've put yourself in question. Both the body and the "I" appear within consciousness. Consciousness is, we aren't. Keep observing.

It All Happened on Its Own

When it came time to read my poem in front of the group, I had told myself that I would read from intellectual and then emotional centers. The intent to do this was there, but it wasn't enough to actually be there. When I was trying to read from the intellectual center, I got a picture that it was really just formatory. As I began to read the second time, without any intent or specific effort, there was a shift to emotional center that was very strong and unmistakable. It happened all on its own.

The attention shifts between centers, but we usually do not observe it.

What Is My Aim?

When I left the seminar, I had an epiphany of sorts. "What is my aim?" I thought. The immediate answer was "Wholeness." It wasn't just an intellectual idea, but a realization felt at a deep level, like it lived in all the centers. The feeling was that wholeness is inseparable from self-remembering. And this led to my being relatively awake for a sustained period. Driving home, I didn't turn on the radio. With the experiencing of the body I had had during CBI and from this "space" my driving habits, their mechanicality, became apparent. So it was interesting. I had a kind of double impression: I was a machine and, in seeing this, I was not a machine. At home, exhausted, I fell into a deep sleep, and when I woke up I had the feeling that something had changed, that I was back to my "normal" mechanical state.

Yes, the seminars are quickeners. Working with the theme and integrating body-senses-mind brings an intensity and duration that changes our vibration, our level of being, and brings the possibility of experiencing the wholeness in all its multiplicity. Do you know the definition of wholeness?

No.

It's the true meaning of the word *religion*, and it was perhaps this wholeness that made an impression deep enough that you didn't distract yourself with the radio going home. This allowed you to more vividly observe your usual mechanicality, the "subterranean" world we usually have no experience of. Of course, the pull of everyday life, its hypnotic momentum, is strong. But having experienced a higher level of being, we know, this is a possibility for us now, not after we die. This is not a "hereafter teaching" but a "here teaching." So the aim is right and real.

Guessing Centers

When people were guessing which centers I was reading from, I was attempting to read from the intellectual center, but by the end of the second reading I became identified with the emotions and how good it felt, and didn't remember to read from that center. So the question became, is my intent enough to come into any given center?

This is a question that comes from your own consciously lived experience. You were present, relatively speaking. Therefore, your question is based on material and not description. This is an important discrimination to understand. Let me repeat: If one isn't present, there is no material. It's simply description.

The attention does not feel like it's in my head but in my chest. There is a tightening and heat experienced in the chest that has been labeled as anxiety and it's hard to breathe.

At the entrance to Prieuré West, in the garden there is a boulder with a large rock balanced on top. It's a symbol, a reminder to stay in balance. To do this, we must first see when we are out of balance. The attention follows the breath, the breath the attention. So, if one center is too active, focus and breathe into another center.

XXV

Self-knowledge and being are the foundations of understanding. If there is only growth in knowledge and not being, then knowledge becomes distorted.

Voice & Body

The other night I was reading All and Everything *out loud and it was observed that the rhythm of the voice was creating a subtle movement in the body. At first I questioned if I was misperceiving this, then it continued, and it was realized that it was just another part of the reading that allowed a deeper connection in the moment.*

Reading in the way the author prescribes, and with the exercise given, means you are initiating yourself into the Work. It's a magical book, a *Legominism*, that works on body, senses and mind.

Thrown into Question

Someone called to give me a task. The person made a strong impression on me. The task was presented with such presence that it gave me a deep appreciation of the Work. It also cut off all the "I"s, the identification that came up, the fear. But then as I did the task, there was fear that would come, but it was not given any energy; it was just accepted, and there was then an exploration of a part of myself that the rest of me had no knowledge of. This had the effect of throwing the whole of me into question—not in terms of having a particular question, rather that there appears to be so much that I don't know about myself—of revealing myself to myself so to speak.

We can help one another by working to be present. To make every exchange a conscious exchange. Then each is a reminder to the other. This is an individual work but also a group work. These two sides can't be stressed enough. The Work in the lowest and highest sense is self-revealing. So many sides of myself are a stranger to me. Only by being present, observing, and not identifying with the content of the observation are these hidden sides seen.

Self-Conscious

When I spoke to people at work in order to do otherwise and give myself a reminder to self-remember, I kept my thumbs and index fingers touching, as was suggested. In the first conversation it worked to keep me active toward myself. I was so self-conscious, though, that it wasn't until the third conversation that I was able to inhabit the body to some degree. But there was never the experience of the whole body.

Self-remembering, as mentioned, has many degrees. Because it absorbs and refines impressions rather than deflecting and aborting them, impressions have more force. This force creates more energy and there is more sensitivity. This makes me more emotional. If I can contain the emotion—not let it explode, identify or fall into fantasy—and at the same time remember myself, then an entirely new level and taste of what self-remembering really is will be experienced. If feeling becomes emotion and you remember yourself . . . well, see what that is like.

Mental Reminder

This week, when the mental reminder came to be present, most of the time there was a struggle. There was impatience or an "I" that was in a hurry and didn't want to take the time. There was another "I" that would make the effort. The impatient "I" would go through the motions, pretending.

We live in a hurry-hurry world, everyone consumed in becoming, so few in being. We live out ahead of ourselves in mental and emotional abstractions, a psychologized time in which time is not of the essence at all. And so we live under the rule of time. But it is not real time. That is only experienced when I am without quotation marks. From what you say, I gather all of this jousting was taking place in the head, therefore it was one-centered. It's only when we remember ourselves that experience becomes two-centered and, with depth and duration, three-centered.

Truth-of-the-Moment

There has been a pattern of observations that has shown me that I use the work for protection and self-calming. When an emotional shock is received there is an immediate reaction to breathe down into the body, amplify the awareness. Something is hiding from the truth of the moment. The Work is being used to protect the false personality and to self-calm with the hearing of a voice saying, "Breathe down into the body and everything will be OK, it will pass." This is in stark contrast to the few experiences that I have had where I was in the body before the shock happened and seeing the emotional energy change to a higher energy.

Motive defines. Two people can do the same thing, but why they do it defines the action. You took philosophy, yes?

Yes. I almost majored in it.

Remember Immanuel Kant? He said there is a difference between a man who jumps into a river to save a woman who is drowning because she is a fellow human being, and a man who knows she is the daughter of a wealthy merchant and hopes to receive a reward. Sincerity must be learned. No "I" in itself, though it may believe it is sincere, can be sincere, because it is simply one "I" among many. Only in wholeness can there be sincerity. I give this to you for free. But, be warned, the Work is a snake. A snake of wisdom or, when used by the egotism, a poisonous snake. We see this with all the "esoteric-I"s, all the "jealous gods." So the action of remembering yourself is right if the motive is right—to be instead of to protect. That can only be seen in the moment. By the way, Gurdjieff said Kant had it right, except for scale.

Replaying Dreams

A sign in a shop window produced an attraction toward the daydream that had come up from seeing that sign last week.

The sign "produced it"?

Well—

You had no choice in the matter?

I suppose not.

There is no "supposing." One is either here or not here. One is either conscious or mechanical. There are many degrees of both, of course. Now go ahead.

I had passed some time in the daydream in a way that was pleasant to me and the "attraction" was an impulse to replay that dream and pass time in a pleasant way. I had also seen other times when I had an impulse to replay certain pleasant dreams; I have a repertoire of dreams.

You say this without any embarrassment.

I imagined a whole scene where I was the owner of the store where the sign was placed, and I was interacting with the person who had placed the sign. This dream played up my "broad-mindedness" and "assertiveness."

Why are we on Earth? As Mr. Gurdjieff asked, "What is the sense and significance of human life on Earth?" To daydream? Or to experience Earth life? Having been given life don't we have a duty to actually live this life rather than dream about another? We can live by the Law of the Sun or the Law of the Moon. It's our choice. Choose wisely. But recognize there is no choice in dream life, only in embodied life.

Inner Something

When I first entered the Work there were times of flatness. But there was also a sense of sadness or loss. So there must have been identification. Now the "flatness" is experienced not as dullness but as an absence of inner drama. There is an inner something that is constant and with that a sense of peace, a sense of all-rightness however things or situations arise, a deep taste of the temporal nature of things and situations and of something that is not temporal.

Remember, knowledge is state specific. When the state changes, the knowledge changes. What is reported needs to become crystallized. That takes remembering oneself in the fire of the moment. Let life show us where we are, as opposed to where we think we are. The Work is a snake. A snake of wisdom or degeneracy, depending on the growth of knowledge and being, not one or the other.

The Presumption of "I"

I am sitting here and there are voices telling me, "You don't have to say this." "You don't have to talk about this . . . it's not important." Someone called me this week to ask a question and I gave them my answer. I told you about this, but then a part of me lied to you. Just before this lie, I was telling myself "Yes, you know what you're doing . . . you do have the best interest in mind. Yes, you know what is right."

So what's your question?

I don't have a question, just that there is this shock of the fact that there is this something "foreign" in me, that there really are these "I"s, these different parts, and that there is some part of me that really doesn't want to believe that.

This idea that we are one, have individuality, consciousness and can do usually takes a long time to break. Only then can real inquiry take place. Otherwise, there is always the presumption of I. As mentioned, I always start from the wrong place.

I'm amazed at how strong that part of me is, it insisted that it was nothing, that I didn't have to say it.

We all have good lawyers.

My Father's Death

My father passed away. He had been housebound for some time. He had been a man with a strong and forceful personality. As he aged he softened and as his condition worsened his personality peeled away and it seemed for the last seven months he lived in essence. During these months I felt I was finally able to know him. His condition was such that there was no way for him to intellectualize what was happening to him, yet we were so deeply connected that there was no need for many words. When I visited him there would be a look of simple joy and recognition as he would greet me.
The night before he died I was awakened at three o'clock in the morning with a strange sensation that lasted for ten minutes or so. I thought he must have died that night, but when I saw him in the

morning he was breathing, but I sensed he was not there. He truly looked like a machine with no being present. This was the first time I felt detached from him when I was with him. He passed some time in the early morning of the next day. Throughout his last days I tried to remember myself and observe, which gave the experience another dimension. The grieving that I had experienced for his decline passed with his death. I feel my world is somehow different and that I have changed in some subtle yet real way.

When a loved one dies it creates an emptiness in our heart which we can fill only with God. Thank you for offering this to us. You might look up what is said about prayer in *Search.*

XXVI

Futurizing the Immediate

When you asked me to write my question after the meeting, I told myself I would do it when I got home. When I got home I listened to the voice that said to write it now wouldn't be a challenge, so why not wait a few days or even a week? All week long I reviewed the question. It is now a week later and I cannot remember the question at all. There are so many other memories associated that I can't separate what was really said from what came later. It brings up a number of feelings. There are feelings of rebellion and thoughts of rationalization and justification— "It's not really such a big thing." I find myself promising to do what you ask in the future, and somehow not really believing it.

Struggle always with the "tomorrow disease." Never bargain. Be ruthless with yourself. Let it always be, as Ibsen says in *Brand*, "All or nothing." There are many "taboos" about self-remembering. You just encountered one. We talk of getting the "taste" of self-remembering. Well, to get to a real taste, one has to first taste all the taboos. They don't taste good. But, as they are only psychological, you learn to bite right through them. Once you see the taboo is only a thought-form, a projection, it disappears. That is, it's not a snake lying in the road, it's a rope. All our efforts to remember are a preparation to remember, for we can only truly experience that in the fire of emotion when we have the consciousness and will to stand in our being. But isn't what's really at issue here my unwillingness to give up my self-will?

Pause in the Thought-World

Sitting down tonight the thoughts were very fast. As I began to self-remember the thoughts slowed down slightly. The attention was going back and forth between the mind and the body. As I relaxed further, the thoughts continued to slow down and I was able to observe the thoughts while maintaining awareness of the body. With further relaxation there were spaces between the thoughts. I also saw that there were times when my thoughts would pause.

Tension, both psychological and muscular, is a contraction and compression that not only eats energy but helps to create thought. Relax into the awareness by breathing into the body. Observe not only the pause but the space between thoughts, the silence. Merge with it.

Blockage

You asked that I write to you about the ideas given at the last seminar. The dialogues were some of the richest I've experienced, yet something in me refused to write about them. I suppose it is my sense of individuality and independence, my resistance to subject myself to a higher authority. I feel a strong awareness of a blockage in myself. There's a blockage in my personal life as well.

I'm just a stand-in for your father. What you are experiencing with me—not in a real sense but in terms of your projections and interpretations—you played out with him. This is an opportunity for you to consciously observe the mechanicality. In doing so, you'll suffer yourself, what you take to be "yourself," and then the inner fire of that will melt the blockages. It won't happen overnight. But it's lawful that it will happen, not by your doing anything other than making yourself available to be in Being.

How Can God Be Real?

I was out with some friends after a week in bed with a bad back. I hadn't taken any pain killers but sensed the body and breathed into the pain. I kept my mind free of negative thoughts and kept my aim in view—to heal myself. It happened, but then, as I said, out with some friends and not getting my way and being refused, my back began to act up. I asked to be taken home, but my partner ordered another round of drinks. I took this as an affront and walked home. I was fuming. Suddenly, I came to and observed. It was like observing a stranger from the outside, yet sensing all the reactions of the body. One "I" after another coming up, one justifying, another commiserating, another hurt, another saying "I'll show you." Then there was an "I" that I've rarely noticed—it wanted to be in this state. It loved all the fury, the misery.

This is real work on yourself. Working with the physical pain and then the mental, and look what was observed—that which loves all the chaos. It feels like this is living! Isn't the deeper truth that in us there is that which loves to suffer. It's a denial of real life, of God. It is suffering, so how can God be real?

Preserving Face, Breaking Bonds

Over the past several weeks there have been subtle impressions that a part of me wants to hide, and remain in hiding, particularly with you. The personality wants to maintain or preserve how it is seen or regarded by you. And it also happens at other times. When someone asks me a question that I don't know the answer to, part of me wants to hide then, too. No, what I want to say is that all I can do is listen to it, feel the impulse, sense the sensation, because it is already there . . . when it happens, it is already there.

That this is finally seen and admitted is an important step. And I see that by admitting the truth I don't go up in smoke. In fact, I feel lighter, more spacious, connected, yes? Now, isn't it stupid to avoid admitting one's ignorance? To indulge in this hiding is a drain and misuse of energy, a breaking of relationship with oneself and others. No lie comes free. It resists and bottles up the truth-of-the-moment, keeps it down. This is why so many people are so heavy, have so little space, both psychologically and often physically. We get to keep what we lie for and so become "weighted down." We become fat with lies. Become an authority on "the art of hiding."

Magic Circle

I have been wondering lately when I am going to get real with the

Work. I had a dream last night . . . in the dream I was in a retail store at the cash register complaining about something. You were in the customer service line behind me. As I was complaining to the clerk I was aware that I was just going on and on, just to be noticed, to be difficult, it's just what I do. I kept looking back at you in line trying to get some response, but you were just waiting in line patiently with no expression or reaction. You were not going to comment. There was a strong sense that you were just waiting for me to "get real," to commit to working on myself.

Most dreams are just an off-loading of energy. But this is a teaching dream, a communication from a higher source. Remember in *Meetings with Remarkable Men* where it talks about being trapped inside a "magic circle." Your "black magician" has put you there and will keep you there unless you give up self-will and do as your "white magician" directs.

"I-Know-Best"

I was writing down the "I"s that I had observed over the last few days. One of the "I"s named was I-Know-Best. "She" likes to give her husband advice. "She" is very powerful because she knows she's right and she has a good cause—to help him. Also—and I don't know how I know this—this "I" is modeled after my mother, who was very good at telling people how to do things. As soon as I finished writing about this "I," my husband walked into the room and told me that he was going to do something. I immediately suggested that he do it another way. I heard what I said and laughed. I could just as easily have cried in despair.

Naming one's "I"s is like the power Adam was given in Genesis of naming the creatures in the Garden. To name is to have dominion over. Otherwise, the "I"s enslave. Keep looking for your "mother."

Subject-Object Relationship

Thinking about what has been said about subject-object relationship I tried to see where my attention was. Was it inside myself or going out? I see that I tend to be inside myself. During the week I feel like I'm not really present. I observe how different my experience is in meetings.

As has been said, we think we live in subject-object relationship, but if we follow our attention we will see that either I am
all object—my attention is totally directed at the object outside
myself—or it is focused on me, the subject. It can move very
quickly between the two, which gives the illusion of subject-object
relationship, but there is really no relationship; it is all one or the
other. Now, the attention can be divided between the subject and
the object, so that there is an awareness of both simultaneously.
But this is usually within the head brain. Intellects are particularly
susceptible to this. As to meetings, yes, we practice establishing an
authentic relationship. Then we do the same with the rest of our
life.

Lying to the Teacher

I have been practicing to remember myself as you advised. This is
when the real valuation of what we were given began to appear. There
was no resistance. It is just a part of me. And as I was doing this,
a thought came that when you asked me the second time if I was
remembering that part, I was able to reply and not lose the connection
completely. I could not say for sure if I said the truth to you at that
time. Many times I have observed "I"s who like to take the credit
jumping out and signing the check and other "I"s have to pay the bill.
And there is not much I can do about it. Also from Search *we know*
that the first barrier is overcoming lying to one's teacher. So, how can
one remember not to lie to his teacher?

Lies come in many flavors, gross to subtle. Then it's a question—to what degree is the lie intentional? Mechanical? The study
of lying on the formal level is as broad as it is deep. Its basis is
avoidance. When the young boy in Ingmar Bergman's *Fanny and*
Alexander is asked why he lies, he says—"To keep the advantage."
One also keeps one's face, one's position.

I'm glad that the Day of Exploration wasn't over for you on
Sunday. Yes, there are many "I"s, "I"s that talk, "I"s that sign checks,
and "I"s that pay this check. There were at least three "I"s while
you said only one sentence. How can you remember yourself with
all that? This is the time when one can get angry at oneself. Many
people think that anger is something bad. This is the way to use
anger. Get really angry at yourself for losing connection with the

body. It is very hard to remember ourselves with other people. That is why we practice in neutral moments—washing the dishes, doing body impressions, sitting. And everybody goes at their own speed. If one wants to go fast he needs to set the bar higher.

XXVII

Have you seen the cartoon that shows a fellow slumped on a couch, watching the boob tube, holding a remote in one hand and a cell phone in the other? God has just called and the fellow says—"Say, would you mind if I put you on hold?" Isn't that how we are with everything that doesn't fit into the moment that is living us? Self-remembering will always be "outside" that moment. We have to say "no" to becoming and "yes" to being.

I Thank You So Much!

You told me when we first met that if I would sincerely work on myself I would know who I am. I've been wading through a lot of past, which has colored my present in the wrong way, and slowly learning a little of who I am and I thank you so much! Now I wish for more than to know who I am. I wish for what you cannot give me—understanding, consciousness, a soul. I'm sure if I were to see a videotape of myself in a meeting, say a few years ago, I would be filled with horror. I know I'm different. I think differently. I feel different, even if I'm still at the bottom of the ocean; the chains are breaking and I pray I live long enough to be free.

Observe the tendency to drown yourself in overdramatizing, dig into the motive behind spiritual ambition. Understand, emotion by itself, intellect by itself, leads nowhere. The only currency accepted is seeing and admitting who I am not. The rest is filthy lucre.

My Dirty Little Secret

Yesterday, something was seen and reacted to all day. I observed an "I" in myself that wants power, wants to be looked at as an authority, wants to have control. There were many "I"s that came up and rationalized and tried to minimize this observation. It has been seen a number of times in the past and not spoken about. So it was never publicly acknowledged or revealed, but it's there.

The desire for power is everyone's dirty little secret. Everyone is into power in some form, even the hermit who rejects life does so to retain his power. But see that the "power" referred to is a desire for a specific kind of power. Observe what that is. Please don't analyze it, observe it in the moment.

Throwing a Wrench

I changed my way of walking as you suggested. I was shocked at how the change made me feel—as though someone else was walking. A fear came up. I could see that my personality was bound up not only in my thinking and expression but in the body itself.

A way to see how the system works is to throw a wrench into it. Do otherwise than we have conditioned ourselves to do. Create friction within oneself and observe. This will take real will because we are programmed to do things as we have always done them. That's what feels comfortable and so feels right. It's part of why we are asleep to ourselves.

The Speed Freak

In trying to do otherwise, one thing I've been attempting is to drive more slowly. I have the habit of driving fast. I can keep my speed down only when my attention is on it, but as soon as an association comes in I find I'm speeding up again.

Isn't that's a feature of yours—speeding?

It's a very old habit—it goes back to the way my dad used to drive.

It's not just driving, is it?

What do you mean?

Have you listened to how you are talking?

I don't always talk so fast…

Some people are running away from something, but I get the

feeling you are running *to* something.

If I knew what I was running to that would be helpful to me.

If you got there what would you do? Would that be enough? Wouldn't you run to something else? Are you right-handed or left-handed?

Right-handed. I also tried washing my hair with my left hand...

See, there you go—you're anticipating. When someone is talking, you're running ahead of them, anticipating what they are going to say.

Yes, I'm usually racing, I guess, so it's hard to hear.

Perhaps my speed is my fear of being present, of experiencing people, the space. Try doing one thing slowly, with attention and conscious awareness of the body.

Different Ears

I was hanging out clothes to dry on the balcony when I overheard women speaking in the garden next door. The first impulse was to judge, thinking they were speaking about nothing at all. Then it struck me—I had a real perception of the fact that if I could truly hear myself speaking, would I really utter so many useless words? It was a moment of true understanding of something I had only read about and thought I knew. Now I observe, really observe, my speech, not changing it, not judging it, just listening with different ears, wondering who I am. The tones of voice belong to one "I" or another. I hear how the tone changes when I am not sure of myself. And then memories of sensations and feelings of my reactions come up, like how I feel when someone really pays attention to what I say, and the sensation connected with the tone becomes "self-sure" and almost euphoric. I feel like I am discovering "me"—not "I"—day by day.

Deeper than seeing is listening. Please continue.

Commit Thy Work to God

Recently I reread where Gurdjieff answered a question saying that as a result of work on themselves, people experience an improvement in health, enlarged horizons, and a new interest in life. I've experienced some of those, and feel I'm beginning to understand some of what is meant about the benefits of self-remembering and self-observation.

Each time I come to presence my inner tempo changes, as does the quality of my blood. I bring a stillness, being, to the incessant becoming of life. I reconnect myself to what is, not to what isn't, and so in time there begins to be an integration of body-senses-mind. This makes for an inner harmony of parts.

I come out of the word world. A space, a separation, appears, and so the experience is I am the body and I am not the body, I am the feelings and am not the feelings, I am the thoughts and am not the thoughts. I am. I am not. And I am and I am not. Ultimately, I am not. On my teacher's gravestone are these words—Commit Thy Work to God. Let's keep that before us.

Thoughts of Different Types

You spoke to me about observing different types of thoughts. I was not able to observe this, but I did observe that the act of self-remembering slows down thoughts. This was especially observed tonight. Sitting down, the thoughts were very fast. As I began to self-remember the thoughts slowed down slightly. The attention was going back and forth between the mind and the body. As I relaxed further, the thoughts continued to slow down and I was able to observe the thoughts while maintaining the experiencing of the body. With further relaxation, I saw there were spaces between the thoughts. There were times, too, when there would be no thought. I looked at someone when they were talking and for a moment there was a looking without thinking. Later on, I saw someone making movements with his hands that I did not understand and there was a looking without thinking. Once I understood what he was doing a thought came labeling his activity and the thoughts resumed.

You went beyond observing different types of thoughts to the thoughts themselves, their various tempos, and how they fill up the space, obscuring it, giving a "crowded feeling," which may be what motivates people to talk so fast—they hope to empty themselves of thought so they can feel more spacious, which is, of course, impossible. Now that you have experienced the space behind thought, relax still deeper into the Silence.

Sleep, Shame & Blame

As I prepared my clothes to take for the January 13th Celebratory Dinner, I discovered my good jewelry was missing. I had misplaced it and had no idea where. I had such a feeling of being asleep, this whole part of my life was missing. It's like what I do regarding the Work—disregarding what is of value. There have been other incidents since then. I am deeply asleep.

To admit to oneself truly that they are asleep—based on one's own verification—is a big step. Though it is talked about, the recognition is not lived. Some people in the Work, and many especially in pseudo-work, really never come to it. That is, it never penetrates emotionally. It creates a lot of "esoteric-I"s.

In observing I've noticed that besides the shame there can also be a blame which brings a sense of righteousness and separation, a shifting of responsibility. On rare occasions there is no identification and the blame passes over or through me with no effect.

Was there a lot of blame in your family?

Yes, I was the oldest but my sister was favored over me. It led to anger and resentment.

The Elephant Maker

I had a phone conversation with a friend whose mother recently died. My friend said she was angry, hurt and disappointed that friends and family members had not lived up to her expectations during this time. I said most people don't live up to our expectations, we don't live up to other people's expectations, and most of the time we don't even live up to our own expectations. Then I touted that my relationships are much healthier now because I've been able to let go of expectations. That same evening, I expected a telephone call that I never received. I spiraled into my own feelings of disappointment, hurt and anger at myself for allowing these feelings. The next morning I still felt it and

*knew that this would be something good to work on, but I couldn't
separate myself enough from it. All I wanted to do was send a sarcastic
email. I fought with myself to keep from doing that, but finally ended
up sending a milder version of what I had intended. I made something
so insignificant into a big deal. How do I stop myself from doing that?*

What is significant is what is inherent in what I report but
do not directly say—I was lying to my friend, acting as though
I had reached a level of understanding that I have not come to.
Intellectually, there can be an understanding, but that is only conceptual. One expected phone call that doesn't materialize and I am
brought to my knees. What happened to this idea of myself as being
able to let go of expectation? Poof! It disappeared, that's how real
it was. And know this—the "I" that talked to my friend is not the
"I" that reacted to not receiving a phone call, which is not the "I"
that is making a judgment about what happened and who wants
to stop from doing it again. From fleas we make elephants.

XXVIII

God's Image

*You spoke of Gurdjieff saying that the only true thing one could say
about man was that he was made in the image of God. You said to
meditate deeply on that and at that moment I sensed, saw, a sheet
descend over my face and I recognized how mechanical I was, full of
self-image and personality. It shrunk into a ball and fell away.*

Yes, this experience is the result of your work on yourself, your
resolve to break the first barrier, not to lie. This is an important
moment. Don't let it fall back into the sea. We are like a camera
with the shutter closed. Open up, take pictures of yourself. The
images will be negative. To develop them, they must be put through
a solution in the darkroom. Then hang them out to dry. What is
negative will turn positive.

Challenge & Initiation

*I have been reading the First Series aloud before I go to bed at night.
One night I was so tired, I went to get in bed, saw the book, sighed
and picked it up and went into the other room to read. I observed my*

voice was deep and seemed to come from deep within. I noticed also an energy that wasn't there before. I read on and on and followed what was being read. I put the book away outside of my bedroom and went soundly to sleep.

Where there is resistance that's where the work begins. We can never know what is on the other side of the resistance unless we test it. Super efforts, on whatever scale, are necessary, for they challenge "the comfort zone," take us beyond where all the centers have had enough. The *First Series* is written as a challenge and initiation. How much of myself will I give to awaken? How sincere can I be?

I remember when I was in New York and a woman said she had left the book on the subway and was so fearful that she had lost it. She went to the Lost & Found at Grand Central and told the man the title and described what it looked like. A curious smile came over his face, she said. He motioned her into the back room where all the lost items were kept. He pointed to the long sidewall. It was lined with copies of the *First Series*. "What the hell is it about this book," he said. "Everyone keeps losing it!"

Where Words Fail

I had a nourishing sitting this morning. The experience of the body was different than it has been. There was an energy, a certain movement, a vibration. I'm not sure what the right word is. In the past when I experienced this I tried to keep it going. Now I just let it happen. It changes. It's not always the same. I came to a place where words fail.

To allow, to accept, to be with whatever is, however it is—this takes knowledge and self-discipline. Otherwise, as you saw, the mind traps and levels the experience. Once the current appears simply allow it, knowingly merge, know it from the inside, pass beyond subject-object perception. Metaphorically, it's like deep diving. You relax and go down fifteen feet and relax still more, acclimate; go down another fifteen feet and so forth. Soon you find yourself gliding along the bottom of the ocean. You've passed beyond ego awareness. There is simply a deep awareness. Each time the bottom is touched the awareness is taken, but then it returns and it's finer. In this way, awareness reaches finer and finer levels. And then the blank state is reached.

What's that?

It'll make itself known. Just keep relaxing, accepting, merging, staying aware.

Eating Maggots

During lunch I was working to be in the body and there was some relative presence. As I tore a piece of bread in two, it looked like there was a maggot in it. A whole series of reactions came up, all of which I lived inwardly but didn't manifest outwardly. I lived the inner shudder; the sound, as if I'd screamed; the hand shaking the maggot off the bread, but didn't. Then a simple observing of the "thing." Slowly there came a seeing of what it actually was—a piece of garlic. The whole experience was like a metaphor for how to work. Later it was remembered what Mr. Gurdjieff said about categories of influences, one of which is the influence of form. In that nanosecond of misperception the "garlic form" totally influenced me organically, but there was also that which was separate from the reactions. So, it was odd, I was the body and its reactions, and also, and at the same time, I wasn't.

To someone not in the Work this may not sound like very much—I tore a piece of bread in half and I saw what looked like a maggot and went through a whole series of reactions, though I didn't express them outwardly. Then I saw it wasn't a maggot but a piece of garlic. Okay, so what? But this is a vivid example of consciously living life, experiencing what is perceived and the ensuing organic reactions but, at the same time, also being separate from them—but not disassociated—and so not identifying, not saying "I," keeping it below the neck. And then having "eaten" the energy of the reactions . . . simply observing the form of what had been perceived and seeing it now for what it was, a misperception. This shows a control and a maturity that can only come from long and sincere work on oneself. To be able to work with our senses in this way shows that we have ceased to be a machine.

The Razor's Edge

The last two days I've woken up cleanly, not groggy, with a very strong sensation around the body, a high vibration, kind of like electricity. Yesterday I tried to stay aware of it during the morning sitting. It created a deep sensation. This morning when I woke up a voice said, "This is how the body should be." I got dressed and went into the kitchen and heard, "You give your energy to objects." I saw how I give all my attention to something, like making coffee, all my attention, and immediately the sense of the body dimmed.

As has been said, divide the attention. Stay in the center between going out and staying in. The razor's edge.

Survival of the Most Conscious

When I returned home from the seminar I was more open and clearer than usual as a result of the CBI, meditation and teaching. At home I received a big shock and reacted violently. I wanted to take revenge. I would have thought that my more open state would have allowed me to absorb the shock without a major reaction. Can the openness be easily turned into a major reaction?

In terms of the shock itself, it's the strength of the shock compared to the strength of my presence, the vibration. The stronger the shock, the stronger my vibration must be. There is also a question as to the depth of my understanding of the content of the shock itself. The shock, as said, either eats me or I eat it. That is, either the shock is absorbed or it absorbs me.

Sounds Darwinian.

Survival of the most conscious. Now, what is it about revenge that it's such a prevalent reaction? It's a reward on the machine level.

Stepping Back

There's been a realization of a need to step back into a more elementary place in terms of my work. There have been a lot of fundamental exercises and practices I have been remembering that I have not done in a long time, or have done a few times and then stopped. I need to come back to working on the level of being embodied and not worrying about coming to something big or important. There has also been the realization of how much of my motivation comes from personality and the fear that if I let go of that there might be no motivation at all.

How old are you?

Thirty-four.

No, in terms of the Work.

Four and a half.

You're still a toddler. When we catch a fish we let it take as much line as it wants. Eventually it gets tired and we reel it in. But if we work for results, the fish breaks the line. As Lord Pentland often said, "We can't go slow enough." What you say should be a reminder to everyone of how easy it is to get lost and not know it. As to the fear of losing motivation, if false personality is weakened that is only self-will. Understand this, no person in this room, or anywhere, will ever be liberated, become enlightened, be realized—however we term it. The person is a construct, an assemblage of "I"s. All motivation that has this as its origin is simply self-will. Also, it's important to make a distinction between false and real personality.

What's that?

It manifests in being connected with Being.

Emptiness & Potato Chips

I found myself not having anything to do and wanting a bag of chips. I saw what I really wanted was to fill up the emptiness with food. Then I saw that in my past I had gotten involved in various events, situations and relationships, sometimes lasting years, to keep from facing the emptiness.

Obesity, if it's not a genetic condition, is a defense against life. It limits movement, responsibility and guards against undue involvement and the attraction of others. It also keeps me in the forefront in a way. In any group of people I always stand out. My obesity allows me either to feel my superiority or my self-pity. At the bottom, the emptiness, the lie of it all, shadows whatever I do. And what do I do—I stuff my mouth. If you stay with the Work at some later time when you have more clarity and weaken your self-will—to the point where you can admit that everything you achieve is not of your own doing—then we can work on this. As to the "emptiness" you are speaking of, it's a psychological emptiness.

Keeping It Below the Neck

I see that just before the point of blowing up, there would be a split second, like a flash, in which I'd be outside it, like being outside a room looking in. But the identification was so strong it would pull all of me back into itself. Then later, really wishing to work with this, there was a moment in the midst of the beginning of an identification. You've talked before about keeping the reaction below the neck. Though I had in the past attempted this, this time it was a very new experience. I made an effort to relax the face, and allow what was happening below the neck to continue. The sensation was very, very new. The head was completely clear, quiet, full of space, while below the neck there was this roaring furnace, principally in the chest. There were no thoughts saying, "Don't do this, do it that way." No thoughts at all, just the experience of space and the raw energy being generated below.

Exercises are given as a means of exploring what previously remained mechanical. We want to bring these into view, objectify what is subjective. Consciousness expands—I'm speaking from your point of view—the gradient between it and the subconscious lessens, and if sustained the two become one. Remember, as we read in the *First Series* once there was only consciousness but then a split developed. It is our being-duty to heal that split.

XXIX

Before I took myself to be all one. I was unified in my dream of myself—the meta-belief of an indivisible I. Now I have become two. Before I was whoever I took myself to be. Now, there is the observing of whatever "I" is manifesting itself in the moment, There is a real taste of it, because the impression is not filtered. These glimpses of awakening, milliseconds of observing, loosen the head armor, the jamming system.

The Moon World

When resistance has arisen in the past, I've just pushed through it. Lately, it has become very persistent, or perhaps I am just more aware of it. I awoke in the middle of the night and found myself experiencing resistance. It was decided to really explore it and as I did I found myself enveloped in a leaden, low vibrational state. I felt I was in the Moon world, world 96, though there was something that remained outside it. A fear arose that I would become stuck in this world. Help was asked for, and I found myself in a very light state of high vibration, much like I experience when I am remembering myself.

If we look at the Ray of Creation—which shows each level of existence from the very densest to the lightest—we might ask why is it that these various levels of vibration exist; that is, what keeps the levels "separate"? What maintains the Ray of Creation? Not only reciprocal maintenance of energies, but also resistance to becoming anything more or less than that level's existence. If there was no resistance, Creation would be all One, which, of course, it is and isn't. The same is true for psychological resistance. Beyond the ordinary resistance of "I"s to anything other than what they take themselves to be is the resistance we meet when we are on the verge of being moved to a new level. That you resisted the impulse to run from this resistance but explored it shows a clarity and control that can only be the result of a hard-won maturity. That you prayed, asked for help, is further evidence of that.

Hard as Nails

The person appears to be soft and caring on the outside, but inside she's hard as nails. Only when there is a real contact in the emotional center do I have a genuine softness and understanding.

You once said that what you most hated about others and most liked about yourself was the ability to lie. Mechanical lying is not an ability but a disability.

You can't make genuine contact with the emotional center as long as you indulge a weakness. You cannot stop lying immediately as it is a habit you protect yourself with, but you can suffer it by being present to it when it happens . . . and weaken it later by not justifying it and admitting it to whomever you've lied to.

What do you mean protect myself?

Imagination exaggerates your fear . . . a fear that is not based on what has happened but what could happen. The one is concrete, the other limitless.

Missing Father

My father wasn't there for me. We had no relationship. I never really suffered this, as my mother gave me a lot of love and maybe I was too wrapped up in myself to care, or I took it that his being that way was somehow natural. I don't know. I just feel now that there is a hole in my life. Though I had a father, I really didn't have a father, if you see what I mean. So in a way I became my own father. So I see that my relationship with you is one of need and also resistance.

Whatever relationship or lack thereof the student had with their biological father, it is bound to be projected on one who, as Mr. Gurdjieff says, "takes the role of the teacher." The relationship between the student and teacher, who in essence is one's spiritual father, is many leveled. Instead of fighting with the need or resistance, experience it directly. Let it tell you about itself. What you find out, share with me.

What Is Real?

As I sit here and listen to others speak I am observing a voice come up inside me and I begin to go off into imagination. I catch myself and come back to the room, but I still find it difficult to follow the questions being asked. It's different when you speak. It's as if my mind isn't involved, I just sit and listen. The space expands around me. My question is how much of this difference in my experience is the result of my own projection or attitude and how much is a perception of a real difference between the speaking?

Without moving . . . take in an impression of yourself sitting there. Now, without looking, where are your knees in relation to your feet?

They are further out in front.

So take a deep breath. Now again, simply by the inner experiencing, adjust your feet so they are under your knees and take another breath. How is that?

The breath went much deeper.

Right. That is a small taste of what I am talking about. You were under tension. For a long time you will only be interested in yourself. Then one day you might open up to others. You might even find that you are not afraid of others when you do open up. All of the questions asked here are your question and all of the answers are your answer. That is how it is for everyone. We are not here to judge you but simply to provide the conditions by which you can observe yourself in the Immediate, and, in so doing, bring the light of intelligence to that which has been hidden from you.

I Am My Judgments

I've been really struggling with whether to say this or not. I was with someone I know, and I identified with judgments about this person. I was angry at the person . . . very angry. At one point I said to him, "What's wrong with you!" The person didn't say very much to me. Later, "I"s kept coming up that were still identified with the judgments about this person. When this happened, I saw that I was the judgment. Reflecting about this later, I saw these judgments revolved around a fixed idea about this person.

Yes, we are our judgments. We embody them in that moment. Chemically and psychologically. So why the resistance to speaking?

There was a feeling not to talk about it, that it was too risky, that I would be exposing too much.

And so I internally consider, say nothing, or paint over what I report. Of course, truth exposes the lie which is why I live in half-truth and lies. We come together here to wake up to this general state, to see how it holds me.

As I was speaking tonight I could hear in my voice that I wasn't telling the truth . . . not completely. There was a lot more there I wasn't saying.

To hear myself as I am speaking takes a special effort of attention and separation. Otherwise, we live in the meta-belief of ourselves as an indivisible I.

Castes & Classes

I was struck by the reading in All and Everything *about castes and classes. I had read Gurdjieff's aversion to castes before and had thought only of the Indian caste system, but this was the first time I had seen mention of classes. He said we always relate to others "up" or "down"—with deference or false humility to those above or with contempt or condescension to those below. He says we need to be sincere to relate in any other way.*

Then, at the grocery store, I saw myself on a level above the clerk, not relating as an equal. A German woman pushed past me at the checkout stand, asked if I was going to bag my own groceries; I shook my head no. She proceeded to do the bagging with an air of moral superiority that seemed to put her "above" and the clerk and myself "below." It was a shock.

We live in our "I"s, in becoming, not Being. The "I"s have not only their agendas but the beliefs that bolster them. Our "societal-I" believes we live in a classless society. Our class system is founded not on blood and breeding as it is in Europe but on Mammon, on what Gurdjieff calls "dollar fever." Ever wonder why there are so many ads for watches? Is everyone losing their watch? Of course not. The watch you wear is a sign—and there are hundreds of them—about where you stand in society, what you can afford. He also speaks of "Mr. Bellybutton," lost in mechanical sex and eating.

"Mussolini-I"

An "I" comes up and takes control quite often. It is very strong, powerful and gives a sense of unity. In the past it was appealing due to its power and apparent unity. No longer. It has no compassion, gives a cocky confidence but doesn't speak much. It came up in the meeting. Afterward, I went out to dinner with a friend. I drove his car to the restaurant because I knew the way. But I had become disoriented—I suppose because of what I had

seen at the meeting—and had to really focus to get a sense of direction.
Though there were easier spots to park at the restaurant, I chose a difficult
one. I looked down at the gearshift and there was no light. Apparently,
I had been driving with the lights off. I barked an order at my friend to
turn a light on. I have named it my "Mussolini-I." It makes the trains
run on time. It doesn't suffer fools lightly.

This is a keen observation and report. Mussolini is somebody
I'm going to have to live with. He's a very strong feature and, as
said, doesn't talk much, so is not readily seen. He obviously doesn't
like to be talked about, so this is a real step in controlling him. First
we see him, then we name him and report on him. That weakens
his influence and, like a panther, we use him when needed but
otherwise keep him caged but well fed.

Denying Myself

Last week I tried to deny myself something as a means of coming to
myself. I first tried leaving the car radio off. I soon got used to the quiet
and decided this was too easy. I have a habit of reading the paper at
lunch and at night after dinner. The idea of giving up the paper was
a shock. I didn't want to embrace it at first. It felt almost too big to
handle. I glanced at the paper on the kitchen table, making out a few
headlines without picking it up. I resolved not to read it; instead I
gathered it up and put it into the recycle bag.

I didn't suppose Sunday would be a problem since we don't
subscribe to the Sunday paper. But when I left the house Sunday
morning the first thing I saw lying in my path was the Sunday paper.
It felt like a cosmic joke. I decided to ignore the paper, not bring it
inside, not touch it. The challenge now is to come to myself when I
see the newspaper, not simply work to deny myself.

What is it that denies? From where does the denial originate?
I can do the work from my self-image, you know. It takes a long
time to really make that discrimination. I do the exercise because
I have the dream of becoming conscious. Remember the third
being-obligolnian-striving where it speaks of Self-perfection. This
isn't the little self which is referred to. And the modifier afterwards
declares "in the sense of Being." So we are not speaking of the self-
perfection of the person. Many people in the Work, and especially

those who leave, often make this mistake. All that said, you are really working with yourself, experimenting. However, who gave the radio exercise?

What?

Ponder that.

Expressing Negativity

You talked about not working with nonexpression of negative emotions, but on the contrary expressing them in order to see them. As I was in a faux-Work where expressing negative emotions was taboo, your words were very surprising for me. I am confused now with what my attitude should be, as Ouspensky talks about the necessity of working with this idea.

To not express negative emotions before one consciously experiences them and sees their effect on oneself and others is simply to cement over the psyche. Their nonexpression is, yes, preparation for the second shock, but if we are just beginning to work with the first shock aren't we being a bit premature? It makes for good crowd control and allows students, particularly those given to idealism, to unwittingly enhance their self-image.

What do you mean "crowd control"?

For faux-teachers it's a way to protect themselves from criticism, which, of course, is of prime concern. When you represent yourself, say, as "The Teacher of the Planet," stroke your students' vanity and self-love by telling them they are "the Elect of Jesus Christ," and make all sorts of world-ending prophecies . . . well, wouldn't you live in fear of being exposed? Weirdly, the more outrageous the presentation the better, for it forces students to deny their reason and conscience and thus totally commit themselves.

XXX

Sea of Influences

In looking at influences, it was seen that those that are intellectually

*based have a very strong hold on me and immediately suck me in,
but when the body is included with the breath, the influences dissolve
away. In contrast, emotional influences are still felt even with the body
and breath being present. It was also seen how at all times during the
day I am under one influence or another.*

We live in a sea of influences. It's to first see what are the predominant influences I live under, what they give and don't give me,
where they lead. Take influences as a line of observation—whenever
you remember to remember, or are remembered, become aware of
the influence present. There is no way I can live influence-free, but I
can choose the influences under which I live. Everyone, everything,
is an influence, changing of course, but a definite kind of influence.
The same with what I do and don't do, think and not think. The
books I read, films I see. The world-time and society I live in. All
this needs to be observed, known. There are higher influences and
lower, ascending and descending. Become aware of conversation,
where it begins, the shocks, the deflections. Make a study of it all.
With any decision point, ask yourself: Is this in accord with my
highest aspiration? We put ourselves under higher influences each
time we step out of our time, our societal life, and come to being.

"The Shrew" on Stage

*Yesterday I was offended by someone's behavior and I watched as very
quickly "the shrew" surfaced and raised her voice and yelled at this
person. I observed this character as she went through her emotivity,
but as usual had very little control over her. Then last night I went
to a play and at one point a woman character was offended by a
man's comment and she immediately began yelling at him. I saw her
become the exact same character that I had been earlier in the day.
It was a huge shock to watch this character in myself on the stage. I
wanted to sink down in my seat, I was so disgusted and repulsed by
that behavior. It was similar to when I am in that state and part of me
is watching, but with even more impact because I wasn't emotionally
distraught while watching the character on stage. The shock of seeing
this stayed with me all night and through today.*

You saw the truth of an "I," but who was it that was "disgusted
and repulsed"? There was the shock of seeing your "shrew" but

then identification. So now that you have observed the shrew, take it as a line of observation. That is, look for how she plays out in your life, all the little ways, not the big dramatic scenes. See what she believes, what she fights for, what supports her—observe, but work to do so impartially.

Being Cut Off

I was driving home from work and in a relatively present and peaceful state. Many of the drivers were driving erratically, but I wasn't affected by it. Then all of a sudden somebody cut me off. Because I was present I immediately noticed a very intense sensation in the solar plexus, as well as a very hot sensation around the body. I felt trespassed against. And what was the most surprising was the violence that came out in feeling, how much anger and hatred flared toward this person who had cut me off. What was really surprising was that some peace came back. Usually I'd be playing out what had happened over and over again. But it just fell away.

What happened in terms of the negative emotion? Look at it in terms of centers.

The negative emotion came from the place in the solar plexus. And it was completely taken over; that was where the energy was, in that center. The other two centers were completely blocked out by it.

Do you think it's possible that the instinctive center—the three centers exist at different rates of vibration, instinctive being the highest—do you think that the instinctive center likely reacted first? You wouldn't know that, but given the difference in the speed of centers you would think that, right? So the instinctive center is shocked and the emotional center borrows this experience and then adds imagination—remember your words, "and he trespassed"? And then you've got a whole world of negation.

And so we have negative emotion. It wasn't Freud but Mr. Gurdjieff who introduced the idea of negative emotions. It's not there quite so sharply with Freud. In all these years has any psychologist ever come forward and explained how is it that we have negative emotions, in a functional sense? Of course they explain everything in terms of psychology because that's where they're trapped. I want to know how I function. And I can only know how I function if I'm present to myself, if there's self-remembering. And then I'll see, as Mr. Gurdjieff says, there is no center for negative emotion; it's artificial. And this is an example of it.

What Is My Chief Feature?

I asked myself, "What is my chief feature?" A single-word answer came—self-absorption. It really hit me. I decided to take a walk around the neighborhood. I felt like a giant walking through an architect's model of the houses in the neighborhood. When I returned I was very aware of the body and how relaxed most of it was. I observed the exhalation of the breath was very long. I looked at objects through each center. The TV was turned off. Looking at it through the intellectual center brought the idea of "squareness." The emotional center was disappointed because there was no picture; the instinctive center felt the weight of the TV.

This is the lawful result of all the small efforts you have made. The world expands. Time changes. New impressions arise. Was there any fear in walking around.

No.

Are you afraid now?

Yes, there is a fear of saying something that no one else has said before.

One reason we work in groups is that everyone benefits from other people's work. We must be true to our experience and not internally consider. We have to learn to eat our fears. And yes, by the way, "self-absorption" is just an aspect.

But I thought—

Now don't run off to one of these enneagram personality books to find your chief feature. Unless you really want to confuse yourself.

What's wrong with them?

Read *Taking with the Left Hand.*

Soup of the Person

A friend whom I've known for a long time said something to me that really shook my self-image. I had always thought of myself in a certain way and they said the exact opposite.

How do you know your self-image was shaken?

Sincerity.

No, that isn't what knows. Sincerity is how one relates to what is known.

I don't want to say consciousness.

Let's say perceiving then. Your self-image was shaken—that was the content of the perception. The content was identified with and so the content was suffered, right?

Yes.

But the perception did not suffer. Identify with the content and there is suffering, desire, fear and so forth. All the person stuff. One leads to Being, the other to the soup of the person.

Letting Go

I was standing still and a thought came to be present. For a moment, I thought it was because the inner talking stopped. There was a certain clarity, but then I realized I had not really self-remembered. Once I felt really connected, I started walking. There was much awareness of the separate parts of the body walking. I sat down and an impulse came to read a book I had with me. A fear came up that I would be lost in the intellectual and moving centers as soon as I started reading. So I sat for a few minutes, relaxed and breathed deeply into the body then started reading. While reading, the awareness of the body remained and there was much energy experienced from this. At one point it was seen that an arm would move mechanically, then in an instant before the end of the movement something would bring me back to experience the last part of the arm moving. Then what came up was to not control the body, but to just observe. So there was a letting go during the observation. Once this was done the experience of awareness was sustained for a longer time than usual.

Because of my wish and my work on myself, a reminder to remember comes. The mind stops its inner chatter. An equipoise in the mind is sensed. I feel "clear." I think this is presence, but it's only one center. This is what ordinarily is considered being present. But the body is uninhabited. Two centers are missing. Now, when the attention is redirected into the body, the body appears in consciousness—consciousness does not appear in me, as is ordinarily supposed—I appear in consciousness. Consciousness is, and I am not, unless I am is remembered. I am the body. Or, rightfully said, I am is the body. Sustained, a separation arises. I am not the body but the body is. Likewise, I am and am not my thoughts. I am and am not my feelings, and so on. There is a stillness, a new quality of being free from the ordinary world, of being of it but not in it, of being in it but not of it. The Self in self-remembering. All things, gross and subtle, appear and disappear in this re-membering. The absorption of self in Self may be so expansive that what remains is only the circumference of consciousness, not a center. Consciousness without objects.

Playing a Role

The other day I walked into a room full of computer guys. There was a relative presence in the body and I felt a negative energy in the room coming from them. There was a big contrast between my relative presence and their negativity and I could feel they noticed something as well. A decision was made in the moment to fit in by playing a role of negativity. I said something negative about my day. The energy in the room changed and it felt like I'd been accepted. I played this role for a while and felt how contagious the negativity was.

That you were present and experienced their state and didn't identify but participated—that is, did otherwise and played a role—could only have happened after long work on yourself.

Should this happen again then experiment—say something positive and experience what happens. As to the negativity of others, inwardly bat away all verbal comment, but don't contract in any way or block another's physico-chemical vibrations—let them pass through you.

Brick in the Stomach

I had the realization that I wasn't controlling the breath; the body was breathing without the head interfering. I felt a kind of joy. But since then I notice I do control the breathing.

Head-bound, we are held hostage by the neurotic need to control everything. So we don't breathe from the body but the head. The breathing is psychologized, shallow, not a true rhythm, and so a cause of dysfunction and disease. You obviously identified with the joy and so initiated the return of the person. Let the breath gradually descend to the abdomen. Many people experience a tightness there, like carrying a brick in the stomach. In time, the breath of an embodied body will dissolve this of itself. Do not do anything. Just impartially observe and be. You may find the sides of the body and the back coming alive, the pores of the skin opening and the whole body breathing and expanding.

The Key

My stepson is now in his adolescent years and both my wife and I were very upset over something he had done. I completely lost myself in anger, in the "righteousness" of emotions. I was immersed in negativity, totally convinced I was right and he had to be set straight. The inner talking and judgment went into overdrive, but suddenly I saw where I was and it stopped as the attention shifted to the body. A strong feeling of compassion came over me. There was a recognition that my son was acting in the only way he could act—he was doing his best under the circumstances. I went up to his room, hugged him, and told him it was all right, that I realized he had done the best he could. He started sobbing, expressing how he had seen things. On balance, his view was much more nuanced than I had recognized. Ever since, my relationship with him has shifted—the underlying "tone" has become deeper, more meaningful. You always speak about awareness of the body as being key. I never really took this in before in terms of how profound it is.

We hear about self-remembering, we think we understand, and from time to time we remember ourselves . . . but until there is self-remembrance in emotional moments it is just practice. We need to put conscious flesh to the sharp bone of experience.

XXXI

Killing Fear

I observed how I was afraid to talk. It was like there was a body of fear beside me. I wanted it to go away, to kill it.

Whatever our state it seems omnipresent. All our systems, physiological and psychological, support it. Our chemistry changes, the breath changes, thoughts change—our whole world is in unison with our identification. Or so it seems. Our body and our psychology are one. It seems monolithic; there seems to be no way out. It's as if we are a software program—and everything is in the program, even our resistance and all possible solutions. Every way out has already been defaulted.

Sounds hopeless.

Yes, everything we think and feel—all our reactions and actions—are already in the program.

Everything is preprogrammed?

Yes and no. Have you ever heard of the riddle of the goose in the bottle?

No.

How to get the goose out of the bottle? It can't pull itself through the neck of the bottle. It's too big. And if it breaks the bottle, then it injures or kills itself, so how does the goose get out of the bottle?

[Silence]

It realizes that it's not a goose and it was never in the bottle. It was just a reductionist way of thinking.

I don't see the connection.

The only movement that is not in the program is to intentionally do nothing, because all actions are already discounted in the program. The only action—not a "doing" in the usual sense of the word—is to remember oneself. It's completely inward, invisible. It disturbs nothing on the outside and therefore has no counter. Everything else is a doing of some type and all doings are in the program. Self-remembering is simply a relocation and redistribution of one's attention. Thus, one becomes embodied. In doing so, the attention is freed and elaborated and a new quality emerges. That quality separates one from their state. From this separateness, the state and its manifestations are observed. If there is identification with the observation, then the separateness is lost. One becomes their state again or a successive state. That is, they are absorbed back into the program. But whatever has been observed has been truly seen without buffers or filters. One's intelligence has been awakened to itself. The observer and the observed are then not one. Otherwise, they are.

Suffering the Person

I awoke in the middle of the night in the midst of swirling "I"s. It was seen clearly, not from the head brain but emotionally, that these "I"s were all false personality. The "I"s appeared to be confined in the top of my head. My center of gravity shifted to my chest. Awareness of the body diminished as a strong sense of presence and oneness was experienced that was beyond sensation. I lay in bed in this state for some time, very much alert, and unable to sleep. A question arose: Is this change permanent? There was a sense that the "I"s could be released; and with a feeling like dust sprinkled over the body from head to toe, a sense of the body returned, as did false personality. I was then able to sleep.

Has anyone told you that you are looking younger?

No.

Well, you are. I was smiling at your question. It's an example of how false personality defends itself. It wants to survive and will use whatever means necessary to survive. So, in this case, a question comes to you and you are back where you started. This has to be experienced over and over. Why is it that the last thing a person will give up is their suffering? What is it that suffers? The personality, the person, the self-image suffers and you do not want to give it up. It's not as if it will be destroyed but that it will no longer be king; it will be removed from its throne. It's very devious.

And clever.

Yes, very clever.

Sound-Beyond-Sound

Ever since last Sunday, the exercise has created a state of hearing of a sound-beyond-sound that has continued to be present during observations. Many years back, when I asked you about the sound I was hearing, the experience only happened during meditation when I was very still and silent. Now the sound is present whenever I remember to listen to it. It isn't drowned out by ordinary sounds. It has created sensitivity to other sounds in my environment such as music and other ambient noise. There is a desire to listen to these sounds which register at a much more imperceptible level than is usual.

It may be a sound-beyond-sound. Note where you hear it, what part of the body, in front or behind. When you awaken in the morning, don't get up but listen to it for ten minutes or so. In meditation and with *being-Partkdolg-duty*, use this along with the other supports.

The Courage of Sunglasses

I had to meet with a group of people about something serious. When I walked into the room I had my dark sunglasses on. I immediately recognized that the glasses were being worn as a form of hiding. There was an intention to really take that in, to remember myself and taste this hiding. I had to continually redirect the attention and to keep observing these inner impressions. Then there was an inner recognition that this was an opportunity to act consciously, to actively participate in being-Partkdolg-duty, and take the sunglasses off. All that happened, everything that was involved in that very small gesture, is difficult to put words to. But there was a deep taste and understanding of what the word courage *means. Usually the word is used for big, dramatic events and not for removing a pair of sunglasses. But I realized that genuine, conscious courage begins in these tiny moments.*

I was present, I experienced the Immediate on the physical level, recognized the reactions, and, in doing so, was able to extend the octave still further. So there was conscious experience, not mechanical. Now don't give yourself a medal. This must be done again and again until it rightly crystallizes; otherwise, it simply further coats superiority, self-love and vanity.

No More Excuses

When you told me at the Day of Exploration to take a black marker pen and write "No More Excuses," my reaction was "I don't have a black marker pen." It shocked me how this response appeared without thought and it occurred to me that this is the very essence of what I take to be "me." These clever little humorous statements serve me on many levels: making excuses, shirking responsibility, defiance, procrastinating, and so on. I would now like to understand this part of myself, and I am wondering how to best approach this study?

This is your infantile rebel. You don't need to understand him, you need to struggle against him, to never do as he says as regards the Work. He buffers everything to level it, downgrade it, so he can remain in control. The actuality is that you have yet, after all this time, to enter the Work. You are still picking and choosing, immersed in a self-will that hides behind a "likeableness" and a "poor-me irresponsibility" that evades any self-discipline. It thinks it's winning when it's really losing. How sad, how lawful. People who are attracted to the Work are rebels. They haven't been completely taken in by the carrots society offers. That is what brought you here—you weren't completely hypnotized. But now that you've arrived, it's time to leave the rebel at the door and become a student.

"You're Stupid!"

Several times I had the experience of seeing this "I" appear that said I was stupid and couldn't get anything right. The total experiencing of my body changed from a feeling of lightness and openness to one of heaviness and chaos. It felt mentally and physically unhealthy. I was upset because I couldn't measure up. The more pressure I put on myself the worse it got. I had the feeling that someone was going to start yelling at me or I would be shamed in some way. For the better part of the next day I felt a disharmony from this. Could not stop the tape. I knew I was operating from faulty perceptions. But in spite of recognizing that, I knew everyone on my team knew I was the stupid one. As I was writing in my diary this morning, I had an insight that I often say I can't do this or that to protect myself from failure. It has something to do with my early childhood and school experiences. It feels like I am at a point where I have to revisit my demons, face them.

We only think we live in the present. The past is living us and we rarely recognize it. When we practice *being-Partkdolg-duty,* the gradient between the waking consciousness and the subconscious lessens and a shock on the surface can strike deep into the depths and let us see the origin of our reaction. So we don't go tinkering around as psychologists do trying to plumb the subconscious, but all the time unwittingly supporting the notion of the person. Yes, now psychologists, ever mindful of criticism and ever wanting to be in step, have moved to "transpersonal psychology," beyond the person, a neat move. But who among them has gone beyond the level of the adjusted formatory mind together with the arrogation of spiritualized language and various techniques? The Fourth Way focuses on the present and questions the solidity of the notion of the "I." All manifestations, inner and outer, are observed and felt—felt because we are not just in the head but in the body, in the instinctive center, and possibly, if the awareness is strong and sustained enough, in the emotional center. Then the impressions are direct, not filtered, and the power of the shock, in a context of self-remembering, takes us deep into our origins. In this way, we empty and integrate the subconscious so we can get to what is really of value there, conscience.

"I" Tribes

For the past several weeks I have been seeing many different "I"s from different points of view and with a new intensity. There are circumstances in my life which have shown me these "I"s, the joyous ones and the disappointed ones, in a way that I have not experienced before. I can see that several "I"s are connected or related to each other.

We have tribes of "I"s within us, and they war and pillage just as tribes and nations do. War is just an externalization of what is happening inside us. Many soldiers report that in war, for all its horror, they never felt more alive. That's because the inside meets the outside. But at what cost! And the results can only be temporal.

Exploring Space

Lying in bed I was aware of tension in my feet and legs. I placed my attention on these areas, breathing into them, intentionally letting go, and keeping the mind free from thought. As the tension eased, I became aware of tension in other places. I did the same in those areas. What followed was a direct impression of the body, which became larger and larger as I became more relaxed. I felt like I was exploring space, the space of my body. This impression was vivid and profound. In some way it was deeper yet smaller than what I have experienced with double attention. There was no sense of an observer separate from the observed, only the changing observation. What is the relationship between direct impressions and divided attention?

There first has to be the wish to be. Then the thought or organic reminder to work. A redirecting of the attention, experiencing the tissues of the body, breathing down into the feet, making a conscious contact with the earth, then breathing the current upward, becoming fully embodied, keeping the mind free of associative thought, and dividing the attention between the inner world and the outer, between subject and object. This state of self-remembering—can it be sustained? Can there simply be an awareness of the context without identifying with the content? If so, the impressions are taken in directly and so the impressions octave of the Food Diagram is not aborted and can proceed.

But did you answer my question?

Very good. Direct impressions are unfiltered impressions. A strong shock does that, but then that's only to the mechanism itself. It's only when you are in the third state of consciousness that direct impressions are received.

Faustian Bargain

I'd heard the idea of giving up something that's habitual so I could better see myself—create an inner confrontation—I'd heard that but always forgot. But one morning, at the conclusion of sitting, the question came, "What can I deny myself?" The idea came to give up my morning coffee. Immediately the body felt hot, filled with a charge of energy. The chest was filled, too, with a hot anger. A voice said, "Not that, you don't have to do that." The rejection was so complete I thought that was what I should work with.

Not drinking coffee in the mornings didn't seem that difficult initially, but as the week went on a bargaining started. In some instances I could work with it, in others I couldn't, and the bargain was accepted. I found I would buy myself off by not having the coffee but then having a cherry Danish. I noticed, too, I was irritable, sometimes really negative. The denying of the coffee seemed connected to many other things.

When we create an inner confrontation, the friction, the suffering, creates a new level of energy. We need to absorb it by relaxing, breathing, staying focused, not going into imagination. See that imagination is in the mechanical part of the centers and when we focus this cuts the imagination. If we don't, as this octave proceeds, we will get results opposite to what we wanted. You also encountered "the denier." Maybe you need to understand what a Faustian bargain is. When Jesus goes into the desert and is confronted by "Satan," it's not a tempter outside him but within himself. And the final bargain "Satan" offers is that if Jesus will just worship him, all these worlds over which he says he has dominion will be given to Jesus. Now if you would like to really increase the confrontation and suffering, then do as Gurdjieff says and use your imagination—imagine in the morning that you are drinking a cup of coffee.

Are you kidding!

Of course, just kidding. . . .

XXXII

Awakening again and again to my mechanicality I finally accept it—I am mechanical, asleep. In so doing, I pass from being an unconscious egotist to being a conscious egotist. This is a major step forward in the process of self-transformation, for it is only from this recognition that I can become a genuine altruist.

Body Within a Body

I find I am still taken by postures, moved from one posture to the other, completely out of my control, even when I'm working to be present. While working on a project, I was trying to sense my body, and I watched my hands going up to my hips in a way that they do whenever I'm talking with someone. So I worked to really experience the hands on my hips. Or when I found my hand up on my shoulder rubbing on a sore spot to compensate for the tension in some way, then I brought my hand back down and relaxed the body. But then right away the body had shifted and taken a different posture again. Then I was in a meeting with someone and I had been experiencing a lot of anxiety, and I saw my posture leaning forward and the talking pace was very fast between us. So I sat back with my spine straight and I relaxed the body and things slowed down—but then in a few minutes the posture was right back again sitting forward in a more assertive posture.

That you have the sincerity to speak about this is important—and I'm sure you're speaking for many others—for the work with mechanics and postures requires great persistence. Your history with postures is as long as you are old. You don't take postures, they take you when you're not embodied. This is something to see and admit over and over again until the body remembers itself. That is, the cells and tissues of the body have been so coated with the chemical and alchemical effect that takes place in self-remembering and self-observation that a body within a body has developed.

"There Need to Be Limits"

Last week I came to the meeting dressed in a white shirt and good pants. I had shined my shoes. I had worked physically all day and enjoyed a shower and dressing in fresh clothes. At the end of the meeting, you asked me to help load a truck. Outside, I realized I was not appropriately dressed for the task and became negative. I experienced a lot of resentment. I moved into a central position with a shovel and began working. The negativity faded and there was experienced a sense of enjoyment working with other men. When I got home and saw my dirty clothes the negative "I" started up again. "There need to be limits on what we are asked to do. I should have been told to bring old clothes. Others knew and were dressed appropriately. My clothes will have to go to the cleaners now. What the hell does he think he's doing asking us to work at 10:30 in the dark in a pile of cinders and ashes!"

This was a lot to see. A wonderful exposition of self-importance of the self-image. We have been so covered in it. We have to have a clean appearance at all times. Do you know what that comes from?

My father. He was irrational. Would fly into a rage for no reason at all.

Was your father alcoholic? Children of alcoholics are always scanning the environment for any sign that might trigger violence.

No, he was just violent, irrational. He would punish me for some infraction and then demand that I kiss the ring on his hand.

There is a fish called the wolf fish which you sometimes see in aquariums. It has to be kept in its tank alone. It can't tolerate other life. People can be like that psychologically.

Terror of the Situation

I read the chapter "The-Terror-of-the-Situation" in the First Series. At first there was a lot of resistance, but I kept reading. At some point I actually became interested and found myself at the end of the chapter.

I went back and reread certain paragraphs and tried to understand them. Resistance arose and a voice said, "I don't understand this. I'm not getting it." Then I heard another voice saying, "I'm never going to get this." It was a shock. It was the first time I had heard it.

Have you read *All and Everything* three times, as its author directs?

No.

Why not?

[Strained silence]

It's true—"I'm never going to get it." I want to understand. But on my own terms. I think I can circumvent the direction and read as I usually read—to understand it with the head brain. That's a one-centered understanding at best, which is no understanding at all. The foundation of understanding is self-knowledge and being, which can only arise through learning the meaning of the word *student*. Do you follow?

Need to Be Loved

I have always had this need to be liked, to be loved. That's my first concern. I was the baby of a large family and was adored, so I've never questioned the need. But observing myself, the postures, the voices really reek of it. Where am I to start?

My friend, you are a turd. Start from there.

A turd?

Or *merde*, as Mr. Gurdjieff says. But that's French and does not have a dry enough and condensed taste. One can't get lower than being a turd eaten by the flies of life. It will help in seeing the "Mama's darling." What's been said is a shock, right?

[Nods]

Stay in the space of the shock. Don't level it by personalizing it, by taking it as an attack. It's clean, a wake-up call, an act of love.

Anticipate Always

I see that I always anticipate the outcome of events without waiting to see how life will unfold. [A long description of anticipating follows.]

Is what you report material derived from self-remembering and observation? Or is it analysis?

Well, a summing up of experience.

Seeing is seeing in the moment. Otherwise, it is a "backfilling," a mental reconstruction to convince ourselves and others that we were there. Anticipation kills our relation to what is. We are always ahead of the moment. This gives a certain separation and a security, as we are not really fully present. We keep thinking the moment rather than truly experiencing it.

What would be a true experience?

To experience directly.

How would I do that?

Learn how to listen.

And?

See that you don't.

Well, I think I do. I think I could repeat pretty much what I've said and you've said.

Have you ever had the experience of speaking to someone who is not really listening and when you tell them this . . . they can repeat what you've said?

Yeah.

They were only half-listening, right?

Hmm, well, I guess so.

Feel like the moment is getting away from you, don't like where it's going, so you're confusing yourself, stalling?

[No answer]

Are you here?

You mean remembering myself? I wasn't, but I am now.

I don't mean merely clearing the mental center but being in the body. . . . Okay, now work to stay here. Forget what has been said. That's gone. Gone is gone, by definition. See that you can't be here, if you're in back of the moment. Or, out in front of it, anticipating. Behind the curve, ahead of the curve, you never connect. By the evidence of your own experience verify this. Accept what you are. Become a conscious egotist.

Higher & Higher Levels of Sleep

In doing the morning exercise, I suddenly saw that I was "pushing" the attention into the body and limbs. I hadn't known what I was doing. So I relaxed and just allowed the attention to permeate and elaborate. The pushing was too subtle, I suppose, though now it seems so apparent. I'm surprised it took so long to observe this.

We wake up to higher and higher levels of sleep. There are many different kinds of attention, for example, sensorial, intellectual, active and passive. As we become embodied, and the duration increases, our attention becomes more and more refined. We come to a conscious attention, to a purified self-attention, an absence of the egotism, and finally, at times, a double absence. This discrimination you've made is quite keen and the beginning of a real adventure of attention.

Attraction to Negativity

In observing the attraction to negativity, working to not identify with it, there was a freedom, and also a sense of how I had not really worked, how it had become so much a part of my life. I think it was because I took psychological suffering to be work.

Being-Partkdolg-duty brings a rare quality of suffering, not physical or psychological but moral. It forces me to face my love for the self-image of "The Victim Queen." It's a deep line of observation and one I am strong enough to explore, as long as I discriminate between useless psychological suffering and moral suffering. You tend to cut yourself off from others and then suffer your isolation and in reaction live in judgment of yourself and others. Remember what Gurdjieff said: "I cannot live alone. Aloneness—not loneliness, which is bad thing—but can be good thing for man, very necessary for life, but also necessary learn not live alone because real life depend on other human beings and not just self."

Connections of "I"s

This week I had several experiences of states, states of irritation, tiredness. This was a new way of seeing, suddenly there was a glimpse of what a state is. Just for a moment there was a clarity, and the connections between different "I"s and how they manifest could be sensed. It was as if there was this umbrella under which the rest of me manifested, and the umbrella was the state. But this perception was so new.

First the impulse, then the identification which evokes the "I"-of-the-moment. The "I" is connected to a state, then a "world." Airtight and seamless, totally self-justifying. We become a lock-in. And we are privy to none of this ... unless we remember and observe. A *being-obligolnian-striving* is to understand more and more about the laws of World-Creation and World-Maintenance. We take that usually in what we consider the positive sense, but creation is involution. It's a descending octave, not ascending. Also, viewing this psychologically, how do we create and maintain our negative state, as they, too, are "worlds" of a type?

Waking Up to the "Radio"

I woke up this morning and began hearing the voice in my head. I tried to focus attention on the body, but I didn't have the energy to do that. I remembered what you said about when you first wake up in the morning to try to listen and be aware before the "radio" comes on. I've never been able to catch that moment.

The intellectual center sometimes awakens before the other centers. So the head is awake, the body asleep. There is a stillness, an expansiveness, perhaps an oceanic feeling. Simply allow it. At some point, the "radio" turns on, that is, the formatory mind kicks in and the person's "day" begins. Now look for what in radio terms is called the "dead air." That's where real life resides.

XXXIII
All the Same Message

I had done the morning exercise and it brought me to a sense of being relatively present. Then I read an email from you that I interpreted as violent. After the first couple of sentences, I couldn't read anymore. Later, calmer, I re-read it. And the interesting thing is that you were telling me that I don't listen; I just react. So here was this shock of being told what I had just done. I went back through other emails and saw that in different ways you were saying the same thing over and over. It was all the same message.

Yes, it's true. I hear selectively. I only hear what I want to hear. It's mechanical, not intentional, but, of course, I don't realize it. So, please, no blame. That's just another "I," the one that delights in beating myself. Rather, understand that the only way to really hear is to surrender the person and come to being. You realize I have said this many times in many different ways. And, yes, you take it in intellectually and so you think you understand, but you only "think." You have no direct experience of it.

What Do I Want?

I don't seem to be able to decide, really decide once and for all, what I want. I see that one "I" wants one thing, another "I" something else. But what do I want?

You speak as if you have a real I, one without quotation marks. Mme Ouspensky kept asking Lord Pentland, "What do you want?" "I"s want many things, often contradictory. And there are "I"s that easily come to waking consciousness while many others remain in shadows, working by stealth, by forgetting, by limiting, by making elephants from fleas. All this and more first needs to be seen for the question to be real and not imaginary. So aim for that and the question will disappear.

The Pleasures of Negativity

I find I'm often caught up in negative imagination about what may befall me or my family. It's all a waste of energy, I know that, but I still can't seem to stop it.

Why the negativity? We must be getting something from it? If you observe, you'll see, strange as it may sound, we take pleasure in being negative.

It's an indulgence that we allow ourselves. Makes us feel superior. Really verify and admit this to yourself so it touches your emotional center. We need to have the right attitude toward it. Now, be sly—make a positive out of the negative. Every time you find yourself on the edge of becoming negative use it as a reminder to remember yourself. See if you are ready to begin the work of not expressing negative emotions.

Speaking & Tingling

As I was speaking I was self-remembering at the same time. Suddenly, I felt this tingling in the solar plexus and when I spoke it was as if I was a separate person.

To experience a vibration in the solar plexus and to hear oneself speaking as if "I was a separate person"—the separation of this—is keen. Note that the separation is not a disassociation but an inclusion, a wider reception. The quality of the moment will change with extended presence. Time may appear to enlarge or slow down because I have stepped out of head time, that is, psychological time. Space changes as well.

But Then It's No Fun

My experience has been that if I come to myself in the middle of imagination, the imagination stops. I can't be present and in imagination at the same time.

Imagination, fantasy and the like, doesn't want to be seen. But if one is more nimble one can be present to their imagination, to their fantasy. Everything appears and disappears in real presence. So you must choose, no? But you want the power of pleasing yourself don't you?

Well . . . it's tough to resist.

Tough for whom? Instead of escaping into it, or blaming yourself about it—be present to it. Remember yourself. You can do anything you want. Just be present to what you are doing.

Birth of the Little Monster

As punishment for some infraction, real or imagined, my father often sent me to bed without dinner. After dinner, my mother would come up the backstairs and bring me some food. During my first marriage, my wife frequently complained that I was difficult around dinnertime. She said I would become controlling, insisting on a time and definite process. I was aware of this tendency and thought I had worked on it sufficiently. I would take responsibility for cooking dinner. I would eat snacks before dinner trying to eliminate excessive hunger and develop patience. Recently, my new partner has informed me that though "You are a wonderful man to live with . . . between the hours of three and seven you become a little monster." She said I speak in commands and declarative statements and insist on not eating before dinner to avoid ruining one's appetite. I know this is related to the irrationality of my early childhood experiences, but many years of working on this tendency have not eliminated or modified it.

Just as we do not live in the physical dimension when we do not inhabit the body, we aren't in the present either. Our past, as I've said, is living us. Much of it will fall away when we work with it consciously, but there are some imprints that have struck so deeply that they can only be weakened and contained. They will always be there. They are a part of the person. So tag the memories so that when they arise, or when I know I am entering a situation when they usually arise, I remember myself—make consciousness, intelligence and will present. Now I have put myself in a position to either inhibit the playing out of the past and observe the reactions, or observe its actions, its words, its breathing. Either keeping it below the neck, not saying "I" to it, or observing it, regard it as an object. Self-remembering has brought you into the present. A space has been created so that an inner separation can take place—a separation between the observing and the object, that which is being observed. Look at the object, the manifestations of this "I" of the moment, as if you were a doctor looking at an X-ray of a fractured bone.

So-o-o Patient

I talked with my mother recently and asked her questions about my childhood. It was a very long conversation. Many angry "I"s came up that wanted to say things like, "But why didn't you do x, y and z?" or "How could you have done that?" But there was just allowing them to come up, listening, breathing into them. I began to ask questions like, "How did that make you feel?" "What was that like for you?" She would say things like, "I was so-o-o patient," "I was so-o-o understanding," "I was so-o-o tolerant." And as I heard her, it was like I was listening to myself, how I have spoken. I could hear myself in how she was speaking and it was such a shock. Then, she began to talk about her fear. It was really wonderful—she had never done that before. And I had a sense of her as a human being, much bigger than my image of her as my mother.

A living parent is a living museum. If we stop blaming and genuinely strive to listen to our parents, we can come to new levels of understanding. Ordinarily, we should not practice *being-Partk-dolg-duty* with our parents and loved ones, but in some instances it is right. Being present—working to give ourselves and our parents our full attention—is a great gift that can unlock many closed passages and help to repair what has been hurt or misunderstood.

Shocks & Centers

There was a shock received while being relatively present. It was the cleanest experience I've ever had of the different centers. The shock caused a strong sensation of heat at the nape of the neck and then spread up the back of the skull and then went down the body, more like energy than heat. Then came a sensation of fear followed by voices of calming and comforting. The first sensation seemed instinctual. The fear seemed emotional and the talking intellectual.

Because there was a degree of presence, not absence, so much material was perceived that otherwise would be lost. There was working at a level beyond words, and so when the words came, the voices could be seen for what they were. Now, let me leave you with a question: Who was the seer?

Faith in Consciousness

Last week I had given someone my phone number, but he didn't give me his and didn't call. There was a very strong emotional reaction to this, and my issues of control with my father all came up. It was extremely strong, the energy really whirling. The only thing I could think to do was to sit with it. Sitting, the reaction was even worse, tears streamed, I felt I was being overwhelmed. Yet at the same time, there was a recognition that this was a lie, that it was all an "I." But that didn't seem to make things any better. In the face of this "I," came a real feeling of helplessness and hopelessness. There was a prayer to save me from this "I." A number of different "I"s came up—what I would call "helper-I"s who said, "This will pass. It isn't real." I finally got up, thinking, "Well, this didn't do any good," as there was an expectation that I would "will" this away by sitting. And so I went about doing other things around the house. And I was shocked shortly afterward to realize that this "I" and its suffering weren't there any more! What would normally have been my state for perhaps hours was gone in just fifteen minutes. And it was the first real experience of faith in consciousness that I can recall ever having in the Work.

How long have you been in the Work?

Ten years.

Well, that's not too bad.

[Smiles]

We practice in neutral moments—and it's just that—practice. Self-remembering only happens when we're in an emotional state, the stronger the state the stronger the need to self-remember. Like riding a wild stallion, bareback. And when we do ride the horse— what happens?

The impressions increase double fold.

Yes, we "suffer" twice as strongly—which is one reason why people do not remember themselves. Self-remembering is homeopathic. And we don't do it, don't cure ourselves—we only make ourselves available. The action of bringing Being into our lives creates a separation between what we really are and how we are acting. We suffer that separation and that is what "cures" us.

I prayed.

Yes, real prayer.

Yes.

XXXIV

In remembering ourselves time and again, and verifying through the immediacy of our own direct experiencing that we are nothing but "I"s ... we experience a "nothingness." Only from that nothingness does the question genuinely arise—"Well, who am I then?" Analysis cannot answer the question, because the answer does not lie on the level of the question. See that the very posing of the question is a resistance in itself to the admission and experiencing of one's nothingness.

Let It Be

I feel relaxed. I had a nourishing meditation this morning. The experience of the body was different than it has ever been. There was a strong current. In the past when I experienced movement I tried to keep it going. Now I just let it happen. It changes. It's not always the same. I try not to make it be the way I think it should be.

Be, don't "think." Don't trap the experiencing in the word world. Let it be. Breathe, relax and knowingly merge with the current. Keep the mind quiet. Let it be the foreground and the consciousness of it the background. Be passive.

The Weight of Words

When we spoke privately last week I had a question about the "nothingness" in terms of the weight that words carry and the "nothingness" behind them. You told me to meditate on this. I did, and the first thing that came up was breath and the second thing was the father.

What is the connection?

I held my breath at times when I was around my father. He was very stern.

He made you feel like nothing?

Yes.

How did your father discipline you?

He either paddled me or cut a switch from a tree and beat me. He did this until I was eight years old.

So when you feel authority or judgment you hold down your breath, yes?

Yes.

Don't force it. Instead relax the muscles, experience the body, the diaphragm. Release the body and the breath will come on its own, otherwise you psychologize it.

I Was Remembered

One morning I was working at the computer, and suddenly there was a remembering. I didn't remember, rather I was remembered. There was a deep experiencing of the body, its posture, the expression on my face. The stop was so complete that any movement to relax, to assume a "good" posture, would have taken me. I went more deeply into the posture and the expression without changing anything. The experience continued, nothing changing, for I guess about thirty seconds. Then things went on. But there was a "something else" that continued after that and is still with me.

This is an example of an organic self-remembering. It is the lawful result of all the work previously done when to remember oneself was a thought that was acted upon. When we repeatedly imprint the cells and tissues with attention and oxygen, they experience a new level of life and call us to it. That not only the posture was experienced but the facial expression—and that the impulse to change them was resisted—indicates a new level of understanding. Next, you could experiment by making an intentional gesture.

Salvation Army

You told me to experiment and go to the Salvation Army to look for clothes. After fighting with this I finally realized it was all self-will and went. The first thing I observed was that my head was down. I was reluctant to straighten up. I avoided people's faces. I became fearful that someone who knew me would see me. I thought, "What am I trying to hide? What image am I devoted to? Were the clothes an attempt to hide my insecurities with women?" I saw that dressing up made me feel refined, desirable and successful. It communicated credibility. It hid my sense of nothingness. The smell of the old clothes repulsed me. Detergent and old clothes smell. I left the clothing department. That took the pressure off. I could be looking for used gardening tools now. Suddenly there were flashbacks to shopping in expensive stores. I remember buying ties, shoes, Italian merino wool pants, justifying the decision to buy expensive clothing. I remembered, too, having to wear my older brother's pants and my fat cousin's clothes. They all had to be altered. My parents never took me shopping for clothes.

You paid in the coin of the realm and look at what you received.

Ring of Fire

My old ways of vows and intentions, even my wishes, now seem like phantoms. Even the word wish *seems flat. It's not because the word has no real meaning, but because the word, up to now, has been associated to some "doing." The words are the same words, but now they have a new resonance.*

It saddens me, too, to see that others are made the object of all my stuff, and that I can do nothing about it. All that's possible is to keep my mouth shut, but even that is not as easy as it sounds. It seems like I should be able to do more, but I am powerless to do so. All my previous resolves, intentions, wishes, the belief that in the future it would be otherwise, have not been enough.

From an ordinary point of view this is a horrible place I've come to. I'm nothing, I can't do anything, everything I believed in is just ashes at my feet. But from the Work point of view—from the point of view of Being—all the work you have done has brought you to a real "taste of knowledge," as spoken about in *Search*. One's life is how it is because we are what we are, and it cannot be different because we have not been different—did not even understand the possibility that we could think and feel and act in a new way. Now can I continue to stand in the psychological flames of the truth of myself—my nothingness—and not give in to self-pity, and strive to do nothing other than, as you say, "keep my mouth shut?" To do that would take a great deal of clarity and real will. And it is crucial that this is done not for myself but for Being. For otherwise, it devolves to mere egotism and I'm caught again.

Being Bodyless

There is an anxiety about dying, some fear of what is to come, a lack of control, a not-knowing. Just the other day, for example, I experienced myself getting up from a chair. It was like an old man making the effort to stand up. Or, quite similarly, when I brush my hair and the comb is filled with loose hairs, I see it as another sign of death coming closer.

People speak of "rebirth," but the fact is one has yet to be fully born. Everyone is living a half-life. Your recognition of bodily death is a first step toward genuinely being bodily born. Death is a great reminder. None of us knows how much time we have left in the body. It could end at any moment. What would life be without a physical body? We can't know. What we can know now is whether I have a body or not; that is, is there a conscious awareness, a self-sensing, of the physical body? If so, I am preparing food for the growth of a higher body, one which can withstand the shock of being without the physical, being bodyless. But this can't happen unless I have worked to first have a body.

Maya

Many times I feel like I am walking around in a dream state. Every time I wake up I seem to wake up in a dream of some type. It's either a past situation or a future one, some more outlandish than others, others simply like what I'm going to do tomorrow.

What is the Hindu concept of Maya? We don't use the term in the Work, but is there any corollary? Maya is illusion, the hypnosis that prevents us from seeing and being what is real. That said, what causes the delusion?

The belief in "I"s?

"I"s are what? They are surrogates we mistake for the indivisible I. So now we see that there are many "I"s—do we really accept that? That is, admitting to ourselves that we are many and not one. Are we striving to remember ourselves, break the momentum of the ongoing hypnotism of the "I" world? No, why is this?

Trying to protect myself, what I take to be myself?

The root belief of myself is what? Self-love and vanity. This creates the fundamental delusion. This is the origin of Maya. Gurdjieff gives it a direct taste and body, takes it from simply being a concept to an experiencing.

But I am not responsible for self-love and vanity. Kundabuffer was an organ implanted in us so we would see life upside down. Then it was removed, okay, but the specific properties remained. We are all suffering for what we are not responsible for.

Yes, but we can work with *Kundabuffer* to destroy or mitigate the power of "I"s and thus come to real I.

But the so-called original sin, if there is such a thing, is not ours!

Let's say original mistake. But we've gotten way off point. I deny the truth of what I hear, either misinterpreting or arguing about it, to keep making myself right. That's how afraid I am of being wrong. Please ponder why this is.

Mr. Hypnotist

While sitting this week, some very vivid memories have come from my early teen years. I was quite taken with hypnotism. These ideas were combined with psychological science fiction stories about mind control and manipulation. I was very interested in trying these things out on other people and especially when it came to desires, physical desires—to get girls to do what I wanted with them. It was all very juvenile and full of fantasy, but I can see that's when an "I" was born and developed. I've been seeing that "I" operating even today. A woman I was with remarked to me that something I had tried to do was rather obviously manipulative. It was really painful to see that, but it was true.

This is an "I" with a long history. It's not going away, so I must be ever on the alert. For just as it wishes to manipulate others, it will also manipulate me. It is true, you know, that I do reap what I sow.

Suppressing

While sitting and experiencing a sense of being very grounded in the body and a quietness in the mind, I suddenly became aware of having slipped into a fantasy. I saw how it was fueled with fear, desire and ambition. Also, the center of gravity of my attention had shifted to my head. There was an automatic suppression of the fantasy, as is my habit. I recognized this as my pattern, that is, to suppress "bad thoughts." It suddenly dawned on me that there is no need to censor any part of myself. This realization brought a very strong emotional sense of liberation that spread throughout the whole body and brought me to tears.

As we divide the world, so we divide ourselves, and all in the name of what? The "God of Goodness." It is to observe oneself impartially. That means to allow the contents to be what they are, to follow them and see what they do and where they lead. This takes genuine clarity and will. Through your long work on yourself, you now have the right foundation to pursue this. But you've lived your life in division, in this self-calming. Are you sincere enough to struggle? Do you have the courage to give up what needs to be given up?

XXXV

Chemical Connections

I have a very deeply ingrained fear of not being loved, and being alone for the rest of my life and of not having a woman with me. When I meet someone I have a chemical connection with, I either go with it, unable to resist, or I fight it with all my strength, which is, for the most part, with my head. I have been attracting the same kind of person, the same situation, over and over again for years. When the chemical connection happens, I get involved way before I can even think about anything. The emotions are fed and I run crazy.

It is all chemistry, from the lowest to the highest. Observe your whole life in terms of chemistry, not just your "love life." And remember the higher emotional and intellectual centers. Don't soil the purity of your brains.

Separation

During the morning sitting an "I" kept arising that wanted to replay an interaction I'd had a week earlier with an attractive woman. This "I" has a long history of this. Being embodied allowed some separation from it. I saw there were whole new worlds waiting to be born—ones that in the past would have used up a lot of energy. This "I" finally withdrew and has not reappeared.

We can't control what comes into the mind. If we're present, we can control how we relate to it, what we do or don't do. You really worked with it, didn't give yourself up to it. That took self-knowledge and will. Something else is forming in you. Keep feeding it. The separation will increase.

Question Inner Authority

Listening to the other speaker there was an "I" that came up that said, "I already know that." It was seen and dropped. But the first part of what the speaker was talking about was missed. Secondly, I woke up today with the feeling of good energy. I had done some CBI the night before. But I told myself I will stay in bed a little longer. I woke up an hour later completely devastated and that bad energy lasted all day.

You know the bumper sticker that says, "Question Authority"? Well, it needs to read, "Question Inner Authority."

People Watching

I was sitting in a cafe experiencing my right leg. Usually I move my attention from one spot to another. I observed I could see activity in the foreground and the background at the same time. There was the sense of a dance and there was enjoyment in drinking it in. A man was talking to a woman and waving his arms and eating, all at the same time. My judgments of him as a clod and a buffoon began to creep in. But when I again breathed into my leg he was just a man happily communicating with a woman who was enjoying his attention. And seeing his animal joyfully devour the food was just interesting—like here is an animal feeding. My running negative comments were missing when I was present.

Presence eats negativity. Usually we are taken by images, dream into them, spin-off into worlds of our own creation. But simply experiencing the right leg roots me in the physical world, and so I am not just a thought, a feeling and impulse, but a palpable presence that receives and transmits.

"Nothing" & "Something Else"

When I compare this teaching with others, say Buddhism or even New Age teachings, there are a lot of similarities. How should I think about this?

Don't "think." It's only formatory thinking, the mechanical part of the intellectual center. This type of thinking always roots itself in comparison. It thinks extreme examples are a form of mentation. It keeps everything on a superficial level. Your experience of this teaching is only intellectual at this point. To try to compare it to others is simply resistance, withholding, a way of letting the person remain "free." As for the so-called modern "teachings" of the New Age, they are just psychological eclecticisms, mixtures of imagination, invention and practices that entomb one in the "esoteric-I."

What about Buddhism?

There are similarities, as there will be with any authentic teaching of self-transformation, but Buddhism is monastic, a retreat from the world. Its aim is to realize Sunyata, the void, no soul, no Self. It is an Eastern approach.

This teaching—which, amazing as it is, precedes Buddhism, as it does all the known teachings and religions—in itself has no aim. But it grounds itself in the ordinary world, doesn't reject it. It uses the conscious reception of the impressions of ordinary life— the negativity, uncertainty, suffering, illusions and pleasures—to come to real life, to become an Individual. It trains one in how to use one's experiencing to awaken to how one really is and not how they imagine themselves to be, and in so doing, to develop one's bodies, come to conscience and understanding, to make a soul, to become immortal within the solar system.

What about engaged Buddhism, one that engages with life?

This is a very recent movement and one in the right direction, though, of course, it comes with all its monastic baggage. See what Gurdjieff says about Buddhism in *All and Everything*.

Initiation by Pit Bull

I was walking in the woods when I heard a rustling of leaves. Suddenly a reddish-brown pit bull barking ferociously raced out of the brambles and headed right at me. It stopped about four feet away. Without thinking about it I immediately became embodied, sensing my feet and hands, becoming aware of my breath, keeping my eyes soft, looking without looking. I knew that to look a dog in the eyes is to challenge it. If I moved backward, he charged at me. I suddenly became aware of the silence between the barks. Three barks and then silence. The silence opened a space. Hearing and focusing on the silence gave a strange sense of power. The inner stillness I was experiencing was equal to his ferocity. Suddenly a little girl's voice called out and the dog took off.

I touched my forehead. It was soaking wet, the whole body likewise. Something seemed comical.

Well done. Yes, the Work in action.

Silence & Thinking

It was recently seen that I wasn't listening to silence. While trying to do so for the past few days, I recognized how much association is going on, even when there is awareness of myself. And though I have resolved to guard the mind and listen to silence many times, I still don't do it. The question is, how to remember it?

Experience the space first. Listening is a very fine and increasingly rare art. There is an instant, mechanical erasure of what we don't want to hear. The parts that we don't remember are the ones we need to most remember. One needs to be and to listen to what is being said in more than one center, allow it to enter the emotional and instinctive centers and to act upon them. Listen without listening.

What does that mean?

Listen without the person.

Courage in the Muck

I've been working on delegating several Work projects. There are feelings like leaves scattered in the wind. Anger, hurt and impulses to blame people for doing things that are different from the way I expect something to be done. When this is seen there's an acceptance of what people do, an acceptance of them just the way they are.

Why the need to hold on to everything, control everything and everybody? It's more than a fear, it's a deep compensation, no? But "I," the esoteric self-image, doesn't want to be like this, so it convinces me I have accepted people "just the way they are." Like *Peer Gynt*, alluded to before, one has to have the courage of a "melting down," of standing naked in the muck, accepting what is seen without falsely coating it.

Dealing with Divorce

Returning home, I saw from the distance a female figure jogging. The eyes focused in until I saw it was my ex-wife. A struggle ensued. Should I stop? Should I drive by? The decision was made it seems without "my" conscious participation—I stopped. Social greetings were exchanged, a few comments and then the realization she doesn't really want to be talking to me. I am imposing myself on her. A few more insignificant gestures and words, an awareness of the need to be in the body for the required presence and tension of the meeting and then the impulse to share with her everything that has occurred since the old life fell apart. A desire to mention my participation in this Work—we both left a faux group together—and everything I've learned about being in the body, sitting, etc. I suddenly felt what I was doing—trying to present myself as a positive, happy, and vibrant survivor after the betrayal.

Observe the words, "The decision was made it seems without my conscious participation." What do you mean "it seems"? You were taken. You didn't stop. You were stopped. There is a conceit of agency. There was no doer. We are still holding on to being an independent I that can do.

Yes, I see that.

And why the "required presence"? There's something underneath this, but let's not go into it now. The issue at hand—the divorce. Are you looking for vindication?

No, what I want is to be seen as "not such a bad guy after all."

Why can't you just accept there was a relationship, it worked for a while and then it was over?

Because I want some kind of closure, we had shared so much of our lives together, and now, not even an acknowledgement of each other's existence.

It's closed, you're divorced. If you like, go away for a weekend, sit in the morning and evening. In a book write down on the left-hand page all the dates you remember beginning with when you first met. On the right-hand page, write down any impressions or memories connected with those dates. Now pick what you think are the important dates. Put aside all blame, guilt, right and wrong and enter into a state of self-remembering; visualize you and her together at these times. Observe like you are watching a movie. Go through your whole life together, and when Sunday comes close the book, return home and begin your life anew. With gusto.

I feel like a little child drowning in emotional indulgence, unable to think.

What knows this?

XXXVI

Let me read this passage from Kathryn Hulme's *Undiscovered Country*. She was Mr. Gurdjieff's student for the last fourteen years of his life:

> Gurdjieff had given us a pledge to say each time before beginning a new exercise—that we would not use this for the self, but for all humanity. This 'good-wishing-for-all' vow, so deeply moving in intent, had a tremendous effect upon me. For the first time in my life, I felt that I was truly doing something for humanity as I strove to make my own molecule of it more perfect. The meaning of this Work, which at first had seemed quite egotistical and self-centered, suddenly blossomed out like a tree of life encompassing in its myriad branchings the entire human family. The implications of it were staggering. By my single efforts toward Being, I could help sleeping humanity one hairsbreadth nearer to God.

Who Is Mr. Gurdjieff?

On the Internet I read an article you had written, "Who Is Mr. Gurdjieff?" When I read the conversation between Gurdjieff and Bennett, there was a mechanical reaction in the body. I stood up, turned away from the computer and placed my hands over my face. Then I sat back down at the computer and finished reading the article. What was it about the conversation with Bennett? It was when Gurdjieff told Bennett he could write a check with seven zeros, meaning he was Number Seven, immortal within the solar system. This idea had been heard before, but to hear him say it came as a great shock.

Yes, when people are asked who Mr. Gurdjieff was, most never mention the seven levels of man that Gurdjieff speaks about. This is true even with many people in the Work. It's as if, as some have commented, he is like a crazy uncle who shouldn't be mentioned.

There was a strong feeling of having undervalued who he was.

Origin of The Teaching

When I first read Search I was amazed at the quality and scale of the ideas I was reading. I'd never read anything like it, and my interest has been comparative religion.

Ouspensky says that when asked in Russia about the origin of The Fourth Way, Gurdjieff said it was esoteric Christianity. He must have spoken those words in a special way because Ouspensky italicized them. He also said that this Christianity he speaks of existed long before the birth of Jesus Christ and that its origin was prehistoric Egypt; that is, the Egypt that existed *before* 4,000 BCE, before the sands, when Egypt was green. And that this earliest form of Christianity was constituted of the same principles and ideas, even the same form of worship, as the one commonly known.

I've been under the impression that this teaching came from the Hindu Kush or Tibet.

If the teaching that Gurdjieff brought originated in the Egypt of 4,000 BCE, and likely much further back, that makes it older than all the religions we know, and especially Tibetan Buddhism and Sufism, which, comparatively speaking, are very late; the first being a compilation of Buddhism and Bon, a shamanic religion, and Sufism being a more mystical version of Islam. Because of the rich scale and power of the teaching, both Buddhism and Sufism have tried to "own" it, but this is nonsense. There are, of course, certain similarities, which is true of all authentic paths, but the teaching at heart and in aim is quite different. Moreover, Gurdjieff was neither a Buddhist nor a Sufi but a Christian.

I never heard any of this before.

Interesting that you've been in the Work this long and have never come to it. Most likely because you've accepted what others have said and not done your own research. There's much more information about this in the video trilogy.

Golden Time

Reading what Gurdjieff's direct students write, it seems like "the golden time" of the Work is over. There don't seem to be as many opportunities today.

Who here could work with Gurdjieff? Could make the sacrifices he demanded, put up with his so-called unpredictableness? And none of the ideas were in books. Can we imagine what it must have been like for his students to read the transcripts of the *First Series*? You work all those years without a book and the first thing you read is what looks like a weird and unreadable science fiction fable. Or later, after his death, you read *Search*. There it is—all the scraps of knowledge brought together in a unified whole! We have all of Gurdjieff's books and those of his direct pupils, but do we read them? Maybe once, if that. And how many of us study them? We don't have time, we say. Remember, time is counted. No one is counting, but all the same time is counted. Ponder that. In between commercials, of course.

Working with Purpose

There are many observations connected with the work of making the Gurdjieff video trilogy. All the travel to different countries, the difficulties that had to be overcome, and the on-going intensity and purpose created a strong field of energy. The pressure could get enormous and when it did there was the usual whining, anger, guilt, projection—the whole set of mechanical but seemingly very real feelings that ate me up. But the project and others brought me out of it. Time and time again there was a coming together on a level I've never experienced.

This is well said. Whenever some new work is going on it creates new energy. And there will be a reaction of resistance not only on the outside but inside the Work as well, so it must be expected and taken into account. You have seen quite a bit of yourself; this also may give you a different look on *Tzvarnoharno.* It was a perfect work project. We started from scratch. No one had any experience. We all had to work closely together for what—seven years!—and to not lose focus. The aim was to finish the video trilogy and to make it on a professional level. Of this we can be justifiably proud. Now, let's go on. . . .

Real Prayer

What is an example of real prayer?

When there is only wish, not person.

Black Magician

I did something you've been suggesting I do for a long time. Afterwards I felt a number of things. There were moments of anger. Those were familiar. But the head was more quiet, there wasn't as much noise. And also something else that didn't get observed and almost got thrown away, a feeling of being younger. . . I don't know any other way to put it.

False personality defends itself in many ways, primarily with self-will, by not doing what one is asked to do, thinking that I know better, or that I won't do it unless I understand it—but what "I" is going to understand it? Most people are too old. Even in youth they are almost senile. The "knower-I" completely took over. It entombed them in itself, sealing them off from any true experience. Everything has to be on its own terms. The least of which in its terms, but the most overriding, is that this "knower-I" must first understand and agree with what it is asked to do. What's the motive? To maintain control.

The knower is one's black magician. There is a continual struggle, cold or hot, going on between the black magician and the teacher who represents the white magician. It's like Horus and Set. A struggle between the animal and the spiritual, Set is the great lord of materiality, the animal; Horus, the spiritual. Set is sluggish, unchanging, resistant, worshipping memory and history, with a penchant to reduce everything—especially the spiritual—to the understandable and thus the meaningless. Horus is light, open, spacious, nimble and creative. There is a constant struggle between the two. If Set wins, the student returns to material life. If Horus dominates, Set becomes his helper, and the student enters real life.

Expanded Body

After CBI yesterday one side of the body opened. I felt as though it expanded by one or two feet. Then, after doing the body impressions today it provided a similarly exaggerated sensation. I mean one leg was sensed to be twelve inches or more lower on the ground than the other. Was this real or an exaggeration?

How do you know it was exaggerated? In one state of relaxation that was what was felt. Afterward, in another state, you reported on it. It is important how we re-present experience to ourselves. The lower cannot contain the higher. However, if we speak and there is not complete accord inside us with what is said, then one center may be confronting another. Or a certain psychology may have entered. All is grist for self-observation.

I Did Not Want It to Stop

After the morning exercise and sitting, I was having breakfast when suddenly a wonderful state of self-remembering appeared spontaneously and the body was flooded with wave after wave of energy. The mind was still and I believe I "observed" the body for the first time so clearly—the posture was a direct impression. All the muscles, bones and facial expression were taken in and there was a sensation of heat in the solar plexus. There arose an inner voice saying "I Am, I Am"—it was strong and deep and I did not want it to stop, but as soon as the mind thought this it stopped.

As said, there are two types of self-remembering. The first is mental, the thought arises to remember oneself. After a long time of repeated practice of obeying this reminder to redirect the attention into the body, the second may emerge, an organic and spontaneous experiencing, one in which "I am remembered." If a thought arises ignore it—whatever the thought, it is still a thought, a formulation. Instead, use it as a shock to open to a deeper level. Only in this way can we learn. The reaction, of course—"I did not want it to stop"—psychologized what is beyond psychology. Self-knowledge has many tiers of experiencing.

Dissolving

During meditation the sensing of my body began to change. I don't know how to describe it because any words related to temperature or form don't seem to fit. There was an experience of dissolving into that inner body. But an "I" jumped in with a thought and a fear. The fear was voiced as, "I won't be able to get back. I'll go crazy." The voice was very quick and quiet but it stopped the "dissolving." There was an immediate feeling of regret.

Also, I'm experiencing a funny kind of chemical imbalance.

Initially, the head is the active force, the body the denying. Then, when the body comes alive, this changes. There is a sense of dissolving as expansion takes place. I experience space and the silence beyond the surface. The foreground dissolves and the background appears. But if there is identification with the old, there is negative emotion and I become recidivistic. As to the sense of imbalance, just as false personality defends itself psychologically, the body may do so as well. The body is used to a certain sense of itself, tempo, and so forth. Self-remembering changes one's chemistry and sense of oneself. The body may need time to adjust to a new level of being and so it undergoes a purging.

My Old Life

There was a shock the other day when I visited my old house with a friend. He drove into the driveway, stopped the car and started to get out. I had told him to drive to the house, but I didn't mean to stop and get out. There was a recognition that this was an important moment, to really be there to take in the impressions directly. As I walked around there was a sense of being in a kind of silence, and the quality of time changed. The new people are remodeling the place and there was an expectation that peeking through the front window would be a big shock. But it wasn't. It was simply seen and taken in. But then when I walked around to the back and saw the old dishwasher outside, everything changed. So many things connected with my old life came back. And, it wasn't that it was all negative ... there were many wonderful memories, I hadn't realized how much of my old life hasn't been digested.

We can't say hello to the new until we say goodbye to the old.

Fourth Way Probes

*Probes are spontaneous talks
on various aspects of the teaching.
They are given at the beginning of
every Day of Exploration.*

Who's Flying This Plane?

LET'S ROLL!

Just a few years ago that was shouted in a plane high above the state of Pennsylvania. We all know that story. The black-bearded, angry-eyed guys with box cutters defending the plane's cockpit, the passengers no longer in their seats, the impending fight for survival.

No, the passengers were no longer in their seats telling themselves this was not a hijacking, or if it was, then they'd soon be landing at some airport, thinking to themselves, "We'll be hostages for a while and then negotiations will begin, and we'll get out of this."

No, they were not self-calming with these thoughts or the idea that God would protect them, that everything happens for the best, and if something was to be done, let someone else do it.

When a stewardess reported that ground control had confirmed that the hijackers wanted to crash the plane, maybe target the White House, the recognition dawned: *This was a suicide flight!*

"Let's roll!" the passengers screamed, and rushed the cockpit. Slashes, punches, blood, screams. They must have gotten close to opening that cockpit door, because the hijacker piloting the plane suddenly nosedived straight into a farmer's field in Pennsylvania.

By analogy each one of us is a passenger in our own plane, alone. And our plane only has so much fuel. At one point it's going down, too. Just a matter of time. Whether it's in a Pennsylvania farmer's field, or the mountains near Denver, or a California desert, our plane is going down somewhere, sometime.

Can I get that through my head? *That I am going to die at some point…* Yes, intellectually I can admit that I'm going to die, but emotionally it still doesn't touch me. And anyway, well, there's always life after death. I have a soul, so only the body's going to die.

I tell myself stories like that just like the passengers did before they realized what was up. Do I think I'm going to land at another airport? That this plane isn't going down? Is that why I keep sitting in my seat? But then I look around: *there are no others on this plane.* I'm the only passenger. And then the question finally breaks through the jamming system—*who's flying this plane?* Who's in that cockpit? Where are we headed? I get out of my seat now and start up the aisle, but as soon as I do the plane hits turbulence. Warning lights start flashing. I feel queasy. So I go back to my seat, sit down, buckle up, turn on the TV. Surfing the channels, I discover a strange, esoteric station. There's an interview with some wacko talking about everyone "being mostly disembodied," about not really having a body. Now how ridiculous is that? I've *got* a body! What's he talking about? But suddenly I see what he's saying. Yeah, there's a body, but I don't have a *conscious awareness* of it.

The question recycles: The wacko's talking again about redirecting the attention out of the head brain, amping up the body's vibration, becoming embodied. The warning lights are still flashing, seat belts must stay fastened, but I'm not buying it. I need to know the answer—*Who's in the cockpit?* I make my way up the aisle. The closer to the cockpit door I get, the more fear I feel. Like there's some unstated taboo to not open that door. That if I do, I'll be "poisoned for life." Life will never be the same. The voices in my head roar, but the question nags—*who the hell is flying this plane!* I yank open the cockpit door—empty! The plane's on automatic! The whole flight is programmed. *There's nobody here but me.*

Me? Who is this "me"? Yeah, "me," but what do I mean, what am I referring to, when I say "me"? Certainly not just the body. I could lose a limb, an eye, and still be "me." But, like that wacko guy said, this sense of "me" keeps changing. So many different "me"s, so many voices all saying "I." He said something about egotism, believing in, worshiping really, an imaginary "I."

I remember once reading this incredibly frustrating book in which there is original sin, but Adam didn't do anything. Adam was manipulated. He had an organ put into him that made him see things upside down. Made him think he was the center of the universe.

I look out the window. The plane is landing. Over the intercom, a disembodied voice says this is the Holy Planet Purgatory, that we're just going for a "look-see." Purgatory isn't at all what I imagined. Absolutely beautiful. Everything you would want. Movies, great food, golf, tennis, parties, gorgeous women, skinny dipping, casinos, self-help groups, therapies and a drug-of-choice for every occasion. But there's this flashing sign saying the aim for those on this planet is to cultivate an unflagging, instinctive need for *being-*

Partkdolg-duty in order to purify ourselves.

I lived in a cave when I first got here. Didn't care for it, complained, so I was moved to the penthouse suite atop the local casino. No problemo. Round-the-clock room service. Dynamite chicks. Then late one evening I notice a lot of planes taking off from the airport. I call the control tower. Yeah, they're going straight back to a former state of mind, Earth.

Hey, there's a knock on my door and under it slides what looks like—yes, an airplane ticket. My name's on it. Flight 1-2-3, Destination Earth, one-way.

Hmm…why me? What did I do?   ✗

City of Life, City of Death

Mr. OUSPENSKY ONCE SAID THAT ALL LIFE IS STREETS AND CROSS-ROADS. What did he mean? But first, before examining that, we need to know where we are. St. Augustine wrote of the City of God and the City of Man. Which city are we in? Before answering, we need to realize that there are not really two cities. There cannot be. If there were, that would be an essential Manichean duality. *The two cities are the same city.* But the first is a city of self-awareness, the second a city of sleep. The level of vibration, the quality of perception, the essential orientation—these are what make the difference.

Given St. Augustine's metaphor, those of us in the Work can be said to be nearing, or in, the City of God, the City of Life, when we are walking on the street of the Work. We'll come to many crossroads. Some are detours, some cul-de-sacs, others are one-way streets that may take us in a completely different direction from which we may never find our way back. Once off the "main street" we may even forget entirely why we were walking the street of the Work in the first place.

Walking on "Main Street"

Have you ever found yourself in a foreign city, one whose language you didn't speak? You ask for directions. You pretend you understand because you don't want to appear stupid. But the directions mean nothing. So you keep walking, but you don't know where you're going. Suddenly, you make a left turn just because it "feels right." But it isn't intuition—you're just guessing, hoping this street will be the short cut. Then you realize that the street is just a stage set—all the buildings are facades, the people just acting, pretending.

This said, now what does Ouspensky mean when he speaks of life as a kind of city map with streets and crossroads—what's he referring to? What comes quickly to mind is the Law of Seven, what Mr. Gurdjieff calls *heptaparaparshinokh*, best exemplified by the musical octave. Think of the practice of self-remembering as the Law of Seven. It's only when we remember ourselves that we're on main street, the street of the Work. Otherwise, we're on a cross street, a cul-de-sac, or we've taken a detour. But when we actualize ourselves, come into the present moment, when we break the mechanical momentum and redirect the attention out of the head brain—only then are there possibilities. Everything else is determined.

Time and again making the effort to be, the simple, immaculate truth will dawn: *there is only main street.* There might seem to be crossroads, but in fact there are no cross streets, no detours, no cul-de-sacs. They only appear to exist. There really is only one street. All the rest are dream streets. Once that is understood, self-remembering takes on a new, deeper valuation. Either I am here or I'm asleep. Period. There are many degrees of both, of course.

What Is My Wish?

I am called to remember, either organically or by mental reminder. Out of the dream street I am called to the main street. Do I heed the call? Deny it? What is my wish? To be awake? Or not? That's my choice, my free will. If I don't heed the call, I must see why, unambiguously, without excuse or rationalization. Otherwise I lie to myself. There are lies and there are lies. A lie here between the "yes" and the "no" isn't a little white lie. It's part of the archetypal lie, the general law that keeps everyone in the hands of Morpheus, the god of sleep. A thousand times I may lie to myself at this crossroads. But one day I will see it. Only then will the self-understanding dawn and I will both see and feel what I have hidden from myself: *that I am not sincere.* Only then will Mr. Gurdjieff's words ring true, that we must "learn to be sincere."

Everything More Vivid

Let us say we have heeded the call. That we've come out of the dream state into the Immediate. "Life is real only then, when 'I am,'" says Gurdjieff. When he first spoke in England and was asked what it is like to be conscious, his rapier-like reply was—"Everything more vivid." Yes. In a state of self-remembering everything outer and inner is more defined; the impressions increase double-fold. Then, as we see with the musical scale, there comes a gap, a shock point, a *Stopinder*, as Gurdjieff calls it. Self-remembering has increased, however subtly, the quality of our vibration. Whatever the shock, we can absorb it if our vibration, and the clarity that accompanies it, is equal to or greater than the shock. Life, in this sense, is really "eat or be eaten." Absorbing the shock, we assimilate its energy; we become more awake. Otherwise, we descend to a lower state in which our lives are nothing but the drama of walking a city of dream streets.

So where do we live? In the Immediate? In the City of Life? Or the City of Death? 🕱

Knowledge Is Not Enough

WHAT IF WE HAD COME TODAY KNOWING NOTHING ABOUT THE TEACHING? What if we had really searched, are led to the door, we knock, enter, and for the first time hear about the Ray of Creation, the Diagram of Everything Living, the Food Diagram, internal considering, imagination, buffers, self-remembering, self-observation, and that we have to make a soul, one that we didn't get gratis? If we were to hear all this right now for the first time—how would we experience that moment?

This was likely Ouspensky's experience in April 1915 in Moscow when he first met Mr. Gurdjieff. To Ouspensky, widely read in matters esoteric, these ideas were all amazingly new. He had been searching unsuccessfully for what he called "a new or forgotten road," "a teaching of a more rational kind." Until Ouspensky's *In Search of the Miraculous* appeared in 1950 there were no articles or books on the ideas he heard at Gurdjieff's table; these ideas were not in that day's occult marketplace. When Ouspensky returned to St. Petersburg he burst into Phillipov's café to meet another seeker and exclaimed—

"I have found the miracle!"

Gurdjieff gave Ouspensky everything he was searching for, and more. But as we know, it was not enough. Isn't that also our experience? No matter what we are given, it's not enough. Why is it never enough? When we are introduced to a whole scale of ideas, when we are struck with the sense that we are hearing as close to a formulation of the truth as we have ever experienced—why is that not enough?

Knowledge—A Passing Presence

We want knowledge, and part of that wanting is the belief that if we just had enough knowledge we would act differently. If we just understood what we were doing, we would act more intelligently. Well, to a degree that's true, but the problem lies in the words *knowing* and *understanding*. One can have information and even knowledge, to some degree, but it is on our level. "Knowledge is a passing presence," as Gurdjieff says. Knowledge is state specific. A lower level of vibration cannot know and understand that of a higher level. The higher encompasses the lower, not the lower the higher. Knowledge can even be an obstacle. Gurdjieff warned J. G. Bennett about this. "With too much knowledge," he said, "the inner barrier may become insurmountable."

In India, the Upanishads were kept secret, discussed only among the Brahmans, the priestly class. All the lower classes—Kshatriya, the warriors; Vaisya, businessmen; Sudras, untouchables—were not allowed to hear these ideas. Those who did break this taboo had hot liquid glass poured into their ears. Why? It must have something to do with knowledge, esoteric knowledge, its power to transform and, equally, to corrupt. Esoteric knowledge is a snake. In the right hands it leads to wisdom; in the wrong, it is self-poisoning. Esoteric knowledge in the service of egoism only enriches *Kundabuffer*, self-love and vanity.

The hot new field is neurology, the science of the brain and spinal cord. It's exploring what consciousness is and isn't. In time, it will define in its powerful but reductionist scientific method what it means to be human. When science informs society that the "I" is just a construct, that it has no conscious will, and so forth, is that going to be a breakthrough? Or a breakdown?

Corrupting Society

None of this strikes Gurdjieffians as new knowledge. After all, in many ways the Work has been waiting for science to catch up. But to give this knowledge to society at large is to corrupt it. Years ago, Robert Ruark wrote a book called *Something of Value*. It was about Christian missionaries in Africa who took away the native religions and gave Christianity in their place. Everything fell apart. We took something of value from the Africans and didn't give back anything they could use.

The present period seems to be an attack upon the human being, his identity and his purpose in the world. Will society be able to stand up under this? Not if it does not come to a new level of consciousness.

Listen to what Albert Camus wrote in his *Notebooks 1942–1951* some sixty years ago:

> Modern intelligence is in utter confusion. Knowledge has become so diffuse that the world and the mind have lost all point of reference. It is a fact we are suffering from nihilism. But the most amazing things are the admonitions to "turn backward." Return to the Middle Ages, to primitive mentality, to the soil, to religion, to the arsenal of worn-out solutions. To grant a shadow of efficacy to those panaceas, we should have to act as if our acquired knowledge had ceased to exist, as if we had learned nothing, and to pretend in short to erase what is inerasable. We should have to cancel the contribution of several centuries and the incontrovertible acquisitions of a mind that has finally (in its last step forward) re-created chaos on its own. That is impossible. In order to be cured, we must make our peace with this lucidity, this clairvoyance. We must take into account the glimpses we have suddenly had of our exile. Intelligence is in confusion not because knowledge has changed everything. It is so because it cannot accept that change. It hasn't "got accustomed to the idea." When this does happen, the confusion will disappear. Nothing will remain but the change and the clear knowledge that the mind has of it. There's a whole civilization to be reconstructed.

The question is: what part will the Gurdjieff Work play in the reconstruction of civilization? Fritz Peters in his *Boyhood with Gurdjieff* recounts Gurdjieff saying, "If enough individuals could develop themselves—even partially—into genuine, natural men, able to use the real potentialities that were proper to mankind, a complete disaster could be avoided."

Gurdjieff brought this Work not for you and me but to help avert a world catastrophe. So when we work on ourselves we need to understand it is not for ourselves alone but—as large as it may sound—the future of mankind. To do so is to have faith not in knowledge but in the consciousness in which all knowledge inheres. ⚡

Shocks—Eat or Be Eaten

[Sound of a hand clap] What is that? A sound? An energy? A force? It is all those, but primarily it is a shock.

[Sound of hand clap] What kind of shock is that? It's an intentional shock, not accidental. In life the preponderance of shocks are accidental. But what is a shock in itself? It's something that breaks the continuity, disrupts, rends the virtually seamless hypnotic momentum of ordinary life. By its nature, the shock is unexpected. *[Sound of hand clap]* Each of the senses, alone or in combination, has its particular kind of shock. One could explore this at some length, but the question is: *How do I relate to the shock?*

Well, to begin with, the shock is against something. What? It's against my world as I know it and have deliberately—and not—constructed it. In the case of the hand clap just now, the shock disrupted each person's expectation. At the very least, the expectation that the silence would be broken by spoken words—by the speaker speaking rather than clapping. The presumption is of the continuity of what we've known, the presumption of memory; that as the past has been, so will the future be. Though time and again we are confronted with the obvious fact that people, situations and things never are what they were, yet we continue to believe otherwise. That's very strange, isn't it—to have something in your life, these shocks, that totally throw us off the tracks…and yet, after the shock eats us, or more unlikely that we eat and integrate it, we still go back to the old belief that we know what's happening, that we can judge how things are going to be. The base assumption is that

I know—that against all evidence to the contrary, *I know.*

Shocks strike directly at what? This knower. Each shock momentarily unseats the knower. It isn't that we can't know at all, of course we can. We can know in the moment. Or, rather, the nanosecond. Let us call it the Immediate, the what-is. When we exceed the bounds of direct knowing we leave the Immediate. Unfortunately, the knower, undisciplined, is always either ahead or behind of the Immediate.

Djartklom & Faux-Reality

You go out in the morning, your car is there, the engine starts, you go to work. But one morning your car isn't there, or the key doesn't work, or the ignition doesn't start, and suddenly at that moment what happens? What happens at the exact moment of the shock? In a word—*Djartklom*. (I won't go into the meaning of the term, as I assume you have read and studied Gurdjieff's *Legominism* in the manner he suggested.)

So, suddenly there is a rent in my life, a disruption, a separation, the sudden appearance of a new Immediate. There is a knowing, but of nothing. Or let us pronounce the word differently—*nothing.* There is a knowing of no-thing which, if I am not attuned to this subtlety, is interpreted as a nothing and is dismissed. Of course, all this isn't deliberated. It's an instantaneous cognition, based on one's previous experience and conditioning. But when this happens—and it happens in less than a nanosecond—the world opens, stands still. The stillness is either eaten or it eats me. *Me* being my attention of the moment. I am eaten when my attention—a higher, finer degree of attention or awareness than is normally experienced—cannot withstand the aftershock of stillness, of no-thing, of Being. And so, mechanically, awareness devolves into an ordinary attention, which devolves into person-attention, and in all the shocked space a "person-world" is reborn. (Remember the third *being-obligolnian-striving*—"To know more and more about the laws of World-Creation and World-Maintenance"?)

Well, let's not take "world" in the objective sense, as is primarily meant, but psychologically. A psychological world, based on my identifications, known and unknown, is now born. It's a construct. It has nothing to do with the reality of Being. And because this world I've created is not in accord with reality, I must suffer. Suffer what? Suffer the consequences of having created a separate world. And in this suffering—because I refuse to believe that I, and only I, have thus created my suffering—I dig myself deeper and deeper into my faux-reality, rationalizing it, defending it. It engages me in a continual battle, hot and cold, to make my reality the only true reality. Hence, all arguments, at bottom, are essentially my person-world against yours. And as yours is likely to also be a faux-reality of your own construction, it's "The Battle of the Faux-Realities!" One psychically either enslaves or becomes a prisoner in the world of another. Faux though they be, they can be murderous psychically and sometimes physically.

Not having the understanding, the vibration and stillness to absorb the shock, the descending octave carries my attention to its lowest point of world creation and self-calming. All compensatory. And then what? No matter how I protect myself, another shock is sure to come. Again, the same rent, and so forth, and another person-world-of-the-moment is created. The worlds aren't haphazard; they're linked because the linking component is me, whatever I take that to be. Just as the world so created is a construct, so is the person. And the person, as the faux-god or goddess, creates a chain of worlds with himself/herself at the center. (Remember the biblical admonition: "Ye shall have no other gods before Me"?) And so how do we gods and goddesses live? Well, we live to prevent shocks. Our whole world is set up to prevent shocks. As much as we try to impose order to prevent shocks, disorder happens, must happen, because we live, principally, in the unknown.

No Guarantees

When we go to sleep at night the unconscious assumption is that we will not die in our sleep, so we can relax enough to sleep. Going to sleep—at night or sleepwalking through our day—is really the assumption of "as I have been, so I will be." But this is to discount *Rascooarno*. There are no guarantees, and never have been, of anything remaining as it was. As David Hume, the great Scottish philosopher, famously pointed out, "Just because the sun has risen in the east, as long as we've ever looked at it and our ancestors have ever looked at it, doesn't say that it's going to do so tomorrow." You can't prove the present by the past and you certainly can't prove the future.

So we are left with the recognition that shocks happen. And the shocks are of all types. There's the shock of losing a loved one, the shock of divorce, the shock of losing your job. These are the three biggest shocks, we are told. Why? Well each is a definite world. A world very close to us, a world we identify with deeply. But you could go into a toolbox and not find your hammer, a hammer you expected to be there, and it's a little shock. And what happens? You react to it with irritation. How do you offload that irritation? By blaming somebody else—known or unknown—it doesn't matter. Or, if self-love has a masochistic streak, you blame yourself. The point is, you get rid of that irritation. Why? It upsets the psychological structure, the person-world you've worked so hard to put in place. We do this with all kinds of shocks. Besides friends and lovers and bosses, the biggest recipients are usually parents, those fallen gods and goddesses.

Well, what to do about all this? Nothing—if you're not in an authentic way of self-transformation. You just take the shocks on the chin and get more life insurance, live in a gated community, whatever. But that is not going to help, because shocks are built into the world. Remember *Trogoautoegocrat?*

Thank goodness for shocks! Shocks open closed doors and closed minds. The shocks aren't the problem. It's how we relate to them. The world on every level is eat or be eaten, reciprocal maintenance. In both cases we grow, if we are open to growing. Otherwise, we live a life of contraction. Is my attention/awareness free and strong enough to absorb the shock? If not, why? If it is absorbed, there is more energy, more openness, the activation of more intelligence. If not, it instructs me in what I still have to understand, let go of, decrystallize. That is, if there is sincerity.

[Sound of hand clap] ⚶

Present at the Creation

WHY DO I WISH TO REMEMBER MYSELF? Isn't the deep reason *to be present at the creation?* Yes, Being in the Becoming. The Becoming of Creation is ceaseless, it never stops. At every moment, with every breath, I am re-created. But when I am not present at the creation, I'm where? Seesawing between past and future, denying creation, and so I am automatically being re-created.

Presence & Choice

When we are remembered as "I am" or "I Am," creation still happens, but my relationship to it has changed. "I" have stopped creating the dream state, the waking state. In that denial there is the affirmation of being in the Being of Becoming. "No" is said to the ongoing hypnotic momentum, and "yes" to self-remembering. I can still create, I can still build something, think something, feel something, take something apart, but being present at the creation I can elect to go deeper and deeper into the world of Being. Instead of going automatically forward in time, the movement is backward, outward, upward.

In *All and Everything* Mr. Gurdjieff speaks about this. He affirms there is only one energy. This is the energy that flows out and the energy that flows back, just like our breath. Habituated by society and the impulsions of our own lower nature—man is a two-natured being—we go forward into time, constantly creating. Every creation is in itself 1-2-3. Involution. No manifestation can be higher, encompass totally, the original idea from which it sprang. But what happens when I am present to the doing? Aren't there two creations simultaneously, the one higher, the other lower?

What Is It that Changes?

When we have time on our hands, what do we do? Don't we either get bored, irritated, fall asleep, do something, anything to fill the time. To just "be," to do nothing, is very difficult in the midst of a constant creation ceaselessly going on not only outside me but inside me. If physiological creation wasn't going on inside me on all the various levels—molecular, chemical, and so forth—I wouldn't be here. So though I can affirm my being in Being, live more deeply, I must realize that the impetus, the momentum, is always to go forward. By the act of self-remembering that is denied. Time changes, space changes, awareness of the body changes, awareness of the environment changes. Does it *change*, really? Isn't it that I change? Isn't it that I've stepped up to a higher vibration, a higher relationship? It's not the world of name and place and form and history. It's an *Immediacy*, a simultaneity, a nonlinear experiencing of a scale beyond the Kantian categories of mind (words, being symbols, can only reflect, can never be what they reflect). The chatter stops. Yes, errant thoughts or feelings may arise, but they are given no attention, are immediately assimilated. We don't say "I" to them, we "eat" them. They are food. If we don't, they eat us, and we are taken down into the person again; we slip back into the static world of history, heroes and villains. That world is constantly being created by people who, without choice, have taken a position in that world, the world of the diplomat, general, politician, criminal, business-man, citizen. The position is unconscious; that is, unconscious of being in Being. Not that such people are unintelligent, lack tal-ent or character—though, of course, they may—but they live in the domain of the automatic unconscious. Not affirming being in Being, they must constantly affirm their becoming and fight to maintain it. Intellectually, they may admit it is transitory and can only end in disintegration, but were they to act with this knowledge they chance losing the one thing they strive to keep: their power.

The idea, let alone the experience, of both not acting and acting simultaneously is completely foreign. They are all action when they act, all thinking when they think. To be and to not be simultane-ously is beyond their comprehension. For them, one either is or is not. The idea that one can be and not be at the same time is simply mumbo jumbo, sophistry. And so they remain pawns of power and glory. When reaching the last rank on the world's chessboard they become queens or rooks, knights or bishops, whatever the historical moment calls for.

A Higher Creation

To be present at the creation, we must deny the becomingness of creation for *the higher creation*, the 'creation' of consciousness. We are speaking of this from the standpoint of the person, because in reality there is no creation. Being is always, I am and I am not. I am no-thingness and I am nothingness. I Am.

Gurdjieff speaks of our Common Uni-Being-Endlessness, the primordial, that which is and is not, beyond description, metaphor. The ancient Egyptians speak of a primordial darkness, mystery, water, out of which emerges an island, the "homeland of the pri-meval ones." It is the urge for creation of the Creator God that creates all the other gods and all that exists in the descent of this primordial octave that manifests this God's Ray of Creation. And with time, *Heropass*, that island must eventually slip back into the primordial sea. The Hindus speak of Brahma creating on the out breath, Vishnu maintaining the out breath, then Shiva appearing, the dissolution of the in breath, a whole world like a bubble popping and on the next breath, a new world coming to creation. Is that the same Brahma? Is Brahma #1 the same as Brahma #2? In Absolute essence, of course, it would have to be, but could there possibly be different aspects that are highlighted with the emergence of every new Creator God? Could it be that there isn't one God but a number of gods? That the god of the ancient Egyptians is not the Yahweh of the Jews, the Father of Christianity or the Allah of Islam? And yet it is. And it is not. Is this difference in Creator Gods at the core of the conflict we see between people of different religions? Could it be that the Creator Gods of the different religions are really different, and yet one and the same? Is it for us to expand our being to the point where we can simultaneously understand these supposedly irreconcilable points of view?

The End of Religion?

People say that God has spoken to them. Gurdjieff says that God doesn't speak, the angels speak. There must be a telepathy between the Creator God, gods and angels. And so when we are spoken to, we are spoken to by angels. Martin Heidegger, the great philosopher of ontology, says the only thing that could save us now is the speaking of a new god. His essay, "The Question of Technology," cuts to the root—unless man awakens and consciously guides and controls technology, it will enframe him in the automatic. Joseph Campbell says we live in "a terminal moraine of myth." There is no more myth, no more central belief. Others say God has left us, is dead. Perhaps it is we who have left. By being present at the creation, by denying automatic creation, we make a call not only on ourselves but to That which is higher.

The great religions appear to have come to their final manifestation. Fundamentalist extremism is carrying the day. That can only portend a new step. As many historians have pointed out, modernity is always presaged by a return to fundamentalism. At an accelerated time when we are flung into the future, we look back. As Marshal McLuhan put it, "We're driving into the future, looking into the rear view mirror." Why? Because we are not in the car, we're not driving it, we're not present at the creation.

In the midst of the Russian Revolution, Gurdjieff guided his people between two opposing armies and over the bandit-infested

Caucasus. Before setting out he told them that "Conscience must guide us, that conscience is innate. We only have to awaken it." We awaken it by being present at the creation. ⅍

Our Perfection & Why We Refuse It

MR. GURDJIEFF SAYS THAT THE WORK FOR SELF-PERFECTION CHANGED after the *Choot-God-Litanical* period, "that all-universal calamity, a terrifying cosmic event," when the purity of the *Theomertmalogos*, the Word-God, the Emanation of the Most Holy Sun Absolute, the most sacred substance, began to issue with "the admixture of subjective properties of extraneously caused arisings." This produced a disharmony in the inner functioning of certain of the planets, which then began to effect the crystallizing of the higher-being-parts of those working for Self-Perfection.

What was this *Choot-God-Litanical* period? Gurdjieff doesn't say, but I intuit that it is when the fiery youth Beelzebub confronted Our Endlessness and almost caused a universal rebellion. The root cause of his rebellion was that our young rebel, who had become "an attendant on His Endlessness," saw something he considered "illogical" in the government of the World and, as Gurdjieff tells us, he "interfered in what was none of his business." What did Beelzebub see? I intuit that it was the apparent injustice that seems to reign in the World.

Gurdjieff speaks of himself early on as a "Compassionate Idiot." I intuit that this is precisely what Beelzebub was and why he was exiled to the solar system Ors and the planet Mars. In a word, he felt for our suffering and all the suffering of creatures throughout the World.

It was only after his long exile in which he performed many duties that he became acquainted with *Kundabuffer*, the self-love and vanity that dominate those not awakened to their real self. *Kundabuffer* was an organ implanted in human beings so they would be blinded to their reason-for-being. A colossal blunder, the organ was removed, but its properties still persisted.

So, our quest is to rid ourselves of our identification with our self-love and vanity and develop and perfect our bodies so we can be in the Self-perfection of That which eternally Is. However, Gurdjieff reveals to us that even if we attain to becoming worthy of living on the Holy Planet Purgatory, because of the resulting admixture of the *Choot-God-Litanical* period, we will remain apart from His Endlessness as long as we are not completely purged of these subjective qualities.

This admission, I believe, is at the root of Gurdjieff's *Legominism*. It is he, as a representative of Beelzebub, or Beelzebub himself incarnated in the body of a young Greek-Armenian of a low caste, much the same as Gurdjieff tells us happened with Ashiata Shiemsh who was "actualized in the planetary body of a three-brained being of a boy of a poor family as a definitized conception of a sacred Individual," who is speaking to us.

He is giving us the necessary esoteric teaching and practices which will enable us in turn to create a *Kesdjan* body, an emotional body, an intellectual body, and finally a soul which will be immortal with our solar system.

But I sense he may also be confessing—his *Legominism* is a confession as well as many other things—that because of his youthful rebellion we will likely never attain complete Self-perfection.

Does that mean we should give up and indulge ourselves and garner as much earthly pleasure as we possibly can? If we wish to.

That's one stream. He offers us another.

And who is "us"? Those of his Tribe and those who wish to become part of his Tribe. That is, he offers it to those like him in essence—rebels!

That context laid out, what about this notion of perfection? We are all striving for it, but the striving is for the person to become perfect. In doing so, we not only see our own imperfection, but we see that of others and, of course, constantly chide them to become perfect.

Why do we do this? We will get to that.

But first we should understand that as persons we are already perfect. We don't have to do anything, become anything—we are perfectly imperfect! Why do we resist this? Because we want to become better persons than we are. Not better beings but better persons.

This is an impossibility as the person is already perfect but does not see or accept this. Hence, all the striving, struggle, tension, psychic and physical warfare.

The person is, as Gurdjieff says, an overlay on the three-centered bioplasmic machine that we are. The machine itself, given its hereditary nature and nurture conditioning, is perfect. That is, perfect in its imperfection. Each of us has always been, perfectly been, what we are. That is, three-centered machines which function and misfunction. If you are a genius machine, you are a perfect genius. If a retard, then a perfect retard. And everything else in between. Of course, the centers are rarely, if ever, equal in their development, and so one might be intellectually quite brilliant and emotionally quite naïve, or instinctively a barbarian. As persons we are perfect in our imperfection and cannot be otherwise.

This, fortunately, is not entirely true. If we can recognize, that is observe impartially, that we are simply functioning and misfunctioning machines and that we have overlaid this with the notion of being a person, an individual, that we can observe what we are—bioplasmic machines!

We can begin to see how the machine acts in the world, its postures, gestures, facial expressions, tones of voice and so forth. We can see the dreams and attitudes and lies and omissions of each of the centers of our machine, and we will see the imperfections of its perfection.

Now what is that sees?

That which sees is not what it sees.

The machine, high efficiency or low, occurs in our seeing. If there is not identification, that is, no arising of the so-called person, then the seeing is impartial.

To the degree one still takes himself to be a person there will, of course, be suffering. That is, as said earlier, necessary. Suffering is an essential principle of creation, something our Compassionate One had to learn, like all of us, the hard way.

But to the degree the self-observation is impartial then an inner space is created between the object and the subject in which Intelligence can appear. The emergence of Intelligence so influences the machine that it becomes more than a machine. It becomes physical in the real sensing of that word and so lays the ground for the *Kesdjan* and the other bodies. This of course with the breathing and sensing that occurs with the advent of Intelligence.

The machine, then, begins to operate at its most efficient level, given its limitations of hereditary nature and nurture. But as one knows that they are not the machine, and that they are the machine, this is simply a grounding factor. One day the machine will stall out and Intelligence will be set free from earthly limitations.

However, as long as we insist on taking ourselves as persons, then we will try to perfect our persons, and to the degree we do—because every machine can be perfected to a degree beyond its comfort zone—our very success will be our entombment, for it will trap us in the person.

Through the Beelzebub-given practices of self-remembering and self-observation, the latter impartial and directed at dissecting the workings of the three centers, we can rid ourselves of the person concept, the self-image, the false personality, and see ourselves starkly as what we are—three centered bioplasmic machines.

As long as we persist in thinking the person is observing the machine, all perceptions are skewed and discolored with the conceit of agency, the person.

The person is a construct, a way of avoiding the truth of the machine. And the resultant attitudes of utopian perfection that will some day happen, if only . . . If only what? If only we were rational? But machines are not rational above the binary degree of being a machine. Therefore, all attempts to improve the world, to improve oneself, while rooted in the notion of the person, are by definition, impossible of creation, for the simple fact that no matter how far we go in perfecting our machine life, we will still be machines, deny it to the very end though we will. Hence, the folly of ordinary human life, the eternal weeping and waling and grinding of teeth, all in actually so unnecessary.

It is only by accepting our perfection, as previously defined, that true self-observation can begin, true release from the functioning and misfunctioning of the machine, can rightfully occur.

And we can realize that which we truly are, have been, and will always be, so help us God.

And thank you, Mr. Beelzebub, rebel extraordinaire! ⟋⟋

Have a Soul, Make a Soul

How often do we remember ourselves? How many times on any given day and for what duration? Whatever our answer, what's happening the rest of the time?

When I'm not in the state of self-remembrance, what state

am I in? We've read about it, we've all talked about it. But does this other state come readily to mind, this state other than self-remembering?

I mean, I get through the day. I get by. Some days better than others. I work, relate, eat, return home. Go through the habit-honored routines and go to sleep, physical sleep. And so it goes.... Not to worry. I have a soul. It won't be dust to dust. I'm too important. *I have a soul.* Isn't that the root belief?

Some 5,000 years ago there was another belief. The ancient Egyptians believed one had to make a soul. At first the belief was that only the pharaoh could make a soul. Later, the idea of soul-making included the nobles. Still later, everyone could make a soul. At some juncture the belief passed from everyone *making* a soul to everyone *having* one. That was certainly comforting. But having a soul also meant you could lose it, depending on the way you lived. The soul had to be light as a feather or you would be fed to the rhino.

About 3,000 years ago Moses went up the mountain, spoke to God, and returned with the Ten Commandments. It was God's prescription for how we should live. Over time, these ten rules were expanded to over five hundred rules. About 2,500 years ago the ancient Greeks introduced philosophy, rationality, the love of wisdom. In *Phaedrus,* Plato spoke quite beautifully about his vision of the soul, its fall and incarnation. Some 500 years later, Jesus Christ introduced the idea of salvation and resurrection of one's soul through faith in God. Some 600 years later, Allah spoke through Mohammed, saying that Allah is everything, and one must surrender their life to Allah otherwise they were infidels. Some 1,300 years later another Messenger from Above appeared. He told us we had no soul but could make one. With that the long trajectory of ideas about the soul comes full circle—*we have to make a soul.*

But the consensual belief, constantly reinforced for thousands of years, is that I was born with a soul, God-given, no strings attached. So while intellectually I find the idea interesting that a soul has to be made—it's food for the intellect—do I emotionally accept that I don't have one?

I have read, of course, that I have no indivisible I, no free will, cannot do. I am just a bundle of "I"s. Now something strange happens, a kind of mental jujitsu I am not aware of. Because I comprehend the idea linguistically, I unconsciously assume I am not reading about myself but about other people. It's not volitional. A psychological buffer separates me from what I am reading. It keeps me asleep in the belief that I am an indivisible I.

Now when I remember myself or, better, when I am remembered, and observe—what do I observe? I observe the "I-of-the-moment." Another "I," the "self-improvement-I," almost instantly appears that wants to improve the previous "I," followed by another "I" that thinks it futile, and so the "fight-of-the-'I's" begins, a "yes" against a "no," and so it goes. Though this is observed time and again, some part of me simply won't accept that I am all "I"s and not a real I. It takes a great sincerity—*and sincerity must be learned*—to admit without justification or excuse that almost all my life is lived in the waking sleep of my meta-belief in myself as an indivisible I.

Four states exist: physical sleep; waking state, which is a waking sleep; self-remembering; and the fourth state in which self transcends itself—but is there a conscious awareness of them? The waking state has a seamless quality—a stream not of consciousness but its opposite. Attention is rarely in the Immediate but either ahead or behind it. Only a shock, a disruption, internal or external, breaks the hypnotic circuitry. Momentarily, the revolving mental wheel of future-past and past-future is shocked to stillness. Psychological time ends. An awareness of space appears, a certain separation. But then, almost immediately, the space is psychologized by the "I-of-the-moment." This "I" either eats me, my attention, or my attention eats it. That is, if the self-remembering is strong and lasting enough to allow for self-observation that does not devolve to reaction, then this "I" is eaten. In this eating of "I"s, the false personality, which substrates the "I-structure," weakens and allows a space for essence to grow. Will and self-knowledge develop, as does being, and a commensurate level of understanding appears. The tempo of life changes, as does one's chemistry. The physical body now well-fed gives birth to a *Kesdjan* body, and, like Russian dolls, the emotional and mental bodies then develop, and finally, we are told, a soul is formed. This self-transformation can only occur if one is consciously working with one's sleep. But how can this happen if I can't admit that I'm asleep?

About states, Mr. Gurdjieff says:

> In order to understand what the difference between
> states of consciousness is, let us return to the first state
> of consciousness which is sleep. This is an entirely sub-
> jective state of consciousness. A man is immersed in
> dreams, whether he remembers them or not does not
> matter. Even if some real impressions reach him, such
> as sounds, voices, warmth, cold, the sensation of his
> own body, they arouse in him only fantastic subjective
> images. Then a man wakes up. At first glance this is a
> quite different state of consciousness. He can move,
> he can talk with other people, he can make calcula-
> tions ahead, he can see danger and avoid it, and so on.
> It stands to reason that he is in a better position than
> when he was asleep. But if we go a little more deeply
> into things, if we take a look into his inner world, into
> his thoughts, into the causes of his actions, we shall see
> that he is in almost the same state as when he is asleep.
> And it is even worse, because in sleep he is passive, that
> is, he cannot do anything. In the waking state, however,
> he can do something all the time and the results of all
> his actions will be reflected upon him or upon those
> around him. *And yet he does not remember himself.* He
> is a machine, everything with him *happens.* He cannot
> stop the flow of his thoughts, he cannot control his
> imagination, his emotions, his attention. He lives in a
> subjective world of "I love," "I do not love," "I like," "I
> do not like," "I want," "I do not want," that is, of what
> he thinks he likes, of what he thinks he does not like, of
> what he thinks he wants, of what he thinks he does not
> want. He does not see the real world. The real world is
> hidden from him by the wall of imagination. *He lives in
> sleep.* He is asleep. What is called "clear consciousness"
> is sleep and a far more dangerous sleep than sleep at
> night in bed.

So the great and precious invitation we've all been given is the
word he brings and the practices he gives in which there can be an

awakening. One can bring a soul into life. And so the aim: Being in the Becoming of life, and so to consciously eat the inertia and negativity, and to experience the peace and the harmony, and the joy and the pleasure, the creativity, the self-expression. But it must be worked for. Conscious life, incarnation, immortality—they do not come cheaply.

Fourth Way Essays

The essays are selected from those published in
The Gurdjieff Journal *and other publications*
that pertain to the theme of this book.

Son of Man: The Spiritual Machine

EVERY TIME HAS ITS QUESTIONS. HOW IT ANSWERS THOSE QUESTIONS not only defines that time but, more importantly, the time to come. The adage "as a man thinketh, so he is," might be better formulated "as a man defines himself, so he is." Within a time period, the defining questions are difficult to discern, but certainly in our time a likely candidate is: Can a machine be conscious?

Through the drumbeat of commercialized propaganda (let us call advertising by its real name), computers are referred to as "friendly," "intuitive" and "intelligent." Consciousness, then, certainly seems "doable."

But, how to define consciousness?

Ray Kurzweil, a pioneering computer scientist and inventor, and author of the book *The Age of Spiritual Machines*, defines consciousness as "The ability to have subjective experience, the ability of a being, animal or entity to have self-perception and self-awareness. The ability to feel. A key question in the twenty-first century is whether computers will achieve consciousness (which their human creators are considered to have)."

That Kurzweil does not directly ascribe consciousness to human beings may place him with Behaviorists, like the late B. F. Skinner, but he doesn't want to put forth, as Mr. Gurdjieff does, the idea that humans are not conscious, have no indivisible I, no free will, and are, in fact, machines. No, he sidesteps the issue—his great love, idée fixe, being machines. His interest in humans appears to be only as they relate to, and can be reverse engineered for, the benefit of binary machines.

Because of the continual doubling of memory capacity and computing speed, Kurzweil predicts computers will achieve the capacity and speed of the human brain by about the year 2020; this means computers will be capable of twenty million billion calculations per second. And that, he says, is just the beginning.

He reasons that because the human brain follows the laws of physics it must be a machine. By reverse engineering the human brain to see how it works, and then applying that to a neural networking scheme, computers will be able to "match the human brain in subtlety and complexity of thought." Neural networking is a computer simulation of human neurons. It is "a system (implanted in software or hardware) that is intended to emulate the computing structure of neurons in the human brain" of which there are one hundred billion.

Nonbiological Intelligence?

Recognizing that time is not constant but has periods when it speeds up and slows down, Kurzweil says that we are now entering the "knee of the curve." This is a time when "the exponential nature of the curve of time explodes inwardly or outwardly" and major events multiply. And so machines, which he refers to as "nonbiological entities," will quickly outpace human evolution. "[There will be] a new form of intelligence on Earth," he says, and inasmuch as he equates intelligence with consciousness, and consciousness with spirituality—the next New Age spirituality is the nonbiological, not the biological. "Nonbiological entities," according to Kurzweil, "are going to vastly expand in the breadth, depth and subtlety of their intelligence and creativity," so much so that we will "be able to download our minds onto computer hardware . . . the essence of our identity will switch to the permanence of our software."

Here we come to the question behind the question—which is not whether nonbiological entities can become conscious but, rather, can human beings become conscious? That is, how do we define human identity? Gurdjieff's answer, and we suspect Kurzweil would agree, is that "Man is a machine" . . . until he becomes conscious of himself. "There are moments," explained Gurdjieff, "when you become aware not only of what you are doing but also of yourself doing it. You see both 'I' and the 'here' of 'I am here'—both the anger and the 'I' that is angry. Call this self-remembering, if you like. Now when you are fully aware of the 'I' and what it is doing and which 'I' it is—you become conscious of yourself." (And, of course, this is only the beginning.)

A Fundamental Mistake

In his review of Kurzweil's book "I Married a Computer," the philosopher John R. Searle points out that Kurzweil makes the fundamental mistake of equating a computer simulation of human functions with true duplication. (In his book Kurzweil seems to be overly identified with virtual reality as it relates to human sexuality—whereby you create your own custom tailored, simulated partner—which is, all bells and whistles deleted, simply cyber-masturbation.) Whatever it is doing, whether playing chess against Gary Kasparov or having sex, the computer can never know, be aware of, what it is doing. "From everything we know about the brain," Searle points out, "and everything we know about computation, increased computation power in a machine [Kurzweil's primary argument] gives us no reason whatever to suppose that the machine is duplicating the specific neurobiological powers of the brain to create consciousness."

Of course, just as computer terminology has incorporated other human attributes such as "intuition" to the workings of a binary digital machine, Kurzweil and his followers will likely begin to discriminate between "machine knowing" and "human knowing."

Calculating Isn't Thinking

Kurzweil asks, "Are computers thinking, or are they just calculating? Conversely, are human beings thinking or are they just calculating?" A wonderfully incisive question for the answer is—for anyone who has observed himself or herself—calculating. That is, when not dreaming. The philosopher Martin Heidegger in his book *What Is Called Thinking?* explores the question in depth and says, "Science does not think." Rather, it mostly calculates. True thinking originates in silence. Quoting the pre-Socratic philosopher Parmenides, Heidegger says, "For it is the same thing to think and to be." But he goes further: "The essential nature of thinking is determined by what there is to be thought about: the presence of what is present, the Being of beings."

Deeper still than the question of thinking is that both Kurzweil and Searle take the intellectual human brain as the be-all and end-all of human cognition. But what is being simulated or duplicated (take your pick) is only the formatory brain, the mechanical part of the intellectual brain. They know nothing of the two other ordinary brains of which Gurdjieff speaks—the emotional and the instinctual—let alone the higher emotional and higher intellectual brains. And so in creating their "conscious" nonbiological entity, Kurzweil and followers can only be replicating the lowest part of the brain. *But believing it is the highest, they will define it as such.* In emulating the Creator, who created mankind in his image—all human beings, potentially, being the Son of God—the cyberists will create their very own "Son of Man," the so-called "spiritual machine." To the extent our children accept this infernal delusion, they will be so defined. Humankind will be thus well on its way to becoming bees and ants, while the "Son of Man"—made in man's own formatory image—is on full parade.

Heidegger, in his seminal essay "The Question of Technology," declared that the essence of technology is to "enframe" life, to include all and everything within its unknowing but powerful binary grip. "The rule of enframing," he warned, "threatens man with the possibility that it could be denied to him to enter into a more original revealing and hence to experience the call of a more primal truth. Thus where enframing reigns, there is danger in the highest sense." ⚔

Notes

1. *Consciousness.* The question was first raised in our time by C. Daly King (1895–1963), who met A. R. Orage in 1924. He met G. I. Gurdjieff a few years later. Of Gurdjieff, he said, "He is the only person ever met by the writer who gave the indubitable impression that all his responses, mental, emotional and practical, were mutually in balance and thus the further impression that everyone else was out of step, but not this man himself. It is just what would be expected, though unpredictable, by a sophisticated Waking person [a person in the waking state of existence] when confronted by someone else in the state of Awakeness." King studied The Fourth Way teaching with Orage until Orage's return to England in 1931. His books include *The Psychology of Consciousness* (London: Kegan Paul, 1932), *The States of Human Consciousness* (New York: University Books, 1963), and *The Oragean Version*, privately printed, 1951.

2. *A key question.* Ray Kurzweil, *The Age of Spiritual Machines—When Computers Exceed Human Intelligence* (New York: Viking, 1999).

3. *Man is a machine until.* G. I. Gurdjieff, *Views from the Real World* (New York: E. P. Dutton, 1973), 79–80.

4. *Fundamental mistake.* John Searle, "I Married a Computer," *The New York Review of Books*, 8 April 1999. In jest, Searle's title associates to Philip Roth's book *I Married a Communist*, which is his attack on his former wife, Claire Bloom, whose book *Leaving the Doll's House* shows Roth to be schizoid and obsessed with sex.

5. *Creation of consciousness.* Of course, looking at the question in this way, or from this direction, presupposes the creation of consciousness. As Colin McGinn expresses it in his "Can We Ever Understand Consciousness," *The New York Review of Books*, 10 June 1999, "The problem, precisely, is how it is that the higher-level biological processes of consciousness result from

lower-level physical properties of neurons." But what if consciousness *is*—and is not created? What if by a redirection and redistribution of attention out of the formatory mind, the mechanical part of the intellectual center, we so maximize our potential vibratory intelligence that the higher emotional and higher intellectual centers are accessed? And in that accessing, consciousness is actualized. This formulation is, of course, made from the perspective of the lower. From the higher perspective of consciousness itself, there never was a time when it was not. And in accessing that perspective, all notions and definitions of higher and lower and so forth are seen to be what they are—state specific. They are applicable to a given world or rate of vibration. At higher rates, they have no meaning.

6. *Thinking.* Kurzweil defines this as "A sequence of rules and instructions that describes a procedure to solve a problem. A computer program expresses one or more algorithms in a manner understandable to a computer."

7. *Science does not think.* Martin Heidegger, *What Is Called Thinking?* (New York: Harper & Row, 1968), 240, 244.

8. *Essential nature of thinking.* Martin Heidegger, "The Question of Technology," *Basic Writings* (New York: Harper & Row, 1977), 309.

From *The Gurdjieff Journal* (TGJ) #20

The Future of Danger & Paranoia

Why are we so afraid of the future? To be sure, we live in a time of great transition, between two great ages—the Industrial and Technological. The transition between the two is likely to be even more profound than in the early 1800s, when society shifted from an Agrarian worldview to the Industrial. The resulting physical dislocations caused a great trauma for rural inhabitants forced to look for jobs in urban factories. But the deeper, more lasting dislocations were psychological and spiritual. The resulting losses of faith and hope, and of identity, customs and values, created a shock whose tremors lasted for generations.

A great many voices are warning against the technologized life we now enter. One of the more interesting is Romano Guardini, who, in his book *The End of the Modern World,* makes the point that the growth of mankind's intellectual and scientific capabilities makes it possible for him to engage in work he either does not, or cannot, experience. Digital technology allows the manipulation of abstraction upon abstraction, as do the experiments of modern physics, all *without* any genuine sensory experience. Guardini does not mention that digital impressions differ radically from analog—digital are received by the left hemisphere of the brain, analog by the right. The brain reaction of telling time by a digital watch, for example, is different from that of older analog watches that have hands instead of readouts. As we digitize life, we become more and more left brained, that is, conceptual, analytical and verbal.

"The rise of technology," Guardini declares, "[in turn] is creating a radically different sociological type and attitude." He calls this new type "Mass Man," a man who is "fashioned according to the law of standardization, a law dictated by the functional nature of the machine." The most highly developed of the mass men are "not merely conscious of the influence of the machine; they deliberately imitate it, building its standards and rhythms into their own ethos." From this imitation will come a new culture; one which will "be incomparably more harsh and more intense . . . a single fact, we must emphasize, will stamp the new culture: danger."

This impending sense of danger permeates modern life in social spheres as well as economic. William Greider delineates a root cause—a kind of musical chairs supply game—in his book, *One World, Ready or Not*. He writes:

> The global revolution has deranged the logic of standard business calculations. The conventional decision-making is not only greatly accelerated (and complicated) by globalization, but also gravely altered. The new machines introduce dramatic opportunities both to reduce costs and to increase output—more for less—but on an exponential scale. *The same machines have given capital wings* and allowed firms to disperse globally, going after shares in markets that were once securely local. Above all, by steadily expanding the potential supply, the breakout of new production methods and products creates pervasive downward pressures on prices. [Emphasis added.]

Digital technology has provided finance capital with a global horn of plenty. Affiliated with no nation or ideology, it moves strictly in accordance with the iron law of maximum return on investment, punishing and rewarding nations and companies accordingly:

> The old standard logic is thus destabilized: the imperative to modernize must be heeded lest a company lose out in the price competition, but the modernizing process also makes the supply problem worse. When companies adopt the technologies that reduce costs and protect their market shares, the inescapable result is to enlarge productive capacity. They do this to keep up, though it means supply surpluses will steadily accumulate somewhere in the marketplace— goods that can't be sold, plants that can't be operated at full capacity. *Someone somewhere will have to eat the losses.* Business people hope that it is not their company. [Emphasis added.]

Several years ago Mexico had to "eat the losses" when billions were pulled out of its market by nervous financiers. Only a large U.S. loan prevented Mexico from plunging into chaos. Mexico then undertook stringent economic measures that sent interest rates and unemployment soaring. The result: rampant prostitution, daylight stickups, carjackings, and crime so commonplace that neighborhoods are privately erecting gates and hiring security guards.

> All companies are thus caught in a continuing scramble to avoid holding the surpluses, protecting themselves by closing factories in a timely manner or unloading excess goods at prices that injure their rivals. To preserve their position, they are compelled to keep doing more of the same: more cost reduction and price-cutting and, in turn, more expansion of potential supply. The circle continues, with its destructive element concealed by the fabulous expansiveness of the system.
>
> The supply problem is not the only way global revolution upends standard practices, but it is the one most central to everything else that happens. *The supply factor and ancillary dislocations explain the desperate edge to the global competition, where even the strongest firms*

sometimes sound paranoid about the future. [Emphasis added.]

The paranoia results in the manic Vince Lombardi "winning is everything" corporate atmosphere, demanding faster and faster time-to-market with fewer and fewer people and a bigger and bigger bottom line.

The future, if the present course is not altered, is not hard to forecast. But that is a very large if, for who can say what new shocks lie in wait? The challenge for those engaged in the process of spiritual transformation is to find a way of working with—and not worrying and speculating about—the societal danger and paranoia. Some years ago, Lord John Pentland spoke about the need to first conceptually understand the cosmology and philosophy of The Fourth Way. Later, having worked on oneself, one could relate it to, and thus better assimilate and understand, one's experience. The same is true with delineating what is happening, and why, to the societal and economic worlds. To be able to be—as is often said—in the world but not of the world. ⋌

Notes

1. *The rise of technology.* Romano Guardini, *The End of the Modern World* (Wilmington, DE: 1998), 76.
2. *The global revolution.* William Greider, *One World, Ready or Not* (New York: Simon & Schuster, 1997), 46.

From TGJ #13

Periods in the Life of Humanity

There are periods in the life of humanity which generally coincide with the beginning of the fall of cultures and civilizations, when the masses irretrievably lose their reason. . . . Such periods of mass madness, often coinciding with geophysical cataclysms, climatic changes, and similar phenomena of a planetary character, release a very great quantity of the matter of knowledge.
—G. I. Gurdjieff

Does what Mr. Gurdjieff says about periods in the life of humanity correspond to what is happening now in the world— 9/11, the Afghan and Iraqi wars, occupations, beheadings, torture, suicide bombers, the Israeli "wall," the extinguishing of plant and animal species, global warming? Does all this correspond to what Gurdjieff is saying about "periods of mass madness"?

Correspondence? Possibly. But how can we know? What can be said is that the world is in the midst of a radical transformation as it moves from an older, industrialized, nation-based society to what may be called a scientific-technologized-global society. This transformation proceeds not only on the level of how we live our daily lives but, more deeply, through redefining human identity and the meaning and purpose of human life on earth.

"Spiritual Fascism"

It is likely that religion as we have known it is in its last days. Weakened by historical time and the increasing power of the materialistic-technological-scientific forces pitted against it, religion may disappear in a matter of decades. The power we see today of fundamentalism, be it Christian, Judaic or Islamic, is not a sign of renewed strength but their last stand against the sandstorm of modernity that is burying them. While there has been a confluence of impelling factors that has resulted in "the clash of civilizations," it is religion that waves the most visible banner.

There are many ways to characterize the reciprocal destruction playing out in historical Palestine and Mesopotamia, but from a Work perspective it could be perceived as a clash between a mental-centered world and an instinctive one. It cannot end well. Identifications are too primary. Whatever its end, both sides will likely be so morally-spiritually-economically weakened that just as America rose to its full power in the aftermath of World War II, so Asia will rise. When it is asked how we blundered away our good reputation, turned the world against us, and lied our way into a no-win quagmire, religion will be the most visible scapegoat.

Even excluding this scenario, the religions of the book, be it the Torah, New Testament or Koran, are unfortunately doomed to irrelevance by modernity. (Unfortunately, because they are the templates upon which civilizations have been founded, and when

they crack what is to replace them?) The way forward into an acceptance of modernity thus blocked, religions rigidify the past, cloak
themselves in fundamentalism, so literal and violent in their interpretations as to become a "spiritual fascism." Of course, the softer
versions of religion, along with the feel-good, God-is-your-friend
megachurches with their prosperity pitches, will buck and sway,
but this will only hasten their end.

Counter-Initiation

Living in a time without religion is exceedingly dangerous.
Psychic trapdoors to humanity's underside expose people to the
lowest and most infernal influences, along with a "counter-initiation," as the Orientalist René Guénon has warned. The culture
may refract into a myriad of belief systems held together only by
the common belief, if not worship, of the economic. But, rightly
or wrongly, as Guénon argued as early as 1942:

> The all too common illusion consists in imagin-
> ing that relations established in the field of trade can
> serve to draw people closer together and bring about
> an understanding between them, whereas in reality the
> effect is just the contrary. Matter partakes essentially of
> the nature of multiplicity and division, and is there-
> fore a source of struggle and conflict.... The economic
> sphere remains and cannot but remain one of a rivalry
> of interests. In particular the West cannot count upon
> industry, any more than upon modern science which
> is inseparable from it, to supply a basis for an under-
> standing with the East; if Orientals get to the point of
> accepting industry as a troublesome, though transitory,
> necessity—and for them it could hardly amount to more
> than that—it will only be as a weapon enabling them
> to resist the invasion of the West and to safeguard their
> own existence.

The Reign of Scientism

Some sixty years after World War II, the world watches as the
United States tries to spread democratic capitalism by force and

threat of arms to what was once the Ottoman Empire. That it guards Iraq's oil ministry and not its museums, which hold artifacts dating back to early Mesopotamia, the beginning of civilization as we know it, epitomizes the ignorant and arrogant mind-set involved.

With the weakening of religion, a new octave is bound to emerge—and it has already begun. Just look at the chain bookstores—paganism, pseudo-religions, pseudo-esoterica. Man needs to believe in something higher than himself—and so the substitution for organized religion is channeling, Wicca, theosophic blunderbuss, New Age "conversations with God" and the like. Generations of fatherless and weak-fathered young people are sure to be drawn into these comforting cults, the word *cult* used in its contemporary rather than its time-honored sense. But greater than this will be the reign of Scientism, the worship of science and technology, which, too, is already empowering itself. Where Wicca and its sister manifestations will offer a comforting entanglement in a spidery web of psychic imagination—the false anima—Scientism will offer a reductive reasoning that trumpets the destruction of human identity and aspiration as a breakthrough rather than breakdown, rendering humans into little more than "machines"—the false animus. A machine identity, once accepted, allows for the basest instincts to play out. Hence, people become subhuman and animalistic in behavior and belief.

Of course, Gurdjieff also proposed that people were machines, that is, having no individual I, but only an "I" in quotation marks, an "I" that changes with outer and inner shocks and circumstances. Having no real I, he says, we have no free will and cannot do, are asleep and thus mechanical. It is the darkest of images, its very darkness calling forth the light if one will sincerely and persistently practice *being-Partkdolg-duty*. Gurdjieff said that of all the so-called cosmic truths we think we know, "the only true one of them all is 'We are the images of God.'" We have taken this to mean that we have a soul and continually comfort ourselves with this notion. In accepting it, and its concomitant idea of salvation, we then enter the iron grip in which whatever we do and say might cause us to lose this soul, be sent to Hell. Hence, the tyranny of the fundamentalist pulpit.

But, according to Gurdjieff, we first must make a soul. As images of God we are undeveloped, that is, negative images. Like camera film, we must undergo chemical solutions in a dark room in order to develop the positive image. Those solutions and that dark room are the esoteric work on oneself through the conscious assimilation of impressions that allows not only the seeing of what is but the feeling through the intentional habitation of the body by means of attention, sensation and breath, which leads to an alchemical transmutation through the stages of *Stopinders* leading to the octave of real I.

A Teaching for Our Time

The teaching Gurdjieff brought a century before the shock of 9/11 and its mechanical aftermath, based not upon dogma and ethics but individual verification and conscious exploration, is a teaching for our time. The origin of the teaching, he said, was esoteric Christianity. And furthermore, "It is completely self-supporting and independent of other lines and it has been completely unknown up to the present time." This declaration has never been sufficiently appreciated, which is why neo-Sufis Idries Shah and Anna Challenger could publish their fictions and polemics in regard to the Work and be taken seriously.

Gurdjieff speaks of "a great quantity of the matter of knowledge" being released during the periods of which he speaks. All is composed of vibration from the slowest and densest matter to the very fastest, least dense vibration. "Knowledge," says Gurdjieff, "like everything else in the world, is material. . . . One of the first characteristics of materiality is that matter is always limited, that is to say, the quantity of matter in a given place and under given conditions is limited." Periods of reciprocal destruction release this knowledge, which can be used by those not identified with the mass madness for not only their own transformation but as the seeds of a new and more intelligent and harmonious movement.

Whatever the time period we are in, it is certain reciprocal destruction, strife and misery will continue to discolor and distort human life as long as we refuse to take responsibility for the "war" in our own lives. As Gurdjieff said: "War has many causes. Some are in us, others outside. We must begin with the causes in us. How can we be independent of external influences when we are slaves of all that surrounds us." 𝒳

Notes

1. *Counter-initiation.* René Guénon, *The Reign of Quantity & The Signs of the Times* (Baltimore, MD: Penguin Books, 1972), 313–20.
2. *All too common illusion.* René Guénon, *Crisis of the Modern World* (London: Luzac and Co. Ltd., 1975), 87.
3. *It is completely self-supporting.* Ouspensky, *In Search of the Miraculous,* 286.
4. *War has many causes.* Ouspensky, 104.

From TGJ #37

How to Work with a Historic Confrontation

THE YEAR IS 1907 AND P. D. OUSPENSKY, JOURNALIST FOR THE Moscow daily paper *The Morning*, must write an article on the Hague Conference, which preceded the First World War.

> I have just received the foreign papers, and I have to write an article on the forthcoming Conference. Phrases, phrases, sympathetic, critical, ironical, blatant, pompous, lying and, worst of all, utterly automatic, phrases which have been used a thousand times and will be used again on entirely different, perhaps contradictory, occasions. . . . What is the use of attempting to expose lies when people like them and live in them? It is their own affair. But I am tired of lying. There are enough lies without mine.

Thirty years later he was to say:

> When power got into the hands of this party [Bolshevik], which was a very small and despised party, all evolution stopped. In the last twenty years Russia has produced not a single book, not a single picture. If there are people who write or paint there, they are people who have been doing it before the revolution. And I saw what happened. I saw what an enormous progress Russia had made in the twenty years preceding the revolution—it was quite a different country; literature, art, everything was developing rapidly. And

> now all this has stopped. At the same time there are plenty of words and promises.... People who use force to make other people accept their own formatory ideas are criminals. ... There is nothing worse than war. But one must make a distinction between those who are responsible for war and simple participation in war. A soldier taking part in a war is not a criminal.... What particularly makes them criminals is spying, lies and pretence. They pretend that they have cultured aims. Actually it is all simply paid propaganda.

So it was then, so it is now and will always be. It is not true that you cannot fool people endlessly. As the German Field Marshal Herman Goering explained at the Nuremburg trials before poisoning himself, one simply has to create an external threat and cast all dissenters as unpatriotic and worse. "It was a good ride," he said when captured, having thrown lavish parties at his castle right up to that moment. Millions upon millions dead, whole cities bombed to the ground, and for what? To stop communism and spread fascism, trying to turn back the clock on what was seen as the disease of decadence and mercantilism and create the Thousand Year Reich. In the end neither fascism nor communism ultimately won out, but rather what one might call democratic capitalism.

Now rising to challenge this view of the world are what are called militant Islamic extremists. The West sees it as a war of terrorism; Osama bin Laden sees it as a defense of Islam. What is behind this conflict? Well, one could argue that it is the final willing out of an age-old historic confrontation that began with the Crusades of the Middle Ages. But if so, why is it happening now. Two reasons perhaps. Because it *can* happen. And because of technology. It is the pervasive power of technology that is opening up and confronting the Islamic way of life. It isn't that the West means to do so, that is, deliberately seeks to undermine Islam. It is more that technology and the globalism it produces (along with a media/Internet/Hollywood confluence of cultural and mercantile sewage) are undermining the Islamic way of life.

This is simply a point of view. There are others, of course. Which is the more valid is not the question. What *is* the question is how those on the path of self-transformation can and should

relate to what is happening. It would be well to remember what
Mr. Gurdjieff says in this regard:

> There are periods in the life of humanity, which
> generally coincide with the beginning of the fall of
> cultures and civilizations, when the masses irretriev-
> ably lose their reason and begin to destroy everything
> that has been created by centuries and millenniums of
> culture. Such periods of mass madness, often coincid-
> ing with geological cataclysms, climatic changes, and
> similar phenomena of a planetary character, release a
> very great quantity of the matter of knowledge.

The question then becomes what are we to do in order to
receive this knowledge. The answer can only be that we identify as
little as possible with world madness, with the reciprocal destruction. That is, we do not indulge negative emotions. We begin to
observe what these emotions are based on—identification and
negative imagination—and, importantly, that they have no real
center. As Ouspensky says:

> All our violent and depressing emotions and,
> generally, most of our mental suffering has the same
> character—it is unnatural, and our organism has no
> real center for these negative emotions; they work with
> the help of an artificial center—a kind of swelling—
> which is gradually created in us from early childhood,
> for a child grows surrounded by people with negative
> emotions and imitates them.

How to deal with negative emotions has been a question in the
Work and was an early source of argument. Ouspensky wrote quite
plainly that negative emotions were not to be expressed, that one
must begin with that. But others held that one first had to express
them to know what they were, since so many people are brought
up not to express them. A social good, nevertheless their mechanical suppression can give one a sense of superiority but keep him
blind to how negative he really is. So how one initially works with
negative emotions really is based on one's conditioning. It also is

important to say something about the other side of the emotional coin. As Ouspensky saw:

> Too much of an indiscriminately positive attitude can spoil things in the same way as a persistently negative attitude towards everything can spoil things, but sometimes a negative attitude is useful because there are many things in life which can only be understood through having a sufficiently good negative attitude towards them.

With all of the aforementioned acknowledged, the next level of study of negative emotions is to not express them. False personality, which acts as a center for negative emotions, begins to weaken, first fiercely defending itself and its views.

By refraining from their expression, we learn to eat negative emotions raw and so not only come to gain a control over them but learn how to transmute their energy. We see that intense negative emotions burn mi 12 of the impressions octave (provided, of course, we have given the necessary shock at doh 48 by remembering ourselves), si 12 of the physical food octave in the sex center, and sol 12 of the air octave in the instinctive center, the lower story being the site of the implosions, the aborting of the octaves. This is why one feels so depleted but self-calmed after a good rant.

Objectively speaking, however, one has burned up the higher hydrogens. We can work on mi 12 only by not identifying with impressions, which, having passed doh 48, are now much stronger. It is more difficult because mi 12 makes one more emotional, not less. Therefore, a certain "distance" or "inner separation" is needed in order not to implode, and this can only be created by *being-Partkdolg-duty*. Genuine results can only be had with the transmutation of mi 12. In doing so, we make our necks "amber," so to say, like the emblem of the society Akhaldan. And thus we prepare for the second conscious shock.

Working in this way, we not only help ourselves but help others and the general situation. We do not give ourselves up to the mass psychosis but strive to Be in the midst of all the chaotic posturing and becoming. ⚔

Notes

1. *I have just received the foreign papers.* P. D. Ouspensky, *A New Model of the Universe*, 2–3.
2. *When power got into the hands of this party.* P. D. Ouspensky, *A Record of Meetings* (New York, NY: Arkana, 1984), 153–54.
3. *The revolution.* In *A Record of Meetings*, 156, Ouspensky says: "I think it is a good idea that the cause of the Russian revolution was an argument in the seventeenth century that arose in the Russian church. Some people said you must cross yourself with two fingers, and some said with three. As a result it created two sects, and destroyed the possibility of the existence of middle class in Russia. And absence of middle class was the cause of the revolution.
4. *There are periods in the life of humanity.* Ouspensky, *Search*, 38.
5. *All our violent and depressing emotions.* Ouspensky, *The Fourth Way* (New York: Knopf, 1957), 61.
6. *Indiscriminately positive attitude.* P. D. Ouspensky, *Conscience* (London: Routledge & Kegan Paul, 1979), 133.

From TGJ #36

The Individual, the Bestial & the Primacy of Nature

Remembering that one of Mr. Gurdjieff's primary principles is the law of reciprocal maintenance, what to make of an article in *Nature* by an international group of nineteen scientists stating that because of global warming and the steady encroachment on creatures' habitats by humans, 15 percent to 37 percent of the Earth's 1,103 species will be extinct by 2050?

Essence Duty

Putting this in the context of the argument J. G. Bennett makes in *Making a New World*, that mankind must adhere to the primacy of Nature in its relating to the world, opens up a provocative perspective. Bennett writes that every mode of existence in the universe is grouped into twelve essence classes, each class supplying the maintenance for another and both being maintained by a third class. Essence classes are defined not biologically but by their pattern and range of possible experience. Think of the possibilities of one-, two- and three-centered beings. The range of experience of each class extends from the one directly below it to the one above it. Man's range, in this scheme, is from the Two-brained Beings to the angelic host (see table below). Man as a three-centered being is positioned at the crossroads between the animal, plant and mineral kingdoms and higher forms of inorganic life. It is man's cosmic duty, performed consciously or mechanically, to receive and transmit energies. (If he does so consciously, then he can use part of these energies for his own self-transformation.) His other duty to those essence classes below him only comes into play as his numbers and actions begin to threaten the extinction of species. It is his responsibility to see to their survival primarily by restraining his actions in their favor and not in his. Bennett makes a very crucial point in this regard:

> There are serious consequences of our wholesale destruction of animal species, inasmuch as the energies they should release have somehow to be made good. Since man alone has the required range of emotions, it follows that the human species has to replace the energies needed for cosmic harmony that animals should be furnishing. Mankind thereby unwittingly condemns itself to a quasi-animal existence. This partly accounts for the terrifyingly inhumane behavior that has become so prevalent in our time. Fear and anger lead us into bestial cruelty that bewilders those who believe in the nobility of the human essence. Gurdjieff's Reciprocal Maintenance may be hard to accept in all its details, but we must admit that it makes sense of much that is otherwise unaccountable.

Bennett speaks of the prevalence of "bestial cruelty" in the world—man's inhumane treatment of man and other species—and certainly there is enough evidence of that. But one wonders about what seems to be a quickening slide into the primitive and animal domains by so many people. There seems to be a general confusion wherein, to take one example, "freedom" is considered and defined on the instinctual level. It is to act as one likes and feels regardless of circumstances, for to do otherwise is to be insincere, phony. Certainly the young have always rebelled, and so they should, but the tattoos, nose rings, tongue studs, Goth dressing, drugs and raves and the like, along with music that makes Johnny

Rotten and the Sex Pistols tepid in comparison . . . could all this, as well as the political and corporate corruption and greed, be the result of what we have been doing to animals? Strange, but then on first thought isn't *Solioonensius* as a cause of war also strange? Whatever is propelling our culture on every level from the religious to the political to the everyday, we do seem to be in a free fall, temporary or not.

Great historical forces appear to converge as the old industrial world fades over the horizon and the new global-technological world locks into position. What it portends cannot be clearly seen. Seers, like the philosopher Martin Heidegger, who believe they have grasped its essence, are not hopeful. As Heidegger said in the *Der Spiegel* interview before he died, "Only a god can save us."

Self-transformation Is Key

But Heidegger was a philosophical pre-Socratic, not an esotericist. The idea of man's self-transformation through working on himself—through the conscious receiving and transmitting of energies—does not seem from his writing to be an idea familiar to him. (Sartre remarked that in Heidegger's 488-page masterpiece *Being and Time* there were only six lines about the body.) Fearing the spread of Communism and enframing of technology to hasten the devolution of being of what he called *Das Man*, the mechanical "they-self," Heidegger, like many intellectuals of his time, hoped for a political transformation, and so supported the National Socialist Party.

But Gurdjieff had seen that politics, as well as religion and other mass movements, were no answer. As he said in the mid-1920s:

> History had already proven that such tools as politics, religion, and any other organized movements which treated man "in the mass" and not as individual beings, were failures. That they would always be failures and that the separate, distinct growth of each individual in the world was the only possible solution. . . . As an individual developed his own, unknown potentialities, he would become strong and would, in turn, influence many more people. If enough individuals could develop

themselves—even partially—into genuine, natural men, able to use the real potentialities that were proper to mankind, each such individual would then be able to convince and win over as many as a hundred other men, who would, each in his turn, upon achieving development, be able to influence another hundred, and so on.

The Essential Question

Can enough people transform themselves to a degree of individuality such that they can help others to do the same? This is the essential question. What Peters reports and what Gurdjieff's own actions indicate—his wanting "clubs" to be established in all the major cities of the world and *All and Everything* given to as many people as possible—is that he envisioned the teaching being taken out into life. Fifty years after Gurdjieff's passing, the Work has come to a new place in the octave where it must either enlarge its perspective and responsibility or risk going the way of the Ephrata Cloister, New Economy and the Shakers, all at one time strong nineteenth-century religious movements.

While clearly "religion," as we commonly think about it, is not the way, there is a shadow side of the Work, a self-centeredness which can only be transcended by understanding the Work as sacred. Writes Katherine Hulme in *Undiscovered Country*:

> Gurdjieff had given us a pledge to say each time before beginning the new exercise—that we would not use this for the self, but for all humanity. This "good-wishing-for-all" vow, so deeply moving in intent, had a tremendous effect upon me. For the first time in my life, I felt that I was truly doing something for humanity as I strove to make my own molecule of it more perfect. The meaning of this Work, which at first had seemed quite egotistical and self-centered, suddenly blossomed out like a tree encompassing in its myriad branchings the entire human family. The implications of it were staggering.

Place this against what Bennett said about man's responsibility toward animals (as well as the Earth itself). For all his quixotic behavior and wrongheaded sense of democracy in esoteric matters, Bennett was a seer. He said it plainly enough: to avert a catastrophe man needed to come to the recognition of "a fundamental change in values which will consist in putting Nature first and man second. This is a bitter medicine to swallow, but unless we take it we shall perish."

A deep understanding of the primacy of Nature, in the sense of which Bennett speaks, is needed if mankind is not to sink to a bestial level. But, paradoxically, the development of this understanding of the threat of the bestial is, as Gurdjieff said, "a work against nature." It is an esoteric perspective and as such cannot be commonly held. Of course beyond the bestial is the environmentalist's fear of the demise of the Earth as a living habitat for humanity and other forms of life. That can be clearly understood on its own terms. The questions are: what kind of shock will be necessary before the primacy of Nature is heeded? And will there be enough time? ⚔

Table of Essence Classes

12.	Endlessness	The Supreme Creative Will
11.	Trogoautoegocrat	The Spiritual Working by which Creation is maintained
10.	Cosmic Individuality	The Divine Will
9.	Demiurges	The Angelic Host
8.	Man	Three-brained Beings
7.	Vertebrates	Two-brained Beings
6.	Invertebrates	One-brained Beings
5.	Plants	Static Life Forms
4.	Soil	The Sensitive Surface Layer
3.	Crystals	Static Non-living forms
2.	Simples	Primary combinations of matter
1.	Heat	Unorganized energy

From *Gurdjieff: Making a New World* by J. G. Bennett

Notes

1. *103 species on the Earth.* "Scientists Predict Widespread Extinction by Global

Warming," *New York Times*, 8 January 2004.

2. *Wholesale destruction of animal species.* J. G. Bennett, *Making a New World* (London: Turnstone Books, 1973), 210.

3. *Only six lines about the body.* Martin Heidegger, *Zollikon Seminars*, ed. Medard Boss (Evanston, IL: Northwestern University Press, 2001). Heidegger answered, "I can only counter Sartre's reproach by stating that the bodily is the most difficult to understand and that I was unable to say more at the time." He then proceeds to speak about the body, 231–33.

4. *History had already proven.* Fritz Peters, *Boyhood with Gurdjieff* (New York: E. P. Dutton & Co., 1964), p. 161.

5. *"Good-wishing-for-all."* Katherine Hulme, *Undiscovered Country* (Boston: Little, Brown and Co., 1966), 112–13.

6. *Nature first and man second.* Bennett, 272.

7. *Against nature.* P. D. Ouspensky, *Search*, 47.

From TGJ #34

Zoonoses & Zoostats

"THIS IS A TIGHTROPE. WE ARE BALANCING A REAL NEED FOR treatment versus some very real risks. There are a lot of unknowns," declared Dr. David Kessler, commissioner of the Food and Drug Administration.

What Dr. Kessler is referring to are the guidelines developed for the transplantation of animal organs, cells and tissues into human organisms. What was earlier called "genetic engineering" and now presents itself as the amorphous sounding "biotechnology" has allowed man to break the species boundaries with which Nature has differentiated one species from another. Heretofore, the genetics of every species was sacrosanct. Through biological rejection mechanisms, each species was protected from the introduction of organs, cells and tissues from all other species. No longer. Now through a kind of Trojan horse biological trickery science has been able to transplant baboon bone marrow and fetal pig cells into human organisms. Baboon livers have also been attempted—so far unsuccessfully—and pig livers will soon be included on the transplantation menu.

Diseases May Leap Natural Barriers

When Dr. Kessler speaks of "very real risks" and "a lot of

unknowns," he is referring to possible transmission of infectious animal organisms to humans. Microbes, harmless in their native animal organism, can radically change when inserted into the totally alien human environment. AIDS, for example, is believed to have somehow "jumped" from African monkeys into humans. Society risks being beset with an entirely new spectrum of diseases of animal origin for which there are no treatments or cures. And already there is evidence of cross-species genetic viral mutations. For example, at Lund University in Sweden, Dr. Jonas Blomberg has shown it's possible to stimulate harmless endogenous viral sequences in human and monkey cells into a form that could cause disease. If monkey cells were put into humans, could disease occur? "Sometime it probably will happen," said Dr. Blomberg.

Why would we take such a risk? It is said that there are thousands of Americans dying each year because they cannot get the necessary organ transplant. It is said there are some 50,000 needy patients on ever-growing waiting lists and only 5,000 annual human donors. With the addition of animal organs, say researchers, the supply would far outstrip the demand.

So are we risking our species security to possibly save some 50,000 lives? A strange thanatological wager.

"I see the guidelines as a show of support from the government, from society, that the need is definite," said Dr. Steven Deeks, the San Francisco doctor who recently transplanted the baboon bone marrow. And, he added, "No one really wants to stop science cold."

Science as Business

Science, of course, is all agog with the endless possibilities of xenotransplantation, the catch-all, kitchen-sink word for any type of genetic tinkering. Big business, too, is falling all over itself as it views the new markets and problems (and hence need for solutions) that xenotransplantation and, its corollary, zoonoses, would provide. *Zoonoses?* Yes, that's the name given diseases transferred from animals to humans. It calls up visions of all these animals falling out of one's nostrils. What this word evokes as well, is Gurdjieff's use of the word *Zoostat,* which he defines as "the functioning of their [human] 'being-consciousness,' and which was divided into two entirely different consciousness having nothing in common with each other." The first is our waking-state consciousness and the second our subconsciousness. We function primarily from the first. "Objective-Conscience," wrote Gurdjieff in *All and Everything*, "is embedded in that consciousness which is here called 'subconsciousness,' in consequence of which it takes no part whatever in the functioning of their ordinary consciousness." Could any person or persons with Objective-Conscience seriously propose so radically altering humankind as to 1) make them part animals, and 2) risk new animal-derived diseases and, yes, possibly plagues? Such a question gives one a sense of the absurd and vulgar *logicnestarian* growths that mark our time. The breaking of species boundaries is so extreme an act that no dialogue or appeal is possible.

If science/big business, à la Dr. Deeks, is not stopped cold, then to Gurdjieff's Diagram of Everything Living there will be a new level interposed between man and vertebrates, that of the animal man. The diagram shows that every degree of being is defined "by what serves as food for this kind of creature or being of a given level and for what they themselves serve as food." The lower circle shows what the given class of creatures feeds on; the upper circle shows what class feeds on it; and the middle circle shows the average for the given class. Being an average, of course, it means that some people are higher and some lower. In the case of man, that would mean that some men tend toward the vibrational state of angels, or 12; and some toward that of vertebrates, 48.

Ray of Creation Deflected

Between the average level of man, 24, and that of vertebrates, 48, we will have an artificial level interposed between the two. This can only be a bastardization, some quasi- or pseudo-human state of being. As suggestibility and the egotistic desire to prolong human life at any cost catches hold, an increasing percentage of society will exist in a pseudo-human state. It would mean that in the process of *Harnelmiaznel*, in which "the higher blends with the lower in order to actualize the middle and thus becomes either higher for the preceding lower, or lower for the succeeding higher," mankind would have taken an irrevocable step downward and backward. We would have rendered ourselves human capons shorn of all possibility of spiritual evolution—our destiny only further devolving into a monster or animal state. Fortunately, there are conscious forces moving into place to contest that fall. In the meantime, we must become as clear as possible about what is happening and why. ⨎

Notes

1. *Trojan horse biological trickery.* Human genes have been transplanted into animal organs to make later rejection less likely when they are implanted into human beings.
2. *Objective conscience is embedded.* G. I. Gurdjieff, *All and Everything*, 359.
3. *What serves as food.* P. D. Ouspensky, *Search*, 322–23.
4. *The higher blends with the lower.* Gurdjieff, 751.

From TGJ #12

Sex on the Brain

In his 136-page chapter "Beelzebub in America," the longest in *All and Everything*, and, interestingly, preceding the chapter on war, Gurdjieff prophesied that what would destroy the power-possessing beings of America was sex and food. It was not our "feverish existence" whose "predominant urge" was this "love of 'dollar business' and of dollars themselves." It was not our malefi-cent invention of advertising which he viewed as "one of the chief causes of the continued dwindling of the psyche" of three-brained beings of this planet with the sacred being-function of conscience being completely atrophied among contemporary journalists and reporters. The major problem was food and sex with almost half of the Americans he met. He saw that the "proceeding functioning of the transformation of the first being-food is disharmonized," which is to say that "their digestive organs are spoiled," and almost a quarter were candidates for impotence. If this continued at the present rate, he said, then what befell monarchic Russia will befall us—that is, we will be destroyed. The death of Russia came because of the abnor-malities of the Reason of the power-possessing beings there, whereas with America it would be the consequence of organic abnormalities. The death of Russia came from 'mind' whereas the death of America will come from the 'stomach and sex' of its beings.

Occultism & Russia's Mind

What Gurdjieff is pointing at with Russia can be seen in

The Occult in Russian and Soviet Culture, a series of essays which give a vivid portrayal of the predominance of Spiritualism and Satanism in Russia's "Silver Age" (1890–1914). Contrived by Allan Kardec (1804–69) in France, both Spiritualism and Spiritism had reached Russia by the late 1850s and gradually infected the minds of many of its nobility. Before Rasputin, there were many other charlatans. The Satanism virus came via the Symbolist writers, such as Baudelaire, Rimbaud, Verlaine, Villars and Huysmans. "The widespread Russian interest in the fashionable forms of occultism," says Maria Carlson in her essay "Fashionable Occultism," "was a middle- and upper-class response to the larger crisis of culture and consciousness. . . . Seances, mediums, [theosophical] mahatmas, and magic soon became part of the language of daily communication." Russia's enchantment with the occult is attested to, she says, "by the publication of more than thirty Russian journals, as well as over 800 discrete book titles (exclusive of belles-lettres) dealing with such subjects between 1881 and 1918."

The effect of occultism on Russia "contributed massively to the politics of myth and cult that culminated in Stalinism," states Bernice Glatzer Rosenthal in her essay "Political Implications of the Early Twentieth-Century Occult Revival."

> In the twilight years of the empire, politicized occult doctrines had helped to structure perceptions of and receptions to contemporary events, nourishing the maximalism and utopianism of the extreme left and the conspiracy theories and anti-Semitism of the extreme right. . . . During and after the Bolshevik Revolution occult ideas were a major factor in Soviet utopianism. Occult-derived symbols and techniques informed early Soviet mass festivals and political theater, as well as the Lenin cult, the Stalin cult, and Socialist Realism.

The situation in Russia today is little better, if not much worse, than it was before Yeltsin's quasi-democratic government. "The Satanic principles of lies and fraud" are rife in Russia today, says the Russian Patriarch Alexy II, the spiritual leader of the Russian Orthodox Church. Concerned by the collapse of Russian society's formerly strict moral code, the Patriarch says that Russian society is imbued with "the cult of violence, cruelty, betrayal and lechery," with a pervasive propaganda of egoism, pleasure and entertainment corrupting the people. The Patriarch decried the constant "mocking and ridicule" of traditional Christian values, noting that the teachings of the Bible were being "pushed into the background, toward oblivion." He also blasted the continuing Russian fascination with paganism, spiritualism, cults and black magic, all of which have flourished since the collapse of the officially atheist Soviet Union.

Sex on the Left, Sex on the Right

Meanwhile, in the United States the outbreak of "neo-Puritanism" rages unchecked. At the core of this neo-Puritanism, as with "political correctness," as well as certain forms of feminism, are a fascism and a negative identification with sex; this can be seen, for example, in Arthur Miller's *The Crucible*.

In his trenchant and too little studied essay "Sex and Evolution" in *A New Model of the Universe*, P. D. Ouspensky states:

> It is necessary to understand that almost all the morality which has been imposed upon the human race, almost all the laws controlling sex life, almost all the restrictions guiding people's choice and decision in these cases, all taboos, all fears: all these have come from infra-sex. Infra-sex, precisely in virtue of its difference from normal sex, in virtue of its inability to become normal, and in virtue of its non-understanding of normal sex, began to regard itself as superior, began to dictate laws to normal sex. This does not mean that all morals, all laws and all restrictions relating to sex were wrong. But, as always occurs in life when right ideas come from the wrong source, together with what is right they bear within them a great deal that is wrong, that contradicts their fundamental essence, that brings about new confusions and new complications.... The whole history of mankind is nothing but the rule of pathological forms over normal.

A Psychic Virus

If the media is the outer form of the societal mind, it looks as though we have sex on the brain. The vehemence and righteousness with which our power-possessing pols fulminate and flagellate about sex, lies and a fallen society, all this egged on by fundamentalist religicos, bespeaks a very dangerous mental parasite which once let loose infects everything. As Gurdjieff said, "one must always and in everything guard just against the initial impetus, because on acquiring momentum, it becomes a force. . . ."

Likely, that has already occurred. To not be infected by this psychic virus is our societal work of the near future. ⨊

Notes

1. *A series of essays.* Bernice Glatzer Rosenthal, ed., *The Occult in Russian and Soviet Culture* (Ithaca, NY: Cornell University Press, 1997).
2. *The Lenin cult.* When Lenin's body began to decompose, it was decided to embalm him after the fashion of the recently discovered pharaonic tomb of Tutankhamen. Rather than a pyramid, however, Lenin's tomb was shaped like a cube, as this signified the fourth dimension. The idea of the cubic shape originated with artist Kazimir Malevich, who believed that entrance into the fourth dimension enabled the escaping of death. Aleksei Schusev (1873–1949) designed a three cube structure in evocation of the Holy Trinity (before the Revolution he had designed churches). The idea of the resurrection of the dead was that of Nikolai Fedorov (1828/29–1903) who believed that "The resurrection of all mankind will result in a complete victory over space and time." His ideas have today led to what is termed "Russian cosmism." Says George M. Young Jr. in his "Fedorov's Transformations of the Occult," "The focus for ancient lost power and knowledge for Fedorov is not Atlantis but the Pamir mountain range. . . . This is one of the most desolate spots on earth, a range of icy windswept 24,000-foot summits. But even before Fedorov, this region was a center of mysteries, wonders, and legends. . . . Early Islamic literature names this as one of the seven gates of Paradise. In the deserts that stretch north of the Pamir range, along the silk trails of the caravans, the nineteenth-century traveler Arminus Vambery, and thirty years later Sven Hedin, passed beside the minarets of ancient cities buried in shifting sands, and long after Fedorov, Gurdjieff [who may not have known Fedorov's work] set much of his *Meetings with Remarkable Men* in this very region."
3. *Neo-Puritanism.* It has been called "sexual McCarthyism." Interesting that the same militant right wing that gave birth to the Communist witch hunts in the 1950s gives birth now to what may become another kind of witch hunt. Where liberals err on the side of sentimentality, indulgence and secular utopias, the conservative shadow is always this political "cleansing." Ouspensky, like many seekers, was more attracted to the conservative viewpoint, but meeting its

secular practicing in the flesh he withdrew. "They smelled bad," he said.
4. *"Sex and Evolution."* For an explanation of what Ouspensky means by "normal" and "infra-sex," one should read and reread his exposition.
5. *Fundamentalist religicos.* One sees the distortion in Jimmy Swaggart's sexual voyeurism. It is a sex without sex, a sex on the brain.
6. *The initial impetus.* G. I. Gurdjieff, *All and Everything,* 945.

From TGJ #19

Work Love

THE WORK SOMETIMES IS CRITICIZED FOR LACKING IN LOVE. WHAT is meant is a lack of warmth, of good feeling, of affection, a spirit of friendship and encouragement. In a word, a lack of brotherhood. These qualities are all really there, but not in the conventional outward way except at certain appropriate times. What has to be realized and a point that is often missed—and it is a vital point—is that the aim is to wake up from the sleep of the self-image, from self-love. And awakening is not to a glorious sunny morning but to all the explanations, the "could haves," and rationalizations that obfuscate the primary fact of our existence: that we are mechanical and awash in dreams. Mr. Gurdjieff's aim, and that of all authentic teachers, is to create the conditions by which we can see ourselves as we really are, not as we imagine ourselves to be. That engenders a necessary moral suffering, an inner heat that dissolves the false personality and leads to genuine self-transformation and transcendence.

Not surprisingly, just as we attribute to ourselves that we have a real I, free will, and the capacity to do, we also believe we can be sincere, that we can love. But how can a sleeping person love? Isn't the 'love' we experience a 'sleep love,' a personal love? When Hindus meet they say *Shanti,* which means "I honor the light within you." Not you as a person but the light, the truth, the being that is manifested. True love, spiritual love, is impersonal, yet intimate in a way that can never be known until it is experienced. So all criticism really is based on the conventional idea of love, of person-love, not Being-love, Work-love.

Personality Defends

What does impersonal mean? Certainly it does not mean cold,

indifferent, callous. As we are, we have no experience of the impersonal; the closest we come is disassociation, a psychological state of frozen reaction. So to begin to understand we must begin where we are: with the personal. That we personalize everything, possessing and setting boundaries, is what we rarely notice. Personalizing taints whatever awareness we have. In our perceptions, we always include others, objects, situations, but rarely do we include ourselves. We do not live in a subject-object world, as we take for granted, but rather on investigation we will see that we live in an object world in which the subject, ourselves, is missing. By means of a correct practice of self-observation and self-remembering, we seek to include the missing subject. In time, we see that this subject is not one but many. We are not one indivisible I but many "I"s, each of which has its special dreams, fears and identifications. We wake up to the observed fact that everything we think, say, and do is largely personality—false personality. In the beginning, observation is a marvelous telescope that allows us to see what has long been hidden, but once personality awakens to the fact that its supremacy is threatened, it fights. As Gurdjieff says, "Personality defends itself."

When we are hit—shocked on the funny bone of our chief feature or chief weakness, around which all of false personality and the "I"-structure revolves—we run amok. Like a fish who has bitten the worm and found itself hooked, we dart and dash and make a run out to sea—anything to get the hook out of our mouths. At the neutral moments when we have made the effort to be present, all the reverse conditioning comes into play. We struggle to stay awake in the maelstrom and so record what would ordinarily be lost. It's all blame and justification, dark vows and dreams of revenge. And should the shock be direct enough, personality will even conjure thoughts of suicide. False personality would rather die than see itself. It can be that extreme.

So when love is mentioned, are we speaking of love between false personalities, self-images? If so, in the world of the personal—that is, of A influences—the impersonal has no place. The impersonal, C influence, can appear only as B influence, a book, poem, art, architecture or some like secondary manifestation. At best, these can only reflect C influence, but that reflection can call forth a remembering. For C influence to be received, we have to short-circuit the hypnotic momentum of ordinary life and our identifications and create a stop, a space, allow ourselves to become knowingly available to receive such an influence.

But this has to be learned, learned in the only way we can learn: through continual failure. For as we will see, we can't remember ourselves. And yet, nonetheless, we must continue to make the effort and, in so doing, understand that the effort cannot be an ego-effort, a willful effort, for then its source of origin taints and disfigures all results. False personality projects itself as the spiritual "I," a spiritual parody endemic to our times.

A Work Effort

Work love has many levels of meaning. Here is one example. Years ago, in the late 1970s, Christopher Fremantle, who had met Mr. Gurdjieff and for many years been a teacher in the Work, was chosen to speak one evening in the weekly lecture series in New York. A handsome man, a mathematician, and every bit an English gentleman, he was now suffering from cancer. In his seventies, he had undergone chemotherapy and so had lost most of his hair. Pale and frail, his clothes too big for him, one might easily conclude that he was half the man he had been. But then one only had to look into his eyes, still lightest of blue and shining with remarkable intelligence.

He mounted the few steps of the platform with some effort and took his seat on the hard-backed chair atop a small Persian rug. Looking out on some hundred and more people filling the hall, all of whom were in the Work, he began to speak in the soft and sensitive way that was his custom. The subject of his talk is not remembered but he spoke for upwards of a half-hour. Then the floor was opened to questions. Immediately, in the third row off to his left, a woman stood up. She did not look familiar. Later it was said she had come down from Canada. Her voice was as sharp as it was clear.

"Mr. Fremantle," she began, pronouncing each syllable, "it is all well and one supposes good what you say . . . but you don't define any of the terms you use."

The room crackled with the directness of her words.

His answer is not recalled, but his demeanor is. It never changed. He remained as he had been, as if nothing had happened.

The Kiss of Life

The woman again stood up, allowing no time for the last word of his answer to settle in.

"But Mr. Fremantle," she now declared, her voice edged with a dash of sarcasm, "you haven't answered my question. Your terms— define them, please."

The force and the presence conveyed were such that the great hall itself seemed to shatter. A wave of anger swept through some of the younger people. How could she attack Mr. Fremantle like this? Doesn't she see he is ill? What kind of person is she!

Still sitting in the cushionless chair as he might sit before his fireplace at home, nothing visibly changed about him, showing no trace of identification, he again spoke.

And the woman again attacked him, now taking some of the phrases he had used and turning them in on themselves, then contrasting them with other "airy comments," she said he had made.

And so it went . . . back and forth, neither giving any ground, she attacking, he receiving and not being moved.

Finally the evening came to an end and he left the platform, now with a great deal of energy, looking much better than he had. He was later seen speaking with the woman in the foyer, both smiling and nodding.

Of course, he might have crumbled. The woman's force, the power of her logic, was formidable. She gave as strong a challenge as was ever witnessed in public and amid all that energy—the energy of people who had worked on themselves and who sat there present, witnesses to the evening. Even a slight identification on his part and he might have gone up in flames.

But he didn't. Instead, he was coated anew, and what might have been the kiss of death was the kiss of life, the kiss of love—the kiss of Work love.

Said Gurdjieff of love, "All accumulated vibrations create a current. This current brings the force of love. Real love is a cosmic force which goes through us. If we crystallize it, it becomes a power—the greatest power in the world."

In one of his last letters, Mr. Fremantle said to a student, "The idea of 'intentional' or 'voluntary' suffering is the last in the Work—and it implies the ability to be free from the automatic need to evade, reject, or react mechanically to suffering. This freedom cannot be acquired without a change of state and long self-study, evidently."

Not too many months after the talk, Mr. Fremantle died. ✗

Notes

1. *The Work sometimes is criticized.* Which is not to say that the Work is beyond criticism. Gurdjieff many times insisted that the methods he used were for him alone and not to be imitated. Creating the conditions by which another person suffers is a delicate matter. One's hands must be clean of all things personal.
2. *True love.* G. I. Gurdjieff, *All and Everything,* 357, speaking about what humans take for love, says that it is "firstly also the result of certain crystallized consequences of the properties of the same *Kundabuffer*; and secondly this impulse of theirs arises and manifests itself in the process of every one of them entirely subjectively . . . not one in ten could describe even remotely, the sensation of genuine Love."
3. *A spiritual parody.* Aren't we fortunate to have so many liberated, enlightened or, as is currently said, "fulfilled" people. To think that this has been the goal of traditional societies such as India for so many thousands of years and they have, quantitatively, produced so few in comparison to what America has spawned in but a generation.
4. *The force of love.* Private conversation, Solita Solano Archives, Library of Congress, Washington, DC.
5. *He wrote to a student.* Though Mr. Fremantle gave many talks and wrote many essays and letters, none were published during his lifetime. Some have been collected in his book *On Attention* (Denville, NJ: Indications Press, 1993).

From TGJ #15

Who Is Mr. Gurdjieff?

WHAT IF EVERYTHING YOU HAD BEEN SEARCHING FOR ALL YOUR life, all your questions and concerns, were to be answered *right now* and in a way that went far beyond anything you yourself had come to?

Take a moment—what would be your experience?

Go into it deeply.

If you allow yourself to experience the wonderment of all your questions being answered—then you would be experiencing something of what P. D. Ouspensky must have felt when he first met G. I. Gurdjieff in that noisy merchant's café in Moscow.

How is it, you might ask, that this Greek-Armenian—sitting

across from you and speaking Russian with a Caucasian accent rarely associated with the authority and presence he emanates—could know all this?

You, who are heralded in theosophical and literary circles. You, who have lectured before thousands on "The Problems of Death" and "In Search of the Miraculous." How could it be that *you*—despite your many gifts and seriousness of search—have not even remotely approached the scale of this strange man's understanding?

The question is there from this first meeting and will continue all your life—*Who is this George Ivanovitch Gurdjieff?*

It is no less the question today than it was in April 1915. Today, it is ours to meet him not in the flesh but through the ideas in his magnum opus, *All and Everything*, the *Legominism* he hurled into the future.

Many, if not all of us, have shared in Ouspensky's wonderment and his question. So it was, too, with the members of the early St. Petersburg group who often wrestled, as Ouspensky reports, with the question of Gurdjieff's identity.

"What he [Gurdjieff] had been born with," said Ouspensky, "and what had been given him by schools, if he had passed through a school—we often spoke of this, and some of us came to the conclusion that Gurdjieff was a genius in his own domain, that he had scarcely had to learn, that what he knew could not be learned and that none of us could expect or hope to become like him."

This from Pyotr Demianovich Ouspensky, a man not given to easy praise. Ouspensky's standards were high. His formidable intellect, the earnestness of his seeking, were apparent in early childhood. At the age of six young Pyotr was reading books by difficult authors such as Lermontov and Turgenev. As an adult he had actively searched for the miraculous, studying, writing and making two journeys to the East in search of what he called "a new or forgotten road . . . a school of a more rational kind." He had met many teachers and schools but none that suited his independent spirit and discerning intellect. Ouspensky was a seeker of a very high type and not one to be easily won over. And so for him to admit that Gurdjieff was *a genius in his own domain, that he had scarcely had to learn, that what he knew could not be learned and that none could expect or hope to become like him* indicates the level of being which he first perceived in Gurdjieff.

He was not alone. The normally reserved Dr. Leonid Stjoernval, one of the Petersburg group's earliest members, had once exclaimed:

"Yes! I believe that Georgi Ivanovitch is not less than Christ himself!"

Later in Paris the diva Georgette LeBlanc, who spent the summer of 1923 at the Prieuré and who later was a member of the group known as "The Rope," gave this impression of Gurdjieff:

"The light that came from the little salon illuminated him fully. Instead of avoiding it, he stepped back and leaned against the wall. Then, for the first time, he let me see what he really is ... as if he had torn off the masks behind which he is obliged to hide himself. His face was stamped with a charity that embraced the whole world. Transfixed, standing before him, I saw him with all my strength and I experienced a gratitude so deep, so sad, that he felt a need to calm me. With an unforgettable look he said, 'God helps me.'"

Of course, one can easily explain all of the foregoing and many similar reports in terms of suggestibility. But such an explanation is only that. An explanation, not proof. And so we are left with the reports from a highly intelligent and accomplished cadre of people who worked closely with Gurdjieff.

Let us leave the question of Gurdjieff's identity for the moment and ask what brought him to the West. Here, opinion will likely be more unanimous. It is quite clear that Gurdjieff believed he had a mission. That mission was to bring to the West an ancient teaching, formulated and calibrated to exigencies of the contemporary world. From his first appearance in Moscow in 1912 until his death in Paris in 1949 *never once* did Gurdjieff ever refute or contradict himself on this point.

His coming to the West was no wild idea. And he came not as a holy beggar or ethereal saint but as, of all things, a businessman who by his own effort and ingenuity had been able to amass a million rubles and two invaluable collections, one of old and rare carpets, and the other of Chinese cloisonné.

But what brought Gurdjieff to the West? What was the impelling factor, and why at that time? At the Prieuré in the late 1920s Gurdjieff summed it up succinctly: "Unless the 'wisdom' of the East and the 'energy' of the West are harnessed and used harmoniously, the world will destroy itself."

Gurdjieff had seen mankind's future, the impending terror of the planetary situation, and understood that all the old ways were useless to avert the coming man-created catastrophe.

Wrote one young resident of the Prieuré:

> He [Gurdjieff] predicted that a day would come when the eastern world would again rise to a position of world importance and become a threat to the momentarily all-powerful, all-influential new culture of the western world, which was dominated, according to him, by America—a country that was very strong, to be sure, but also very young.... Among the purposes of all leaders, messiahs, messengers from the gods, and so forth, there was one fundamental and very important purpose: to find some means by which the two sides of man, and, therefore, the two sides of the earth, could live together in peace and harmony. He said that the time was very short—it was necessary to achieve this harmony as soon as possible to avoid complete disaster. ... If enough individuals could develop themselves— even partially—into genuine, natural men, able to use the real potentialities that were proper to mankind, each such individual would then be able to convince and win over as many as a hundred other men, who would, each in his turn, upon achieving development, be able to influence another hundred, and so on. ... History had already proven to us that such tools as politics, religion, and any other organized movements which treated man 'in the mass' and not as individual beings, were failures. That they would always be failures and that the separate, distinct growth of each individual in the world was the only possible solution. ...

Gurdjieff came to the West to establish a new teaching, ancient in origin, that was specifically formulated for individual growth in the technologized world. It was stripped of the past, stripped of all mysticism, philosophy, religious rites and dogma. It was, and is, the great bequeathing. It is a teaching that gives to contemporary man and woman the great gift—the gift of practical knowledge and techniques by which he can, by his own efforts and intention, transform himself, and, in so doing, free himself from the abnormal being-existence that is the soul-death signature of our time.

And this can be achieved *without* withdrawing to a mountain top or monastery. In fact, the genius of the teaching is that it uses ordinary life, with all its uncertainty, negativity and suffering, to come to Real Life. The Buddha said, "Life is suffering." Gurdjieff said, Let's use it—but *intentionally*. Jesus said, "Love thy neighbor." Gurdjieff said, Yes, but first see that, *as you are*, you can't love.

The teaching that Gurdjieff brought—The Fourth Way, he called it—like all real teachings, has been plundered and leveled and explained away. New Age psychologists and other spiritual predators among us make unattributed wholesale "borrowings" to spice up their own self-styled eclectic brands of "bon ton" teaching. They attempt to legitimize what they've done by proclaiming that this Fourth Way teaching is, after all, nothing new, just a modern repackaging of many teachings.

Critics point to elements of The Fourth Way being found in other teachings, but cannot the same be said of all teachings? That one can find in The Fourth Way elements of other teachings does not mean, let alone prove, that the teaching is simply a synthesis. One could turn the argument just as easily, arguing that the elements found in, say, Christianity are the remains of the ancient Fourth Way teaching as it was wholly given. Gurdjieff is quite clear that the teaching he brings is different and in no way a derivative. He speaks of the four principal lines, Egyptian, Hebraic, Persian and Hindu, and two mixtures of these lines, theosophy and occultism. Both of these mixed lines, he said, "bear in themselves grains of truth, but neither of them possesses full knowledge and therefore attempts to bring them to practical realization give only negative results." He then declares, "The teaching whose theory is here being set out is *completely self-supporting* and *independent of other lines* and it has been *completely unknown* up to the present time. . . ." [Emphasis added.]

Could Gurdjieff be any more emphatic?

Still, whenever the subject of Gurdjieff's teaching is mentioned, one invariably hears contemporary exponents and propagandists of these principal teachings and their derivatives pointing to this likeness or that. But Gurdjieff has been quite clear on this point. "In order to understand the interrelation of these teachings," he said, "it must always be remembered that the ways which lead to the cognition of unity approach it like the radii of a circle moving towards the center; the closer they come to the center, the closer they approach one another."

Many of these teachings have had their day in the sun and, alas, great as they were, have all but spent their seed. No longer are they the potent historical forces they once were. Which is not to say that for the individual or small groups they cannot be effective, but as teachings to move masses, their voices no longer galvanize. True, fundamentalist movements rage everywhere. Is their emergence a sign of renewal or that of a desperate last stand?

As there has been a concerted attempt to cast The Fourth Way as simply a derivative of Eastern Orthodox Christianity, let's examine this contention more closely. Proponents of this view point to the uses of attention in the *Philokalia*, the writings of the early church fathers. But attention is the basis of spiritual work of all traditions; it is the "gas" without which no engine runs. After Ouspensky left Gurdjieff he devoted much time to studying the New Testament and the writings of St. Simeon and others. But Ouspensky left because, as he said, "I ceased to understand" Gurdjieff and what he was teaching. One can easily argue that Ouspensky, in trying to find the origin of The Fourth Way in the Eastern Church, was unconsciously trying to justify his break with Gurdjieff. Whatever the case, The Fourth Way is a way in ordinary life. It is not the monastic way of Mt. Athos. The Fourth Way is not a withdrawal from life.

Orthodox proponents also point to when Gurdjieff was asked about the origin of the teaching and he replied that "if you like, this is esoteric Christianity." *If you like. . .* that is, if you must have a familiar category (Russia at that time was heavily Christianized). Gurdjieff was simply speaking to Ouspensky in a way that would not at that time arouse his imagination. He would later tell him that the origin was prehistoric Egyptian.

Many years later in Paris, Gurdjieff was again asked about the link between Christianity and the teaching.

"I find the system at the base of Christian doctrine," declared one curious man, the Russian intellectual Boris Mouravieff. "What do you say to this subject?"

Gurdjieff replied, "It's the ABC. But they didn't understand at all."

"Is the system yours?"

"No. . ."

"Where did you find it?—From where did you take it?"

"Perhaps," said Gurdjieff, "I stole it."

As to the latter point—his stealing the teaching—one must remember how Gurdjieff taught. Mouravieff, as his writings show, was negatively fixated on Gurdjieff. He believed the worst of him. Gurdjieff's answer to Mouravieff was merely mirroring what was in Mouravieff's mind.

About the teaching's origin, what Gurdjieff is saying is that the teaching *passed through* Christianity, but they did not understand it, that is, how to properly use it. Not only did the church fathers not understand this but they were confused about their own origins. Ouspensky reports that Gurdjieff said Christianity was "not invented by the fathers of the church. It was all taken in a ready-made form from Egypt, only not from the Egypt that we know but from one which we do not know. This Egypt was in the same place as the other but it existed much earlier. . . prehistoric Egypt was Christian many thousands of years before the birth of Christ."

Which is not to say that Gurdjieff—who says he was initiated four times into Egyptian mysteries when in Egypt—did not hold Christianity in the highest regard. His first tutors were Dean Borsh and Father Evlissi of the Kars Military Cathedral, the latter eventually joining an Essene Brotherhood. Many years later, in writing about Christianity, he declared: "In none of the ancient religious teachings were so many good regulations for ordinary everyday life laid down as in just that teaching on which this same Christian religion was founded."

However, the usual wiseacring, mixing and deflections occurred. Wrote Gurdjieff:

"And into this teaching [Christianity] of truth and verity, they began also to mix for various egoistic and political reasons, fragments taken from other religious teachings already existing there, but fragments such as had not only nothing in common with the teaching of Jesus, but which sometimes even flatly contradicted the truths this Divine Teacher taught." And because of what he calls "criminal wiseacring," the "genuine faith in all this Divine and uniquely accomplished teaching of salvation of the All-Loving Jesus Christ was totally destroyed."

Gurdjieff realized Christianity's reign as a powerful historic force, had, collectively speaking, eroded. Gurdjieff understood that to yoke a new formulation of an ancient teaching to a Christianity that had lost its force would have neutered the teaching. Gurdjieff was looking forward—not backward.

Stymied in his own time from establishing the teaching, he sent his *Legominism* into the future, into our time, to us.

Speaking of *All and Everything*, A. R. Orage said, it "is a sort of Bible; the anomalies that seem to us incongruous and absurd may be a text within a text, which, when rooted out, may comprise an alphabet of the doctrine . . . Gurdjieff's book, perhaps, is a kind of Bible for the future."

And Gurdjieff himself said: "I not wish people identified with me. I wish them identified with my ideas. Many who never will meet me, simple people, will understand my book. Time come perhaps when they read *All and Everything* in churches." Neither Gurdjieff nor the ideas are to be worshipped, but rather worked with and understood. He was not bringing a religion but a teaching of self-transformation to be practiced in ordinary life.

Finally, the charge that it is not really new is meaningless. Gurdjieff has said the same himself:

"All the great genuine religions which have existed down to the present time, created, as history itself testifies, by men of equal attainment in regard to the perfecting of their Pure Reason, are always based on the same truths . . . the saying is fully justified which has existed among people from of old—'there is nothing new under the sun.'"

Given the foregoing, there cannot be any doubt—from Gurdjieff's point of view—that:

1) He had a mission to bring the teaching to the West.

2) The Fourth Way is whole and independent of other lines.

3) *All and Everything* is a *Legominism*.

As empathic as Gurdjieff was about the human condition, he didn't come to the West to save any individual person. His mission was not personal but planetary. Gurdjieff came to save the world from destruction.

Others may have come to save people. Gurdjieff came to save

the planet through the awakening of the aforementioned hundred people. Consequently, he was in search not of students, but of those he might quickly prepare to help to establish the teaching. He was in search of what he called "helper-instructors."

A final point: what has befallen Christianity and other great teachings is the mixing of various extraneous elements and wise-acrings which can only result in a loss of force. And do we not see the same thing happening with the Work today? To speak of an Ouspensky "line," or Bennett or Nicoll "line"—to say nothing of all our other latter day "lines" that have arisen—is absurd. Does anyone seriously consider that any who were students of Gurdjieff's, great seekers though they were, were on the level of George Ivanovitch Gurdjieff? There can only be one authentic line.

Let us now return to what the crux of the matter is in determining why Ouspensky, Orage, Bennett and so many nameless others left Gurdjieff. Answers on a certain level are specific to the person. But, more deeply, what is the common factor that Ouspensky, Orage and Bennett shared? To approach this let us first return to the question: *Who was George Ivanovitch Gurdjieff?*

How we relate to the teaching, its usefulness to us, depends on how we answer this question. If we take him as simply another spiritual teacher, say a crazy wisdom master, to borrow a category from the Tibetan Buddhist tradition, then of course, all is well. There are more than a few whose Pure Reason is developed to that level. Putting Gurdjieff among them makes no trouble for us. But if we move the level to that of a Messenger from Above, to use Gurdjieff's terminology, then are we not forced to live in total question? For what is our criteria, what are our referents?

Are we so confident in our own impartiality and level of spiritual development that we can really decide who Gurdjieff was? Can we really judge the understanding, composed of knowledge and being, of a man the stature of Gurdjieff? Many do, of course, but then this is a time when there is a scarcity of many qualities, self-love and vanity, unfortunately, not among them.

Lacking revelation or recognition, we cannot say with good conscience who Gurdjieff was. But we can recognize who *he* took himself to be. We can agree that he saw his mission as bringing a teaching to save the world from destroying itself. His actions matched his aim. He voluntarily put himself into the swirl of abnormal conditions that make up contemporary life and was largely misunderstood, vilified, and he suffered accordingly.

What an individual or a thing is, is directly related to the function they perform. A screwdriver cannot perform like a hammer, call it what we will.

Let us recognize that our conceptions of the great spiritual messengers to mankind, such as Jesus Christ, Moses and Buddha, are idealized in the extreme. They are portrayed as perfect in a way no incarnation taking human form could be. Therefore, since our picture of them is essentially unreal, any who come afterward—whether his mission is to speak to all or a part of mankind—will fail greatly in comparison. So, the simple fact is, can any of us truly define, let alone discern or judge, a *Messenger from Above*? The experience lies outside all ordinary categories.

As Gurdjieff uses the phrase, let him define it.

"Genuine Messengers from Above [are] sent for the purpose of aiding the three-brained beings in destroying in their presences the crystallized consequences of the properties of the organ *Kundabuffer*."

And having destroyed the crystallized consequences, then the three-brained beings would be open to the impressions of what would be—for them—a new world but is in actuality the world that has always existed.

Gurdjieff wrote his *Legominism*, divided into three series, to help provide the solution to what he saw as three cardinal problems.

His *First Series* was written "To destroy, mercilessly . . . in the mentation and feelings of the reader, the beliefs and views, by centuries rooted in him, about everything existing in the world."

Second Series: To provide "the reader with the material required for a new creation and to prove the soundness and good quality of it."

Third Series: "To assist the arising, in the mentation and in the feelings of the reader, of a veritable, nonfantastic representation not of that illusory world which he now perceives, but of the world existing in reality."

So Gurdjieff, in accord with his own definition of Messengers from Above, has come to destroy illusion and to help three-brained beings regulate their being-existence, that is, make it more harmonious.

As he said in the *Third Series*: "My Being is necessary not only for my personal egoism but also the common welfare of all humanity."

"My Being is indeed necessary to all people; even more necessary to them than their felicity and their happiness of today."

Less formally, Gurdjieff once was asked what his whim was. "He said it was to live and teach so that there should be a new conception of God in the world, a change in the very meaning of the word."

Of all his pupils, perhaps Frank Pinder, a no-nonsense British mining engineer, a colonel in British Intelligence, and a longtime student, summed up why Gurdjieff came. Said Pinder:

"Gurdjieff came to strike a big Doh to help the upflow of the Law of Seven against the current mechanical life.... Gurdjieff came to give us a New World, a new idea of God, of the purpose of life, of sex, of war."

But then Pinder asked a very potent question—

"Who are 'Us'?

"Us" are those who accept him and his teaching and help to carry out this work. This world of ours cannot be saved in our measure of time. Had it been possible it would have been 'saved' long ago by prophets and teachers who have been sent. *Those who look for the world to be saved by a single teacher in a given time are shirking their own responsibility.* They wait in hope of a 'second coming' with no effort on their part—indulging in the disease of tomorrow." [Emphasis added.]

No single teacher in a given time can save the world. But each teacher who comes can speak to those who are his to speak to. It is up to those who are attracted to him to listen and to practice the teaching and to help to carry it forward.

At this point, do I register in myself a resistance to an impartial consideration of the possibility that he is actually who he says he is? That this new formulation of an ancient teaching is whole?

To be sure, there is a certain danger in even pondering who Gurdjieff was and what his teaching was meant for, because the answers, if affirmative, impose a responsibility so serious that no one wishes to face them.

If answered in the negative, then, of course we are free to do as we like. But isn't continuing to think of ourselves as connected with

Gurdjieff in any serious way simply to indulge in the very beliefs and views he came to destroy?

In my book *Struggle of the Magicians,* I show at great length the many factors involved in why Ouspensky, Orage and Bennett left Gurdjieff. In sum, what it came down to was that each man would not intentionally suffer his chief feature. Ouspensky would not give up, as he said himself, his "extreme individualism." He would not work on his emotional center to the depth Gurdjieff demanded. Orage would not give up his need to love and be loved. Bennett was simply too enthralled with himself, his opportunities, abilities, and his need to be "free."

Each, of course, believed they left Gurdjieff for what they took to be legitimate reasons. Otherwise exemplary and serious students, they did not realize that their chief feature had blinded them to the unique quality of a man of Gurdjieff's level, and the dire need for the implantation of the teaching in the face of the impending planetary catastrophe.

"Unless the 'wisdom' of the East and the 'energy' of the West . . ."

Of the three, Orage was the student closest to Gurdjieff. It was he who saw deepest into the dilemma Gurdjieff posed. For several years and more Orage had found himself in the middle between his young wife and Gurdjieff, each of them pulling in opposite directions. Gurdjieff finally forced a choice in 1930. Orage chose family life. In a letter of explanation to a student of his, Orage admits that he left Gurdjieff because, as he termed it, he did not have "the absolute faith." Orage then wrote:

"What I pray for is that my own friends, the best I have on earth, the New York group, may not only not suffer on my account, but that, through me, like another Moses, they may find themselves led to the Jordan and transported across by Joshua Gurdjieff!"

Four years later Orage suddenly died. Learning of Orage's death, Gurdjieff wiped a tear from his eye with his fist, and declared, "This man my brother."

Pyotr Demianovich Ouspensky was never that close or clear. His aim had been to penetrate "the labyrinth of contradictions" of ordinary life to the "unknown reality" beyond. This, he called the "miraculous." He was in search of this miraculous and understood there was no escape from "the thin film of false reality" except by, as he said "an entirely new [or forgotten] road, unlike anything hitherto known or used." Ouspensky found that new or forgotten road and walked a good ways down it before becoming confused. This brave, questing, earnest soul thought he could keep the message but throw out the messenger. Ouspensky died in 1947 without comprehending that the messenger who came to him in that noisy Moscow merchant's café was a living embodiment of the message.

A very young John Godolphin Bennett had spent six weeks at the Prieuré and, by his own lights, had amazing experiences, yet he left, promising to shortly return. Twenty-five years would pass before Bennett would see Gurdjieff again. It was to him that Gurdjieff whispered, only a few months before his death in 1949—"For a long time now, I can write a check with seven zeros. . . . Even your King cannot do that."

To understand that to which Gurdjieff alludes we must recall that the ancient teaching he brought postulates there are seven different possible degrees of men, the highest being man number seven—he who is immortal within our solar system.

Who is George Ivanovitch Gurdjieff?

For Gurdjieff it was not a question. He told us who he was and why he had come.

We do not have to believe him. In fact, he would certainly not want us to do so. But how is it that we miss the mark so often in discussing him and the teaching he brought?

Might it have something to do with self-calming? If so, it's time to become serious. The state of the planet and human life demands it. ⋀

Notes

1. *What he [Gurdjieff] had been born with.* P. D. Ouspensky, "Fragments of an Unknown Teaching," draft (New Haven, CT: Sterling Library, Yale University).
2. *A new or forgotten road.* P. D. Ouspensky, *Search*, 5.
3. *Yes! I believe.* Anna Butkowsky-Hewitt, *With Gurdjieff in St. Petersburg and Paris* (London: Routledge & Kegan Paul, 1978), 67.
4. *The light that came from the little salon.* Margaret Anderson, *Unknowable Gurdjieff* (New York: Arkana, 1962), 149. A quote from Georgette LeBlanc's *La Machine à Courage.*
5. *Unless the 'wisdom' of the East.* Fritz Peters, *Gurdjieff Remembered* (York Beach, ME: Samuel Weiser, 1971), 122.

6. *He [Gurdjieff] predicted that a day would come.* Fritz Peters, *Boyhood with Gurdjieff* (York Beach, ME: Samuel Weiser, 1964), 160–61.

7. *The teaching whose theory is set out.* Ouspensky, *Search*, 285–86.

8. *In order to understand the interrelation.* Ouspensky, 285.

9. *If you like, this is esoteric Christianity.* Ouspensky, 102.

10. *I find the system at the base.* Boris Mouravieff, *Ouspensky, Gurdjieff et les Fragments d'un enseignement inconnu* (Brussels: Revue Synthèses, 1957), 8. Mouravieff's question in French was, "Je trouve le système à la base de la doctrine Chrétienne." This question is ambiguous in that it can be taken as meaning that Christian doctrine is at the base of the system. Inasmuch as Gurdjieff was not a native French speaker, the question remains as to why Mouravieff phrased his statement so ambiguously, and also how Gurdjieff understood it. Mouravieff met both Gurdjieff and Ouspensky in Constantinople in 1921. His last contact with Ouspensky was in 1937 and with Gurdjieff probably earlier. Robin Amis, a former Gurdjieffian now leading the Mouravieff camp, says Mouravieff's father gave him information on the relationship between Gurdjieff's Fourth Way, Russian monasticism and Tolstoy, Dostoyevsky, and some lay circle. If true, why did Mouravieff, whose views of Gurdjieff are so rigid as to be pathological, wait until after Gurdjieff and Ouspensky died to publish his *Gnosis*, a three-volume work that attempts to hinge The Fourth Way to Eastern Orthodoxy? Mouravieff gives no real concrete proof of this connection yet proceeds to pirate the teaching. The level of Mouravieff's writing is far below that of Ouspensky (let alone Gurdjieff) so, to those able to discern and not imagine, that gives a strong indication as to what is going on here. In terms of energy, it should be noted that a few years after Mouravieff's death the institute he founded to propagate his views closed.

11. *Christianity was not invented.* Ouspensky, *Search*, 302.

12. *In none of the ancient religious teachings.* G. I. Gurdjieff, *All and Everything*, 1001.

13. *And into this teaching of truth.* Gurdjieff, 702–03.

14. *Criminal wiseacring.* Gurdjieff, 736.

15. *It is a sort of Bible.* C. S. Nott, *Teachings of Gurdjieff* (York Beach, ME: Samuel Weiser, 1961), 194.

16. *I not wish people identified.* Gurdjieff, 1002.

17. *All the great genuine religions.* Gurdjieff, 233.

18. *Genuine Messengers from Above.* G. I. Gurdjieff, *Life Is Real Only Then, When 'I Am'* (New York: E. P. Dutton, 1975), 2.

19. *He said it was to live and teach.* Philip Mairet, *A. R. Orage: A Memoir* (London: University Books, 1966), 105.

20. *Gurdjieff came to strike a big Doh.* Nott, 224.

21. *In my book.* William Patrick Patterson, *Struggle of the Magicians: Exploring the Teacher-Student Relationship* (Fairfax, CA: Arete Communications, 1996), 157.

22. *What I pray for.* Louise Welch, *Orage with Gurdjieff in America* (Boston: Routledge & Kegan Paul, 1982), 117.

23. *For a long time now.* John Godolphin Bennett and Elizabeth Bennett, *Idiots in Paris* (York Beach, ME: Samuel Weiser, 1991), 34–35.

Keynote Address, First All and Everything Conference, 1996

What Is the Origin of The Teaching?

THOSE WHO DO NOT KNOW HISTORY ARE NOT ONLY CONDEMNED to repeat it, but they also allow history to be distorted. A graphic example is the new edition of P. D. Ouspensky's *In Search of the Miraculous.* Its cover shows a Middle Eastern man, presumably a Sufi, and the book is described as being "The Classic Exploration of Eastern Religious Thinking and Philosophy." The foreword is by Marianne Williamson, the millionaire spiritual doyenne of the New Age (now renamed "New Thought"), teacher of the channeled teaching known as the *Course in Miracles.* She tells the reader that if you hadn't read this book "then you hadn't learned your mystical basics"; Ouspensky's text is just a primer by which one can evolve into the spiritualism of the mystical channeled teachings. This reorientation—"repackaging" to use a marketing term—will no doubt broaden the appeal of this esoteric text and, of course, boost sales.

It will, no doubt, make Gurdjieffians angry as well, but this new "Sufi" edition is a lawful result. For too long the essential questions—who is Gurdjieff? and what is the origin of The Fourth Way teaching?—have been left unanswered. Time and again we see Mr. Gurdjieff referred to as "a philosopher and mystic" or some such safe appellation. Nothing much is said about the teaching's origin, but the suggestion is it is either a compilation of teachings or mostly Sufi.

Why is it so difficult for otherwise intelligent people to understand that Gurdjieff is a Christian and the origin of the teaching is also Christianity (though the term "Christianity" should be taken in an expanded sense)? Why do people keep saying Gurdjieff's identity and the teaching's origin cannot be known?

Let it be declared without reservation: Gurdjieff was a Christian. Why? If a man is baptized a Christian, and his earliest teachers are the dean of the Kars Cathedral and a priest who later becomes the abbot of an Essene monastery—what is he? If, when finally establishing the teaching at the Prieuré, he declares that "The program of the Institute, the power of the Institute, the aim of the Institute, the possibilities of the Institute can be expressed in a few words: the Institute can help one to be able to be a Christian."—what is he? If in writing *All and Everything* he begins with the Christian prayer "In the name of the Father and of the Son and in the name of the Holy Ghost. Amen."—what is he? If, at his death, his funeral is held at the Russian Orthodox Church and his burial is performed according to that church's prescriptions—what is he?

How, then, could anyone believe that Gurdjieff is anything but a Christian?

Is there an unconscious bias at work here against Christianity?

The teaching—its approach practical and scientific with its admonition to believe nothing until one can verify it—has appealed to intellectuals who disregard Christianity. The people initially attracted—Ouspensky and Orage, for example—were very much influenced by Theosophy and Nietzsche and had a low opinion of Christianity (although later on Ouspensky's viewpoint would change). Considering themselves caretakers of the teaching, intellectuals have been vigilant about maintaining its "purity." This is both laudable and understandable, but in doing so have they been blind to its obvious Christian ancestry?

When asked about the teaching's origin, Gurdjieff says it is "esoteric Christianity, if you like." The reason he adds the words "if you like" is because he doesn't know how much the questioner knows about Christianity. For the Christianity of which Gurdjieff speaks has its origin in prehistoric Egypt. "It will seem strange to many people," Gurdjieff said, "when I say that this prehistoric Egypt was Christian many thousands of years before the birth of Christ, that is to say, that its religion was composed of the same principles and ideas that constitute true Christianity."

The Christian Church Was a School

And after much discussion he adds:

> The question of the origin of the Christian church, that is, of the Christian temple, is much more interesting than we think. To begin with, the church and

worship in the form which they took in the first centuries of Christianity could not have been borrowed from paganism because there was nothing like it either in the Greek or Roman cults or in Judaism. The Jewish synagogue, the Jewish temple, Greek and Roman temples of various gods, were something quite different from the Christian church which made its appearance in the first and second centuries. The Christian Church is a school concerning which people have forgotten that it is a school.

The idea that what Gurdjieff brought was the esoteric teaching of a Christianity that existed *before* Christ seems to be a taboo subject. Other than in articles in this journal, it remains unexplored (see also the investigation of the subject in the video *Gurdjieff in Egypt*). If the subject is engaged at all, it's never with intelligent argument but name calling, which in itself suggests a psychological repression.

Sufi Merchandising

Is this why the covers of Gurdjieff's books frequently show Oriental rugs or Arabic writing—though Gurdjieff wrote his *Legominism* in Armenian and Russian and was fluent in those languages as well as Turkish? Yes, he did sell rugs, but the usual association of Oriental rugs is to Sufism and not to Christianity. Yes, there are references to Sufis in Gurdjieff's writings, and possibly he was initiated into one or another of their orders. But the Christianity of which he speaks—and out of which he teaches—*predates* Sufism, contemporary Christianity and Judaism by many thousands of years. In his search, yes, he did visit Mecca, but in disguise, because he was not Muslim. There are those who would divide Sufism from its Islamic base, but as William C. Chittick, a noted scholar of Islam and Sufism, shows in his *Faith and Practice of Islam*, one can't be a true Sufi and *not* be a Muslim.

If a Sufi, then Gurdjieff must have kept the Five Pillars of the Islamic faithful. Did he? Of course not. Moreover, as we see in *All and Everything,* he certainly did not accept Muhammad as God's only prophet. Are some of the songs and dances he taught Sufic in origin? Yes. But this doesn't make The Fourth Way a Sufi teaching.

One could only argue for the teaching's not being Christian in origin if most of what Gurdjieff lived and wrote is glossed over. Because the teaching's origin has never been definitely stated, such New Age exemplars as Williamson feel free to pick and choose what pleases them from Gurdjieff's teaching and drop the rest (just as Robert Burton, E. J. Gold and a host of others have done before her).

It can be clearly and unequivocally stated: Gurdjieff was not a Sufi but a Christian, who, like the teaching that he brought, is centered in a "Christianity *before* Christ." These are essential questions that must be argued, if necessary, but finally and definitively answered. Otherwise what this new edition of *In Search of the Miraculous* presumes will be the beginning of both Gurdjieff and the ancient teaching of The Fourth Way being made *Tchik.* *K*

Notes

1. *Esoteric Christianity.* P. D. Ouspensky, *Search,* 102.
2. *See* Mary Ellen Korman, *Prayers in G. I. Gurdjieff's* All and Everything (Fairfax, CA: Arete Communications, 1998).
3. *Orthodox funeral and burial.* See J. G. Bennett and Elizabeth Bennett, *Idiots in Paris* (York Beach, ME: Samuel Weiser, 1991), 52. Here, two months before his death, Gurdjieff recounts, as he did many times before, that Roman Catholicism had degenerated entirely, only the Orthodox Church had retained at least something.
4. *The program of the Institute.* G. I. Gurdjieff, *Views from the Real World* (London: Arkana, 1984), 152–54.
5. *It will seem strange.* Ouspensky, 302.
6. *Greek or Roman cults or in Judaism.* Ouspensky. The common idea is that Christianity grew out of Judaism. That it does not, changes the relationship entirely. For a learned discussion of the subject see Karl W. Luckert's *Egyptian Light and Hebrew Fire: Theological and Philosophical Roots of Christendom in Evolutionary Perspective* (Albany, NY: SUNY Press, 1991).
7. *Anything but a Christian.* See Kathryn Hulme in *Undiscovered Country* (Boston, MA: Little Brown & Co., 1966), 112–13.
8. William C. Chittick, *Faith and Practice of Islam* (Albany, NY: SUNY Press, 1992).
9. *Five Pillars.* Consists of saying the double *Shahadah,* or testimony, that there is no god but God and that Muhammad is His messenger, performing the ritual prayer, fasting during the month of Ramadan, paying the alms-tax, and making the hajj if one has the means to do so.

From TGJ #27

Gurdjieff & Christianity

WAS GURDJIEFF A CHRISTIAN? THE ORIENTATION OF THE TEACHING— is it Christian? Entering the new millennium, some fifty years after Mr. Gurdjieff's passing, it is important to begin to understand the part that Christianity played in his life and in the teaching he brought.

Certainly, as Gurdjieff makes clear in *Meetings with Remarkable Men*, he was raised as a Christian—"I know the rituals of the Greek Church well," he would say many years later, "and there, underlying the form and ceremony, there is real meaning." His first religious tutor was seventy-year-old Dean Borsh, the highest spiritual authority of the region. As Dean Borsh aged, he asked the young deacon Bogachevsky to tutor Gurdjieff and confess him every week. For two years, Bogachevsky tutored the young Gurdjieff and then, when the priest was posted elsewhere, he had Gurdjieff continue his confessions by mail.

It is interesting to note, regarding Bogachevsky's caliber, that later he went to Mount Athos as a chaplain. Soon, however, he renounced monastic life as practiced there and went to Jerusalem. Bogachevsky joined the Essene Brotherhood there and was sent to one of its monasteries in Egypt. He was given the name Father Evlissi and later became one of the assistants to the abbot of its chief monastery. According to Gurdjieff, the Essenes had preserved the teaching of Jesus Christ "unchanged" and that as it passed from generation to generation it "has even reached the present time in its original form."

The depth of what Gurdjieff felt for this man was expressed when, in his maturity, he declared, "Father Evlissi, who is now an aged man, happened to become one of the first persons on earth who has been able to live as *our Divine Teacher Jesus Christ wished for us all*." [Emphasis added.] Gurdjieff's choice of words would seem to indicate that for himself Gurdjieff accepts the divinity of Jesus Christ. He speaks, for example, of Jesus Christ as "a Messenger from our ENDLESSNESS," "that Sacred Individual," "Divine Teacher Jesus Christ," and "Sacred Individual Jesus Christ."

Although Gurdjieff speaks highly of Christianity and of Jesus Christ, there are also many stories of his making fun of Catholic priests, even shouting at them on occasion. For example, his niece Luba reported in her *Luba Gurdjieff: A Memoir with Recipes*, "My

Uncle never taught us how to go to church, or pray, or anything like that. And he never liked priests or the nuns. When we were out driving and he saw a priest, he would say, 'Shoo! Son of a bitch.'"

Gurdjieff certainly knew a great deal about Christianity—not only its religion but its esoteric foundation as well. This can be seen when he came to Russia in 1912 and took the guise of a Turkish prince, calling himself "Prince Ozay." Within a year of his arrival in St. Petersburg he met the young English musicologist Paul Dukes, later an officer in British intelligence. Dukes reports that the prince wore a turban and spoke in Russian with a marked accent. He was of medium height, sturdily built and the grip of his hand "was warm and powerful." His dark eyes, Dukes said, "piercing in their brilliance, were at the same time kindly and sparkling with humor." After a chess game which the prince won handily, he spoke knowledgeably to Dukes in English (which Dukes said he preferred) of the Lord's Prayer. The prince told Dukes it was designed "as a devotional breathing exercise to be chanted on a single even breath."

"I have been in many churches in England and America," said the prince, "and always heard the congregation mumble the Lord's Prayer all together in a scrambled grunt as if the mere muttered repetition of the formula were all that is required."

Ozay informed Dukes that the incantation of prayers as a devotional breathing exercise was practiced in the earliest Christian Church, which inherited it from the ancient Egyptians, Chaldeans, Brahmins, and others in the East, where it is known as the science of Mantra. This esoteric side, Ozay said, was lost in the Western Church centuries ago.

Gurdjieff had intended to found the Institute for the Harmonious Development of Man in Russia, but the revolution precluded this. It was not until eight years later, in 1921, that he was able to establish it in France. At the time, he stated the Institute's aim unequivocally: "The program of the Institute, the power of the Institute, the aim of the Institute, the possibilities of the Institute can be expressed in very few words: the Institute can help one to be able to be a Christian." He spoke of a Christian as being "a man who is able to fulfill the Commandments . . . both with his mind and his essence." St. George the Victor was proclaimed as the Institute's patron saint.

The Original Christianity

The opening of *All and Everything*, begins with a prayer: "In the name of the Father and of the Son and in the name of Holy Ghost. Amen." And within, Gurdjieff speaks of Christianity as based on "resplendent love," saying also that among all of the ancient religious teachings none had so "many good regulations for ordinary everyday life." He believed that Christianity is the best of all existing or future religions "if only the teaching of the Divine Jesus Christ were carried out in full conformity with *its original*." [Emphasis added.] It is not clear what he means by the words "its original," but presumably a religion or teaching that came before Christianity.

It is clear he believes that Christianity—the religion—was mixed with Judaism, and that Judaism by that time "had already been thoroughly distorted." During the Middle Ages, Christianity was further distorted by the fantastic doctrines of hell and heaven imported from Babylonian dualism by the church fathers. Christianity, Gurdjieff says, had been "the religion and teaching upon which the Highest Individuals placed great hopes"—note how he separates religion from teaching—but, as a result of what he calls "absurdities" and "criminal wiseacring," genuine faith in Christianity was "totally destroyed."

Messengers from Above

Perhaps more significant for determining whether or not Gurdjieff was a Christian is that while he obviously held Jesus Christ in very high regard, he does not take him as the only Son of God. Rather, Jesus Christ was but one of a number of Messengers from Above, though of these He apparently holds a special place. Although Gurdjieff speaks of Jesus as a saint, as he does of Saint Buddha, Saint Mohammed, Saint Lama, and Saint Moses, it is only Jesus and Buddha that Gurdjieff also speaks of as being "Divine."

Gurdjieff's view of the resurrection of Jesus Christ differs radically from accepted doctrine. He holds that if a person dies and is buried, "this being will never exist again, nor furthermore will he ever speak or teach again." However, in seeming contradiction, he views the Last Supper as being a preparation for the sacred sacrament *Almznoshinoo* on the *Kesdjan* body of Jesus Christ. *Almznoshinoo*, he says, is a means of materializing and communicating with the higher-being bodies of a deceased physical body by the *Hanbledzoinian* process of intentionally coating its *Kesdjan* body. In order to accomplish this, a particle of an individual's *Hanbledzoin* must be taken while he is alive and either kept in a corresponding surplanetary formation or taken in and intentionally blended with the *Kesdjan* bodies of those who will afterward participate in the *Almznoshinoo* process.

Because Jesus Christ did not have the necessary time before he was crucified to explain and instruct his apostles in certain cosmic truths, he had to resort to a magical ceremony so that he might complete his mission while still in a cosmic individual state. It was at that moment, according to Gurdjieff, that Judas put forward an ingenious plan—the conscious betrayal of Christ—that would gain them the necessary time. Gurdjieff refers to Judas as a saint who, of all the disciples, was the most devoted and had the highest degree of reason.

Concerning religion per se, Gurdjieff tells us there are seven levels. The religions of the first three are subjective and correspond to people who are primarily instinctual, emotional, or intellectual. It is at the fourth level that religion begins to become objective, free from the distortions of personality. At this level, the practitioner is beginning to emerge from the hypnotism of ordinary life and engaging in a struggle with what it means to be a Christian. Only at the fifth level does one have "the being of a Christian," for only at this level can life actually be lived in accordance with the precepts of Christ, because one has now achieved a commensurate unity and will that is free from external influences.

Good & Evil Nonexistent

Concerning good and evil Gurdjieff is quite clear. "The fantastic notion," he says, "namely that outside of them [outside of people] there exist objective sources of 'Good' and 'Evil' acting upon their essence" is without foundation—there is no external good and evil.

Our present notion of good and evil, Gurdjieff believes, is based on misunderstanding. He says that long ago a being of Beelzebub's tribe, Makary Kronbernkzion, who was a full member of the society Akhaldan, an esoteric brotherhood, was the first to employ the words. In an essay he wrote, entitled "The Affirming and Denying Influences on Man," he spoke of the trinity of forces in the conscious evolution of human beings. The first force he characterized as arising from the causes proceeding in the Sun-Absolute, and issuing from it by momentum. This force, like the other two, is totally independent. Kronbernkzion called this force "Good." When the momentum of this force is spent, there is then a striving to reblend with its source, the Sun Absolute. This fundamental World Law is characterized as, "The effects of a cause must always re-enter the cause." This second backward-flowing force, which must continually resist the momentum of the first force, he called "Evil," or the active force. From the clash and friction of these two forces is formed the resultant, which in relation to the two other forces is considered neutralizing. This trinity of forces issues from one cause, the Prime Source of all creation. As long as people project a good and evil having some objective existence outside of themselves, spiritual evolution becomes curtailed.

Gurdjieff, although raised as a Christian and no doubt baptized, had a deep understanding of Christianity, held its regulations and commandments in high regard, as he did its Divine Messenger from Above Jesus Christ, would nevertheless not be accepted by either the Roman Catholic or Eastern Orthodox Churches as a practicing Christian. And yet Gurdjieff, it is quite clear, would insist that he was a Christian—a genuine Christian.

Clearly, for Gurdjieff, the word *Christianity* has a meaning different from that of contemporary churches. After his arrival in St. Petersburg, the subject was broached when Gurdjieff was first asked, "What is the relation of the teaching you are expounding [The Fourth Way] to Christianity as we know it?"

"'I do not know what you know about *Christianity*,' answered Gurdjieff, emphasizing this word. 'It would be necessary to talk a great deal and to talk for a long time in order to make clear what you understand by this term. But for the benefit of those who already know, I will say that, if you like, this is *esoteric Christianity*.'"

In the account it is important to note that the first use of the word *Christianity* is italicized. That he then again uses the word *Christianity*, but modifies it with *esoteric*, underscores the point he is trying to communicate. When he says he does not know what the questioner understands by the term Christianity, Gurdjieff adds that in any case he will answer, but "for the benefit of those who know already." On the basis of these remarks, some, such as

Boris Mouravieff and Robin Amis, have believed that Gurdjieff was referring to Eastern Orthodoxy as it is practiced at Mount Athos. But this is simply an external reading, which, even at that, contradicts itself.

In continuing the discussion, in the very next paragraph, Gurdjieff speaks about "the desire to be *master of oneself*, because without this nothing else is possible." Then he addresses the subjects of love of mankind and altruism, and concludes with "In order to help others one must first learn to be an egoist, a conscious egoist. Only a conscious egoist can help people. Such as we are we can do nothing."

In sum, one must strive to become a true individual and to do that one must practice esoteric Christianity.

Rediscovery of Original Christianity

From the remarks discussed previously, it is quite clear that Gurdjieff, in his quest for the origin of esoteric knowledge, rediscovered what he called a Christianity before Christ. "The Christian church," said Gurdjieff, "the Christian form of worship, was not invented by the fathers of the church. It was all taken in a ready-made form from Egypt, only not from the Egypt that we know but from one which we do not know. . . . This prehistoric Egypt was Christian many thousands of years before the birth of Christ, that is to say, that its religion was composed of the same principles and ideas that constitute true Christianity."

After rediscovering the essential principles and ideas, Gurdjieff traveled to Persia, the Hindu Kush, and elsewhere to reassemble the complete teaching from the many elements that had migrated northward over time. He then reformulated the teaching, which he called The Fourth Way, for our contemporary understanding and introduced it to the West. In first speaking of its origin he declared—"The teaching whose theory is here being set out is completely self-supporting and independent of other lines and it has been *completely unknown* up to the present time." [Emphasis added.] It is "completely unknown" because its origin is prehistoric—predating the ancient Egyptian religion, Judaism, Zoroaster, the Avesta and the Hindu Rig Veda.

So, in sum, Gurdjieff is, and is not, a Christian. The Fourth Way teaching is, and is not, Christian. It depends on what we know about Christianity, our definition of it.

For Gurdjieff, there are two forms of Christianity, its original form and its contemporary form.

The Fourth Way, for Gurdjieff, is *esoteric Christianity* in its highest form. That is, if it is so recognized and practiced. Otherwise . . . ✗

Notes

1. *Greek Church.* G. I. Gurdjieff, *Views from the Real World,* 86.
2. *"Passing from generation to generation."* G. I. Gurdjieff, *All and Everything,* 703.
3. *"Messenger from our endlessness."* Gurdjieff, *All and Everything,* 99, 701.
4. *"Sacred Individual."* Gurdjieff, *All and Everything,* 701.
5. *"Divine Teacher Jesus Christ."* Gurdjieff, *All and Everything,* 703.
6. *"Saint Jesus Christ."* Gurdjieff, *All and Everything,* 737.
7. *"Shoo! Son of a bitch."* Luba Gurdjieff, *Luba Gurdjieff: A Memoir with Recipes* (Berkeley: Ten Speed Press, 1993), 64.
8. *English.* Did Gurdjieff speak English? James Moore in private conversation said that Mme de Salzmann told him that Prince Ozay was Gurdjieff. Paul Dukes reports that the prince's friends spoke in Russian. "Ribald stories made up part of the conversation, some of which my host [the prince] translated to me with gusto." *The Unending Quest* (London: Cassell & Co., 1950), 104. Dukes, an intelligent young man with a fine ear, makes several references to the prince speaking English. As he said he visited with the prince off and on from 1913 until February 1917, it is inconceivable that Dukes could have been misled. By making reference to Gurdjieff speaking English, was Dukes protecting Gurdjieff? As Dukes published his book after Gurdjieff's death, there was no reason to protect him. Did Gurdjieff feign not being able to speak English to make it harder for his English and American students to understand him? That's a possibility. As with many things about Gurdjieff, we are left in question. Paul Beekman Taylor, in his essay "Gurdjieff and Prince Ozay," argues against the two being the same. He quotes Moore but never mentions that it was no less than Mme de Salzmann who told Moore that Gurdjieff was Ozay. Strange omission.
9. *Prayer.* Ozay told Dukes that a greater measure of the mantric art survived in the Greek Orthodox Church, especially in its Russian branch, on account of its devotion to pure song without instrumental interference. The Orthodox Church has never allowed its singing to be debased by organ 'support,' and indeed does not permit organs to be placed in churches. Dukes, 110.
10. *The Institute and Christianity.* Gurdjieff, *Views,* 152–54.
11. *Relation of Fourth Way to Christianity.* P. D. Ouspensky, *Search,* 102–03.
12. *Resplendent Love.* Gurdjieff, *All and Everything,* 702.
13. *"Full conformity with its original."* Gurdjieff, *All and Everything,* 1009.
14. *"Definite utterance."* Gurdjieff, *All and Everything,* 3. Given this, it is wondered

whether Gurdjieff's admonition "Do not do to others what you would not wish them to do to you" is an example of an original formulation, later changed.

15. *"Thoroughly distorted."* Gurdjieff, *All and Everything*, xx.
16. *Mouravieff and Amis.* William Patrick Patterson, *Taking with the Left Hand* (Fairfax, CA: Arete Communications, 1998).
17. *"All taken in ready-made form from Egypt."* Ouspensky, 302.
18. *Makary Kronbernkzion.* Gurdjieff, *All and Everything*, 1138.
19. *I do not know what you know about Christianity. Search*, 102–03
20. *The Christian Church.* Ouspenskly, 302.
21. *"Completely unknown."* Ouspensky, 286.

From TGJ #22

Gurdjieff, Sufism & Mohammed

Ever since Mr. Gurdjieff's death, Sufis have claimed him as one of theirs. Either that or claimed that the teaching he brought is really Sufism in disguise. Parallels between Sufism and the ancient teaching of The Fourth Way can be pointed out, of course, certain of his dances, music and perhaps some practices. No one reading the first two series of his *Legominism, All and Everything*, could doubt his familiarity with and respect for Mohammed, Islam and Sufism. But does that make Gurdjieff a Sufi?

Gurdjieff is a Christian. But not of contemporary vintage. He often made fun of contemporary Christianity. The Orthodox, he said, had retained at least something, but Roman Catholicism had degenerated entirely. He held that Jesus Christ was not the only divine messenger to the planet, which would of course exempt Gurdjieff's adhering to the Nicene Creed. Still, in even a casual look at his life, his Christianity is so obvious as to make one wonder why it would remain a question. Gurdjieff was baptized a Christian, educated by Russian Orthodox priests, and at his death services were conducted at his request in the Russian Orthodox Church in Paris by a Russian priest.

Gurdjieff's Vision of Christianity

Four months after finally succeeding in opening his Institute for the Harmonious Development of Man, he declared, "The program of the Institute, the power of the Institute, the aim of the

Institute, the possibilities of the Institute can be expressed in a few words: *the Institute can help one to be able to be a Christian.*" [Emphasis added.] He went on to say, "Christianity says precisely this, to love all men. But this is impossible. At the same time it is quite true that it is necessary to love. First one must be able, only then can one love. Unfortunately, with time, modern Christians have adopted the second half, to love, and lost view of the first, the religion [of being able to do], which should have preceded it."

He then added, "Half the world is Christian, the other half has other religions. For me, sensible man, this makes no difference; they are the same as the Christian. Therefore it is possible to say that the whole world is Christian, the difference is only in name. And it has been Christian not only for one year but for thousands of years. *There were Christians long before the advent of Christianity.*" [Emphasis added.]

This last statement accords with what P. D. Ouspensky reports Gurdjieff said in Russia some seven years before. When asked what is the origin of The Fourth Way, Gurdjieff said that to understand what is meant by the term Christianity one would have to "talk a great deal and to talk for a long time." Then he declared: "But for the benefit of those who know already [that is, know what he means when he says 'Christianity'] I will say that, if you like, *this is esoteric Christianity.*" [Emphasis original.]

Later on, Ouspensky reports Gurdjieff saying: "It will seem strange to many people when I say that this prehistoric Egypt was Christian many thousands of years before the birth of Christ, that is to say, that its religion was composed of the same principles and ideas that constitute true Christianity. . . . The Christian church, the Christian form of worship, was not invented by the fathers of the church. It was all taken in a ready-made form from Egypt, only not from the Egypt we know but from one which we do not know. This Egypt was in the same place as the other but it existed much earlier."

What isn't commonly understood, though the clues are there in *Search*, *All and Everything*, and *Meetings with Remarkable Men*, is that Gurdjieff discovered the teaching of The Fourth Way in Egypt and Ethiopia (Abyssinia). That was his first journey. His second was to rediscover, reassemble and reformulate elements of the original prehistoric teaching of Christianity—existing in Egypt before 3,000 ʙᴄᴇ—that over time had moved northward with Pythagoras and into Central Asia.

Bennett's Bias

One of the advocates for the notion that Gurdjieff's teaching is based on Sufism is J. G. Bennett. In his *Making a New World*, an otherwise interesting study of Gurdjieff and his teaching, Bennett clearly overlooks the importance of Gurdjieff's connection with Egypt while greatly emphasizing that of Central Asia. But he does write:

> We know that the Eastern churches have admirable spiritual exercises, some of which Gurdjieff taught his own pupils. He refers to a journey to Abyssinia with Professor Skridlov. He stayed for three months in Abyssinia where he followed up indications he had found in Egypt of the importance of the Coptic tradition. At the end of his life, I more than once heard him speak of Abyssinia, even referring to it as his 'second home,' where he hoped to retire and finish his days. He also mentioned the special knowledge of Christian origins possessed by the Coptic Church that had been lost by the Orthodox and Catholic branches of Christianity.

So, like a good bit of what has happened to the Work since Gurdjieff's death, the Work has largely brought this confusion upon itself. The recent new edition of Ouspensky's *Search* shows on the cover a Sufi in a turban. This is congruent with covers of Gurdjieff books which show either Arabic writing or Persian rugs. This denial of the origins of Gurdieff's Fourth Way, intentional or otherwise, now with a historical clash between Judeo-Christianity and Islam coming to the fore, must be righted if Gurdjieff and the teaching are not to suffer by association.

Thus, with the understanding that Gurdjieff is a true Christian and that The Fourth Way is an ancient teaching rooted in prehistoric Egypt—and therefore, *being the original source teaching for all subsequent teachings*—let us look at Gurdjieff's connection with Islam and Sufism.

In *The Herald of Coming Good* Gurdjieff speaks of a

brotherhood—a word he puts in quotation marks apparently to signify that it is something more than a brotherhood as commonly understood—which exists in the heart of Central Asia. Later he will refer to it as a "certain Dervish monastery" where he spent two years studying Oriental hypnotism. Because, he says, "I foresaw certain possible changes in the conditions of ordinary life [there would be a world disaster, if the "wisdom" of the East and the "energy" of the West were not integrated and made harmonious— see Fritz Peters' *Gurdjieff Remembered*] and decided therefore to confide my intentions to a 'brotherhood' with a view to securing in certain ways their future co-operation." He mentions that long discussions followed concerning mutual obligations "which, on my side, were chiefly on the grounds of my future religious and moral actions, and, on their side, were on the grounds of guiding, in strict accordance with the means indicated by me, the inner world of people whom I would confide to them."

Gurdjieff is not going to the East as a disciple or student. He is directing the brotherhood in how the students he will send will be taught—"in accordance with the means indicated by me." In the translator's note to *Meetings with Remarkable Men*, it states that "Gurdjieff was a master . . . an actual incarnation of knowl-edge." (This is heartening, as Gurdjieff is often characterized as a "philosopher and mystic," but unfortunately speaking of him as a master was not continued.)

Certainly Gurdjieff was well acquainted with Islam and the Sufis. After his sojourn in Egypt he adopted a disguise and traveled to Mecca, and later he and Professor Skridlov disguised themselves as a direct descendant of Mohammed, a Seïd, and as a Persian der-vish, respectively, in order to explore Kafiristan (if Gurdjieff had indeed become a Sufi, why the disguise?). Gurdjieff certainly holds dervishes in high regard, for he writes in the *All and Everything*: "By the destruction of this 'dervishism' those last dying sparks will also be entirely extinguished there which, preserved as it were in the ashes, might sometime rekindle the hearth of those possibilities upon which Saint Mohammed counted." He speaks in high terms of the founder of Islam, calling him "the Sacred Individual Saint Mohammed" and of Islam as "the fourth great religion." With time, however, the purity of the religion was diluted by mixing into it "something from the fantastic theory of the Babylonian dualists" and "about the blessings of the notorious 'paradise' which as it were, existed 'in the other world.'" He notes that Islam "from the very first split into two schools the 'Sunnite' and the 'Shiite'" and that the "psychic hatred of each because of frequent clashes now transformed completely into an organic hate." He warned: "Beings of certain European communities have during recent centuries greatly contributed by their incitement...in order that the animosity should increase should they ever unite, since if this was to happen, there might soon be an end there for those European communities."

If one brotherhood stands out above all others for Gurdjieff it is clearly the World Brotherhood. "Among the adepts of this monastery there were former Christians, Jews, Mohammedans, Buddhists, Lamaists, and even one Shamanist. All were united by God the Truth."

This World Brotherhood is Gurdjieff's Brotherhood. ⚿

Notes

1. *Orthodox had retained at least something.* J. G. Bennett and Elizabeth Bennett, *Idiots in Paris* (York Beach, ME: Samuel Weiser, 1991), 52.
2. *The program of the Institute.* G. I. Gurdjieff, *Views from the Real World* (London: Arkana, 1984), 152.
3. *Christians long before the advent of Christianity.* Gurdjieff, 153.
4. *This is esoteric Christianity.* P. D. Ouspensky, *Search*, 102.
5. *Prehistoric Egypt was Christian many thousands of years before the birth of Christ.* Ouspensky, 302. To follow Gurdjieff's search in Egypt, see the video *Gurdjieff in Egypt* (Fairfax, CA: Arete Communications, 1999).
6. *Certain Dervish monastery.* G. I. Gurdjieff, *The Herald of Coming Good* (Edmonds, WA: Sure Fire Press, 1988), 59, 19.
7. *I foresaw certain possible changes in the conditions of ordinary life.* Gurdjieff, *Herald*, 59.
8. *Gurdjieff was a master.* G. I. Gurdjieff, *Meetings with Remarkable Men* (New York: E. P. Dutton, 1963), x.

From TGJ #31

Gurdjieff's Cheek

"I DO NOT PRETEND TO UNDERSTAND GEORGY IVANOVITCH," SAID Mme Ouspensky. "For me he is X." That January 1924, her husband had left Mr. Gurdjieff for good. Ouspenky's leaving—with the added admonition to his students forbidding them to see or speak about Gurdjieff—put into high relief the by-then perennial question: who was Gurdjieff? A great many people have attempted to answer that question, but in many ways he remains, and will continue to remain, X. The reason has to do with scale. Attempts to see him invariably bring him down to the level of the inquiry as well as the inquirer. Factually more is known about Gurdjieff than any other spiritual figure, but beyond a certain point one is still left in question. Mme Ouspensky said, "It is useless for us to try to know him," and while in the essential sense that is true, still it is helpful to keep returning to what we do know about Gurdjieff's life, for his life was a living demonstration of one who both embodied and lived the teaching. In doing so—focusing on the facts and applying our reason to the point where intuition speaks—here and there edifying glimpses emerge.

The usual focus is on what an individual does, not what he doesn't do. This is normally passed over, not as the consequence of a conscious decision, but because the focus itself is not considered deeply enough. To know what is left out we must first know what is put in; but we become so focused and entangled with that that the question of what has been left out, what has been denied, never appears.

Greek & Armenian Forebears

A noteworthy example is Gurdjieff's heritage. That his father was Greek, his mother Armenian is well known. We know that his family suffered at the hands of the Turks and Kurds, yet in none of his writings does he ever excoriate them. Nor does he express personal grief at the murder of his father, or speak of the genocide of the Armenians, his mother's people. Only when Gurdjieff tells us about the "skeletons" arriving at his door in Essentuki in July 1918 does he give us an idea of what he felt. In February 1918, he had sent for his family in Alexandropol to come to him in Essentuki to escape the impending Turkish invasion. His mother, brother Dimitri and his wife, younger sister Sophie Ivanovna and her fiancé Georgilibovitch Kapanadze came, but Gurdjieff's eldest sister, Anna Ivanovna Anastasieff, had stayed behind in Alexandropol with their father who refused to flee. That May, with the Turks advancing, she and her husband Feodor and six little children fled, along with twenty-two other relatives, losing their home and homeland, and, cold and hungry, walked on bare feet over tortuous mountains. In mid-July, looking like skeletons, they arrived in Essentuki, bringing the news of the murder of Gurdieff's father by the Turks. Said Gurdjieff, "The enemy, stronger and better armed than their own troops, will inevitably mercilessly and indiscriminately massacre not only the men, but the women, the aged and the children, as was the order of things there."

The only reference Gurdjieff makes to this persecution is in the "Armenian" chapter of *Meetings with Remarkable Men.* "The Aïsors suffered very much in the last war, having been a pawn in the hands of Russia and England, with the result that half of them perished from the vengeance of the Kurds and the Persians. . . ." In this chapter he also speaks of the destruction by invasion and earthquake of Ani, the ancient Armenian city of churches, and then makes a curious statement, that this is the only time he has, or will, "take from information officially recognized on earth."

If we do look at ordinary information, one fact leaps out: after centuries of enduring killings and persecutions by the Turks, Armenians suffered two horrific genocides, the first in 1895 and again in 1915–16, under an official Turkish government policy of annihilation. On April 24, 1915, during World War I, the Armenian Holocaust began. By the time it was over 1.5 million Armenians, 750,000 Assyrians, and 400,000 Greeks had lost their lives.

We know that shortly after the 1915–16 genocide, from March to July 1917, Gurdjieff stayed with his family in Alexandropol and then went to Essentuki. With events of the Russian Revolution worsening, in August 1919 Gurdjieff left his family in Essentuki and undertook the hazardous journey of guiding his students between the Red and White armies and then over the bandit-infested Caucasus mountains. Arriving in Sochi, they took a boat to Poti and then went overland to Tiflis, where they arrived in January 1920. That Easter, Dimitri arrived in Tiflis to say that their mother and sisters and families had survived a harsh winter with famine and typhoid rampant. In June, with the Red Army having conquered the areas north of the Caucasus and threatening to take Georgia, northern Armenia and Azerbaijan, Gurdjieff left for Constantinople, arriving there in early July. Meanwhile, with his mother and family staying on in Essentuki, Anna and her family returned to Armenia. In November 1920, when the Turks once again invaded Armenia, Anna and everyone in her family was killed except a son, Valentin, one of only thirty people who escaped out of four hundred villagers.

No Haven in Turkey

In Constantinople, Greeks were only marginally accepted, Armenians not at all. Only five years earlier most Armenians in the city had been sent to concentration camps to die or were taken into the wilderness where they were bludgeoned to death. With what Gurdjieff called the "wiseacring" of the "Young Turks"—Kemal Attaturk and other young military officers and reformers bent on making Turkey a secular state—becoming more virulent, he says that since the situation began "to have a particular smell, I decided—without waiting for the various delights which were bound to develop in connection with these wiseacrings—to get away with my people as quickly as possible, with our skins whole." Leaving for Europe in August 1921, the following year he was able to establish the Institute in France and bring his mother and the remainder of his family to safety.

Years later, when living in France, Gurdjieff said the Armenians were "a wonderful people of great antiquity. They had not let their country be overrun by Western civilization. They had kept up their old customs, particularly the roots of their language, which was full of old sayings, old customs of the past, and this kept their people clean and unspoiled by the slime of the West." Family was important to Gurdjieff, and he understood the objective meaning of war and destruction. No more than alluding to the immense suffering endured by the Armenian people, and the personal suffering he and his family endured, never did Gurdjieff vilify the Turks. In the true Christian meaning, he turned the other cheek. Of this, he said in *Search*:

> Let us suppose that a man decides according to the Gospels to turn the left cheek if somebody strikes him on the right cheek. But one "I" decides this either in the mind or in the emotional center. One "I" knows of it, one "I" remembers it—the others do not. Let us imagine that it actually happens, that somebody strikes this man. Do you think he will turn the left cheek? Never.

He will not even have time to think about it. He will either strike the face of the man who struck him, or he will begin to call a policeman, or he will simply take to flight. His moving center will react in its customary way, or as it has been taught to react, before the man realizes what he is doing.

Prolonged instruction, prolonged training, is necessary to be able to turn the cheek, and if this training is mechanical—it is again worth nothing because in this case it means that a man will turn his cheek because he cannot do anything else.

Gurdjieff turned the other cheek often in life. As he said many times, "Exterior play a role, interior never."

This can be seen at the time of Gurdjieff's death. When Attaturk and the Young Turks came to power in 1923 they immediately banned men from wearing the traditional fez, women the veil. Though he wore Western clothes, Gurdjieff remained traditional. In 1949, dying of cancer, Gurdjieff was taken on a stretcher from his apartment to the American Hospital. He was sitting up, smoking a cigarette, and on his head he wore a red fez. ⚜

Notes

1. *I do not pretend.* J. G. Bennett, *Witness* (Santa Fe, NM: Bennett Books, 2007), 128.
2. *Left Gurdjieff.* Ouspensky then started his own "line" of the teaching. He was seen several more times thereafter at the Prieuré, but what transpired is not known. In midsummer 1931, Ouspensky met Gurdjieff at the Café Henri IV in Fontainebleau. It was the last time they would see one another.
3. *Skeletons.* G. I. Gurdjieff, *Meetings with Remarkable Men,* 278.
4. *The enemy.* Gurdjieff, 278.
5. *After centuries.* Robert D. Kaplan, *Eastward to Tartary* (New York: Random House, 2000); Christopher J. Walker, *Armenia: The Survival of a Nation,* rev. 2nd ed. (New York: St. Martin's Press, 1990).
6. *Take from.* Gurdjieff, 88.
7. *To have a particular smell.* Gurdjieff, 283.
8. *A wonderful people.* Cecil Lewis, *All My Yesteryears: An Autobiography* (Rockport, ME: Element, 1993), 174–76.

TGJ #28

Gurdjieff & Money

W<small>HEN</small> M<small>R</small>. G<small>URDJIEFF</small> <small>ARRIVED IN</small> R<small>USSIA IN</small> 1912 <small>HE DID NOT</small> come as a beggar but as a man of some wealth. He came with a million rubles, a fantastic sum at that time; one ruble could feed a lower-class family of five for about three days. He came as well with two invaluable collections, one of old and rare carpets, and another of porcelain and Chinese cloisonné. He came, as he said, with a "sacred task"—to establish the ancient teaching of The Fourth Way in the West.

His plan was to create an institute in which "helper-instructors" would be trained who would spread the teaching throughout the West. Having already solved what he termed "the material question," he was financially independent in the full meaning of the term. Thus, he had no need to depend upon or cater to anyone. He did not inherit this wealth, nor was it otherwise given to him, but rather with his wits and hard work he earned it. He speaks of how he amassed such a princely fortune in great detail in an "addendum" to the ten chapters that make up the *Second Series* of his initiatory text *All and Everything*.

America's Predominant Urge

This addendum seems to throw the whole book off-kilter and raises a number of questions about the writer, for he made the money in large part by taking advantage of people's ignorance and credulity. It is all rather distasteful—but then how are great sums of money made so quickly? We expect such of robber barons and politicians and their ilk, but not of a man who is charged with a sacred task. And worse, Gurdjieff appeared to take pride in duping others, saying that "the process itself of earning money never took much of my time, because, owing to the resourcefulness and common sense developed in me by correct education, I was already in all these life matters what might be called an expert, cunning old blade." Money itself, and the love of it, he spoke of as being "despicable and maleficent," and often connected this with America and its identification with money. He spoke, for example, of the American habit of "implanting in children the love of dollars . . . just this love of 'dollar business' and of dollars themselves, has become, in the common presence of each of the native inhabitants of this continent who reaches responsible age, the predominant urge during his responsible what is called 'feverish existence.'"

People's Attitude Toward Money

But Gurdjieff was an eminently practical man and he understood that to accomplish his task he would need money. Arriving with such a magnificent sum, still he asked students for a thousand rubles a year, an amount that caused Ouspensky, who was charged with enlisting pupils for the St. Petersburg groups, much consternation. Ouspensky reports Gurdjieff telling him that "he did not desire and *ought not*—he emphasized this—to spend his own money on the organization of the work. His work was not, and could not be, of a charitable nature and his pupils themselves ought to find the means for the hire of apartments where they could meet; for carrying out experiments; and so on. Besides this, he added that observation showed that people who were weak in life proved themselves weak in the work." Later, he added, "No, even if we needed no money at all it would still be necessary to keep this payment. It rids us at once of many useless people. Nothing shows up people so much as their attitude towards money."

Gurdjieff understood that most people's relationship to money was neurotic or juvenile: "Man never on any account wants to pay for anything," he said, "and above all he does not want to pay for what is most important for him. You now know that everything must be paid for and that it must be paid for in proportion to what is received. But usually a man thinks to the contrary. For trifles, for things that are perfectly useless to him, he will pay anything. But for something important, never. This must come to him of itself."

Ouspensky obviously was of many minds about the "money question," but he came to see that Gurdjieff was establishing the principle so that he might see the question at a deeper level. In practice, Gurdjieff often acted differently. As Ouspensky reported: "Many people indeed could not pay. And although in principle G. put the question very strictly, in practice he never refused anybody on the grounds that they had no money."

After the Russian Revolution broke out, Gurdjieff lost most of his money but had to support many of his students. Circumstances in revolutionary Russia became so chaotic that Gurdjieff and his group were finally forced to leave. In doing so, what remained of his rubles was absolutely worthless. In Essentuki he pointed out to Ouspensky: "Now do you understand why we collected money in Moscow and St. Petersburg? You said then that a thousand rubles was too much. And will even this money be enough? One and a half persons paid. I have now already spent more than was collected then."

Arriving in Constantinople in July 1920, this man who eight years earlier had come to Russia with a million and more rubles now had urgent money needs. What he called "the material question" would follow him for all but a few years prior to his death. Within a year he and his followers would embark for Europe where, after many difficulties, he would finally establish in France his Institute for the Harmonious Development of Man.

The Pressure for Money

In Europe Gurdjieff was literally a stranger in a strange land. Not only did he have to teach himself a working knowledge of English, French and German but he also had to deal with European customs, almost all of which he found abnormal. And besides providing for the needs of his extended family, he continued to support many of those who came with him from Russia. The enormous strain and pressure required an unceasing struggle.

Seeing how identified Westerners were with money, Gurdjieff quickly saw its use not only in practical terms, but as a means of putting his students "in galoshes"—that is, totally psychologized between a 'yes' and a 'no.' It was a painful experience, as we will see shortly. But, initially, his asking students for money was no problem. Orage said, for example: "Gurdjieff says that the attitude to finance is all part of the dream state that we live in. If men could wake up it would very soon be changed. Gurdjieff's attitude to money is different from that of anyone I have met. . . . Gurdjieff may appear to be throwing money about, but he calculates and uses it for certain non-personal ends."

But under Gurdjieff's constant insistence for money, Orage's attitude began to change. Six years later Orage was saying, "The situation is anything but bright and I confess to a little fatigue with Gurdjieff and his ways. Perhaps that is because I've just had to find over two hundred dollars with which to discharge the debts he failed to remember." [During his last visit to New York.]

Along with Orage, Gurdjieff pressured other students, especially Jean Toomer, who organized and led the Chicago groups, and regularly had to ask his students for special donations. As the demands never seemed to cease, they caused great turmoil with resulting doubts about Gurdjieff. And so, though he was thousands of miles and an ocean away, Gurdjieff created situations whereby students might see themselves. In this light it is interesting to read how Toomer reacted. It should be noted that Toomer was in a unique position in regard to money, having married Marjorie Content, a woman of great wealth through her father, a Wall Street financier. In what follows it will be seen how Gurdjieff used money to create deep questions and suffering in Toomer. Interestingly, Toomer even saw, albeit only intellectually, what Gurdjieff was doing.

"I have always thought," wrote Toomer, "that he used the money thing as a lever with which to work on you—one of the few and most effective ready-made levers available to him in relation to you, as you live under a system of private ownership and difficult peculiar finances, in short, under the capitalistic order, or disorder. Not that he does not want the money, but that he achieves two results, one for himself, one for yourself, by use of the one means."

One can see Toomer valiantly struggling not to get stuck in regard to Gurdjieff and money: "One surely must think twice and again and again," he said, "before hardening and fixing the belief that Gurdjieff is after money only. To me, this belief never has and does not now seem tenable. Surely also, if one has feeling for the work and good will towards him, one must be on the alert so as not to refuse help if and when the call 'Wolf, wolf,' really means wolf."

Mental Gymnastics

Toomer saw that what Gurdjieff was putting him through mentally was very much like doing the physical movements and dances. Wrote Toomer: "You find your mind and psyche going through *gymnastics* which require your inner world to perform feats of coordination and endurance quite similar to those required of the body in the exercises and dances demonstrated by Gurdjieff and his pupils when he first came to this country in 1924 [when he first met Gurdjieff]. Witness myself. This that I have written and much more was stirred up in me owing to the fact that I was asked for an additional three hundred [dollars] in the circumstances I have described. Not every day does one experience such a plowing."

What follows is Toomer's remembrance of his experience with Gurdjieff in 1934–35 over the said "material question." To understand what is happening beneath the words and events, one has to remember that Gurdjieff used money as a teaching tool. Gurdjieff many times emphasized that no one else was in a position to employ his special techniques. But that, of course, has not stopped a good many faux-Gurdjieffians from financially exploiting and harassing their students in Gurdjieff's name.

Yesterday morning, already informed by Gurdjieff that he would leave America for France today, knowing that he had insufficient money for this purpose, I gave him two hundred dollars. The money was hardly in his pocket when he began working on me for more. He invited me to lunch. I knew what it was for. I accepted. I accepted for a totality of reasons [and] also because I had an immediate matter which I wished to put to the test. At two o'clock, I presented myself at his apartment, a one room and kitchen affair on West 69th Street, piled up with I do not know how many suit cases and loaded trunks.

The Unique Idiot

Lunch, prepared by himself, was ready. His unpublished manuscripts were stretched on the bed. When I entered he arose, saying he was tired. By the feel of things I knew he was not leaving America the next day.

The food, like all the food he prepares, was amazing, original, unlike any food I've tasted elsewhere. As customary, vodka was poured and the toasts to the idiots began. First, to the health of all ordinary idiots. Having drunk half a glass to all ordinary idiots we began eating. Meat of which I did not know the name. Smoked fish, really smoked and really delicious. Salad with a mustard-wine vinegar sauce.

"The Son of man came eating and drinking..."

Always when presiding at a table Gurdjieff has a certain charm and lordliness. He devours his food and thinks well of you if you do likewise. Always when eating he is lavish, unstinted, with instinctive generosity. A young Russian typist had come in to do his afternoon work. Gurdjieff had the youth sit with us at the table and supplied him with all the food he could eat, food he could not possibly buy at any restaurant here or in Europe.

The toasts were drunk, scaling up from ordinary idiots to super idiots, arch idiots, hopeless idiots, compassionate idiots, squirming idiots, square idiots, round idiots. . . . At each toast half a glass of vodka went down the hatch. After each drink a sizable quantity of food was consumed. Life was jovial, mellow, expansive, with just the right amount of gusto to accompany the eating of food by men.

He himself, by the way, calls himself the unique idiot. The unique idiot is twenty-one on the scale: You seldom reach a toast to it. Should you, Gurdjieff guarantees that while everyone is under the table he will dance on the table top. Also by the way, it is generally understood by those who dine and drink with him that God is his heir, and that when he dies God will then become the unique idiot.

The main dish of the present lunch consisted of four young chickens, split in half, potatoes underneath, small cuts of some strange meat on top, all cooked together in a deep pan with a golden colored gravy at the bottom. It really was a delicious dish; and while we were eating it, picking the meat from the bone with our fingers, Gurdjieff remarked with a smile that this food alone, without any extra effort on the part of man, would be enough to take him to paradise. Of course, he added, the food would have to be eaten not once but right along. Lunch finished, we smoked, Gurdjieff momentarily reclining on the bed, propped on an elbow. He had to get up in order to show the typist where to begin. And, on his feet, he bethought himself of his business with me.

An Original Office

For this business we repaired to the bathroom, an "original office" as Gurdjieff had said before on the occasion of previous visits to its privacy, the only private place in the apartment, what with two typists in the main room and of the clowning sort, typewriters banging there. In this original office there was barely enough room for the two of us. Into my mind came the line, "'Won't you come into my parlor,' said the spider to the fly."

To the bathroom, then we hied ourselves, not without fitting ceremony. The gist of the business was this. He would not leave tomorrow on the *Île de France* which I already knew. He would leave a week hence on the Paris. Now this delay made certain things necessary. Of course, said I to myself. It necessitated that he send two hundred and fifty dollars (Ah-ha, said I to myself) to France by cable in advance of his arrival. It necessitated that he have money to live on while still in America. In short, he needed about three hundred and thirty dollars. For this sum he depended upon me exclusively, naturally. It was possible for him to get it elsewhere, but for reasons growing out of his policies with different people, and also because of his aims, he did not want to call upon those people at this time for this need. It is up to me. He gave his essence-word that in four months he would pay me back. Not only would he pay me back but I'd have a place in his future creations. If, however, I failed him, he and the entire work would go up the chimney, as this was the critical hour.

I listened. I nodded. I smiled. Inwardly I had the same disquieting feelings aroused in me by similar situations in the past when he had worked on me for money, feelings similar to those he had aroused in others, feelings which in some instances had driven them off from him with disgust and anger and the conviction that he was using his power merely in order to obtain money, money, and more money without cease.

I remembered other times, other "critical hours," in which he had put it up to me, I being cast for the role of the only one who could save the situation. I squirmed, because I resented being worked on in this way. I squirmed. I knew, and I knew he knew, that it was only because of my positive sense of him, because of my positive experience with and belief in his work, and his ideas, that I had let myself in for such a situation where demands could be made of me with some effectiveness. I squirmed and was incredulous that he would try to work the same old trick again, seeing that just this trick had driven me away from him the previous spring soon after his arrival in this country. I felt awful, because just this behavior of his was again putting my belief in him to a severe test, threatening to collapse every positive feeling I had, threatening to undermine the very beliefs and hopes upon which my life had rested and moved ever since 1924.

Who Is Gurdjieff?

What could be in the man's mind? Who and what was he? What were his purposes? What aims did he have for me, if any? What aims for the people of the world? Was I a mere tool? Was I not even that, so nothing from his point of view that he need not even consider the way he used or misused me? Was he, as some claimed, insane? Did he, as some also claimed, know psychic laws but was essentially stupid in his practical dealings with people? If he knew anything at all about me, how could he fail to know that I was ready and willing to do all I possibly could as regards any real need of his that I could grasp and understand, whereas just these tricky manipulative tactics were sure to throw me off?

Or on the other hand, was he under the guise of this, to me, distasteful proposal, trying to do something for my good? I recalled a saying of his—"The means are mine. You look for the results in yourself." I also recalled—" You can see only the present. I see in terms of a hundred years." So then was he producing in me some necessary tension? Was he showing me, so that I could not possibly fail to see for myself, that for all of my professed great and deep belief in the work, I could be thrown off by some comparatively trivial thing simply because it rubbed me the wrong way? Obviously my declarations of value were but declarations if I suddenly faced about and disavowed everything merely because he put a screw in me and turned it.

This is what is so awful about the situations with Gurdjieff. The situations themselves are always taxing—and you can arrive at no sure reconciliation or fixed understanding because for every fact there is a counterfact, for every reason a counter reason, for every bit of "bad" behavior another bit of "good" behavior, for every son-of-a-bitching thing a counter saintly thing.

Why Manipulate?

Gurdjieff was talking away. He said, among other things, "It is not for me. I am nothing." Suddenly with utter sincerity, I said, "I feel the same way. I am nothing." And I did feel it. I felt I wasn't important, not the slightest. I felt I had reached the limit of my possibilities. I felt there was no further use that I tax myself, not in relation to him, not in relation to anything, but mainly not for myself. I felt selfless, without ego. I felt I would gladly willingly give all I was and all I had if it would be of any service to others. I felt that an additional three hundred dollars was nothing at all to contribute to his work, if it really were a *work*, if it really was destined to be of vast service to mankind. What were three hundred dollars? What was three thousand or three hundred thousand dollars? Every American month and year such sums are squandered on nonessentials, staked and lost on projects of no real benefit to anyone even if they do succeed, such sums and vastly larger sums are sunk into battle ships and the various instruments of man's war against man. Three hundred, for a creative service? It was far too little to give.

But if just this sum was needed for just this need, then why manipulate? Why not a straight request so that I could respond with a straight hand? Why not do it in a way that would assure me that the sum would be thus used, that after I had given the three hundred I would not at once find myself being worked for an additional five hundred, and so on and so on as long as I could scrape together a cent—or until I, like others before me, became disillusioned and embittered and broke off from him completely.

We left the bathroom and took chairs in the main room, the typewriter pounding and clacking. We smoked and joked. I asked Gurdjieff certain questions about myself. He said I did not deserve to know. I asked, "If I do not deserve, then who does?" His reply was that nobody deserved. I asked, "Then for whom are you doing all this work?" "I will live for coming generations," he said. "It is for them."

Again, as in the past, he thwarted these kind of questions, refused to give me this kind of assurance that I would get anything in these terms from him.

In my mind was the thought, "I do not count. Not finished but not important." In my feelings was the feeling, "Nothing more is possible for me." So then, of what use can I be to others? I could not feel that to give an additional three hundred dollars would be any real use. It would be burnt up quickly as the sums in the past had been burnt up, going like smoke up the chimney. When I went home I'd have to face my wife with it. My wife would be thrown off because she, like any sane human being, would be thrown off convinced that my leg was being pulled, convinced that Gurdjieff had wanted to see me again only so as [to] get money from me again, he knowing that I had married into a wealthy family. What a devilish hellish situation. Or, perhaps, a situation of purgatory. I recalled his idea of the value of suffering. I was suffering. I recalled his saying, a memorable saying that is a key to the meaning of the entire work and method, "You here already having realized that you have only yourself to contend with; therefore thank those who give you the opportunity." I was contending with myself, wondering if I would be wise or a fool to thank him. "Oh ye of little faith," a voice in me said.

He was ready for his afternoon rest. Beginning at 6 or 7 a.m. he writes of his latest work at Child's. If you go up to see him you find him there at a table, as inconspicuous as any of the restaurant's patrons except for his unusual practice of writing there all morning completely absorbed and concentrated, pausing for brief intervals to drink coffee. Around noon he goes out to shop for lunch. Then, returned to his apartment, he cooks. He eats and drinks, and drinks a fair amount of vodka or apple jack so as to relax. We had gone through it all.

Now, about 3:30, he wanted to get the full benefit of relaxation. He invited me to dinner that same night saying he would cook a special dish for me, whatever I wanted. I smiled. As I went out he was pulling back the bed cover, preparatory to sleeping for an hour or so in the midst of the typist and the clacking machine.

As I walked to the subway and thence home, I recalled many things. With the vodka in me I too waited to relax. The situation would not let me let myself.

I recalled my meetings with him the previous spring soon after his arrival from Europe. I had not seen him for several years. Learning that I was in New York he asked someone to call me, saying that Mr. Gurdjieff wanted to see me at Child's that evening. I went. He was in a bad way. His health was poor. He looked it, liverish, looked as if he had been drawn through a mill, was laboring under a heavy ceaseless strain physically and mentally and every way. Leaning towards me he told of certain difficulties in France, said that now he really needed me. In the past he had not. Now he did. He spoke about the future and hinted at certain rewards that [would] be mine then if I helped him now. I, moved deeply, replied that already he had done an inestimable amount for me and that out of gratitude, with no thought of further reward, I would gladly do all I could [to] help him meet his present extremity.

A Changed Man?

My mind flashed over subsequent happenings, the sum result of which was that I felt a great relief when I left New York and thus left him. To me he seemed a changed man, changed for the worse. I felt his work was dead. Whether dead or not, there was no place or function for me in it. It was a travesty and hollow mockery of the work I had entered in 1924 with all my heart. I would have nothing to do with what was going on at present. I would have something to do with future work—if there was a future work—on the critical basis as if I were meeting him and his work for the first time, taking nothing for granted.

I recalled the messages from him that reached me in the Southwest. I recalled my return with my family to New York in the fall, and the one abortive overture that was made me via Fred Leighton [one of Gurdjieff's pupils, at whose apartment he sometimes stayed when in New York] the very evening of my arrival when I was fatigued by travel and facing the difficulties of adjusting a young child to strange people and a new environment.

I recalled how I had felt all summer that Gurdjieff considered no one but himself, that he had a way of making his needs and difficulties seem a thousand times more vast and portentous than mine or yours, that he was stranger and wiser than any of us [and] had a way of calling upon the weak and stupid to help him out— and we, the idiots he so freely called us, fell to and did help him, feeling that he was weak and in grave need whereas we were able to do things for him, to do things for him even at the neglect of those actually depending upon us.

Was this the meaning of St. Matthew 10: 34–39, "For I am come to set a man at variance. . . ." I recalled how, from October to the following January, I had been cut off from him, not seeing him at all, he making no effort to have me see him.

During these months I heard of goings on, later, scandals, God knows what not, all at second or third hand. On the face of them, these stories piled up to substantiate the feeling, not only of myself but of many of Gurdjieff's former followers, that the work was dead, that Gurdjieff was like a wheel gone off its axle careening smartly down the road with mad velocity smashing into things right and left, caring for nothing and nobody. Only his writings, his great books, remained. Whatever people had come to feel of Gurdjieff himself, everyone and of course I myself, still maintained and upheld the greatness of his ideas. They are *source*. There are none to be classed with them in any literature of my acquaintance, his vast works with their incomparable psychology of man, their truths, their convincing knowledge of reality.

His Behavior Was Awful

His behavior during these months as reported to me by a few people who had seen him was awful. Hearing these reports strengthened my own personal impression of him gained the previous spring. Heretofore my position had been this: Though I would have nothing to do with him in his present phase, though I would certainly not bring any new people to him, neither would I judge him one way or the other. He seemed to be tearing down everything he had created, his life seemed a blight, he was alienating people and throwing them off right and left, of all those formerly interested in him only Fred Leighton remained faithful, but I would not put myself in the judgment seat and judge him. Who was I to judge him? Now, however, everything piled up in me and quite deliberately I moved myself out of the state of suspended judgment. On certain occasions to certain people who were in a position to critically weigh what I said, I let fly.

A for me interesting situation developed. Now that I was apparently turning against him, certain of those whom I had taught to have a positive sense of him now turned about and began instructing me to have a positive belief in him. That I, the erstwhile teacher, found myself in the role of a student to my own former pupils who had now risen above me because they saw and believed whereas I was blind and skeptical. The situation was not without its humor. Not without irony too, irony and several disquieting elements involving my responsibility as the person instrumental in bringing them into the Gurdjieff world.

Time passed.

The "Old" Gurdjieff Returns

One day in early January Fred Leighton phoned to say that Gurdjieff asked me to a special meeting. I said I would be there. In general I thought it possible and expected that at any time Gurdjieff would really "start something," that the pendulum having swung to one extreme would begin its swing to the other. Perhaps this special meeting would mark the turning point. I felt sure that Gurdjieff would speak. I was extremely curious to see him again, to sense him again, to test for myself first hand if any changes had occurred in him during those months of which I had had such wild reports.

I presented myself. Gurdjieff, to my eyes and senses, seemed much the same as ever, much the same as the man I had known in years past, his health obviously improved over the condition I had last seen him in the previous spring. Indeed he seemed happy. He had the air of a free man. I recalled what Leighton had told me of what Gurdjieff had told him, that just during this period he was as happy as he'd ever been in his life. To me personally he was as affable as I was to him. It seemed that we both tacitly agreed to let bygones be bygones. Insane? He was in full possession of every one of his extraordinary faculties. Debauched and slovenly? Nothing of the sort. Afraid of the dark and of being alone? It was ridiculous. Whatever he had gone through, the thing that showed plainly was a decided improvement in every respect.

Leighton and Israel Solon [an American student of Orage's] were there when I arrived: others had been asked, a picked number. No others showed up. After waiting a while Gurdjieff asked first myself and then Leighton to read aloud from the manuscript he was then working on, an introduction to his books which would replace *The Herald of Coming Good*. With this latter book, the only one of his writings to be published to date, Gurdjieff said he was dissatisfied.

Before the reading, at intervals during it, and after the reading, Gurdjieff made remarks in his unique way, remarks about myself and my position and condition, remarks about Leighton and Solon. Some were obviously jokes. Others were just as obviously of a different category, in the manner and tradition of his way of teaching, one of his ways.

Teachings? Yes, one can so utilize it for himself. As to Gurdjieff's aim, it may not be this at all, certainly it is not so simple, and certainly it includes his interest to see how we respond to his prods.

While he was preparing a late and rather lavish supper, Leighton, Solon and I worked on the translation. It would be more accurate to say that those two worked. For myself, my reflections and questions about Gurdjieff and the events of the evening were of far more importance than any slight help I might have given to the manuscript.

Gurdjieff's "Taking"

Supper began—and, of course, the toasts to the idiots. In the course of eating and drinking quite a number of things came up, among them Solon's accusation to Gurdjieff that Gurdjieff stole or tricked money from people. Gurdjieff denied it. He [Gurdjieff] said he took it. I backed him up. I said he took it. And he does. The distinction may not seem important, but it has, I feel, a direct and significant bearing on the general way in which Gurdjieff operates.

He gives, as he was giving the suppers. He takes. Often as not he will even tell you in advance that he is going to take. Tricks he has, and he uses them apparently without conscience. But believe me he is not and never has been and never will be a petty trickster. His use of tricks is so glaring that they almost shout at you telling you what they are. He knows they are tricks. So do you. If you then fall for them can you accuse him of dishonesty?

He fixes a situation. He leads you into it. You go into it, eyes open. Then he takes—if you let him, and often you do. If you let him, if he takes today, then you may be sure that as long as you have relations with him you will again and again find yourself in a similar situation. If you withhold, then again as long as you have relations with him a similar situation will be repeated.

Why? Why does he work it this way? Might as well ask the sphinx. Is there some profound teaching and training involved? Or doesn't it, on the contrary, argue that he has a most cynical view of human nature, believing that people are but sheep who must be sheared because they wouldn't understand and respond to his need if he presented it as a human being to human beings?

The Great Turning Point

From Leighton I had previously learned that Gurdjieff was now again in a bad way financially, trying to hold on until his birthday, the middle of January our calendar. This date, the middle of January, was to be the great turning point, the ending of one long period during which Gurdjieff, in addition to writing, was building up his body and his physical health. By January 15th his body would be fully restored, his writing would be finished, and immediately thereafter he would enter upon an entirely new phase.

Earlier this evening Gurdjieff had said some extremely interesting things which threw light on his apparently shameful conduct during the past months. The gist of what he said was this. That in order to restore himself, particularly his body, it was necessary that he suffer. In order to suffer he had deliberately done things to people and situations which would enter into his automatic processes and of themselves cause suffering and make him suffer whenever he remembered them. An amazing idea, an amazing intention!

If it was to be credited, it fully explained why he had manufactured scandal after scandal, trouble after trouble, each one worse than the preceding, crescendo, during the past months. True, it did not touch on the benefits or disasters experienced by those others who were parties to his Gurdjieffian nights. True too, it may have been no more and no less than an objective afterthought, a bit of rationalizing that amounted to a strike of genius. But, as I say, if the explanation of intentional suffering were to be credited, it did completely illumine his own conduct, and it did explain how the "maniac" of the past few months was now this eminently sane, sound, rather quiet, even rather circumspect personage who presided at the supper table. And it did somewhat explain the circumstance related by Leighton that throughout the "worst of it" Gurdjieff had treated him, Leighton, in much the same way as he had always treated him, never mistreating him.

A Revival of Feeling

During the course of the supper I felt a revival of my old feeling for Gurdjieff. The drinks helped my subconscious self to come out, and I found myself, with something like a rush of feeling, *once more affirming him*. My mind was working too. I did not want to be importuned for money. I did want to offer it to him voluntarily if he really needed it. Before the evening was over I proposed that we, myself, Leighton and Solon too, *and I had others in mind*, work out a scheme whereby Gurdjieff would receive from us a definite amount each week for the period of a month. Later on, the plan was actually carried into effect. After leaving Gurdjieff that evening I did not see him again for several weeks.

That was early in January. February was over half over when I again got a call. I went to lunch. I went to dinner. The upshot of it all was that Gurdjieff, planning to leave America on March 2nd, needed money for the passage. Practically no manipulation was required, nor resistance against manipulation, for me to promise two hundred dollars. This done, I felt at ease, and, also, just a little virtuous. I breathed a sigh of relief and satisfaction. This time, it seemed pure, the money transaction would occur simply, without "tactics," on the simple real basis of one person responding to another's need.

I soon saw, however, that, for some reason or other, I was in for a period of being called upon to come to lunch, come to dinner, come for Turkish bath. Gurdjieff is that way. If he calls you he calls you. With him it is all or nothing. He wants to take you away from everything else—or, in any case, he wants you when he wants you, often, one after the other—and it is up to you to decide that you too want or else call a halt.

It was just this by me previously known tendency that I had braced myself against when returning to New York in the fall. I had my own life and affairs, my own world; I had not wanted to be absorbed by him into his affairs and his world, even though I liked his cooking, always got something from being with him, and, in a way, really and sincerely considered it a rare privilege to be in his company. I may be mistaken but I also believe that thousands of people also would consider it such a privilege, *if* they had a genuine sense of him, *if* he would discontinue his strange baffling antagonism-arousing tactics. Through the fog which he himself creates around himself there are but few who can see and sense him—and of these few, all are alternatively drawn towards him and repelled, praising, damming, appreciating, cursing.

All fall and winter I had been on my street, he had been on his. Now in February he was asking that I come. What was it? Was he . . . [Copy of manuscript obscured. The previous summer, while in the Southwest of the United States, Toomer had written a letter to Gurdjieff in which he refused certain of Gurdjieff's requests.] . . . strength of the position as stated in my letter? Or did he think that because of several considerations it was time for me to move out towards him and him towards me?

Many reasons lead me to go. I calculated that it would last

only until March 2nd, and for this short period I could manage to harmonize my sessions with him with my personal life and work. I went. I returned. I went. I returned. I looked to see what was happening in me. I looked to see what was happening to those intimately related to me. I thought about the situation of my visits with him. One large thing I disliked. As circumstances were, I was in a passive role in a passive position. Unlike myself in former years, now this year I wanted nothing special of him. I was related to him through no active mutual work. I was like a visitor, a guest, yet not like a guest either because, owing to long established relative positions, he was the master, I the pupil, but, now, he with a master's prerogative, I without a student's initiative and purpose. In this passive position I was a piano to be played upon—and some of the times I did not like, while others I did like, but the main point was that I resented and resisted my passive and therefore relatively purposeless and helpless role. My only struggle was a struggle to maintain my individuality and balance. But, as my totality was passive, I often felt as if I were struggling in a void—not at all a pleasant sensation.

Some interesting things were said. On the whole, he talked more freely than was his former wont.

One evening at Child's he talked to Dahl [identity unknown] and myself about tapeworms. It began as a joke. Pointing to me he remarked that in spite of my good appetite I remained thin. Why? Perhaps a tapeworm, he said. He then began talking of an experience in which he and a physician finally delivered a patient of a tapeworm with two heads, one head having already been removed, a three-headed rascal. Leighton joined us. Gurdjieff told Leighton the joke on me. Leighton thought it was a good one on me. The smile left his face when Gurdjieff turned on him with the remark that he too had a tapeworm. Not one like mine; Leighton's was, if you please, an astral tapeworm. My physical worm made me physically thin. Leighton's astral worm made him psychically heavy. Physical thinness, psychic heaviness, such were the different results produced by the respective worms.

On another occasion in a serious mood, Gurdjieff made plain the distinction between the automatic and the conscious processes of man. He explained also that real mentation, thinking of a thing, thinking about a thing all round from all possible aspects and angles, happened only infrequently in man. To me he suggested the outline of the way in which a man gathers material for the formation of his "I." To me one day he said that I had no notion of how my subconscious, the real part of me, was related to him.

One afternoon in his apartment before lunch he happened to notice the shoes I was wearing, English waterproofs. We fell to talking about the products turned out by various countries, England sewed honest products but expensive, Germany flooding the world, now Japan was rivaling Germany. We spoke about the Japanese, and, in reply to my question as to why the Japanese were so energetic and enterprising he remarked that the conditions of life in Japan discouraged the rearing of parasites and made for the growth of productive men. Not education, he said, but life itself does it in Japan.

Why Gurdjieff Created Difficulties

One morning in Child's we reminisced about the motor trips he used to take, excursions out from the Château at Fontainebleau to the various parts of France. By all ordinary standards they were wild reckless daring exhausting trips. I had always wondered precisely why he took them as he did. Already I knew that while his body was occupied with driving he composed his writing. Now he explained that he had also done it to tire his body so that his body would rest and thus enable him to rest his mind, which otherwise might have burnt up from ceaseless overwork. Said I, "I thought you did it, created all those difficulties, in order to generate energy." "That too," he replied, "Many different combinations all at the same time."

He then told me that following his motor accident he had been compelled to produce energy artificially. To this end, during the few following years, he had consumed enough drink to have killed ten men and, in addition, forty pounds of opium. To my question, "Did you know in advance what you were doing, or was it an experiment attended by a grave risk?" he replied, "It was necessary to create energy artificially, my condition and my means and aims were such. I knew, yet it was also an experiment and risk."

Sometime later, having meanwhile changed moods a thousand times it seemed, we talked about the chapter in his *First Series* in which he formulates the relative understanding of time. He asked me if I had had some sense of the truth before reading the chapter.

"Yes," I said, "I knew that there was no correspondence between what we may call my personal experience of time and a calendar year. How long is a year? How long is a day? In one day I may, so to speak, live a month. I am forty years old. What does that really mean? Who knows how long I've lived in my forty years?"

He nodded. "Speaking just like that, I can tell you I've lived thousands of years. It is possible to know how to live thousands of years in one life." "I believe it," I said, "For instance, I'm sure that in some way you actually experienced Tikliamish and those ancient civilizations you write about in the *First Series*."

"Could not be imagination," he said.

"Could not," I agreed. "Your words and descriptions convey the sense of actual personal experience."

Again later he remarked in a quite different vein, "I tell you something secret, only for yourself. Twenty-one years ago I vowed never to use hypnotism to effect my aims. Recent circumstances have make me struggle with myself to keep my vow. I not want to break it. But recently I lose sixty million francs. Not lose on stock market or by fire or ordinary ways. Combination of forces take away. I not want to break my vow." As this "secret" was told to me by Orage some years ago, I feel quite at liberty to pass it on to you.

In still another mood he recalled to me his chapter which narrates the process by which God created the world, first by emanations from himself, and later the entire work of universe making went on by itself. "Just so," he said, "I create my world. First, emanations. Then everything happens. But my task more difficult than God's. God have to destroy nothing first. Nothing existed. He simply created. But I, I must tear down before I can create. Double work. If you want to put new building across the street you must first tear down old one."

I nodded understandingly. I smiled. "Yes," I said. "I see. Now another answer to 'the burning question of the day' as to how and wherein our Gurdjieff differs from God." He too smiled.

The Ruler of Africa

That afternoon after lunch in his apartment I reminded him of a joking promise he had once made me. "Remember," I asked, "Remember? Once you promised to make me ruler of Africa."

"Something went wrong," he smiled.

"Is my psyche African?" I asked.

"African."

"At different times you have told me it was English and, again, typically American. I don't understand."

"You not as I counted," he said.

"How do you mean?"

"In the very beginning I counted you."

I suppose he meant that when he first saw me he calculated and, so to say, got my number. He went on, "You not as I counted."

"How do you mean?"

"You manifest differently at different times, different from what I expected. You not as I counted, and I get angry."

"Angry? Why?"

"You not as I counted."

Some ten years after Toomer's experience, Gurdjieff gave his perspective on "the material question." He said: "You remember Prieuré and how many times I have struggle with money. I not make money like others make money, and when I have too much money, I spend. But I never need money for self, and I not make or earn money, I ask for money and people always give, and for this I give opportunity study my teaching, but even when they give money still almost always impossible for them learn anything. Already, they think of reward…now I owe them something because they give me money. When think of reward in this way, impossible learn anything from me." ✕

Notes

1. *A sacred task.* G. I. Gurdjieff, *Meetings with Remarkable Men,* 270.
2. *An expert, cunning old blade.* Gurdjieff, 252.
3. *Feverish existence.* G. I. Gurdjieff, *All and Everything,* 920.
4. *Weak in the work.* P. D. Ouspensky, *Search,* 102.
5. *Attitude toward money.* Ouspensky, 165.
6. *This must come to him of itself.* Ouspensky, 178.
7. *He never refused anybody.* Ouspensky, 165.
8. *I have now already spent more.* Ouspensky, 371.
9. *Between a "yes" and a "no."* Said Toomer: "More than one person more than one time has, after leaving Gurdjieff, found himself to be just such a split fool in hell. How he loves to put people in galoshes—as he expresses it. He is

too polite to use such a phrase as split fool in hell. No, he simply puts you in galoshes. If you say yes you are a fool. If you say no you are two fools. If you say both yes and no you are a split fool in hell."

10. *Non-personal ends.* C. S. Nott, *Teachings of Gurdjieff* (London: Arkana, 1990), 35.

11. *Yesterday morning.* Jean Toomer Papers (New Haven, CT: Yale University Library).

12. *I am forty years old.* Toomer was born in 1894.

13. *I owe them something.* Fritz Peters, *Gurdjieff Remembered*, 89–90.

From TGJ #16

The Redeemed Beelzebub
Pondering Chapter XLVII

READERS OF *ALL AND EVERYTHING, BEELZEBUB'S TALES TO HIS Grandson* are met from the outset with what seems like a labyrinth of words undulating riotously in a profusion of ideas, perspectives, insults and asides. And so from the very beginning Mr. Gurdjieff challenges the reader's sincerity of interest, demanding a directed, not captured, attention.

The book, a *Legominism*, that is, "the means of transmitting information about certain events of long-past ages through initiates," has three layers. The first of which is "To destroy, mercilessly, without any compromises whatsoever, in the mentation and feelings of the reader, the beliefs and views, by centuries rooted in him, about everything existing in the world." This assault is unflagging. The result is, if the reader submits, all the artifices of the knowledge he thinks he has about himself and the world will be stripped away. What is left is his quality of mentation alone. Why? Because only then will he truly be able to learn and grow. What is not generally understood is that there is a payment to be made for any genuine transformation. The payment is made in terms of one's time, energy and attention. We give it so easily to our daydreams and our personal life, but when it comes to the study of oneself in the persistent reading and rereading of *All and Everything* resistance arises. We are used to a book capturing our attention, letting us escape into its images. Gurdjieff confronts us with the meagerness of our attention and lack of will. If we accept this and patiently struggle on, not only will our attention and will increase, but also a new perspective will be born.

The interpretation that follows, certainly not definitive, is offered in the hope that those who have resisted Gurdjieff's book might become interested enough to give it another chance.

Colors of Being

Having thus begun, let us first note the chapter could have been titled "The *Lawful* Result of Impartial Mentation." But instead Gurdjieff chose the word *Inevitable,* which means the same but evokes an emotion, and hence more force. Gurdjieff's beginning this last chapter of the *Legominism* with Beelzebub as its first word adds even more force. And the last words of this first sentence tell us that "everything was suddenly lit up with a 'pale blue something.'" So Beelzebub, like everything within the spaceship *Karnak,* has changed color to pale blue. Later, we will find that Beelzebub becomes orange—the sacred rod which is the channel by which his horns are returned emanates the color orange—and, at the chapter's close he becomes pale yellow. It is at this point when Beelzebub's grandson—all references to Beelzebub are now capitalized as "His," "Him," "Your," and "Himself"—asks Him a last question of what would be said to our ALL-EMBRACING UNI-BEING-CREATOR concerning the possibility of saving the three-centered beings of the planet Earth by directing them "into the becoming path."

Note here that the now redeemed Beelzebub is spoken of as being One with the Creator, for as Gurdjieff writes:

> Simultaneously 'something' pale yellow began little by little to arise around Beelzebub and to envelop Him, and it was in no way possible to understand or to discern whence this something issued—whether it issued from Beelzebub Himself or proceeded to Him from space from sources outside of Him.

The answer Beelzebub gives to Hassein each reader should ponder for himself.

Returning to the chapter's beginning, we see that several archangels, a multitude of angels, cherubim and seraphim meet with Beelzebub's tribe in the main hall of the spaceship *Karnak* (the name calling up the great temple complex in ancient Thebes). Gurdjieff observes that these two groups are not the same but are "differently natured three-brained beings." What is this nature? Has the angelic ever been portrayed with horns? And what are horns?

Regardless of difference, the angelic and Beelzebub's tribe jointly sing the "Hymn to our ENDLESSNESS" which, we are told, is sung on such occasions everywhere "by beings of all natures and all forms of exterior coating." As the two different natures spoken of are both three-brained beings, and in an earlier chapter we are told that the difference between human beings and Beelzebub and his tribe is that we are two-natured and they are one-natured, it would be supposed that the angelic are also one-natured.

Passing beyond this, what is our ENDLESSNESS like? The Hymn gives some core attributes such as "Long Patient," "Abundantly LOV-ING," the "CAUSE Of All That Exists," and the "Unique VANQUISHER Of The Merciless *Heropass.*" So He is patient, loving, creative and a warrior—a Vanquisher of Time. We are told, too, that everything that breathes is a maintainer of the Universe on its level and in so doing extols the MAKER-CREATOR. (The capitalization may seem like an impediment to newer readers—presumably why the revised edition eliminates all such capitalization—but the loss is that the reader is not reminded of the magnitude of what is being given.)

The word "merit" is voiced in the Hymn and it will be used several more times in speaking of Beelzebub. To this reader's ears, when the word is first used by the venerable archangel it has a certain loving but sly undertone. He tells Beelzebub that a pardon has been granted to him from Above "and for certain of your merits." Is this a reference to what we read in Chapter II about Beelzebub's "as yet unformed Reason due to his youth" which gave him a "limited understanding" in how he saw the governance of the World and so it seemed to him "illogical"? He therefore rebelled and was exiled, hornless. Horns, we are told, define a being's "potency and degree of Reason."

In the classic edition there is a misprint; the word *variety* is used instead of *virility* (now corrected in the Errata). The revised edition substitutes the word *potency*, which gives a far larger meaning. (Like any revision, it has its strong and weak points; among the former, substituting the word *pentoëhary* for *piandjoëhary* in a previous chapter.)

He and his kinsman settled on the planet Mars, and as an earlier chapter tells us, it is soon after the birth of the planet Earth, as it was still in a cooling stage. Beelzebub, therefore was an eyewitness to all that subsequently took place. Instead of brooding, he made an active exploration of Ors, making several excursions to Saturn, as well as six descents to the planet Earth.

He lived a life of merit during his long exile. (In human time, he resided in our solar system some 14.6 billion years before a pardon was granted.) The number of horns he previously had is not known, but he now receives an awe-inspiring five horns. This means Beelzebub has attained the Reason of the sacred Podkoolad, which is "the last gradation before the Reason of the sacred Anklad," only "the third in degree from the Absolute Reason of HIS ENDLESS-NESS HIMSELF." We understand now that impartial mentation has within it many degrees, each sacred, others being Degindad and Ternoonald.

The sacred Anklad brings to mind the ancient Egyptian Ankh, the symbol of eternal life as well as the word for physical life. In the Egyptian creation story the god Atum emerges from the vast watery darkness of the deep called Nun onto a Primeval Mound from which he creates the gods, an ennead of nine gods, each being a manifestation of his creative powers, and every living thing. In the Memphite creation story, the creator is named Ptah and is located in the Heart and Tongue, one the seat of intellect, the other the weapon of creative power. In essence, what Gurdjieff is giving is a more detailed account of how creation came to be and how the very creation, and even the Sun Absolute itself (the Primeval Mound), was threatened by the merciless *Heropass.*

The Sacred Rod

A deep lesson of this chapter is the way Beelzebub's horns are restored. Active elements are channeled through the sacred rod having a ball at its end (one might conceive something like an ankh). The glowing orange rod, one of four in the Universe, is the sacred rod of the Archcherub Peshtvogner, one of four cardinal All-Quarters-Maintainers. As Beelzebub kneels before him, the venerable archangel puts the "chief end," the ball, over his head, pointing the opposite end—as every stick and spine has two ends—toward members of Beelzebub's tribe.

Previously, the venerable archangel has informed the tribe that those who wish to do so—the act is purely voluntary—can touch the sacred rod and, depending on the length of time touched, an equivalent amount of active elements will "pass from your own horns for the formation of the corresponding horns on this pardoned being of your nature."

One by one, all the members of Beelzebub's tribe touch the rod. The length of time is indicated by the captain of the *Karnak* because, one presumes, their ardency and reverence is such that some, perhaps all, might lose their horns entirely. We learn from this not only the need for a demonstration of gratitude and self-sacrifice, but that in terms of materiality there is not a making of more materiality, there is only an exchange of its gradations.

There is so much more that can be received from the chapter, a mere ten pages in all. Being only an interpretation, this essay cannot be a substitute for the direct experience of self-initiation which can only be had by one's own active reading and pondering. ⫝

Lord John Pentland: In Tribute

THIS YEAR MARKS THE TWENTIETH anniversary of the passing of Lord John Pentland, the remarkable man Mr. Gurdjieff chose to lead the work in America. Under his indefatigable leadership as president of the Gurdjieff Foundation of New York, from its inception in 1953 to his death thirty-one years later, the ancient teaching of The Fourth Way, rediscovered, reassembled and reformulated for modern times by George Ivanovitch Gurdjieff, grew significantly both in numbers of students and the establishment of foundations in many of the major cities of America. In the waning months of his life, Gurdjieff had told Lord Pentland: "You are like Paul; you must spread my ideas."

His Life Mission

Gurdjieff's directive became Lord Pentland's life mission and responsibility, one that he never shirked. He became an unwavering and instrumental force in establishing the teaching and in doing so had to bring together and reconcile many disparate elements. Always diffident and respectful of others, he was open to new ideas and approaches but his perspective was always clear: the need to preserve the teaching and protect it from the introduction of distortions. He had to employ all his considerable political skills and organizational ability to guide the teaching through the many societal and psychic innovations and disturbances of the 1960s and '70s. Not everyone shared the same level of understanding, of course, and so some viewed him as too doctrinaire and unbending.

In February 1976 he had a heart attack. It must have been severe as a pacemaker was installed and he did not return to leading groups until the fall. For months everyone had anticipated his return, and so one Sunday morning at the Foundation's estate at Armonk, New York, when the tall, thin and erect figure occupied the speaker's seat to open the day, a breathless quality entered the room. What would he say after so many months? He spoke in an even tone as always, never excessively underscoring a point, but the theme of his remarks—the questioning of whether or not the Work any longer had a purpose to serve—hit like a bombshell for those who took it as a statement of fact rather than a theme of inquiry. That the man who had been instrumental in creating the Foundation could be questioning its purpose was a red hot pepper for those who misunderstood the point he was making—that just as with a person, any spiritual or secular organization can become too fixed if it does not continually strive to keep its highest aim in view. It was a masterstroke. The work he presented thereafter, rather than energy work that can induce imagination if not properly discriminated, was a reemphasis on core teachings and a probing of self-limiting identifications and beliefs.

The Gift of a Sheik's Hat

In Lord Pentland's final years a student had traveled to Kars, the ancient and remote village where Gurdjieff had grown up, and on his return had stopped in the city of Konya, Turkey, a Naqshbandi and Mevlevi dervish center. Seemingly by chance, he had met an old man on the back street of a bazaar who handcrafted dervish hats. He was the only one authorized to do so, and the hats could only be sold with the permission of a sheik. Permission was granted for the purchase of a white sheik's hat. Upon the student's return, he presented it to Lord Pentland. Lord Pentland, who always eschewed ostentation of any type, was surprised and pleased. "He looked wonderful in it. Perfect," the student recounted.

Lord Pentland died in Houston from a heart attack on Valentine's Day. It seemed fitting that the end came while he was on the road visiting groups. The funeral was held at St. Vincent Ferrer Roman Catholic Church in Manhattan, only a few blocks from the New York Foundation. Following the initial Catholic ceremony, Lord Pentland's daughter, Mary Sinclair Rothenberg, walked to the pulpit and read from the Bible and then from *Sword of the North*, a novel about Prince Henry Sinclair, a thirteenth century warrior-chieftain and ancestor. The passage she read was of Prince Henry's death. Her voice was strong and clear and carried throughout the cavernous neo-gothic church. When she delivered the last line, however, her voice escaped her and the word *dead* shot into the high vaulting of the church and echoed down on the mourners in the pews.

Following her, a longtime and senior pupil and a group leader who later became president of the New York Foundation read from verses in Corinthians speaking of the vanity of man, the two bodies of man, one natural, the other spiritual. At the end of the reading, he noted that "Lord Pentland believed in the mystery of Resurrection."

William Segal, a close friend of Lord Pentland's and a senior group leader, spoke next. "Lord Pentland was the leader of the Gurdjieff Work in America," he said, "and a man who never spared himself in his role as a guide, as a teacher and as an administrator." He drew an intimate and loving portrait of his friend, explaining that Lord Pentland was much more carefree than many realized. "Lord Pentland was not afraid to laugh at himself," Segal said. The Saturday before his death, he said, he and some others had been with Lord Pentland when "a well-known philosopher was introduced to him and said, 'So you are the famous Lord Pentland!' and everyone laughed, especially Lord Pentland." Segal ended with the observation that in directing the work of the Gurdjieff Foundation Lord Pentland had taken on "impossible challenges." He then added with emphasis, "Lord Pentland was not afraid to be misunderstood."

With the Ouspenskys

He was born Henry John Sinclair on June 6th in London and lived from the age of five to twelve in India, where his father served as governor general of the Indian state of Madras. On the death of his father in 1924, he inherited the title of Lord Pentland at age eighteen. His family is from Edinburgh, Scotland, and the land known as the Pentland Hills. Not far away lies Rosslyn Chapel, dating from 1446 and built by his ancestor William St. Clair (more commonly, Sinclair), the Prince of Orkney.

Lord Pentland studied engineering at Trinity College, Cambridge, and graduated in 1929. He traveled widely and entered the worlds of business and politics. At thirty years of age in 1937 he attended a lecture by P. D. Ouspensky. Joining the Work, he regularly attended meetings and weekend work at Lyne Place outside of London. Of the thousand or so students Mr. Ouspensky had at the time, Lord Pentland became one of two deputized by Ouspensky to answer preliminary questions and do readings; the other was J. G. Bennett. With the war mounting, the Ouspenskys left for America in 1941.

Lord Pentland came to America to serve on the Combined Production and Resources Board, a cooperative effort of the United States, England and France, and so was able to resume his work with the Ouspenskys. Besides meetings in New York City, a large farm/estate had been purchased at Mendham, New Jersey, for weekend work. As Mme Ouspensky's work was more practical than her husband's and stemmed directly from Gurdjieff, Lord Pentland came to feel much closer to her. She had fallen ill with Parkinson's disease and was largely confined to her bed. Nevertheless, she directed the household and the daily work. Of this time Lord Pentland wrote:

> Madame, she was always called simply Madame, was constantly arranging conditions, whether through physical labor on the farm, through carefully formulated questions and messages to us, or through talks as we sat on the floor in her bedroom, which had the effect of miraculously renewing our energies and zest for living at the expense of the ugly and sleepy associations inside us. When we felt that renewal, she did not merely tell us to observe and record how it appeared, but confronted us with the question: "What do you want?" ... The meaning of Madame's question had to be felt inside. I heard it outside. So the question did

not penetrate. It bounced. . . . I needed to free myself from a lot of unnecessary tensions and emotions even to have glimpses of the truth of Gurdjieff's ideas. I was facing my life as if it were a surface, oblivious of all the underside.

At Gurdjieff's Table

In late 1947 the shock of Ouspensky's death brought Lord Pentland to the realization that despite all the work he had done on himself, "I hadn't arrived at anything; I came to nothing." That is, like many others at the time, he had come to the place in which he felt his nothingness. Through Mme Ouspensky's introduction he went to Paris and met Mr. Gurdjieff. He found, as he said, that "Gurdjieff had an extraordinary quality of providing encouragement. People, he often used to say, were like motorists who were stalled on a highway for lack of gas and he would come and give them a fill-up." Eight years before, in 1941, Lord Pentland had married Lucy Babington Smith, another student, and a year later a daughter, Mary, was born.

The couple took seven-year-old Mary to meet Gurdjieff at his apartment. Wrote Rina Hands of this time:

> People are beginning to bring their children. They sit at the table with us and participate like everyone else, often being able to choose their idiots. There is a little English girl here at the moment, Lord Pentland's daughter, Mary Sinclair. Today she sat at lunch beside her mother and just in front of Mr. Gurdjieff. The meal was a long one and she was bored. She had been eating an orange and began to tear up the peel and scatter it on the table. Suddenly Mr. Gurdjieff spoke to her. "You know something," he said, "in life it is never possible to do everything." The child looked puzzled, as well she might. We all wondered what was coming. "You see," he went on, "on my table you cannot make this mess. Perhaps at home Mother permits. Then if you want to do this thing, you must stay at home. But if you stay at home, you will not be able to come here

and see me. So you see, you can never do everything.
Now put all orange back on plate and remember what
I tell—never can we do everything in life." She did as
she was told with a very good grace. . . . At the end of
dinner, Mr. Gurdjieff asked her, "Who do you respect
the most?" She did not understand and her mother
said, "Who do you think is the most important person
here?" Without a moment's hesitation, she replied, "My
Daddy." I thought I detected a faint look of consternation on her mother's face, but she need not have had
any qualms. Mr. Gurdjieff beamed at the child and said,
"I am not offended. God is not offended either." He
went on to explain that who loves his parents, loves
God. If people love their parents all the time that their
parents are alive, then, when their parents die, there is
a space left in them for him to fill.

Lord Pentland was with Gurdjieff for about nine months
before he died on October 29, 1949. He returned to New York and
became a permanent resident. The Work being a work in life and
not a withdrawal, in 1954 Lord Pentland founded the American
British Electric Corporation, which specialized in marketing British
engineering services to American clients. He brought together a
very loose arrangement of Gurdjieff people and groups formerly
aligned with Orage, Ouspensky and others, a considerable task at
the time, and oversaw the purchase of a large carriage house on the
Upper East Side as the home of the Gurdjieff Foundation of New
York. He understood the personal cost of taking on such enormous
responsibilities for himself and others, for years later, looking back,
he wrote: "We are educated and tempted to seize the outer forms of
responsibility too soon, before we have understood what is meant
by them, to behave well, to keep one's chin up, to make up for one's
faults by trying harder rather than accepting and seeing them, all
the mannerisms that responsibility can take as a result of a formal
education. The lopsidedness of these deeply embedded habits has
to be seen again and again. . . . Otherwise, the assumption of outer
responsibility may hide from them the subtle movement of wishing
to work and not wishing."
As a teacher the qualities he emanated of integrity, resolution

and restraint, together with his penetrating psychological insight into the origin of a student's foibles and pretences, made for a formidable presence. He had a gift for speaking in a way that eluded the jamming system of the formatory mind and went straight to essence. In his lectures what differentiated him was his ability to ground a subject and then probe it along its full scale before again returning to earth, the everyday.

He was ever mindful in all he said and did to preserve intact those two separate lives in each person which Gurdjieff symbolized in *Meetings with Remarkable Men* as the sheep and the wolf. This is seen by all those who visit Lord Pentland's gravesite at the Kensico cemetery in Valhalla, Westchester County, not far from his home in Riverdale. His gravestone stands on a gently sloping hillside by a large tree, overlooking a pond. It is a rose-tinted granite with a carved design, medieval in style, enclosed by a Celtic border. Within the border are two entwined dragons, one with a lamb's head, the other a wolf's. Between the lamb's and the wolf's heads is a fish which looks as though it had just escaped from water. Below lies the inscription:

Lord John Pentland 1907–1984
And his final message to all who would hear:
Commit thy work to God. 𝒳

Notes

1. *You are like Paul.* J. G. Bennett, *Witness* (Charles Town, WV: Claymont Communications, 1983), 262.
2. *A bombshell.* William Patrick Patterson, *Eating The "I"*, 356.
3. *White sheik's hat.* Patterson, 348.
4. *I hadn't arrived at anything.* Lord John Pentland, Interview, *Telos* [now *The Gurdjieff Journal*], #7.
5. *Madame, she was always called simply Madame.* Lord Pentland, private papers.
6. *People are beginning to bring their children.* Rina Hands, *Diary of Madame Egout Pour Sweet: With Mr. Gurdjieff in Paris 1948–49* (Aurora, OR: Two Rivers Press, 1991), 53–54.

From TGJ #34

Postscript

Fifteen years ago today a man was flying back from Houston.

He had an appointment with a famous playwright who had some ten years earlier left the Work. They were to have met the previous Friday, but the playwright canceled, so the appointment was rescheduled for Monday. This man was returning to keep that appointment. But they never met. He died of a heart attack.

I learned of his death the next day. The funeral was to be held that Wednesday. I called the major air lines and tried to get a ticket to fly back to New York, but all flights were booked. The only possibility was to go by red eye, but I couldn't book a seat over the phone. That night we were to have dinner with B, a woman in my original group. She had been quite close to Lord Pentland. I remembered that once she had given him a candied apple at a meeting. The way she handed him the apple was beautiful, full of respect and caring. But something happened and she had gotten very angry and left the Work.

As it was to be an early dinner, my wife and I decided to go ahead with the plans, and so B came to dinner. It was obvious she hadn't heard of his death. Her reaction when I told her was surprising. It was as if I had said the mailman had forgotten to deliver the mail. But once the dinner was served, B told one story after another about him, all negative. At one point I reminded her that he had just died. She acknowledged that and quickly launched into another story.

My wife and I were in a mild state of shock. It all seemed surreal. Then I remembered that this is exactly what Mr. Gurdjieff wrote about in the *Third Series*. When someone dies all his friends meet afterward and tell their negative memories about the deceased. And so, although it was obviously unconscious on B's part, I saw the evening was turning out just right. I stopped resisting what B was recounting. At one point I even tried to tell a story myself but went completely blank inside.

When I got to the airport, there was a long line in front of the ticket counter. The wait seemed interminable. Finally, there was only one woman between me and the traveler at the counter. Just as he stepped away, the woman suddenly passed out. Without the least consideration, I stepped over her and asked for her ticket, the people behind me rushing to the woman's aid. Like the dinner, it seemed surreal.

"I've got to get to New York. It's an emergency," I said.

The reservation clerk checked her computer screen. There were no direct flights.

"I've got to get there," I told her. I remembered that Mr. Gurdjieff had told Mme de Hartmann when she wanted something to keep the thought in her mind.

The clerk checked and rechecked connecting flights but kept shaking her head.

"There isn't anything," she reported.

"I've got to get there," I repeated. It was a voice I'd never heard before.

Her fingers tapped more keys, her head moving back and forth as one schedule after another came up on the screen. Then suddenly she exclaimed in surprise, "I've never seen anything like this!" The flights I needed to get from San Francisco to New York—Los Angeles, Houston and Atlanta—all lined up with the right boarding times.

When I arrived in New York I went straight to the church at 66th and Lexington where the funeral was to be held. At the main door I saw S, the playwright, acting as an usher. (It was only later that I heard he had come that morning to Lord Pentland's office and, instead of finding him there, found a black wreath hanging on the door. Lord Pentland's daughter, Mary, had asked him to be an usher.) What I experienced at the funeral, you can read about in *Eating The "I"*, it's all there.

A few years ago I went with my wife and friends on a cross-country speaking tour promoting my new book that explored the teacher-student relationship. We arrived in New York in the early afternoon for the talk that evening at the Quest bookstore, so we decided to visit Lord Pentland's grave. We drove north along the Hudson river past the Palisades to Valhalla and to the Kensico cemetery where he was buried. Valhalla, in Norse mythology, is the burial ground of warriors. It seemed fitting, because for me he was the ultimate warrior.

It was a clear day, not like the hazy grey one where once I'd stood with his many other students and watched silently as the casket was lowered. Where each of us, one by one, had said a silent prayer as we threw a handful of dirt onto the casket. There was now a rose-colored granite headstone at the gravesite, the inscription reading:

Commit thy work to God.

Talk given February 14, 1999. Unpublished.

The Art of Asha

Lᴏʀᴅ Pᴇɴᴛʟᴀɴᴅ ʜᴀᴅ sᴘᴏᴋᴇɴ ᴀʙᴏᴜᴛ Lᴇɢᴏᴍɪɴɪsᴍs *ʙᴇɪɴɢ ᴀ ᴡᴀʏ by which high initiates pass esoteric knowledge down through the centuries. I had asked, "Is chess a* Legominism?*" He nodded and several days later gave me a book about Asha, or chess, the royal game, the Game of Kings, thought to originate in India or Persia about 5,000* ʙᴄᴇ*. The book held that chess was a conscious construct that represented the laws and forces governing the world. The primary elements of chess are time, space, force and material. The white and black pieces symbolize the cosmic and natural forces, which constantly struggle with one another for domination. The chessboard is composed of sixty-four black and white squares that theosophically add up to ten, or one and zero, all and everything and nothing. The board is composed of eight rows with eight squares each. Eight is the number of infinity and, when turned horizontally, the symbol of continual return. Each game is a microcosm of the archetypal struggle between Creation and Destruction, Good and Evil.*

A large banner, high atop the chess booth, proclaimed—

*PLAY THE CHESS MASTERS
OF PERSIA
ONLY 50 CENTS!*

The booth was one of many in a bustling bazaar of colorful booths and tents stretching the length of the entire block of Sixty-sixth Street between Lexington and Park Avenues. Overnight, Lord Pentland's groups had transformed the street into a pungent and sumptuous Middle Eastern bazaar offering perfumes and pottery and carpets and candies and clothes and jewelry and belly dancing and fortune-telling and storytelling.

With the two "Persian chess masters" exhausted from a day of playing three boards at a time, and mostly getting beaten, Lord

Pentland stepped into the booth to relieve them. Almost immediately a challenger came forward. He was a well-built man in his mid-forties. He had a hard, unforgiving warrior's face, broad forehead, square jaw, glasses and sharp direct eyes. I had the impression that this man had "crystallized" wrongly. He was dressed casually in a beige sweater, dark brown slacks and loafers, but there was nothing casual about him. His manner was aggressive, cocksure, even defiant.

"Game?" the man challenged.

Lord Pentland nodded, somewhat resignedly I thought. It was as if he knew this man, or this type of man, and had played him many times before. Lord Pentland silently set up the pieces, placing the white pieces on his side of the board. They stood facing one another.

"You always take white?" snapped the man.

Lord Pentland smiled benignly but made no reply. He moved his king's pawn two squares to the center of the board as he had before.

The man's eyes glinted. Instead of countering on the wing with a pawn move, he immediately blocked white's advance by advancing the black king's pawn two squares. He pushed up the sleeves of his sweater, snatched a pack of cigarettes from a pocket, took out a cigarette, and crushed the empty pack, tossing it on the ground. He flicked a light from an expensive gold lighter, inhaled and awaited Lord Pentland's reply. The man gave off a strong animal energy. His movements were confident, powerful. There was a "knowing" about him. He was, to use Gurdjieff's phrase, a "power possessing being." The game evolved into the Four Knights game, symmetrical, a solid and conservative game. The man was no newcomer to the game of chess. He commanded his pieces with authority.

Some seven or eight moves into the game Lord Pentland blundered away a bishop. The man captured instantly with his knight, smacking it down on the board like a rifle shot. The sound hit me right in the stomach.

Lord Pentland, at least outwardly, remained impassive. But I felt inside he was working with his and the man's energy. A bishop down now, white had to go on the defensive. The tempo now was black's. The man quickly built up and consolidated his position, then mounted an attack into the heart of white's pieces. Fortunately,

Lord Pentland had castled his king, but such was the force of the black attack that its forward momentum could only be stalled by the sacrifice of several pawns.

Given black's position and material advantage—white was a bishop and two pawns down—even a draw seemed unlikely. I thought it would be best to concede quickly rather than go through the ordeal of playing out a game that was clearly lost, and particularly so with this man. But Lord Pentland played on. I supposed it was in keeping with the Work. Those students who remained at the bazaar and were free of tasks gathered around the chess table. A student found a comfortable chair and set it down next to the board for Lord Pentland.

"Would you like a chair as well?" inquired Lord Pentland politely.

The man ignored the question. He was bent over the board, bracing his body with one hand, the other on his hip. He had his win, and he wanted it. He was not going to be distracted.

A few moves later, Lord Pentland attempted to engage the man in a little conversation. Instead, the man held up his forearm, checking the time on his watch. His manner signaled impatience. In a clipped, implacable tone he stated:

"Have to be going soon. Let's get on with it."

He resumed his position, hovering over the board. For some moments, Lord Pentland stared at the man. Then he nodded once, twice, three times to himself. It was as if he was coming to an inner agreement with all the parts of himself, galvanizing his will and energy, bringing up his full attention to the total acceptance of the fierce struggle that awaited him. I noticed a sobriety cross Lord Pentland's face; a resolution and seriousness appeared such as I had never before seen. It was the face of a real warrior, a great and ancient warrior.

Looking at the board, white's position appeared beyond the power of any quality of will or intelligence to change. Black had driven a deep V-shaped wedge straight into the heart of white's forces, the lead black pawn standing only two ranks from white's last rank. White had erected a blockade with his own pawn, but how long could it hold? Having an advantage in space, black could quickly shift its attack from side to side. White had to counter shift his pieces to meet the threats. In time, the communication between the pieces, their relationship, would weaken and inevitably lead to a breakthrough. This was exactly black's strategy. Black moved pieces from flank to flank, feigning attacks, laying traps, offering sacrifices of pawns, even a bishop, always with an eye to bulling its way through in the center—but nothing worked. Somehow, I didn't understand it, white held.

With black's attacks blunted again and again, a frustration welled up in the man. He was running out of ideas, his will and energy were flagging. It was evident in his physical posture, which hardened, constricted, inhibited the flow of energy.

Lord Pentland seemed to sense that. He peered solemnly at the man hunched over the board. Finally, the man felt his gaze and looked up. Said Lord Pentland softly: "Perhaps it's only a draw."

"I've got a win here, I tell you!" shouted the man. He glowered and vowed "And I'm going to win."

Lord Pentland smiled wanly, patiently. He understood the man's dilemma. He did have a won game. But that win had disappeared. It was no longer on the board. But the man refused to see the truth of the board. His win was there! Now Lord Pentland brought both his hands to the level of the board. He turned them palm up toward the man. It was as if saying he was sorry, but, well, this is how life is for everyone. The gesture and its execution were extraordinary. Shivers came over my whole body. The man snorted. Some ancient deep anger, hatred even, surfaced in him. He would have his win. Nothing else would do!

Summoning himself to great exertion, the man studied and restudied the board. Throughout, I had felt the will, the resolve, in each of them going up one level after another, each matching the other's will to win. Where Lord Pentland had committed himself, it wasn't in terms of the ego-effort the man made. The effects revealed themselves in little, almost imperceptible ways. The man's posture and facial expression became rigid, less fluid; his movements began to fragment. But the man was a warrior. He fought it all down. He somehow kept control of the mounting somatic chaos within himself. It was as if he was holding apart two angry snakes.

Lord Pentland, if anything, appeared to have gathered strength. Though the stress of such combat must have sapped him as well, he seemed relaxed, contained, still. At one point, he took out a cigarette, lit up and took a long inhalation, his eyes not once leaving the bent angry figure across from him. He closed his eyes then, cocking his head to the sky and exhaling a long funneling draft of smoke.

Suddenly, the man moved. It was as if the move jumped out of him against his will, against his knowledge. Pressure forces such moves when it is not rightly absorbed.

Lord Pentland came up quickly in his chair, moving closer to the board, studying the implications of black's move. Time passed silently. Finally, satisfied he understood, very deliberately Lord Pentland placed his lit cigarette, only half-smoked, on the street, and slowly extinguished it beneath his foot. Then, looking toward his opponent, he asked in a friendly way—"Would you like one?" He extended his hand across the black and white board, offering the man a pack of cigarettes.

Either the man could not speak or would not. In any case, he refused, shaking his head adamantly. Though the play had gone on for over two hours, he would not indulge, not take the chance on letting anything other than the desire to win predominate.

Lord Pentland nodded, understandingly, and returned to the board between them. A slight gust of wind swirled up, blowing the awnings of the booths and lifting the vinyl cloths covering the long narrow chess tables. The sun had gone down. The twilight muted even the bright colors of the bazaar.

Despite the impulsive quality of the man's move, it did not appear to be a blunder. It might not be his best move, but, under the circumstances, he could likely afford it, I thought.

Instead of countering the move, Lord Pentland advanced a pawn, attacking a piece of black's on the left wing. There was a weakness there, as its pieces were overextended. Not having adequate counter play, black had to retreat the piece.

Then Lord Pentland jumped a knight on the right wing and again black had to retreat. That in turn left a weakness on the left wing. Black's forces locked up far inside white's territory, there was no flexibility to regroup and defend against the white wing attack. He had to sacrifice a pawn. Still, it didn't seem too serious.

But then a silent scream went up at the board. The man suddenly saw what that earlier abrupt move had cost. Another black pawn had to be sacrificed or he would be down a major piece. Even so, the capturing white pawn now threatened another of black's pieces. Black had no time to untangle himself. White kept advancing on the wings, driving now behind the center of black's forward position, attacking its soft underbelly.

And then the impossible happened—black's king was mated.

A long deathly stillness hung in the moment; the man leaned over the board in shock, Lord Pentland quietly looked on from his chair. Finally, Lord Pentland stood and extended his hand. The man could barely shake the offered hand and did so without looking. Lord Pentland quickly walked off through the long shadows of the near-empty bazaar.

The skies had been darkening and now, as if on cue, there was a great rumbling in the clouds. It was as if the gods were talking. Lightning flashed and cracked between the buildings and the heavens opened. The hot street was suddenly awash in torrents of water, the rain coming down in bucketfuls, the applause of the gods for *The Art of Asha.*

—Excerpt from *Eating The "I"*

From TGJ #43

Suggestibility & the Formatory Mind

WHEN LORD PENTLAND CAME DOWN THE AISLE TO SPEAK AT THE lecture series, he acted as though he had forgotten something and he left the room. On his return, he mounted the platform hesitantly, nearly tripping on the antique Persian rug that covered its surface. He seemed uncertain as to which of the two chairs on the platform he should take. Beside one of the chairs was a small table with two glasses of ice water. Finally, he took that chair, almost knocking over one of the glasses. He shifted about in his seat, apparently unable to find a comfortable position. Several times he inspected his dark suit for lint and brushed each arm. He smiled, self-conscious and somewhat embarrassed, like a man who has misplaced his door key. Then, he searched the audience of some three hundred Work people horseshoed around the platform, his long neck furtively craning forward, trying to locate a certain face. When Dr. Welch mounted the platform, he nodded and sat back.

Dr. William Welch was a broad, solid-looking man, tanned and square-jawed, ruggedly handsome, with thick, straight silver hair and glasses. A mid-Westerner turned New Yorker, he had the bearing and assurance of a tank commander, one who is used to power. And when he spoke his deep baritone voice and strong analytical mind only increased this feeling of command which he emanated. A trustee of the Foundation, he was the American doctor Gurdjieff had asked for in his final days. Of Gurdjieff's death, Dr. Welch had said, "I've seen many men die. He died like a king." He, along with Lord Pentland and a handful of other teachers, led the Tuesday evening lectures and discussions.

The Idea & Experience of Aim

Tonight was the first in the series of fall lectures, and apparently it had been agreed that Lord Pentland was to speak first, for several times Dr. Welch had glanced at him, but Lord Pentland had taken no notice. Finally, Dr. Welch uncrossed his arms, cleared his throat and began exploring the theme, "The Idea and Experience of Aim." Characteristically, Dr. Welch considered each of the significant terms of the theme and then began probing it with a long series of questions elucidating various aspects of the question: "In essence do the idea and experience differ? How do I come to having a sincere aim? Does this aim change or does it remain the same? How do I stay awake to my aim? How does aim influence me? Who is it that has an aim?" He went on in this manner for ten minutes or so and then checked his watch. He quickly and artfully wrapped up his talk then crossed his legs and took a glass of water from the table. He sat back and waited for Lord Pentland to begin.

But Lord Pentland seemed to be dreaming. Several times Dr. Welch glanced at him, but his look was not returned. Lord Pentland, who always listened attentively, had appeared preoccupied during Dr. Welch's exposition and several times still seemed to be searching the audience for that face. When Dr. Welch stopped, he was caught unprepared. I had never seen Lord Pentland like this. Was his age catching up with him? The heart attack? Perhaps his pacemaker wasn't working properly? I could hardly look. The impression was too painful—my teacher asleep! Lord Pentland sat there like some dunce.

And when he started to speak it was even worse. He began by examining the question of aim from the ordinary viewpoint, but then switched abruptly to the Work's standpoint, then back again, mixing up ordinary aim with conscious aim, floundering, hesitating, making jerky body movements. Several times Dr. Welch looked at the odd figure beside him with some concern. This was not the Lord Pentland he knew. The sense of oddity spread through the big room. People moved uneasily in their chairs, coughed. The more he spoke, the more uncomfortable everyone became, the thought staring us in the face: Lord Pentland was asleep. This was the man Gurdjieff had referred to as his "St. Paul" and had appointed to head up the Work in America. He had been President of the Gurdjieff Foundation since its founding in 1954, had selected this building for purchase, opened other centers around the country; and for most people in the room, certainly the young people, he was the living embodiment of the Work. And now lurching around up there on the platform was this bad joke, this poor, sad mechanical man. Lord Pentland rattled on, the idiocy increasing. The big hall grew deathly silent. Dr. Welch's brow knitted. He folded his arms and stared into the Persian rug. No one looked at the platform. It was as though the enormity of the living unmistakable fact had stopped everyone's mind.

It was then, just when that moment reached its height, that Lord Pentland suddenly stopped speaking. He was in mid-sentence. For a split second he looked into his hands cupped in his lap and then he looked up. Some change had taken place. Slowly, without expression, looking from left to right, he took the measure of the audience. There was a smile then. Small though it was, it radiated throughout the large hall, changing its solidity, lifting the vibration. He again looked through the faces in the room. It was as if he was taking our temperature. Then he sighed and swallowed, and with his head half-cocked turned with an inquisitive expression to Dr. Welch. The two "old dogs" exchanged a secret smile.

Lord Pentland had been acting a role!

Having an Aim

He had talked about aim as a man would who had no aim. His words did not match his being. He demonstrated the lying and distraction, the broken octaves, that go on all the time. And he showed, too, how suggestible we all are. And the teaching he gave did not come cheaply. For he had opened himself to one terrible massive impression—that of three hundred people united in a single heavy thought—*Lord Pentland was senile.* To register the force of that. To absorb the friction. Not to identify. Voluntarily to have taken on that degree of conscious labor and intentional suffering, and submit to it all in public. Well, when he spoke now it was in another manner and tempo altogether and *this* was an entirely different "Lord Pentland."

"I daresay," stated Lord Pentland, his body perfectly erect and relaxed, his voice barely above a whisper but filling the hall, "that these impressions have probably been a distraction. They've put us into our heads. Unless, that is, we have really been listening. For the aim is aimless . . . it is, and can only be, in this very moment. The impressions we receive capture us, if we say 'I' to them. And then, of course, we have a whole host of 'aims.' The mind needs to be quiet for the attention to come into the body. This will change the quality of our energy, bring us to presence. We listen from there, expand from there. All else is to be asleep, aimless. Do you follow?"

Discussion was now to begin. But the shock he had delivered was so full that there were only a few perfunctory questions, mostly by new people. With that, the evening ended and Lord Pentland and Dr. Welch left the platform and strode down the aisle.

"The Nature of the Formatory Mind and the Need for an Exact Language" was the theme of the next lecture. Instead of exploring the subject with another person, Lord Pentland sat alone on the small platform. He was wearing a dark sport coat with a white business shirt, open at the neck. He hitched up the creases of his trousers, cupped his hands in his lap and seemed to totally empty out. It was as though he had collapsed his personality like an umbrella and laid it aside. Then, having slowly regarded the audience, he began to speak. His voice was modulated, rarely emphasizing a word, making no effort to project himself, entertain or captivate. And yet within a few words he had the whole room in his hands.

He began by noting that "we tend to act on our impulses because we are afraid our formatory mind will destroy the impulse with its reason. The formatory mind isn't the real mind at all but one that is forever formulating opinions, attitudes, conclusions, forever talking and imagining. It lives by rote and feeds off the energies of the other centers. The formatory mind has no energy of its own. It is a kind of parasite."

He paused, letting that sink in, and then when everyone's attention was ready, he resumed—

"Mr. Gurdjieff," he declared, "likened the formatory mind to that of 'a secretary.' If she would limit herself to her job, all would be fine. But she insists on intercepting all incoming communications and labeling and confusing everything."

A Challenge Issued

I noticed Isabel, close to the platform, sitting on a pillow, looking like she wanted to speak. She had been in the Work perhaps twenty years. She had stopped growing somehow. She only heard what she wanted to hear. She had a hard shell around her. Rather fearless and strong-willed, she was used to getting her own way. An artist, she always fashioned herself with a dramatic look. Her skin was pale and perfect, her eyes dark, luminous, and her short black hair was close cropped and curled in tight ringlets. It was a style out of the 1920s. Somehow, she was always a little out of synch.

I could see Lord Pentland's use of the word "secretary" had caught her. As soon as the lecture was opened up to questions, she immediately asked:

"Lord Pentland—couldn't we use some metaphor other than 'secretary' for the formatory mind?"

He took a moment before answering. I felt as if he was sounding out the depth of her question. It had seemed so innocent but, in fact, it was loaded. Feminism had had its effect on the Work. Some women questioned Gurdjieff's ideas as being too masculine.

Finally, he responded: "The real trouble is not the metaphor 'secretary' but that the emperor is *all* clothes." Having thus shifted the discussion from the formatory mind to the subject of personality, Lord Pentland went on to make many interesting distinctions between personality and false personality. But I could see by Isabel's face and posture that she was having none of it.

"Thank you," Isabel replied, "but could you answer my question on a more practical level? Specifically, Lord Pentland, what I am asking is this—could some other word than 'secretary' be used for the formatory mind?"

"Computer." Lord Pentland spat the word out quickly and turned away. Everyone laughed.

Others asked questions. All on other aspects of the topic. It was as if Isabel had not spoken. But I felt she had raised an interesting point. For as Gurdjieff was conscious, then his language was exact. If he had used the word "secretary" to describe the formatory mind, it must be exact and have many levels of meaning. I felt he had meant that the formatory mind was passive, not active in a real way. And therefore it had no energy of its own, no life of its own. But as he had been born and raised in an Armenian and Greek society that was heavily masculine, one that in many ways denigrated the female, was there a possibility that he might not be entirely objective on this point?

About the Word "Secretary"

Near the meeting's end, Mrs. Dooling asked a question concerning the exact use of language. She was an older teacher in the Work, a generation after Lord Pentland's. She had sharp chiseled features, more handsome than beautiful, and striking blue eyes. She was not a woman easily "cowed." Her question didn't mention the word "secretary," but it was clear it was that to which she was referring. Lord Pentland spoke at some length, but his answer didn't meet the question. Mrs. Dooling sat stone-faced and unsatisfied. Alongside her sat two other teachers of that generation, Mrs. Flinsch, Dooling's sister, and Mrs. Pierce. I sensed they—"the harpies," as some called them—were unsatisfied as well. Finally Mrs. Pierce, her eyesight fading and her body a bit bent, spoke up, her words ringing out in the big hall—"What we are asking, Lord Pentland, is about the use of the word 'secretary.' It is a word that has many associations that may not be altogether exact."

The room was charged with electricity. Lord Pentland seemed visibly upset. In all these years I had never seen him once publicly challenged by an older teacher.

He clasped his hands together and stared into them for a great while. Finally, he turned toward the two women teachers and threw up his left hand, as if waving them off, his manner as emphatic as his voice—

"I daresay I believe I can speak for fifty percent or more of the people here when I say I think we have said enough about this particular subject. It is time to move on."

He turned away abruptly, looking to the opposite side of the room. A few more perfunctory questions and the evening ended.

—Excerpt from *Eating The "I"*

From TGJ #46

The Question of Truth

THE QUESTION OF TRUTH . . . IS IT A QUESTION FOR US, REALLY? Isn't truth for us simply a living out—that is, thinking, feeling and acting out—of however we believe life to be? Doesn't truth become a question for us only when our belief system suffers a major shock? Otherwise, don't we wander through life being guided unconsciously by whatever "truth" is living us out? And isn't this "truth" itself simply based on our stack of interpretations of what life is and isn't, which in turn is based on prior circumstances and conditioning?

We see that many people mistake their truth for the Truth. The religious, atheistic and agnostic are all dedicated to living out their version and in the wake of their conviction judging others. Wittingly or not they are engaged in trying to convince others of the rightness of what they believe and that to which they are giving up their lives. Isn't extremism and the radical militancy it can evoke founded on this dualistic bedrock?

The Revealed & the Rational

The atheistic and agnostic are each made whole in their denial, their "no," or "maybe yes, maybe no," whereas for the religious it is the "Yes" of that ecstatic moment which brings together all the parts of themselves—intellectual, emotional, instinctive. In time, this moment having passed, they find themselves in a world fraught with temptation, to which, again and again, they must say "No." Isn't the feeling and fear of hypocrisy, of not living what they believe, at the root of their anger toward others and the world at large for not having accepted their truth? How can one live and let live if one believes they are living in a state of sin, a state now amplified by the technology of modernity that crosses all geographic and nationalistic barriers? And so the corrupt world must change so that the person can live in his truth.

If one has not accepted the truth of a religion, Revealed Truth based upon mystical revelation, then one lives out a Rational Truth based on science and philosophy. Where Revealed Truth is fixed and immutable, Rational Truth is a moving target. Scientists and philosophers, those great cerebral thinking machines, have wrestled with the subject ever since the first question—"Why?"—arose. No matter how subtle the scientific discovery, no matter how ingenious the philosophical move, it is only a matter of time until it is countered by still another discovery or move.

Revealed and Rational Truth will always butt heads, the immutable against the mutable. Those in one camp of thought and belief will always see the other as limited—the scientific by its endless questioning, and the religious by its roots in the suprarational. For those living the Revealed life, there are no more questions. For those living the Rational, it can be on a very high intellectual level, but for most people it devolves to the purely personal. They live a secular and personal version, a "Truth" based on what belief is present at any given moment. And rooted as it is in the defense and enhancement of the person, it is always biased and subjective.

Personal truth, by definition unique, is based not only on self-love and vanity but type, polarity and experience, as well as family, group, tribe and nation. Should it be any wonder, then, that so many people live lives of disagreement, denial, argument, and psychic and physical violence? Is it any wonder that at root what everyone yearns for is peace and harmony? So isn't the essential interest not in the question of truth or Truth but rather peace and harmony? Isn't this why zealots and dictators historically always frame their argument by promising to make them a reality ?

Revealed Truth, by definition not subject to rational proof, fulfills a hunger for completion, for certainty. This has been its ageless appeal, which has attracted not only the sincere but the superstitious, mad and megalomaniacal. And even with the sincere there is always an element of the egotistic, for aren't all questions of truth erased in the mechanicality of latent self-love and vanity?

To take one example: the question of the soul. For most people, it's not a question. They simply believe they have one; they cannot conceive that the universe could get on without them. Thus, it's only a question of guarding their soul, not losing it. That one has a soul is a consensual belief. Originally, however, in ancient Egypt only the pharaoh was believed to have a soul. With the passage and pressure of time the nobles were included. Now everyone is thought to have one. It is usually an either/or argument. A third possibility is too esoteric for most to consider. That is, that while we may not have a soul, we can make one. If so, how? But this goes far beyond the probing of the question at hand.

We were speaking of the Revealed and Rational and the person. Can the person ever come to the Revealed through the Rational? The answer is both yes and no. How this can be so can perhaps provisionally be demonstrated by what happened to the author many years ago when he found himself in a confused state in which his personal dream world had suddenly exploded.

Not seeing any future for himself, he wrote a letter to a stranger who was handing out fistfuls of money to passersby, asking for a grant to go to India to research "Death & Life in the Ganges." While the money was real, the fellow was not, that is, he was an escapee from a mental institution (whether he was there because of too much or too little of the Revealed or Rational, the newscast did not report). Weeks later a letter arrived in the writer's mailbox stamped "Undeliverable." By that time, of course, all had been forgotten. Reading the letter, our writer thought to himself that while the words were composed and made sense the premises were unreal. Seeing his own signature at the bottom shocked his mind to stillness, that is, erased his personal or formatory mind. What smacked him right in the face now were questions he had intellectually bandied about but never intellectually-emotionally-instinctively experienced—*Who was this? Who wrote this letter?*

This was a Revealed question, not a Rational one. The letter writer had been living, unwittingly as most do, in the Rational. Unknowingly, the death of his dream left a psychological emptiness, a type of personal void. So the sight of the signature—a signature that was not him *but was him*—instantly formed a question that hit the blank tablet of the mind. His mental center received a shock: *Who am I?* The strength of the shock was such that it also engulfed his emotional center.

An Esoteric Teaching

Centers are spoken about because soon after, our writer, now a seeker after truth, entered an esoteric teaching whose fundamental practices initially aimed at rational verification of the tenets of the teaching. One of these was that three centers make up the human construct: the mental or rational, the emotional or feeling, and the instinctual-moving-sexual. In verifying this, the seeker observed the functioning and misfunctioning of each center and also that each has its own personality. One center desires, another doesn't. Inner conflict. "Yes" and "no" ad infinitum until one side wears out or a shock occurs that tips the balance.

Further observation showed that not only did each center have its own personality, but each had its own truths, its own believers, that is, "I"s who all believe they are the only I and take over body-heart-and-mind. But the seeker's verification, based on the practices of self-remembering and self-observation, rightly conducted, forced him to admit he was not the indivisible I he took himself to be. Observation revealed that each "I-of-the-moment" is a living embodiment of its truth of that moment.

The most radical discovery made at this stage was not only that he was not who he thought he was, but that *he had no body*. He lived in the head, the mental word-world, only aware of the body when it was in lust or fear, in need of food or drink. He spent his life unknowingly listening to the voices in his head, telling him the ever-changing "truth" of the moment, each predicated on self-love and vanity but otherwise disguised.

The Truth of the Moment

To become conscious of the body would mean one would have to turn off the "mental radio" by redirecting one's attention down into the body. In redistributing the attention, the head clears and the truth of the moment is observed. That is, whatever "I" is manifesting. Or, more directly, the unfiltered impression of the Immediate. But this observation is distorted almost immediately by identification. There is the self-image, the false personality, all the "I"s that make it up. It is this that has been unconsciously taken as the truth. It is this with which all the centers have been connected. The self-image is monolithic. There is no way out of it that is not discounted in its program. There is only one thing (and it is not a thing) that offers the way out. It is a redirection of the attention from whatever center it inhabits at the moment into the globality of the body. In doing so, nothing is disturbed on the thing level and so the program cannot note it and react. Remembering oneself incurs no outer resistance from the world at hand. The resistance is only inner. That is, the initial resistance comes from the identification with the self-image. It is the vanity and self-love projected onto the self-image that creates the identification and thus the inner resistance. Observing the I-of-the-moment from the standpoint of the inhabited body, the self-remembered body, is of a different category altogether than merely seeing from the head center, for now there is sensation and feeling of what is observed. This creates a heat that internally begins to dissolve the allegiance to the self-image. With persistence over a long period of time, an inner separation appears, a space in which intelligence can take root and where there is response and not mere reaction to what is present.

Like many serious seekers, our seeker, guided by his teacher (for no one except spiritual geniuses can awaken without one), after many years of practice and questioning, comes to a direct experiencing that what is taken to be our ordinary self and ordinary life is no longer so ordinary. A shift happens. Psychological time stops. Stillness and space appear. Scale changes. Impressions, once static, become dynamic, dimensional. The Immediate expands; the physical world becomes metaphysical ("becomes" from the viewpoint of the seeker). The interpretation of the experiencing may be symbolic, mythological, even archetypal. It might pass into the questioning of the practice itself with "what is the self in self-remembering." One wakes up to deeper and deeper levels of assumption, identification, sleep—all centered on what one says "I" to, what one takes to be "the self." Conscience is uncovered in the living recognition of unity in plurality. One might even expand to where there is perceiving without the perceiver. Or, as it is sometimes put, consciousness without an object (of course, the latent move missing here is that if there is no object, there is no subject).

So we have come full circle, a joining of the Rational to the Revealed. Having great scale, low to high, it is an ongoing experiencing.

Is it the Truth?

Who is asking? 𝒜

First printed in *Revue 3e Millénaire*, #81. TGJ #42

The Question of Rebirth

Rᴇʙɪʀᴛʜ—ᴡʜᴀᴛ ᴄᴀɴ ʙᴇ sᴀɪᴅ ᴛʜᴀᴛ hasn't been said a hundred times over? It's not a horn or a hammer, something you can hold or point to. It's an abstraction and like all abstractions it doesn't give itself up to easy definition. Its weakness in terms of definition is its linguistic power. We can use it to mean whatever we want it to mean.

Let's ask instead when does the idea of rebirth—however defined—become serious? What must happen? Isn't it when the road we've been walking comes to its end? Up until then we didn't think it had an end. Then suddenly the stark and painful recognition and admission that all we believed in, all we gave ourselves to, is so much smoke and mirrors. We thought without really thinking (for the attraction was stronger than thought) that this was the road that would bring all of the parts of me together. It would complete the "I" that I take myself to be. Now, hypnotic suggestion and momentum stripped away, I suddenly see the road for what it is, not what I imagined it to be.

At this point, emptied of dreams, I dwell once again in the I-Don't-Know. But as the poet tells us:

We shall not cease from exploration

Yes, the search continues, but it's still not a rebirth I want—the road was wrong, *not me*. I want a fresh start. And so in time I step onto another road. But now I'm more doubtful, less committed. Now I notice there are roads and crossroads, not just one road. So I begin zig-zagging, one to another, to the point where I feel I'm on no road at all. Of course, the denial is itself an assertion. Being on no road is a road, too. When this dawns I face what I've been fearing: the nothingness that I am, walking an endless circle.

What Does Rebirth Mean?

Now rebirth has become a serious idea. The I am that I am doesn't need a fresh start. I want a new me. I want the real, not the transient. I don't know what I mean. I only know now what I don't want. I've learned to not be afraid to question—not only what other people are saying but what I think, what I feel. And so I ask myself: what does this word "rebirth" really mean? What's the assumption? Doesn't it presuppose I've *already* been born? Yes, we're all possessed of bodies, so there is birth on the physical level. But are there higher levels to which I haven't been born?

I observe myself and see many of my thoughts, my feelings, are contradictory. Desires-fears-dreams—they keep moving me around like I'm a puppet. The body takes postures; I don't take them. Nothing is intentional. All is reaction. The left hand may instinctively know where the right hand is—but does the mind? Often I see I talk, but it's really that I am talked, some inner tape playing out the same old story once again. All empty words. No one, no self-awareness is there. So perhaps—*perhaps*—I haven't really been born at all—I just *think* I have. So this idea of rebirth—it's based on an assumption! This brings me where? Back to the dreaded I-Don't-Know.

Then I find I am reading these words in a magazine whose issue is devoted to the subject of rebirth.

"'To awake,' 'to die,' 'to be born.' These are three successive stages," says G. I. Gurdjieff, a seminal spiritual figure who brought The Fourth Way, the ancient esoteric teaching of self-transformation.

That's it! I've been dead and not known it. I've assumed that being born came *first*. Yes, I have to first awaken so that I can die, so that I can be born. But awaken to what?

"To awaken," says Mr. Gurdjieff, "means to realize one's nothingness, that is to realize one's complete and absolute mechanicalness and one's complete and absolute helplessness. And it is not sufficient to realize it philosophically in words. It is necessary to realize it in clean, simple, and concrete facts, in one's own facts."

Gurdjieff acknowledges this is difficult and impossible to do by oneself. One needs a group of people, he says, with a like aim, all involved in the teaching he brings and led by a teacher. I recoil inside. I find myself between a yes and a no. If the yes wins, there will be a little death, the first of many such deaths; that is, death to all the assumptions I hold about myself. For each time I see the falseness of a deeply held assumption—and none stronger than me as an individual entity; each time a self-image is shattered, there will be a death. And that death will create a space for essence—that which I truly am—to grow. But, as Gurdjieff warned, "False personality will defend itself." It is very canny and will use any and all means to stay in control, for it knows that its loss of power means its death, it being no more than a fabrication, a compensation.

One's attention and energy either serve the real or the false. One is either eating or being eaten, traveling an ascending octave or descending. There are no hybrids.

Learning Sincerity

Self-sincerity is demanded. And yet, as Gurdjieff says, "We must learn to be sincere." Learn? I've been sincere many times, why would I have to learn it? This goes to the heart of the matter. I take myself to be one indivisible I when in actuality I am many "I"s. This has to be experienced deeply. The stark seeing of this will be a suffered death. But what is it that suffers? Not what is true but what is false. This discrimination must be constantly made. If not, the false personality will reassert itself.

So it's a long path, but the only path worth taking, for its direction is vertical, ascending. And I realize, as that poet said:

> *We shall not cease from exploration*
> *And the end of all our exploring*
> *Will be to arrive where we started*
> *And know the place for the first time . . .*
> *When the last of earth left to discover*
> *Is that which was the beginning.*

The Fourth Way is a way of understanding and conscience, and so with every step essence grows and in its wake the recognition of the laws that underlie all phenomena. All else is as another poet sang:

> *The hollow horn plays wasted words*
> *Proves to warn*
> *That he not busy being born*
> *Is busy dying.* ✗

Notes

1. *"To awake."* P. D. Ouspensky, *In Search of the Miraculous,* 217.
2. *To awaken.* Ouspensky, 218.
3. *We shall not cease from exploration.* T. S. Eliot, "Little Gidding," *Four Quartets.*
4. *The hollow horn plays wasted words.* Bob Dylan, "It's Alright, Ma."

Reprinted from *3e Millenaire,* Issue #83. From TGJ #44

The Deep Question of Energy

WE PRIZE ENERGY, FOR ENERGY IS LIFE, GIVES LIFE, ENABLES LIFE. The less energy, the less life. And so the lament of the old adage, "Youth is wasted on the young," meaning not only is energy wasted on the young, but being inexperienced they don't realize the opportunities they have. But with experience, are energy and opportunities used any more wisely? Societally, that can be true, but from the perspective of the aim of self-awakening unfortunately it's not. What we are today, how we are living our life, as Mr. Gurdjieff says, is what we will be and how we will live tomorrow. Only we will be older, have less energy.

Though admitting mortality, most people, particularly the young, live as if they were immortal, the supply of energy endless. It's only with age, the sapping of vitality, that this unconscious assumption of "godhood" weakens and the egoistic assumptions which have taken one's energy may be recognized for what they are and were: diversions from the work of self-transformation. So, whether young or old, if we are not serious about awakening, about learning how to process energies consciously now, then it is unlikely we will be so tomorrow. To begin to understand energy, its uses and misuses, a new perspective is needed, the larger and more comprehensive the better.

When the Universe began what was there?

Given the assumption of a beginning of the Universe, whatever else there might have been there was certainly energy, for without energy there is no life. So: *In the Beginning there was energy.*

And then, what?

The Fourth Way—Sacred Science

Physicists offer descriptions of the development of the world, as do various religions. These are well known, if only superficially. Relatively unknown is the esoteric perspective, especially that of The Fourth Way, the ancient and sacred esoteric teaching rediscovered and reformulated and brought to the West by G. I. Gurdjieff. This teaching, here simply sketched, holds that contained within the wholeness of the Absolute, which is all and everything and no thing, there was the Most Holy Sun Absolute and empty endless space filled with the presence of the prime-source cosmic substance,

Etherokrilno, which is "the basis for the arising and maintenance of everything existing."

The Most Holy Sun Absolute was maintained and existed on the basis of two fundamental cosmic sacred laws. *Triamazikamno*, or the Law of Three, is said to be "a law which always flows into a consequence and becomes the cause of subsequent consequences, and always functions by three independent and quite opposite characteristic manifestations, latent within it, in properties neither seen nor sensed." *Heptaparaparshinokh*, a second sacred cosmic law, exists as well. This law is formulated by Objective Science as: "The flow of forces [*Triamazikamno*] follows a line that constantly deflects at specific intervals and unites again at its ends." The Law of Seven acted in terms of the *Autoegocratic* principle, or design, with no gaps in its seven gravity-centers, or *Stopinders*, processing the Law of Three systematically, thus eliminating all hazard or chance. All seemed well.

But then the Creator God, arisen within the Absolute, observed that *Heropass*, or Time, was diminishing the Most Holy Sun Absolute and so He changed the design of the Law of Seven from *Autoegocratic* to *Trogoautoegocratic*. Whereas *Autoegocratic* is a closed system, *Trogoautoegocratic* is open in that the gaps, or intervals, between certain *Stopinders* were lengthened or shortened. This allowed the entry of new energy from outside which would either spur the processing of the Law of Three or impede and change it; the one allowing the octave to continue to descend, the other to allow it to ascend. While this new processing eliminated the threat of Time to diminish the Most Holy Sun Absolute, it did introduce hazard and chance.

Under *Trogoautoegocrat*, the Most Holy Sun Absolute emanated the prime sacred element *Theomertmalogos*, or Word-God. Within the Most Holy Sun Absolute, the inner forces were One, but when issuing into the *Etherokrilno* it self-divided into a trinity or triad of independent forces [*Triamazikamno*]: Holy-Affirming, Holy Denying and Holy-Reconciling. The sacred Theomertmalogos blended with the *Etherokrilno* that fills the empty space to create the Omnipresent-Active-Element-*Okidanokh*. Its prime arising then is *outside* the Most Holy Sun Absolute.

These forces mixing with *Okidanokh* created the *Megalocosmos*, filling the once empty space with successive levels of worlds known as the Ray of Creation. The farther a given world, and the beings inhabiting it, from the Most Holy Sun Absolute, the more dense, the slower the vibration, the less intelligent and less conscious. Nonetheless, everything is an expression of energy, of vibration, of force, but at *different* levels. Thus, every thing, every manifestation, is *relative* in terms of its potency.

Images of God

Though very far removed from the Most Holy Sun Absolute, we human beings represent in our world the acme of creation—"We are images of God," said Gurdjieff. We are three-brained beings, that is, beings who have intellectual, feeling, and instinctive brains. Two-brained beings are animals; one-brained are insects. Not having a third brain, two- and one-brained beings live mechanical lives. They are what they are and cannot be or do otherwise. A lion is a lion is a lion. A snake, a snake. A bee, a bee. Because we are three-brained beings, we have the possibility of self-consciousness, will and reason, of being capable of transforming ourselves from mechanical to conscious beings. We are then beings of great possibility in which bodies other than the physical are formed leading to immortality within the solar system.

Being-Partkdolg-Duty

We receive the Omnipresent-Active-Element-*Okidanokh* through the three foods: physical food (which is dead) and air and impressions. We receive this energy and transmit it simply by living. But we do so mechanically. That is, we eat, breathe, and see and feel automatically, only occasionally aware of the intake of these foods. It is only when we practice *being-Partkdolg-duty*, aligning ourselves in a triadic configuration, that the *Okidanokh* contained in these foods undergoes *Djartklom,* a dividing of *Okidanokh* into three forces, active, passive, reconciling, which then blend and nourish and coat our three brains, intellectual, feeling, and instinctive, mixing with "kindred-vibrations" which are localized in the corresponding brain. These blendings are known as "*being-Impulsakri*" and it is the quality of these that allows the self-perfecting and coating of the various bodies. If we do not practice *being-Partkdolg-duty*, then there is no *Djartklom* (except when Great Nature needs it), and of the three brains, only the denying-brain in the spine is fed. Hence, if there is no conscious work, then the older one becomes, the more denying, the less conscious.

Being energy systems we absorb and refine energy from lower levels to higher, for example, the eating and transformation of physical food. In maintaining ourselves, energy is used in four different ways. We use it biologically to support the various bodily functions, such as the respiratory system. We use it mechanically to run, climb, lift. We use it psychically or mentally to associate, daydream or think. And, engaged in self-transformation, we use energy to consciously inhabit ourselves and to observe what is present as impartially as possible. These direct impressions, undiluted by personalization, transform themselves to higher and higher levels. (It is all one energy, of course, but of different potencies—the energy it takes to run a race is not the same as that needed to solve a chess problem, or to self-remember.)

At a young age Gurdjieff came to what he termed "the full sensation of myself." That is, he came to the full expression of the energy of consciousness. Observing people's suffering and delusion, self-love and vanity, hatred and violence, the question arose in him: "What is the sense and significance of life on earth, and human beings in particular?" The answers of religion and science he found inadequate. He came to intuit that the ancient wisdom societies had discovered the answer. After making many journeys into remote and dangerous areas, he finally discovered in Egypt an ancient, esoteric teaching which he called "The Fourth Way." He said he was initiated four times into the sacred Egyptian mysteries, in which he says "The Christian church, the Christian form of worship, was not invented by the fathers of the church. It was all taken in a ready-made form from Egypt, only not from the Egypt we know but from one which we do not know. This Egypt was in the same place as the other but it existed much earlier. It will seem strange to many people when I say that this prehistoric Egypt was Christian many thousands of years before the birth of Christ, that is to say, that its religion was composed of the same principles and ideas that constitute true Christianity." Over time elements of this seminal and sacred teaching had migrated northward and so Gurdjieff made a second journey to the Hindu Kush, Siberia and Tibet. This is where the confusion began with people believing that these areas were the teaching's origin and not Egypt.

Mechanical or Conscious?

Unlike the three classical ways of working with the body, emotions, or the mind, this way worked with all three centers at once. Instead of withdrawal to a monastery or ashram, the teaching taught that by consciously receiving and working with the impressions of ordinary life one could come to real life. As to the significance, the purpose, of human beings on Earth? The answer is not for the fainthearted or romantic. Our mechanical purpose on Earth is to do exactly what we are all doing right now. Simply by functioning—breathing, moving, associating, thinking—we mechanically receive, refine and transmit energy. There are higher energies that we can work with, but Nature neither needs nor compels us to do so.

We can breathe, move, associate, think either mechanically or consciously. If we live mechanically, we "die like dogs," as Gurdjieff puts it. If our wish is to live consciously, possibilities abound. The initial barrier to this wish is that most people believe they are already living consciously. In actuality we live in the hypnotic momentum of a seamless stream of energy, a momentum nurtured by societal suggestion, as well as our unquestioned assumption that we are awake. Only when we begin to experience how reactive and conditioned our lives are can we be touched by what Gurdjieff means when he says, "We are unfinished worlds." Within us a germ begins to stir, a seed of our highest aspiration, one which impels a search for *being-Partkdolg-duty*.

I then become a seeker after truth. The search, if sincere, will ultimately bring a genuine teacher and teaching into my life, one that will lead me by the evidence of my own experience to the realization of the obvious—that I am asleep to my real self. My thoughts "think" me, my feelings use me, my postures take me. How to get out of this morass? Do nothing, I will be told. For who is doing it? And why? Simply observe myself, for observation changes nothing and so encounters no outer resistance. I will see that I am not who I imagine myself to be, that I live in a world of words, constantly talking to myself, completely psychologized, moved mechanically by one shock, internal or external, to another, identifying with all, and deeply believing "I" am getting some place, learning something, becoming something. More deeply, self-observation will show I have no conscious awareness of the body. True,

I am quite concerned with how it looks, but other than hunger, desire, fear or injury, I give it no attention. Though I appear to be in the physical dimension, I am somewhere else—in a thought, a feeling, an impulse. All carom off one another and completely envelop me, absorbing all my energy and attention. Objectively, energy is simply manifesting itself in accordance with my conditioning and possibilities of the moment. Energy is being mechanically received and mechanically transmitted. All this is simply to be part of the descending octave of the Ray of Creation.

Necessary Preparation

If, however, I wish to work to become a conscious receiver-transmitter then my life reorients itself to an ascending octave, one of return to the Source, ascending the Ray of Creation, allowing a living at higher and higher levels of consciousness and vibration. Interestingly, one also wakes up simultaneously to deeper and deeper levels of sleep. But to begin with, I simply observe my life, my conditioning, patterns, beliefs.

No, I'm not going to like what I see, because what is seen is how truly asleep I am to myself, to others, the world—that all along a self-image, a false personality, has been living me. In this waking sleep, only the biological energy is spent rightly, because it is self-regulating so that I have nothing to do with it (though I can interfere with it through drugs, etc.). Mechanical energy is always moving me around, and mental and emotional energy is spent in imagination, internal considering, lying, identifying, idle talk and expressing negative emotions. This self-observation, rightly conducted, removes the blinders.

Observing how my life is being lived as impartially as possible (like a scientist looking at a virus through a microscope) allows my natural intelligence to enter and I begin to directly sense and feel what is being observed—direct, unfiltered impressions of postures, breathing, thoughts, feelings, actions, inaction. In this way I begin to recognize by the evidence of my own observation that I am not the indivisible I have taken myself to be, but many "I"s, each with its own agenda, often quite contradictory. These "I"s feed on my energy, capture my attention, lead me here and there.

A Subtle Discrimination

And so by simply observing (when reactive judgment enters, which it will, this is observed as well), one begins to see how energy is used and misused, how its transmission is discolored with egoism and identification. This evokes a real suffering, not a physical or psychological suffering but a moral suffering. This suffering in time will generate an inner heat, one which will begin to create a separation between what is perceived and its perceiving. If one identifies with the perceiving by saying "I" to it, the observing is overlaid with the "observer-I." Thus, the original egoism with which I identify, not to lose control, simply moves to a more subtle level. And so the experience of "the observer is the observed" remains.

However, if the separation between the perceived and the perceiving can be maintained, then an inner space appears for one's natural intelligence to directly absorb the impressions of the mechanicality-of-the-moment as it functions in the service of whatever "I" is in action. If an inner separation between consciousness and the contents of consciousness is maintained, then *one is and is not* what is observed. The transmission of energy is not discolored or diluted to the degree that the energy received is not identified with and psychologized. It is crucial to understand that one can do none of this without a teacher, for if I am asleep to myself, how can I awaken? Moreover, the self-observation referred to is not the usual observation by and of the head with which everyone is consumed. Rather, it is predicated on self-remembering.

Gurdjieff once succinctly explained self-remembering by saying "To know you are angry when you are angry," meaning to experience the anger without identifying with it. That is, knowing how one is manifesting, outwardly or inwardly, with all three centers—intellectual, emotional, instinctual. One can observe how all things, from gross to subtle, appear and disappear within consciousness. A consciousness cleansed of identification with its content is thus without personal referent. One realizes that the body appears in consciousness and not otherwise. Yes, though not generally known or rightly "practiced," the teaching extends from the lowest idea and experience of self to the very highest. Gurdjieff clearly said of the teaching that it "possesses full knowledge" and "is completely self-supporting and independent of all other [spiritual] lines." But this is generally not taken far enough.

Now what was it about "Energy being wasted on the young"? Isn't it wasted on the old as well?

We must remember that as we have the possibility to ascend to higher levels of being and consciousness, we can also descend to lower animal realms. We live not only in possibility but in question.

The deep question of energy is—for what is it being used? ⚡

First printed in *Revue 3e Millénaire*, #82. From TGJ #45

Afterword

ONE DOESN'T KNOW, OF COURSE, BUT THE SENSE IS THAT THIS is my last book. The first, *Eating The "I,"* published some eighteen years ago, was a personal account of my experiences in the Work, with the ensuing books either a chronicle of the introduction and establishment of The Fourth Way in the West—*Struggle of the Magicians, Voices in the Dark,* and *Ladies of the Rope*—or the arrogations and distortions of the teaching—*Taking with the Left Hand* and *The Life & Teachings of Carlos Castaneda.*

The focus of *Spiritual Survival in a Radically Changing World-Time* is on the teaching itself, as it has been practiced, experienced and understood. Obviously, it is not a compendium of the teaching, as its scale and richness no mere book or books could convey, but rather a "taste." Hopefully, its influence might lead the interested reader to seek a direct exploration, for as Mr. Gurdjieff pointed out, intellectual knowledge, while it has its place, can be a barrier to self-transformation if not objectified by practice. And as said at the end of the Introduction, it is simply not possible to teach oneself.

For purists, and this writer counts himself as one, *Spiritual Survival* may perhaps shock some of the Old Guard. Yes, it is understood that the teaching is esoteric and, as recent "New Age history" shows, whatever morsels are put on the public plate are quickly picked over by the ever-burgeoning swarm of teacher-flies endlessly concocting their eclectic mixes of the purported esoteric. Agreed, but I ask in rejoinder—*What time is it?*

If we recall, Mr. Gurdjieff took a personal vow in 1911 to introduce The Fourth Way to the West. As a man of esoteric tradition, why would he do that? Because he realized a major shock had to be given if people were to awaken to the perils they face. Great as the perils were then, today they are many times greater. This radically changing and mercurial world-time we have entered now faces us with spiritual extinction. The only hope, as I see it, is to deeply look in the mirror and discern the true from the false. *Faith in consciousness.*

In closing, I want to thank Barbara, my lovely wife, friend and editor, for her steadfastness and keen eye, Teresa Sanchez Adams for her selfless help and powers of discernment, Henry Korman for his indefatigable labor and creative design, his wife, Mary Ellen, for her faithfulness, character and fine eye, and also to the many readers of the manuscript, chief among them Ron and Claire Levitan, David and Alicia Morley, and Jean Lauderdale. Thank you all! ⚔

—William Patrick Patterson
January 2009
San Anselmo, California

Notes

These notes apply only to the Introduction.

1. *Resource Wars.* Andrew Martin, "Middle East Facing Choice Between Crops and Water," *New York Times*, 21 July 2008. "The Middle East and North Africa are having to choose between growing more crops to feed an expanding population or preserving their already scant supply of water. It can only get worse, as their population of 364 million today (which has more than quadrupled since 1950) is expected to reach nearly 600 million by 2050."
2. *Extreme weather.* James Lovelock, *The Revenge of Gaia* (London: Penguin, 2006). Inventor of a device that helped detect the growing hole in the ozone layer, and originator of the Gaia Hypothesis which held that the Earth is a self-regulating living super-organism, Lovelock predicts that by 2020 extreme weather will be the norm and will cause global devastation. By 2040 much of Europe will be Saharan, and parts of London will be under water. He believes global warming is irreversible, and will cause a catastrophe of mass migrations, famine and epidemics. Holding that solar and wind power are inadequate solutions, he believes nuclear power can solve our energy problem. Food, however, will be the bigger problem. Plants can't grow in extreme weather conditions. Synthesizing food could help. By 2100, he expects 80 percent of the world's population to be wiped out. "There have been seven disasters since humans came on the Earth, very similar to the one that's just about to happen. I think these events keep separating the wheat from the chaff. And eventually we'll have a human on the planet that really does understand it and can live with it properly. That's the source of my optimism."
3. *Highly complex computer generated.* Richard Dooling, "The Rise of the Machines," 12 October 08, *New York Times*.
4. *But we are suggesting.* Dooling. Theodore Kaczinski's manifesto.
5. *People are turning into machines.* P. D. Ouspensky, *In Search of the Miraculous* (New York: Harcourt Brace, 1950), 18. From Ouspensky, *A Further Record: Extracts from Meetings* (London: Arkana, 1986), 43–44, "Suppose somebody invents something to destroy the earth, all life on earth; we are not far from it! ... And these inventions have another side: machines, especially big machines, make people work in a certain way; or things happen in a certain way, because of machines which can only work in a certain way and have to be fed. More and more machines are invented for more and more different purposes, and all these machines have to be fed. I don't mean fed with fuel. I mean they must be kept functioning. ... Machines make people serve them, and really machines control the movements and the life of human beings—the place where they live, the food they eat. ... But the important thing is invention itself. ... The direction of inventions is not controlled and cannot be controlled. ... Suppose people carry dynamite bombs in their pockets. God knows

what might happen! Someone may say quite easily that a small bomb which can destroy the population of London is the most useful thing to carry in one's pocket! From Ouspensky, *Letters from Russia* (London: Routledge & Kegan Paul, 1978), 2–3, "We know now that the whole life of individual men and women is a struggle against these big creatures. We are able to understand without difficulty that a Nation is a creature standing on a far lower stage of development than individual men and women; it is about on the level of the zoophytes, slowly moving in one direction or the other and consuming one another."

6. *Survival as continuing and as persisting.* Raymond Martin, *Self-Concern: An Experiential Approach to What Matters in Survival* (London: Cambridge University Press, 1998), 87, "I claim that so far as our theoretical beliefs are concerned (as opposed to our experiential beliefs) what most of us really want, so far as our so-called self-interested wants are concerned, is primarily to continue as (or to be continued by) some maximally advantaged being with whom we can fully and rationally identify. I call this claim the thesis that *continuing is primarily what matters* most in survival. Its main rival is the thesis that *persisting* (or, identity) *is primarily what matters*."

7. *Porting the brain and nervous system.* Gary Stix, "Jacking into the Brain," *Scientific American,* November 2008.

8. *Paralyzed people's brains directly connected to computers. 60 Minutes* (CBS), October 31, 2008.

9. *Brain-computer interfaces.* See Wikipedia.

10. *Troop enhancement.* Kevin Fagan, "Artificial Brain Project Gets Boost—$4.9 Million Grant," 20 November 2008, *San Francisco Chronicle.* IBM and five universities have received a federal grant to create an artificial brain so small and independently functional it could fit in a backpack and be able to process information from a huge variety of sources, respond almost as if it were reasoning, learn over time, and solve difficult problems as quickly as the smartest humans. Says Stanford bioengineering professor Kwabena Boahen, "It could act like a buddy, looking out for him to tell him what's happening behind him."

11. *Armed border guards.* Cornelia Dean, "A Soldier, Taking Orders from Its Ethical Judgment Center," 25 November 2008, *New York Times,* Researchers suggest that battlefield robots could be created that, according to Ronald C. Arkin, computer scientist at Georgia Tech, who is designing software for battlefield robots, could "behave more ethically on the battlefield than humans currently can." Israel and South Korea already deploy armed robot border guards. Natalie Angier, "In an Age of Robots," 26 November 2008, *New York Times,* reports that "Factory robots encapsulate our drugs, sequence our genes, fabricate our chips, monitor our radiation, spot weld and spray paint our cars, load bricks, rivet bolts, run nuts, make glass, die cast, sand blast…. Moreover, by toting around computationally astute devices like iPhones, BlackBerrys and Garmins, we are at least provisionally solving the embodiment problem of robotics with our own bodies and becoming the smart robots we crave."

12. *Will Technology Kill Privacy? Scientific American,* September 2008.

13. *Uncertainty.* On the ceiling of his library, Montaigne had this sentence by Pliny inscribed: "There is nothing certain but uncertainty, and nothing more miserable and arrogant than man."

14. *Enframing.* Martin Heidegger, *Basic Writings* (New York: Harper & Row, 1977), 304, 307. The word is taken from his prescient 1954 essay "The Question Concerning Technology." (Originally, it was entitled "Enframing" and was the second of a four-part lecture series given in 1949. The three other lectures were titled "The Thing," "The Danger," and "The Turning.") "Because the essence of modern technology lies in enframing, modern technology must employ exact physical science." Speaking of destining, he says, "Enframing belongs within the destining of revealing." He does not believe that technology is "the fate of our age, where 'fate' means the inevitableness of an unalterable course." However, on pages 308–309, "When destining reigns in the mode of enframing, it is the supreme danger. This danger attests itself to us in two ways. As soon as what is unconcealed no longer concerns man even as object, but exclusively as standing-reserve, and in the midst of objectlessness is nothing but the orderer of the standing-reserve, then he comes to the very brink of a precipitous fall, that is, he comes to the point where he himself will have to be taken as standing-reserve. Meanwhile, man, precisely as the one so threatened, exalts himself to the posture of lord of the earth.... The rule of enframing threatens man with the possibility that it could be denied to him to enter into a more original revealing and hence to experience the call of a more primal truth."

15. *Son of Man.* Ray Kurzweil, *The Age of Spiritual Machines: When Computers Exceed Human Intelligence* (New York: Viking Penguin, 1999), 152–53. Kurzweil, inventor of speech–recognition technology, believes that by the year 2020 computers will exceed the memory capacity and computational ability of the human brain. We, "the technology-inventing species," will eventually have our brain and nervous system ported to the computational technology and replace their information-processing organs. "A neurological basis for spiritual experience has long been postulated by evolutionary biologists because of the social utility of religious belief.... When we can determine the neurological correlates of the variety of spiritual experiences that our species is capable of, we are likely to be able to enhance these experiences in the same way that we will enhance other human experiences.... Machines, derived from human thinking and surpassing humans in their capacity for experience, will claim to be conscious, and thus to be spiritual.... And given the historical inclination of the human race to anthropomorphize the phenomena we encounter, and the persuasiveness of the machines, we're likely to believe them when they tell us this. Twenty-first-century machines—based on the design of human thinking—will do as their human progenitors have done—going to real and virtual houses of worship, meditating, praying and transcending—to connect with their spiritual dimension." Not all neuroscientists agree with Kurzweil's "machine world utopia." Gerald Edelman, Director of the Neurosciences Institute at the Scripps Research Institute, in his book *Second Nature* (New Haven, CT: Yale University Press, 2006), 128, does speak of brain-based devices [machine only] which "are capable of perceptual categorization, learning, and conditioning without

instruction and even beginning to display episodic memory and can as a result autonomously locate themselves and designated targets in a real-world scene." But he believes the idea of their being capable of consciousness is quite remote. Says Edelman, 139–40, "[it] would not necessarily have to be alive. Given the presence of a body with sensory and motor systems, what would be necessary is a high degree of complexity in the simulated equivalent of a thalamocortical system interacting with a basal ganglion system. That complexity is presently unrealizable." These structural limitations aside, he says "[it] would have to have a true language, one with syntax as well as semantics. In other words, it would have to have a form of higher-order consciousness. . . . I suggest that someday a conscious artifact could probably be built. But it remains a remote goal. Even if that goal is reached, such a device would hardly challenge our uniqueness. Remember that the brain is embodied and that we are embedded in an econiche [the set of interactions of the body and its particular environment in influencing one another] and culture that could hardly be duplicated or even imitated. The human phenotype with all its complexity is what fuels our particular qualia. The likelihood of matching such a phenotype verges on zero. The precious qualities of our own phenomenal state are safe from preemption or displacement."

16. John Tierney, "Technology That Outthinks Us: A Partner or a Master," *New York Times, 26 August 2008*. Vernor Vinge, mathematician, computer scientist and science fiction writer, in his new book *Rainbow's End*, explores the human-machine interface. He is the author of the 1993 seminal essay "The Coming Technological Singularity," which predicted that computers would be so powerful by 2030 that a new form of superintelligence would emerge. He believes that were machines to come to rule human beings "it's possible that artificial post-humans would use us the way we've used oxen and donkeys." He preferred to hope they would be more like environmentalists who wanted to protect weaker species, even if it was only out of self-interest. One of the earliest warnings about computers dominating humans is found in John Lilly's *The Scientist* (Berkeley, CA: Ronin Publishing, 1988). Lilly is best known for his pioneering work on communication with dolphins.

17. *Royal game.* Ray Kurzweil, *The Singularity Is Near: When Humans Transcend Biology* (New York: Viking Penguin, 2005), 278–79. Kurzweil believes that "The ability of humans to perform well in chess is clearly not due to our calculating prowess, at which we are in fact rather poor. We use instead a quintessentially human form of judgment. Deep Fritz [chess software program that beat world champion Gary Kasparov in 1997] represents genuine progress over earlier chess software systems. . . . Deep Fritz-like programs running on ordinary personal computers will routinely defeat all humans later in this decade. Then we'll really lose interest in chess."

18. *Bar code.* Verichip, an implantable RFID (Radio Frequency Identification) can be inserted into the human hand between the thumb and forefinger. The hand then becomes a credit card with verification by an RFID reader. Credit card companies like MasterCard, Visa and American Express already use this technology in their credit cards. Mexico's attorney general and several of his

staff have had the microchips implanted in their arms, as a protection against kidnapping. See also the bar coding of animals, Mark Y. Stueckle and Paul D. N. Hebert, "Barcode of Life," *Scientific American*, October, 2008.

19. *Knowing awareness of presence.* Martin Heidegger, *Contributions to Philosophy* (Bloomington, IN: Indiana University Press, 1999), 60. Heidegger uses the word "mindfulness" in place of "presence," but he was very much opposed to Buddistic thinking.

20. *Plato.* Martin Heidegger, *Nietzsche*, vol. 1 (New York: Harper & Row, 1979), 200–10.

21. *Descartes.* Martin Heidegger, *Nietzsche,* vol. 4 (New York: Harper & Row, 1982), 119–38.

22. *Preponderance of vulgarity.* Ouspensky, *Search*, 309.

23. *One of man's important mistakes.* Ouspensky, *Search,* 59.

24. *"I"s.* William James, *The Principles of Psychology*, vol. II (New York: Dover, reprint 1950), 371–72. "Each thought is thus born an owner, and dies owned, transmitting whatever it realized as its Self to its own later proprietor. This trick which the nascent thought has of immediately taking up the expiring thought and 'adopting' it, which is the foundation of the appropriation of most of the remoter constituents of the self. Who owns the last self owns the self before the last, for what possesses the possessor possesses the possessed." In his essay "Does Consciousness Exist?," James speaks of consciousness as a process whose function is knowing.

25. *He predicted that a day would come.* Fritz Peters, *Boyhood with Gurdjieff* (Fairfax, CA: Arete Communications, 2006), 195.

26. *Completely unknown up to the present time.* Ouspensky, *Search,* 296.

27. *All the people you see.* Ouspensky, *Search*, 19.

28. *We are the image of God.* G. I. Gurdjieff, *All and Everything, First Series* (Aurora, OR: Two Rivers Press, 1993), 775.

29. *Events are against us.* Ouspensky, *Search*, 342–43.

30. *Mechanics is necessary.* Ouspensky, *Search,* 19.

31. From the dust jacket copy of the 1950 edition of Gurdjieff's *All and Everything,* published by Routledge & Kegan Paul: "*All and Everything* comes at a time when the world is helplessly struggling to control the intensification of technical achievement which threatens to destroy the essential values and purpose of life. This book rediscovers the path which man was destined to follow in the universal scheme and from which he has so far gone away. Gurdjieff expresses his ideas in the form of a cosmological epic based upon the legend of 'Beelzebub'—whose banishment to our Solar System brings him into contact with mankind whose strange customs and problems he describes with deep compassion and at times with superb humor. This 'all-wise Beelzebub,' with profound understanding of the weakness of humanity, points the way towards the regeneration of mankind through the development of the inner possibilities of man and presents a teaching of exceptional value for the world."

Bibliography

Gurdjieff, George Ivanovitch. *All and Everything, First Series.* Aurora, OR: Two Rivers Press, 1993.

The Herald of Coming Good. Edmonds, WA: Surefire Press, 1988.

Life Is Real Only Then When "I Am." New York: Triangle Editions, 1975.

Meetings with Remarkable Men. New York: E. P. Dutton, 1963.

The Struggle of the Magicians. Cape Town, South Africa: The Stourton Press, 1954.

Views from the Real World. New York: E. P. Dutton, 1975.

Ouspensky, P. D. *Conscience.* London: Routledge & Kegan Paul Ltd., 1979.

The Fourth Way. New York: Viking Books, 1971.

A Further Record. New York: Arkana, 1986.

In Search of the Miraculous. New York: Harcourt Brace, 1949.

Psychology of Man's Possible Evolution. New York: Alfred A. Knopf, 1934.

A Record of Meetings. New York: Arkana, 1992.

P. D. Ouspensky Memorial Collection. Sterling Library, Yale University.

Peters, Fritz. *Boyhood with Gurdjieff.* Fairfax, CA: Arete Communications, 2006.

ARETE COMMUNICATIONS

Publishers of Self-Transformation books and videos

Books and videos are available at all serious bookstores or from
Arete Communications by mail or on our website.
When ordering by mail, add $5.00 for postage within the U.S.
Outside the U.S., add $15 for airmail.
Add $1.00 for each additional book, music CD or video.

773 Center Boulevard #58
Fairfax, CA 94978-0058

DISTRIBUTORS

IN NORTH AMERICA:

New Leaf
(800) 326-2665 • Lithia Springs, Georgia

DeVorss
(800) 843-5743 • Camarillo, California

Baker & Taylor
(800) 775-1800 • Charlotte, North Carolina

For a full selection of books, videos and music, see
www.Gurdjieff-Legacy.Org